Dana

THE
BAY OF N......
& SOUTHERN ITALY

Cadogan Books plc
27–29 Berwick Street, London W1V 3RF
e-mail: guides@cadogan.demon.co.uk

Distributed in North America by
The Globe Pequot Press
6 Business Park Road, PO Box 833, Old Saybrook,
Connecticut 06475–0833

Copyright © Dana Facaros and Michael Pauls 1994, 1997
Updated by Michael Pauls, Bill Goodacre and Tory Lindrea
Illustrations © Horatio Monteverde 1994, 1997

Book and cover design by Animage
Maps © Cadogan Guides, drawn by Map Creation Ltd

Series Editor: Rachel Fielding

Editor: Dominique Shead
Copy-editing: Lorna Horsfield
Indexing: Isobel McLean
Production: Book Production Services

A catalogue record for this book is available from the British Library
ISBN 1–86011–002–9

Printed and bound in Great Britain by Biddles Ltd.

The author and publishers have made every
effort to ensure the accuracy of the information in this book at the time of going to press.
However, they cannot accept any responsi-
bility for any loss, injury or inconvenience
resulting from the use of information
contained in this guide.

About the Authors

Michael Pauls and Dana Facaros, their two kids and seven cats live in a leaky old farmhouse in southwest France. They have written over 20 guides for Cadogan.

About the Updaters

Bill Goodacre and Tory Lindrea met in Italy, where they both have lived and studied. They now work in travel and journalism respectively.

Acknowledgements

For this last foray into the Mezzogiorno, the authors' thanks go to all the EPTs, AASTs and Pro Locos around the south who found time to lend us a hand, to Andrew Gumbel and Kathleen Micham, Clare Pedrick and Mario Pinto, and especially Anne and Santino Chianella, for their hospitality and encouragement. As Santino always says about Italy: you cry twice. When you come, and when you leave.

The publishers would like to thank Horatio Monteverde for the illustrations, Animage for the design, Lorna Horsfield for the copyediting, Isobel McLean for the indexing and Map Creation for the maps.

Please help us to keep this guide up to date

We have done our best to ensure that the information in this guide is correct at the time of going to press. But places and facilities are constantly changing, and standards and prices in hotels and restaurants fluctuate. We would be delighted to receive any comments concerning existing entries or omissions. The best letters will receive a copy of the Cadogan Guide of their choice.

List of Maps

Contents

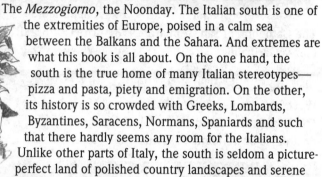

The *Mezzogiorno*, the Noonday. The Italian south is one of the extremities of Europe, poised in a calm sea between the Balkans and the Sahara. And extremes are what this book is all about. On the one hand, the south is the true home of many Italian stereotypes— pizza and pasta, piety and emigration. On the other, its history is so crowded with Greeks, Lombards, Byzantines, Saracens, Normans, Spaniards and such that there hardly seems any room for the Italians. Unlike other parts of Italy, the south is seldom a picture-perfect land of polished country landscapes and serene art towns. Its attractions may be equally compelling, but they always carry a touch of the exotic: the palm trees and whitewashed villages on the long Apulian shore, mirages and bergamots on the straits of Messina, bears and wolves, Greek temples, Albanian villages, crusader ports.

For most of us today, the biggest attraction of all in the Mezzogiorno is obvious enough. Even in Roman times, the land around the bay of Naples was *Campania Felix*—fortunate Campania, the richest and most beautiful province of Italy, its seaside villas the chosen abodes of the Roman elite. History (not to mention the earthquakes and volcanoes) has given it plenty of hard knocks in all the centuries since, but the hints and fragments of paradise are still present on every side: the sweet, fading visions of heaven painted on the ceilings of Naples's churches, or the garden fantasy frescoes from the villas of Pompeii. Or the view down the bay from Posillipo, looking towards Vesuvius (at least when the air is clear enough to see that far). For paradise just a bit compromised, there's the voluptuous if overbuilt isle of Capri; and for paradise perfect, the most unforgettable settings anywhere on Italy's long coasts, we still have Ravello and Amalfi, and the miraculously unspoiled island of Procida.

The manifold delights of the Bay, though, tend to throw the rest of the south into the shade, which is a pity. One of the purposes of this book is to encourage you to move on and experience some of the wonders of three Italian regions that casual tourists do not often see. Rugged Calabria, with its forested mountain plateaux and stretches of coast that rival Campania's, offers Byzantine churches and classical Greek art among its grab-bag of historical surprises. In the remote and wild Basilicata, where people like their pasta with plenty of hot peppers, you may find the cave-city of Matera one of your most memorable Italian sights. Finally there is Apulia, flavoured with a bit of Greece and a bit of Africa, a strange and special world with its wealth of medieval art and architecture, the lovely Gargano peninsula, and some of Italy's best seafood.

Travel

By Air

From the UK

Flying is obviously the quickest and easiest way of getting to Naples, and not ruinously expensive if you avoid the scheduled flights in favour of a charter flying out of London (you can also fly from Manchester or Glasgow in the summer). Scheduled APEX fares to Naples on British Airways, ✆ 0345 222111, with two direct services daily from Gatwick, flying out and returning mid-week are currently around £310 in high season. Booking restrictions apply; you must stay a Saturday night abroad. Ticket changes involve high penalties. If you want to go to Reggio di Calabria, fly from London with Alitalia, ✆ (0171) 602 7111, and change in Milan or Rome to an internal flight; tickets cost £250–300.

London is a great centre for discounted flights, and you should be able to find a good deal if you allow enough time. Seat-only charters to Naples cost about £150 off-peak return; contact a reputable agent (i.e. ABTA-registered), who won't bunk off with your cash and leave you stranded. Check whether the prices quoted include the new airport taxes, currently £16.

Alternatively you can book directly through some charter or holiday operators. The Italian specialist Air Travel Group, at 227 Shepherd's Bush Road, London W6 7AS, ✆ (0181) 748 7575, incorporates Italy Sky Shuttle, Magic of Italy and Italian Escapades. Classified sections of the weekend newspapers also advertise discounted fares (if you live in London, get *Time Out* or other listings magazines, and the *Evening Standard* or the free newspapers like *TNT* or *Trailfinder* which you can pick up near tube stations). Peak seasons are Christmas, Easter and summer, when there are generally at least a couple of flights a day from London (book well ahead). The major charter agencies are: Italy Sky Shuttle, ✆ (0181) 748 1333, who use Alitalia for daily flights from Heathrow to Reggio di Calabria with a change in Milan (about £300 return high season); and LAI, ✆ (0171) 837 8492 (who mainly use British Midland for Naples, Palermo and Brindisi). Rock-bottom fares are generally subject to a number of restrictions, and departure or arrival times may be inconvenient. STA and Campus Travel offer particularly good deals for students.

Useful Addresses

Europe Student Travel, 6 Campden Street, London W8, ✆ (0171) 727 7647

Italiatours Ltd, 205 Holland Park Avenue, London W11 4XB, ✆ (0171) 371 1114

Italy Sky Shuttle, 227 Shepherd's Bush Road, London W6 7NL, ✆ (0181) 748 1333

Trailfinders, 194 Kensington High St, London W8 6BD ✆ (0171) 938 3232

London Campus Travel, 52 Grosvenor Gardens, SW1, ✆ (0171) 730 3402 (for students)

STA, 86 Old Brompton Road, London SW7, or 117 Euston Road, London NW; telesales department ✆ (0171) 361 6161 (for students)

From Ireland

There are no direct flights from Ireland to Italy. The best bet is to travel to London and catch a flight from there. The cheapest flights from Dublin to London are operated by Ryanair (landing at Stansted or Luton), though Aer Lingus and British Midland take you directly into Heathrow which is more convenient and will probably save time and money in the end. From Belfast, both British Airways and British Midland operate to Heathrow. If you're a student, substantial discounts may be available: contact USIT at 12-21 Aston Quay, O'Connell Bridge, Dublin 2, ℰ (01) 679 8833 or Fountain Centre, College St, Belfast, ℰ (01232) 324073.

From the USA and Canada

Transatlantic airlines Delta, TWA, United Airlines and Air Canada all have direct flights to Rome or Milan from a number of cities, including New York, Boston, Miami, Chicago, Los Angeles, Toronto or Montreal, but Alitalia has the most options. Summer round-trip fares from New York to Reggio di Calabria, changing at Rome, cost around $1300, from Toronto about $1100 Canadian. You could travel on southwards from these cities, or by train of course. Alternatively, take a flight to London and change there for Naples, a reasonably economical option. Apex or SuperApex deals are better value than scheduled fares, though you may prefer to pay extra for security, flexibility and convenience on such a long journey (9–15 hours flying time). Beware the restrictions imposed on special fares, and plan well in advance. Obviously, low-season flights (between November and March) tend to be a great deal cheaper than peak-season ones, and mid-week fares are generally lower than at weekends.

As in Britain, a host of cheap deals are advertised in the travel sections of major newspapers like the *New York Times*, *LA Times*, *Toronto Star*, etc. If you are prepared to take pot luck, try for a stand-by or consolidated fare, or consider a courier flight (remember you can only take hand luggage with you on these deals). Now Voyager, ℰ (212) 431 1616, is one of the main US courier flight companies (annual membership fee), based at Suite 307, 74 Varrick St, New York, NY 10013. Both STA and Council Travel are well worth contacting for cheaper charter flights and budget student travel. Both agencies have branches in several major US cities. In Canada, TravelCuts specializes in discounted student fares. Numerous travel clubs and agencies also specialize in discount fares (you may have to pay a membership fee).

By Train

From London the journey time to Naples takes about 31 hours (two rail routes lead to Rome, either via Paris through France, or through Belgium, Luxembourg, France and Switzerland—services run daily in summer). You have to change stations in Paris, from Gare du Nord to Gare de Lyon. Starting at around £190 return (plus £17 for a couchette), rail travel is scarcely cheaper than flying unless you are able to take advantage of student or youth fares, and isn't really a sensible option unless you have an insurmountable fear of flying, or want to see places on the way. **Interail** (UK) or **Eurail** passes (US/Canada) give unlimited travel throughout Europe for under-26s. Buy them before leaving home, from **Eurotrain**, 52 Grosvenor Gardens, London SW1, ✆ (0171) 730 7285 (reservations) or (0171) 730 3402 (information), or **Wasteels Travel** adjacent Platform 2, London SW1V 1JT, ✆ (0171) 834 7066. In the USA or Canada, contact **Rail Europe**, central office at 226–230 Westchester Ave, White Plains, NY 10604, ✆ (914) 682 2999 or (800) 438 7245. If you are just planning to see Italy, however, these passes may not be worthwhile. A month's full Interail pass costs £279, though you can now buy cheaper zonal passes covering three or four countries only. One covering Italy, Greece, Slovenia and Turkey for 15 days costs £189. Check with your agent before you purchase.

Fares on FS (*Ferrovie dello Stato*), the Italian State railway, are among the lowest (kilo-metre for kilometre) in Europe. If you intend travelling extensively by train, one of the special Italian tourist passes may be a better bet, e.g. the **Italy Rail Card**, which allows periods of 8, 15, 21, or 30 days unlimited travel on Italy's trains, including all supplements and reservation fees. Prices range from £110 for 8 days to £190 (second class) for 30 days. To make significant savings, you must do a lot of travelling. **Flexi-Cards** allow a certain number of days' first-class travel within a given period. The **Chilometrico** is valid for up to five people for 20 trips or 3000km, whichever comes first (about £88 second class). Children under 12 travel half-price (under 4 free). The **Cartaverde** is available for young people (26 and under), and entitles you to a 20 per cent discount on all rail travel (L40,000 for one year). Obtain these passes from **Wasteels** (*see* address above) or **CIT** offices (the Italian state-run travel agency) before you leave home. CIT addresses are as follows:

UK: Marco Polo House, 3–5 Lansdowne Rd, Croydon, Surrey, CR9 1LL ✆ (0181) 686 0677

USA: 342 Madison Ave, Suite 207, New York, NY 10173, ✆ (212) 697 2497

Canada: 1450 City Councillors St, Suite 750, Montreal H3A 2E6, ✆ (514) 845 4310.

Naples is a major rail hub and many services from the northern cities terminate here, rather than in Rome. There are hourly trains from Rome to Naples (journey time is about 2½ hours, and you can get a train straight from the airport without going into the city). A one-way ticket costs about L18,000. A convenient pocket-sized timetable detailing all the main and secondary Italian railway lines is now available in the UK, costing £8 (plus 90p postage). Contact Italwings, Travel & Accommodation, 87 Brewer St, London W1, ✆ (0171) 287 2117. If you wait until you arrive in Italy, however, you can pick up the *Sud e Centro Italia* (southern Italy) timetable at any station for about L4,500.

By Coach

Eurolines is the main international bus operator in Europe, with representatives in Italy and many other countries. In the UK, they can be found at 52 Grosvenor Gardens, London SW1, ✆ (0171) 730 8235 or (01582) 404511, and are booked through National Express. Regular services run to many northern Italian cities but terminate at Rome, so you will have to change to another bus or train there. Needless to say, the journey is long and excruciatingly uncomfortable over this distance, and the small savings on price (a return ticket from London to Rome costs about £130, or about £120 for the under-26s) make it a masochistic choice in comparison with a discounted air fare, or even rail travel. However, if it isn't pitch-dark, you'll get a fleeting glimpse of Mont Blanc, Turin, Milan, Venice, Bologna, Florence and Rome on the way.

By Ferry

Besides the whirl of ferries and hydrofoils connecting Naples with resorts further down the coast, and the islands in the Bay, regular boat services also link Naples with Reggio di Calabria, Milazzo, and the Aeolian Islands. International services also run to Tunisia and Malta about once a week. Siremar and Tirrenia are the main long-distance ferry companies operating from Naples.

By Car

To bring a GB-registered car into Italy, you need a vehicle registration document, full driving licence, and insurance papers. Non-EU citizens should preferably have an international driving licence which has an Italian translation incorporated. Your vehicle should display a nationality plate indicating its country of registration.

Distance by road from London to Naples is about 1750km (1050 miles), the best part of 24 hours' driving time even if you stick to fast toll roads. The most scenic and hassle-free route is via the Alps, avoiding crowded Riviera roads in summer, but if you take a route through Switzerland, expect to pay for the privilege. In winter the passes may be closed and you will have to stick to the tunnels.

For more information on driving in Italy, contact the motoring organizations: AA (members only), ✆ (0990) 500600, or RAC Travel Services, ✆ (0800) 550055 in the UK.

Entry Formalities

Passports and Visas

EU nationals with a valid passport can enter and stay in Italy as long as they like. Citizens of the US, Canada, Australia and New Zealand need only a valid passport to stay up to three months in Italy; this can be extended by getting a special visa in advance from an Italian consulate:

UK: 38 Eaton Place, London SW1, ✆ (0171) 235 9371; 32 Melville Street, Edinburgh 3, ✆ (0131) 226 3631; Roadwell Tower, 111 Piccadilly, Manchester, ✆ (0161) 236 9024. Passport information, ✆ (0990) 100495; visa information, ✆ (0891) 600340.

Ireland: 63–65 Northumberland Road, Dublin, ✆ (01) 601 744; 7 Richmond Park, Belfast, ✆ (01232) 668 854.

USA: 690 Park Avenue, New York, NY, ✆ (212) 737 9100; 12400 Wilshire Blvd, Suite 300, Los Angeles, CA, ✆ (213) 820 0622, ✆ (213) 820 0727.

Canada: 136 Beverley St, Toronto, ✆ (416) 977 1566.

Australia: 61–69 Macquarie St, Sydney 2000, NSW, ✆ (02) 2478 442; 509 St Kilda Rd, Melbourne, ✆ (03) 867 5744, ✉ (03) 866 3932.

New Zealand: 34 Grant Rd, Thorndon, Wellington, ✆ (04) 7473 5339.

Special-interest Holidays

Abercrombie & Kent (art and architectural tours, gardens and villas of Campania), Sloane Square House, Holbein Place, London SW1W 8NS, ✆ (0171) 730 9600.

Andante Travels (Pompeii, Herculaneum—archaeology and volcanoes), The Old Telephone Exchange, Winterborne Dauntsey, Salisbury SP4 6EH, ✆ (01980) 610555.

Brompton Travel (Naples opera), Brompton House, 64 Richmond Road, Kingston-upon-Thames, Surrey KT2 5EH, ✆ (0181) 549 3334.

Camper & Nicholsons (specialist yacht charters for motor and sailing boats), 25 Bruton Street, London W1X 7DB, ✆ (0171) 491 2950.

Citalia (tailor-made holidays along the coast), Marco Polo House, 3–5 Lansdowne Road, Croydon, CR9 1LL, ✆ (0181) 688 9989.

Cosmos (Grand Tour, including Vesuvius, Capri, Sorrento), Tourama House, 17 Holmesdale Road, Bromley, Kent BR2 9LX, ✆ (0181) 464 3444.

Magic of Italy (Bay of Naples, escorted tour), 227 Shepherds Bush Road, London W6 7AS, ✆ (0181) 748 7575.

Mark Warner (holiday villages, Campania), 20 Kensington Church Street, London W8 4EP, ✆ (0171) 393 3131.

Martin Randall Travel (archaeology tours to Pompeii, Herculaneum, Amalfi coast, Naples, Campania—guest lecturers), 10 Barley Mow Passage, Chiswick, London W4 4PH, ✆ (0181) 742 3355.

Page & Moy (Easter breaks to Naples and cultural trips to the best classical sites, Vesuvius, the Amalfi coast and Capri accompanied by a specialist lecturer and tour escort), 136–140 London Road, Leicester LE2 1EN, ✆ (0116) 2524433.

Prospect Music & Art (Pompeii, Paestum and Herculaneum—archaeology tours), 454/458 Chiswick High Road, London W4 5TT, ✆ (0181) 995 2151.

Saga (southern Italy for senior citizens), The Saga Building, Middelburg Square, Folkestone, Kent CT20 1AZ, ✆ (01303) 857000.

Solo's (singles holidays in Campania), 54–58 High Street, Edgware, HA8 7ED, ✆ (0181) 951 2800.

Travel for the Arts (opera in Naples and journey along the Amalfi coast), 117 Regents Park Road, London NW1 8UR, ✆ (0171) 483 4466.

Voyages Jules Verne (tours down the Amalfi coast based in Positano), 21 Dorset Square, London NW1 6QG, ✆ (0171) 616 1000.

Itineraries

Campania and the three other southern regions have almost half of Italy's coastline, though most of it is flat and not too exciting. If you are looking for **classic Mediterranean scenery** and a spot on the beach, the first really obvious place to send you is the spectacular Amalfi coast and the islands around the Bay of Naples. If these long-established fleshpots are too overripe for your tastes, or simply too crowded, you'll need to press on further into the region. Try the small resorts of the Cilento (*see* p.178), south of Naples.

Those interested in the **ancient Greeks and Romans** must first visit Pompeii, Herculaneum, the splendid temples at Paestum and then Capua, though the best relics from all these sites are in the great museum in Naples. From the Middle Ages, there is exotic Arab-Norman architecture in Amalfi, Salerno and Ravello. Inland, queer old Benevento is another fascinating place to visit.

A tour of Naples and Campania in less than two weeks should get you through the major sights of Naples and the surrounding region (known as Campania)—almost all of them are along the coast. Begin with Naples (days 1–4), and if you like it enough, you can make the city a base for day-trips to Pompeii and Herculaneum (day 5), the Phlegraean Fields or Vesuvius (day 6), and the islands (days 7–8). Otherwise, Sorrento or any of the islands can provide a more pleasant base. The Amalfi drive along the coast is certainly worth two days (9 and 10; seeing Positano, Amalfi, Ravello, and a look at old Salerno when you finish) though you may never want to leave. Paestum and its Greek temples come next (day 11), and, if you're heading further south, you can continue from here along the Cilento coast (day 12), or else return to Naples through inland Campania, stopping at Benevento (alternative day 12), then visiting Capua and Caserta (day 13).

A seven-day excursion through classical antiquity: for ancient sites and museums, Campania is the equal of Sicily and even Rome itself. Again, start with Naples and its great Archaeological Museum, and a walk through the Spaccanapoli district (day 1). Pompeii and Herculaneum will each require a day if you wish to see them in detail (days 2 and 3), and another day can be spent exploring the sites west of Naples: Cumae, Baiae, Cape Misenum, Pozzuoli, and so on (day 4). Be sure to make at least a day-trip to Benevento to see the Arch of Trajan and the odd Egyptian relics around town (day 5). Capua, with its unique *mithraeum* and amphitheatre, comes next (day 6). Depending on what direction your travels are taking you, you may either begin or end this itinerary with mainland Italy's best-preserved Greek temples, plus an interesting museum, at Paestum (day 7).

Calabrian itineraries: most visitors only take at a look at the region if they're passing through on the way to Sicily, and have some time to spare. If so, drivers should take the old coastal road, the SS18, south through Maratea and Paola; the SS585 that connects with it branches off the A3 *Autostrada del Sole* at Lagonegro-Nord, near Maratea, and it is a much more scenic route than the *autostrada*. It takes longer, but it's a good smooth road, and actually shorter. Take as long as you like: Tropea makes the best stopover along the way. One detour is via Cosenza into the Sila highlands—no little journey, some 89km from the turn-off at Paola to San Giovanni in Fiore in the heart of the Sila. Another, shorter digression would be from Vibo Valentia, around the peninsula to Tropea and Capo Vaticano. This adds an extra 45km to the trip, through some difficult corniche roads, but it includes some of the south's best coastal scenery. Before you make the crossing over to Messina, take an hour or two for the museum in Reggio; even if you have no particular interest in archaeology, the collection contains some of the most beautiful art you'll see in southern Italy. Aspromonte, the broad massif that makes up Italy's toe, is also worth a day's digression for its forests and mountain scenery.

Similarly, travellers en route between Campania and Apulia can with a few detours take in the most interesting parts of eastern Calabria and the Basilicata, such as the cave city of Matera, the dramatic castles built by the Normans and the Emperor Frederick II, and the Greek ruins at Metapontum.

Apulian itineraries: Apulia is a large region—and a long one, all of 405km from the northwestern corner to the tip of the Salentine peninsula. One way of seeing the best it has to offer in little over a week would be to begin with an overnight stay at Vieste, on the Gargano. From there, drive south down this beautiful peninsula to Manfredonia, stopping on the way at Monte Sant'Angelo (55km). Spend a day touring the Apulian cathedral cities or Castel del Monte before arriving at Bari (112km). Apart from its Romanesque cathedral, Bari has little to detain you, so carry on south through Alberobello to look at the *trulli* country on the way to the finest city of the south, Baroque Lecce (158km in one or two days; Ostuni makes a good stop in between). Leave a day or two for the Salentine peninsula before cutting back west to Táranto, with its superb archaeological museum.

If you have more time for Apulia, it might be difficult to choose how to spend it—the region's attractions are many and varied, and spread all over the map. The Gargano and Salentine peninsulas have the best beaches and scenery, and the most engaging towns for a stay are Lecce and Táranto. Apulia's greatest artistic productions are the medieval cathedrals and churches of Trani, Bari, Ruvo, Altamura, Molfetta, Bisceglie, Bitonto and Barletta, all close together in Bari province. The fascinating Castel del Monte west of Bari, and the great castle at Lucera, are only two of the important sites associated with the reign of the 'wonder of the world', the Emperor Frederick II.

By Sea

A complex network of ferries and hydrofoils run by half a dozen different companies links Naples with the islands in the bay and several further afield (Sardinia, Malta, Corsica, Sicily), and other resorts down the coast. In summer, up to six ferries and 20 hydrofoils ply to Capri, and as many to Ischia. There are also regular departures to Procida. In addition, there are ferries and hydrofoils daily from Sorrento to Capri, from Pozzuoli to Procida, and between the islands of Ischia and Procida. All are very short rides, and in most cases day trips are quite viable ways of exploring the local islands. You can usually buy tickets when you turn up at the port; return tickets don't generally offer any savings over two separate single tickets. Services for Capri, Sorrento, Ischia, Procida, Forio and Casamicciola depart from the Molo Beverello in front of the Castel Nuovo in Naples. Boats for Palermo, Reggio di Calabria, Milazzo and the Aeolian Islands leave from the Stazione Marittima. Hydrofoils also serve the bay islands from Mergellina, another important terminal in the western suburb of Naples. Sample costs: Naples–Sorrento return L24,000; Naples–Capri return from L26,000; Naples–Ischia from L17,600 (ferries are predictably cheaper than the faster hydrofoil services, and less affected by rough weather). The daily newspaper *Il Mattino* gives a full list of current timetables.

By Train

Naples, the main rail hub for southern Italy, is served by a full range of *regionale, diretto, espresso*, intercity, EuroCity and ETR 450 fast trains. From the centre (the main station is Stazione Centrale at Piazza Garibaldi), a cat's cradle of funiculars, national and local lines straggles out through the disparate suburbs and down the coast to Sorrento and beyond, via Pompeii and Herculaneum. The state-run (FS) line offers a fast crow's-flight service between Naples and Salerno; for other coastal destinations, you will probably rely on local rail systems. Inland, erratically scheduled and complicated train services head for Caserta, Capua and Benevento from Naples' Stazione Centrale. South of Salerno, Paestum and most destinations on the Cilento coast are served by the main rail route from Naples to Reggio di Calabria.

For coastal journeys, the **Circumvesuviana** is the most useful service, trundling right round the Bay of Naples every half-hour or so from dawn till quite late at night, stopping just about everywhere. This is the best way to reach Pompeii, Herculaneum and Sorrento. The Neapolitan terminus is a modern station on Corso Garibaldi, but trains stop at Stazione Centrale too (on underground platforms). Main lines run east via Ercolano (the Herculaneum station), then diverge, passing Pompeii on opposite sides. One line takes you to Sorrento, the other to Sarno, east of Vesuvius. The journey to Sorrento takes about an hour. You can also get to Nola and Baiano on a separate line. To get beyond Sorrento to Positano, Amalfi, Ravello, etc. it's best to take a bus.

If you're heading westwards from Naples, you have a choice of the Naples underground or **Metropolitana**, which crosses the city centre and ends up at Pozzuoli-Solfatara, a half-hour run. Both the **Ferrovia Cumana** (running along the coast) and the **Circumflegrea** (via Cumae) take you as far as Torregaveta. For information on Italian rail passes, *see* 'Getting There' (above).

Elsewhere in the south, train service is regular along the coasts, and if you plan ahead care-fully you can see all the larger towns in the interior too. It will be complicated, though, involving strange connections and sometimes a trip on one of the several old narrow-gauge private railways still in business: see the 'Getting Around' sections for Calabria, the Basilicata and Apulia for more details.

By Bus

The main bus station in Naples is just in front of the central railway station. From here, a mass of routes heads for all the main towns and places of interest in Campania, and threads through the maze of suburbs and dormitory towns to outlying villages. Many are run by the Naples Public Transport Board (℃ 7001111) which has information offices in Piazza Garibaldi. Other services are operated by SITA (℃ 5522176, Via Pisanelli 3–7) and Curreri (℃ 8015420).

Italian buses are not the easiest system to crack; indications of destination and departure point are often mystifying and it's best to ask before you get on. Buy tickets in advance from tobacconists, news-stands or ticket booths at the bus stations, and validate them on the bus by punching them in the machine (many people don't bother buying tickets, but you can be heavily fined if you are caught travelling without one, or with an unvalidated ticket). In Naples you might want to invest in the travel pass called 'GiraNapoli' (see p.68).

There are regular services to Salerno (SITA), Benevento, Caserta and Avellino (Naples Public Transport Board). Curreri runs a useful service from Capodichino airport to Sorrento. Buses are also the best way to get around the islands in the bay. The Circumvesuviana railway is generally more obvious to use for east bay destinations like Pompeii, but you can take buses too. Buses really come into their own on the Amalfi coast, which is not served by rail, and are far the most enjoyable way to hop from place to place. SITA services ply regularly between Sorrento and Salerno about every 50 minutes. Buy tickets in advance in local bars or shops bearing the SITA sign, or from the terminus depots. Paestum is an easy bus-ride from Salerno, about every half-hour. ATAC buses serve the Cilento coast, from Salerno to Sapri.

In the rest of south, buses are quicker than train travel, and also a bit more expensive. Compared to most of Europe, the Italian inter-city bus system is excellent, and it will take you any place the train won't. The provincial capitals are always the main centres, with a station (usually near the rail station) that has a fat timetable of buses to every outlying village in the province, and a few beyond.

By Car

A car is certainly the best and most convenient way to get to the more remote parts of the Mezzogiorno, but sheer hell in Naples, whether moving or stationary. Driving isn't much fun in any southern town, really. The streets weren't made for cars, and most modern Italians wouldn't be caught dead walking (except maybe for the evening *passeggiata*). In any place of more than 10,000 people, expect solid traffic jams from about 11 am to 2 pm, and again in the evening from about 5 until 10 or 11. If you must drive in or out of a town, try to do it at night or when the Italians are having their *pranzo*.

And if you must bring a car into Naples or Bari, make sure you leave it securely in a guarded parking lot, with nothing valuable inside. On the streets, if the thieves don't get it, a tow-truck may well offer a similar service—take care not to leave it in a *Zona Rimozione* area.

Third-party insurance is a minimum requirement in Italy (and you should be a lot more than minimally insured, as many of the locals have none whatever). Obtain a Green Card from your insurer, which gives automatic proof that you are fully covered. Also get hold of a European Accident Statement form, which may simplify things if you are unlucky enough to have an accident. Always insist on a full translation of any statement you are asked to sign. Breakdown assistance insurance is obviously a sensible investment (e.g. AA's Five Star or RAC's Eurocover Motoring Assistance).

Don't give the local police any excuse to fine you on the spot for minor infringements like worn tyres or burnt-out sidelights. A red triangular hazard sign is obligatory; also recommended are a spare set of bulbs, a first-aid kit and a fire extinguisher. Spare parts may be tricky to find for non-Italian cars. Petrol (*benzina*; unleaded is *benzina senza piombo*, and diesel *gasolio*) is still very expensive in Italy despite price changes in 1992 (around L1900 per litre; fill up before you cross the border). Motorway (*autostrada*) tolls are quite high.

Italians are famously anarchic behind a wheel, and nowhere more so than within the city of Naples, where all warnings, signals and generally recognized rules of the road are ignored. The only way to beat the locals is to join them by adopting an assertive and constantly alert driving style. Bear in mind the ancient maxim that he/she who hesitates is lost (especially at traffic lights, where the danger of crashing into someone at the front is less great than that of being rammed from behind). All drivers from boy racers to elderly nuns seem to tempt Providence by overtaking at the most dangerous bend, and no matter how fast you are hammering along the *autostrada* (toll motorway), plenty will whizz past at apparently supersonic rates. North Americans used to leisurely speed limits and gentler road manners will find the Italian interpretation of the highway code especially stressful. Speed limits (generally ignored) are officially 130kph on motorways (110kph for cars under 1100cc or motorcycles), 110kph on main highways, 90kph on secondary roads, and 50kph in built-up areas. Speeding fines may be as much as L500,000, or L100,000 for jumping a red light (a popular Italian sport).

If you are undeterred by these caveats, you may actually enjoy driving in Italy, at least away from the congested tourist centres. Signposting is generally good, and roads are usually excellently maintained. Some of the roads (e.g. the Amalfi corniche and some of the mountain roads in Calabria) are feats of engineering that the Romans themselves would have admired: bravura projects suspended on cliffs, crossing valleys on vast stilts, winding up hairpins. Buy a good road map (the Italian Touring Club series is excellent).

The **Automobile Club of Italy (ACI)** is a good friend to the foreign motorist. Besides having bushels of useful information and tips, they offer a free breakdown service, and can be reached from anywhere by dialling © 116—also use this number if you have to find the nearest service station. If you need major repairs, the ACI can make sure the prices charged are according to their guidelines. In Naples they can be found at Piazzale Tecchio 49/d, © (081) 5937856; in Salerno at Via G Vicinanza 11, © (089) 226677; Caserta, Via N Sauro 10, © (0823) 321442; and Benevento, Via S Rosa 24–26, © (0824) 314849.

car hire

Hiring a car or camper van is simple but not particularly cheap. In Italian it's called *autonoleggio*. There are both large international firms through which you can reserve a car in advance, and local agencies, which often have lower prices. Air or train travellers should check out possible discount packages. Most companies will require a deposit amounting to the estimated cost of the hire. Most companies have a minimum age limit of 21 (23 in some cases). A credit card makes life easier. You will need to produce your licence and a passport when you hire. Current 1996 rates are around L90,000 per day for a small car (Fiat Panda, for instance) with unlimited mileage and collision damage waiver, including tax (hire for three days or longer is somewhat less pro rata).

Several major companies have offices in Naples; mainly on Via Partenope (near the port), and at the airport or main station: **Avis**, ✆ 7645600; **Europcar**, ✆ 7645859; **Hertz**, ✆ 7645523; **IntalRent**, ✆ 76435423. A hefty surcharge is levied because of the local theft problem, and if you hire elsewhere, check you are allowed to drive within Naples without penalty. You can take a car to Capri or Ischia, but rental facilities are available only on Ischia.

By Taxi

Try not to take taxis if you're on a budget. They are invariably expensive at the best of times, and foreign tourists are unfortunately sitting ducks for overcharging. In Naples, corruption is rife, and even a short trip may clock up an alarming bill because of the traffic jams. Minimum fares are L5000. Try to negotiate the fare in advance if you have to take one. Don't try to flag them down on the street; head for a taxi rank on a main square, or dial through the Radiotaxi system (✆ 5564444). In other resorts taxis aren't such bad news, but they are still expensive, especially on Capri, where a ride may cost up to L30,000.

By Motorcycle or Bicycle

You may have trouble hiring a *motorino* (moped) or Vespa (scooter) in Naples because of theft, but they are available in all the major resorts such as Sorrento, and on the islands. You must be at least 14 for a *motorino* and 16 for anything more powerful. Helmets are compulsory. Costs for a *motorino* range from about L20,000 to L35,000 per day, scooters somewhat more (up to L50,000).

You can hire a bike in most Italian towns. Prices range from about L10,000 to L20,000 per day, which may make buying one interesting if you plan to spend much time in the saddle (L190,000–L300,000). You can usually take your bike quite cheaply on slower trains.

Practical A–Z

Climate

Southern Italy can be diabolically hot in summer, with daytime temperatures soaring to an enervating 35°C, but the drought that scorches every scrap of inland vegetation to a crisp by July is relieved by occasional bouts of violent, torrential rain. On the coast, temperatures are more moderate, refreshed by breezes, while annual rainfall is considerably higher in Amalfi than Rome or London. You can probably manage without an umbrella in summer, but take a light jacket for cool evenings. August is the most unforgiving month to stump through southern Italy. Transport facilities are jammed to capacity, prices are at their highest, Naples and the main sights like Pompeii are abandoned to hordes of tourists, while the locals sensibly remain indoors for most of the afternoon, or take to the beach.

Spring and early **autumn** are much more appealing seasons: spring for the infinity of wild flowers in the countryside, autumn for the colour of trees in the hills. Milder temperatures and fewer crowds make for much pleasanter touring, and you shouldn't need raingear until October. From December to March you can enjoy blissful solitude at reasonable temperatures anywhere close to the coasts, though it will probably be too cold for swimming. Anywhere in the mountains (and even around the Bay of Naples) it can rain and rain, with valleys shrouded for days on end beneath banks of mist.

average monthly temperatures in °C

	Jan	Feb	Mar	Apr	May	June	July	Aug	Sept	Oct	Nov	Dec
Naples	9	9	11	14	18	22	25	25	22	18	15	10
Capri	11	11	12	13	17	22	24	26	21	17	14	12
Bari	6	8	11	13	18	25	27	26	22	18	15	10
Reggio	11	12	14	16	19	26	26	24	22	19	16	12

Consulates

UK: Via Francesco Crispi 122, Naples, ℂ (081) 663511

Via Terribile 9, Brindisi, ℂ (0831) 658340

US: Piazza della Repubblica 2, Naples, ℂ (081) 5838181

Crime and the Police

Southern Italy has more than its fair share of opportunist criminals. Naples and Bari in particular are notorious for street crime; here kindly waiters will tuck your necklace out of sight, and remind you as regularly as bus conductors to hang on tight to your camera. The local brand of *mafiosi* are known as *Camorra* in Naples (crime syndicates who keep a toehold on most walks of life, largely financed by protection rackets, drug-dealing and the proceeds of the *toto nero*, or illegal football pools). Purse snatchings, pickpocketing, minor thievery of the white-collar kind (always check your change, and the taxi-meter), car break-ins and theft are rife. Violent crime is fortunately fairly rare, though injuries are sometimes caused by scooter-born bag-snatchers (stay on the inside of the pavement and keep a firm grip on your property). Pickpockets generally strike in crowded buses and gatherings: don't carry more cash than you need, and split it up so you won't lose the lot at once. Be vigilant in train stations, and don't leave valuables in hotel rooms. If at all possible, avoid taking a car anywhere near Naples. Theft is so tediously common that some car hire firms refuse to rent certain models for use in the city. If your car is stolen, ring the police, © 794 14 35, but don't expect much sympathy. Always park cars in garages, guarded lots or well-lit streets with anything remotely portable or valuable removed or well out of sight. Outside Naples, organized crime is much less evident. For police emergencies, dial © 113, or © 112 outside city areas. The *vigili urbani* take care of minor everyday problems in towns. They are generally more easy-going and courteous than the quasi-military *carabinieri*, who along with the *polizia statale* watch over the rural areas. Traffic offences are dealt with by the *polizia stradale*, who patrol the highways. Possession of any questionable substances could subject you to a very hard time in drug-ridden southern Italy, despite the theoretical legal limit of a few grams of soft stuff for personal use.

Disabled Travellers

Italy has been relatively slow off the mark in its provision for disabled visitors. Uneven or non-existent pavements, the appalling traffic conditions, crowded public transport, and endless flights of steps in many public places are all disincentives. Progress is gradually being made, however. A national support organization in your own country may well have specific information on facilities in Italy, or will at least be able to provide general advice. The Italian tourist office, or CIT (travel agency) can also advise on hotels, museums with ramps, etc. If you book rail travel through CIT, you can request assistance if you are wheelchair-bound.

In the UK, contact the **Royal Association for Disability & Rehabilitation** (RADAR), and ask for their guide *Holidays & Travel Abroad: A Guide for Disabled People*. They are based at 250 City Road, London EC1V 8AS, © (0171) 250 3222. Another useful organization is **Mobility International**, at 228 Borough High Street, London SE1, © (0171) 403 5688 or PO Box 3551, Eugene, Oregon 97403, USA, © (541) 343 1284.

If you need help while you are in Naples or the resorts of Campania, contact the local tourist office. Provincial tourist boards provide lists of hotels with specialized facilities, museums with wheelchair access, etc.

Festivals

In Campania, any excuse will do for throwing a party, especially if it can be combined with having a day off work, and the region plays host to some of Italy's most spectacular and colourful traditional *feste* (festivals). Most of the festivities are linked to religious events and feast days, and the Madonna features prominently, often decked out garishly with bright fairy-lights and gaudy flowers and hauled through the streets atop tiny Fiats

hastily covered with red velvet (with peepholes for the driver), or on platforms stoically borne by the village's fittest and strongest young men. But many of the celebrations also have a strong pagan flavour, especially those linked to the land and the harvest, and some of the feast-day parapher- nalia is unmistakably phallic (towers and obelisks are an obvious give-away).

Whatever the occasion, a village *festa* is a chance to see local traditions and ancient rites in full swing. They are jolly affairs, and outsiders are nearly always welcome. This being Campania, where eating is in itself a second religion, a visit to a *festa* will invariably involve consuming vast quantities of food, often superbly cooked in makeshift kitchens organized by the local women, and served at knock-down prices. The following are some of the best *feste* to look out for, but keep a watch for others by checking billboards in the piazzas of towns and villages.

January

1	Lively New Year's celebration, **Capri**, with musicians playing the *putipu*, a local folk instrument
6	Re-enactment of the Magi's visit to Bethlehem, in **Lizzano** (Táranto)
17	Festa d'o' Cippo di Sant'Antonio (procession for St Anthony, protector of animals), **Naples**; bonfires and games at **Novoli** (Lecce)
Jan–April	Chamber music at the Teatro delle Palme, **Naples**
Jan–mid-July	Opera at the San Carlo, **Naples**

February

First week	Food and liquor show, **Naples**
Carnival	**Putignano** (Bari) has Italy's longest carnival, beginning 16 Dec . The Carnevale Dauno at **Manfredonia** only lasts four weeks (but in both cases, not much happens until the final week). On Ash Wednesday, **Palo del Colle** (Bari) holds its Palio del Viccio, a contest of donkey riders who try to pierce a bladder hung over the street

April

Holy Week	In the south Holy Week celebrations have a definite Spanish flavour, many featuring processions of floats carried by robed and hooded members of confraternities; the most impressive are at **Táranto**; there is a passion play nearby at **Ginosa**, and a torchlight procession for Good Friday at **Nemoli** (Potenza), followed by an omelette feast at Easter; more tableaux and processions at **Sorrento** and **Sessa Aurunca** (Caserta)
Orthodox Easter	Albanian Easter celebrations at **Lungro** (Calabria)

May

Weekends	Cultural and gastronomic events in **Naples**
6–7	San Nicola, **Bari**, night-time re-enactment in Norman costume of the 'Pious Theft' of St Nicholas's relics
8–10	San Cataldo, at **Táranto**, with sea-borne processions
Last half	International music festival in **Naples**
14–21	Feast of the Madonna di Capocolonna, **Crotone** (Calabria)
3rd week	Comic strip and illustration show, **Naples**
28–29	San Gerardo, **Potenza**, with 'Parade of the Turks'

June

2	La Scamaciata, costume parade and festivites in **Fasano** (Brindisi)
7 June–mid-July	Music festival in **Ravello**
27	Sant'Andrea, with fireworks, costumes and processions in **Amalfi**
4th Sun	Festa dei Gigli, in **Nola**, near Naples—procession of enormous 'lilies' (wooden tower floats), recalling the homecoming of Bishop Paolino after his imprisonment in Africa in 394; Challenge of the Trombonieri, arquebus shooting contest in period costume, recalling a defeat over the Angevins, at **Cava de'Tirreni** (Salerno)

July

2	Madonna della Bruna, **Matera**, religious procession with a huge allegorical float that is torn to pieces at the end of the day
26	Feast of St Anne, **Ischia**—a torchlight procession of hundreds of boats, transformed into floats, to honour the island's patron saint

August

6–8	Feast of San Nicola Pellegrino, **Trani** (Bari), waterfront festival
14–16	Madonna della Madia, **Monópoli** (Bari), water festival celebrating an icon of the Madonna that floated ashore

15	Feast of the straw obelisk, **Fontanarosa**, near Avellino—a harvest thanksgiving ritual; feast of San Rocco, **Roccanova** (Potenza); wheat festival, **Foglianise** (Benevento), procession of decorated tractors, with a light pageant in the evening; Feast of the Assumption, **Positano**, an ancient celebration in honour of the Virgin, which also re-creates the landing—and the defeat—of the Saracens
22	Fishermen's procession on the sea, fireworks, etc, at **Porto Cesareo** (Lecce)
29–31	Feast of Santa Maria di Siponto, **Manfredonia**

September

First 10 days	Neapolitan song contest, fireworks, etc. at **Piedigrotta** (Naples)
19	Feast of San Gennaro, **Naples**, where the faithful gather to watch the liquefaction of the saint's blood
end	Apulian handcrafts show, **Fóggia**

November

10	Feast of San Trifone, **Adelfia** (Bari), cavalcade of children dressed as angels, riding caparisoned horses

December

6	Feast of San Nicola, **Bari**
Throughout	Christmas Fair, selling figures and decorations for the *presepi*, **Naples, Bari, Fóggia** and other cities
8	Immaculate Conception sausage and polenta festival, **San Bartolomeo in Galdo** (Benevento)
24	Chrismas cribs (*presepi*) at the Zinzalusa grotto, at **Castro** (Lecce), midnight mass and tableaux at **Grottaglie** (Táranto) and **Nardò** (Lecce)

Food and Drink

There are those who eat to live and those who live to eat, and then there are the Italians, for whom food has an almost religious significance, unfathomably linked with love, La Mamma, and tradition. In this singular country, where millions of otherwise sane people spend much of their waking hours worrying about their digestion, standards both at home and in the restaurants are understandably high. Few Italians are gluttons, but all are experts on what is what in the kitchen; to serve a meal that is not properly prepared and more than a little complex is tantamount to an insult.

For the visitor this national culinary obsession comes as an extra bonus to the senses— along with Italy's remarkable sights, music, and the warm sun on your back, you can enjoy some of the best tastes and smells the world can offer, prepared daily in Italy's kitchens and fermented in its countless wine cellars.

Breakfast (*colazione*) in Italy is no lingering affair, but an early morning wake-up shot to the brain: a *cappuccino* (*espresso* with hot foamy milk, often sprinkled with chocolate—incidentally first thing in the morning is the only time of day at which any self-respecting Italian will touch the stuff), a *caffè latte* (white coffee) or a *caffè lungo* (a generous portion of *espresso*), accompanied by a croissant-type roll, called a *cornetto* or *briosce*, or one of the other fancy pastries that are a special talent of Naples. This can be consumed in any bar and repeated during the morning as often as necessary. Breakfast in most Italian hotels seldom represents great value.

Lunch (*pranzo*), generally served around 1pm, is the most important meal of the day for the Italians, traditionally with a minimum of a first course (*primo piatto*—any kind of pasta dish, broth or soup, or rice dish or pizza), a second course (*secondo piatto*—a meat dish, accompanied by a *contorno* or side dish—a vegetable, salad, or potatoes usually), followed by fruit or dessert and coffee. Nowadays few restaurants blink if you only order a bowl of pasta. You can, however, begin with a platter of *antipasti*—the appetizers Italians do so brilliantly, ranging from warm seafood delicacies, to raw ham (*prosciutto crudo*), salami in a hundred varieties, lovely vegetables, savoury toasts, olives, pâté and many many more. There are restaurants that specialize in antipasti, and they usually don't take it amiss if you decide to forget the pasta and meat and just nibble on these scrumptious hors d'oeuvres (though in the end it will probably cost more than a full meal). Most Italians accompany their meal with wine and mineral water—*acqua minerale*, with or without bubbles (*con* or *senza gas*), which supposedly aids digestion—concluding their meals with a *digestivo* liqueur.

Cena, the **evening meal**, is usually eaten around 8pm. This is much the same as *pranzo* although lighter, without the pasta; a pizza and beer, eggs or a fish dish. In restaurants, however, they offer all the courses, so if you have only a sandwich for lunch you can have a full meal in the evening.

In Italy the various terms for types of **restaurants**—*ristorante*, *trattoria*, or *osteria*—have been confused. A *trattoria* or *osteria* can be just as elaborate as a restaurant, though rarely is a *ristorante* as informal as a traditional *trattoria*. Unfortunately the old habit of posting menus and prices in the windows has fallen from fashion, so it's often difficult to judge variety or prices. Invariably the least expensive type of restaurant is the *vino e cucina*, simple places serving simple cuisine for simple everyday prices. It is essential to remember that the fancier the fittings, the fancier the bill, though neither of these points has anything at all to do with the quality of the food. If you're uncertain, do as you would at home—look for lots of locals. When you eat out, mentally add to the bill (*conto*) the bread and cover charge (*pane e coperto*, between L2000 and 3000), and a 15 per cent service charge. This is often included in the bill (*servizio compreso*); if not, it will say *servizio non compreso*, and you'll have to do your own arithmetic. Additional tipping is at your own discretion, but never do it in family-owned and -run places.

People who haven't visited Italy for years and have fond memories of eating full meals for under a pound will be amazed at how much prices have risen, though in some respects eating out in Italy is still a bargain, especially when you figure out how much all that wine would have cost you at home. In many places you'll often find restaurants offering a **menu turistico**—full, set meals of usually meagre inspiration for L18,000–25,000. More imaginative chefs often offer a **menu degustazione**—a set-price gourmet meal that allows you to taste their daily specialities and seasonal dishes. Both of these are cheaper than ordering the same food à la carte. When you leave a restaurant you will be given a receipt (*scontrino* or *ricevuto fiscale*) which according to Italian law you must take with you out of the door and carry for at least 60m. If you aren't given one, it means the restaurant is probably fudging on its taxes and thus offering you lower prices. There is a slim chance the tax police (*guardia di finanza*) may have their eye on you and the restaurant, and if you don't have a receipt they could slap you with a heavy fine (L30,000).

There are several alternatives to sit-down meals. The 'hot table' (*tavola calda*) is a stand-up buffet, where you can choose a simple prepared dish or a whole meal, depending on your appetite. The food in these can be truly impressive (especially in the centre of Naples, where the sign out front may read *Degustazione*; some of these offer the best gourmet delights to be had in the south, and are always crowded). Many offer only a few hot dishes, pizza and sandwiches, though in every fair-sized town there will be at least one *tavola calda* with seats where you can contrive a complete dinner outside the usual hours. Little shops that sell pizza by the slice are common in city centres.

At any grocer's (*alimentari*) or market (*mercato*) you can buy the materials for countryside or hotel-room picnics; some places in the smaller towns will make the sandwiches for you. For really elegant picnics, have a *tavola calda* pack up something nice for you. And if everywhere else is closed, there's always the railway station—bars will at least have sandwiches and drinks, and perhaps (usually in unlikely locations in the south) some surprisingly good snacks you've never heard of before. Some of the station bars also prepare *cestini di viaggio*, full-course meals in a basket to help you through long train trips. Common snacks you'll encounter include *panini* of prosciutto, cheese and tomatoes, or other meats; *tramezzini*, little sandwiches on plain, square white bread that are always much better than they look; and pizza, of course.

Many Italian dishes need no introduction—pizza, spaghetti, lasagne and minestrone are familiar to all. What is perhaps less well known is the tremendous regional diversity at the table. Naples, of course, invented both pizza and spaghetti, the classic staples of Italian cuisine. A genuine Neapolitan pizza cooked in a wood-fired brick oven is the archetypal local eating experience, and watching it being made, whirled and slapped high in the air with lightning speed, is just as much of an entertainment as consuming it. The popular *marinara* is anointed with tomato, garlic and basil. *Calzoni* are half-moon envelopes of pizza dough, often filled with ham and cheese and sold as street snacks. Pasta often appears with engaging simplicity, smothered in oil and garlic, or tomato and basil. In the south, factory spaghetti gives way to the real monarch of pasta—nothing more than thick home-made spaghetti, but unmistakably different from the mass-produced commodity. Mozzarella, rather than parmesan, appears most often in pasta sauces. *Mozzarella in carrozza* is a fried sandwich of cheese, often sold as a street snack.

Campania tends to be overly modest about its cuisine. Its biggest favourites are simple enough: *pasta e fagioli* (pasta and beans), *spaghetti alle vongole* (with baby clams); the seafood, as everywhere else along the southern coasts, is exceptional. Besides the ubiquitous clams, squid, octopus and mussels (*zuppe di cozze*, mussels in a hot pepper sauce) appear frequently, along with oily fish like mackerel and sardines. Vegetables (often served as *contorni*, an appetising assortment) are excellent too. Aubergines and courgettes make their way into many local dishes, especially *melanzane parmigiana* (eggplant/aubergine baked with tomato and mozzarella), *misto di frittura* (deep-fried potato, aubergine and courgette flowers), or *zucchini a scapace* (courgettes in tomato sauce). In Campania, as elsewhere around the south, specialities tend to be hotter and spicier than in the north, and are often seasoned with condiments like capers, garlic, anchovies, lemon juice, oregano, olives and fennel. Dishes described as *alla napoletana* usually contain tomato, capers, black olives and garlic.

As far as the level of cooking is concerned, Calabria and the Basilicata are probably the most improved regions of Italy compared to ten years ago—a little prosperity makes any corner of Italy blossom. Back in ancient Sybaris, the gourmet centre of the Greek Mediterranean, and in the other towns of Magna Graecia, public gastronomical revues rivalled the athletic contests in popularity; good recipes for fish sauces were treated as state secrets, and slaves who happened to be good cooks were worth enormous sums in the open market. Forget all that—Calabrian cooking today is really not that distinctive, except perhaps in a certain fondness for really hot peppers, but with the simple, fresh local ingredients they use, it won't often be disappointing either. The biggest treat will be the seafood, led by the best swordfish anywhere, caught fresh from the Straits of Messina.

Apulia is more prosperous, and the Apulians take their cuisine a little more seriously. *La cucina pugliese* makes use of all the natural resources at its disposal, especially the seafood; you won't meet anyone in the region who isn't convinced theirs is the best in all Italy. Bari is particularly famous for fish, while Táranto has excellent mussels, mostly from the Mare Grande—and called here *mitili*, instead of *cozze* as they are in the rest of Italy. They feature prominently on the menus of virtually all Táranto's restaurants. You'll learn a lot of new words for shellfish in Apulia, and taste varieties seen nowhere else: favourites include *fasulare*, small and roundish with tan-coloured shells, and *piedi di porco*, small rugged black shells. Apulians scoff at the *vongole* served in *spaghetti alle vongole* everywhere else in Italy. Those tiny clams are really *guttuli*, they say. Real Apulian *vongole* are much bigger, and equally tasty, and you will even encounter *vongole imperiale*, giants among the baby clams.

The local olive oil is dark and strong, closer to that of Greece than the lighter oils of Tuscany and Umbria; the olives too are smaller and fuller flavoured, coming from trees whose roots have to dig deep into the soil to reach water. As in most of southern Italy, sheep make up a great part of the livestock, and the region's sheep's cheeses include the local styles of *pecorino* and *ricotta*—look out for the unusually strongly flavoured *ricotta forte*. It goes particularly well in sauces with the favourite Apulian pasta—*orecchiette*, 'little ears'—formed by shaping the uncooked pasta with the thumb. A popular dish is *orecchiette* with turnip greens: *con cima di rape*.

Puddings and cakes are rich and sweet all over the south. *Pasteria* is one of the most celebrated local sweets, a ricotta pie full of wheat berries, candied fruit and spices, traditionally eaten at Easter. Another irresistible speciality of Naples is *sfogliatella* (flaky pastry, sometimes stuffed with ricotta and candied peel), which is sometimes eaten at breakfast time. If this sounds too much of a good thing, the best deal of all (in season) is a fresh peach, naked and unadorned.

Wine

Italy is a country where everyday wine is cheaper than Coca-Cola or milk, and where nearly every rural family owns some vineyards or has some relatives who supply most of their daily needs—which are not great. Even though they live in one of the world's largest wine-growing countries, Italians imbibe relatively little, and only at meals.

If Italy has an infinite variety of regional dishes, there is an equally bewildering array of regional wines, many of which are rarely exported because they are best drunk young. Unless you're dining at a restaurant with an exceptional cellar, do as the Italians do and order a carafe of the local wine (*vino locale* or *vino della casa*). You won't often be wrong. Most Italian wines are named after the grape and the district they come from. If the label says DOC (*Denominazione di Origine Controllata*) it means that the wine comes from a specially defined area and was produced according to a certain traditional method. DOCG (*Denominazione di Origine Controllata e Garantia*) is allegedly a more rigorous classification, indicating that the wines not only conform to DOC standards, but are tested by government-appointed inspectors. At present few wines have been granted this status, mainly those from Italy's more prestigious Tuscan vineyards, but it is planned that the number should increase steadily.

Italians are fond of postprandial brandies (to aid digestion)—the famous Stock or Vecchia Romagna labels are always good. Grappa (acquavitae) is usually tougher, and often drunk in black coffee after a meal (a *caffè corretto*). Other members of any Italian bar include Campari, the famous red bitter, drunk on its own or in cocktails; Vermouth, Fernet Branca, Cynar and Averno, popular aperitifs/digestives; and liqueurs like Strega, the witch potion from Benevento, apricot-flavoured Amaretto, cherry Maraschino, aniseed Sambuca, as well as any number of locally brewed elixirs, often made by monks.

Campania was known for wine in Roman times. The legendary full-bodied Falerno was highly regarded by the ancients, and praised by Horace and Pliny. Today, the region produces surprisingly little, and not much of any note. The most famous is Lacrima Cristi, grown on the slopes of Vesuvius and only recently granted DOC status. Others to look out for include the white Greco di Tufo or Fiano di Avellino, or the deep, heavy red Taurasi.

Some good wines come from Calabria, though nothing especially distinguished. You're most likely to encounter *Ciró* from the Ionian coast, a strong red wine best drunk in large quantities (also white and rosé). Calabrians claim Ciró as the oldest wine in Italy, made since the time of the Greeks in the area north of Crotone. A new DOC wine similar to Ciró, and made in a neighbouring region, is *Melissa*. Other good, strong DOC wines include *Savuto* and *Pellaro*; there is also a famous dessert wine, *Greco di Gerace*, and similar *Grecos* from the southern *terrazze* of Aspromonte. The Basilicata doesn't produce much wine, but try the excellent *Aglianico* red from Monte Vulture.

Apulian wine, like the cuisine, tends to be strong and full-bodied, and has had a high reputation since Roman times. Today there are about 24 different wines produced in Apulia,
including whites, reds, rosés, sparkling wines and the particularly sweet Muscat. Some
that are worth looking out for are the powerful red, *Cerignola*, from Fóggia
province; other rich reds include *Copertino* and *Salice Salentino* (both these DOC
denominations come in rosé too). Keep a look out for the famous and formidable *Primitivo*
of Manduria, Apulia's oldest and strongest wine—some can be as much as 18% alcohol.
Among the whites, the best is the comparatively light, delicate dry wine from
Locorotondo.

Health and Emergencies

Citizens of EU countries are entitled to reciprocal health care in Italy's National Health
Service and a 90 per cent discount on prescriptions (bring Form E111 with you). The
E111 does not cover all medical expenses (no repatriation costs, for example, and no
private treatment), and it is advisable to take out separate travel insurance for full cover.
Citizens of non-EU countries should check carefully that they have adequate insurance for
any medical expenses, and the cost of returning home. Australia has a reciprocal health
care scheme with Italy, but New Zealand, Canada and the USA do not. If you already have
health insurance, a student card, or a credit card, you may be entitled to some medical
cover abroad.

In an **emergency**, dial © 113 for an ambulance in Italy (*ambulanza*); in Naples,
© 7520696 (24 hours), daytime only © 7520850. The hospital (*ospedale*) in Naples is
Policlinico, Via Sergio Pansini, © 7461111—though this is a regular subject of horror
stories in the local newspapers. Less serious problems can be treated at a *pronto soccorso*
(casualty/first aid department) at any hospital, or at a local health unit (*unità sanitariale
locale*—USL). Airports and main railway stations also have first-aid posts. If you have to
pay for any health treatment, make sure you get a receipt.

Pharmacies are generally open 8.30am–1pm and 4–8pm. Pharmacists are trained to give
advice for minor ills and administer simple first aid. Any large town has a pharmacy that
stays open 24 hours; others take turns to stay open (the address rota is posted in the
windows of pharmacies and in the newspaper *Il Mattino*). The 24-hour pharmacy in
Naples is Carducci, Via Carducci 21–23, © 417283. There is also a public health service
doctor in Naples on call 24 hours on © 7513177.

No specific vaccinations are required or advised for citizens of most countries before
visiting Italy; the main **health risks** are the usual travellers' woes of upset stomachs or the
effects of too much sun. Occasional, much-publicized outbreaks of more serious disease
have occurred in Naples in recent years (cholera, for example), but these are rarely likely
to affect travellers. Take a supply of useful medicaments with you (e.g. insect repellent,
anti-diarrhoeal medicine, sun lotion and antiseptic cream), and any drugs you need

regularly. Stick to bottled water (dehydration is a serious risk in those southern climes) and avoid uncooked shellfish around the polluted Bay of Naples.

Money and Banks

It's a good idea to order a wad of *lire* from your home bank to have on hand when you arrive in Italy, the land of strikes, unforeseen delays and quirky banking hours. Take great care how you carry it, however (don't keep it all in one place). **Banking hours** vary, but core times are usually Monday to Friday, 8.30am–1.20pm and 3–4pm, closed weekends and on local and national holidays (*see below*).

Obtaining money is often a frustrating business involving much queueing and form-filling. The major banks and exchange bureaux licensed by the Bank of Italy give the best exchange rates for currency or traveller's cheques. Hotels, private exchanges in resorts and FS-run exchanges at railway stations usually have less advantageous rates, but are open outside normal banking hours. Remember that Italians indicate decimals with commas and thousands with full points.

In **Naples**, you can change money outside normal banking hours at the post office (*see* p.26), in most good hotels, and at travel agents such as Thomas Cook, Piazza Municipio 70, ✆ 5518399; CIT, Piazza Municipio 72, ✆ 5525426; and Partenotour, Piazza dei Martiri 23, ✆ 7643415.

Besides traveller's cheques, most banks will give you cash on a recognized **credit card** or **Eurocheque** with a Eurocheque card (taking little or no commission), and in big cities such as Naples you can find automatic tellers (ATMs) to spout cash on a Visa, American Express or Eurocheque card. You need a PIN number to use these. Make sure you read the instructions carefully, or your card may be retained by the machine. MasterCard (Access) is much less widely acceptable in Italy. Large hotels, resort area restaurants, shops and car hire firms will accept plastic as well; many smaller places will not. From sad experience, Italians are wary of plastic—you can't even use it at motorway petrol stops.

You can have money transferred to you through an Italian bank but this process may take over a week, even if it's sent urgent *espressissimo*. You will need your passport as identification when you collect it. Sending cheques by post is inadvisable.

National Holidays

Most museums, as well as banks and shops, are closed on the following national holidays:

1 January (New Year's Day)

6 January (Epiphany)

Easter Monday

25 April (Liberation Day)

1 May (Labour Day)

15 August (Assumption, or *Ferragosto*, the official start of the Italian holiday season)

1 November (All Saints' Day)

8 December (Immaculate Conception)

25 December (Christmas Day)

26 December (*Santo Stefano*, St Stephen's Day)

In Naples, the feast of San Gennaro (19 September) is also a holiday.

Opening Hours, Museums and Churches

Although it varies from region to region, most of Italy closes down at 1pm until 3 or 4pm to let everyone eat and properly digest the main meal of the day. Afternoon hours are 4–7, sometimes 5–8 in the hot summer months. Bars are often the only places open during the early afternoon. Shops of all kinds are usually closed on Saturday afternoons, Sundays, and Monday mornings as well—although grocery stores and supermarkets do open on Monday mornings.

Italy's **churches** have always been a prime target for art thieves and as a consequence are usually locked when there isn't a sacristan or caretaker to keep an eye on things. All churches, except for the really important cathedrals and basilicas, close in the afternoon at the same hours as the shops, and the little ones tend to stay closed. Always have a pocketful of coins for the light machines in churches, or whatever work of art you came to inspect will remain shrouded in ecclesiastical gloom. Don't do your visiting during services, and don't come to see paintings and statues in churches the week preceding Easter—you will probably find them covered with mourning shrouds. Many churches are less strict about dress than was once the case but you should cover up for cathedrals.

Many of Italy's **museums** are magnificent, many are run with shameful neglect, and many have been closed for years for 'restoration' with slim prospects of reopening in the foreseeable future. With two works of art per inhabitant, Italy has a hard time financing the preservation of its national heritage; it's as well to inquire at the tourist office to find out what is open and what is 'temporarily' closed before setting off on a wild goose chase.

In general, Sunday afternoons and Mondays are dead periods for the sightseer—you may want to make them your travelling days. Places without specified opening hours can usually be visited on request—but it is best to go before 1pm. We have listed the hours of important sights and museums, and specified which ones charge admission. Expect to pay between L4000 and L8000 to get in. The more important sites such as Pompeii may cost up to L12,000. EU citizens under 18 and over 65 get free admission to state museums on presentation of their passports, at least in theory.

Post Offices and Telephones

Dealing with *la posta italiana* has always been a risky, frustrating, time-consuming affair. One of the scandals that has mesmerized Italy in the past few years was the one involving the minister of the post office, who disposed of literally tons of backlog mail by tossing it in the Tiber. When the news broke, he was replaced—the new minister, having learned his lesson, burned all the mail the post office was incapable of delivering. Not surprisingly, fed-up Italians view the invention of the fax machine as a gift from the Madonna.

If you want to take your chances, post offices are usually open Monday to Saturday from 9am until 1pm, or until 6 or 7pm in a large city. To have your mail sent poste restante (general delivery), have it addressed to the central post office (*Fermo Posta*) and allow three to four weeks for it to arrive. Make sure your surname is very clearly written in block capitals. To pick up your mail you must present your passport and pay a nominal charge. Stamps (*francobolli*) may be purchased in post offices or at tobacconists (*tabacchi*, identified by their black or blue signs with a white T). Prices fluctuate. The rates for letters and postcards (depending how many words you write!) vary according to the whim of the tobacconist or postal clerk.

You can also have money telegraphed to you through the post office; if all goes well, this can happen in a mere three days, but expect a fair proportion of it to go into commission.

In **Naples** the main **post office** is in Piazza Matteotti, © 5511456, near Via Toledo, and is open Monday to Friday 8am–8pm, Saturday 8am–12 noon. You can also send faxes and telegrams from here.

Public telephones for **international calls** may be found in the offices of Telecom Italia (Italy's telephone company). They are the only places where you can make reverse-charge calls (*erre*, collect calls) but be prepared for a wait, as all these calls go through the operator in Rome. Rates for long-distance calls are among the highest in Europe. Calls within Italy are cheapest after 10pm; international calls after 11pm. Most phone booths now take either coins or phone cards (*schede telefoniche*) available in L5000, L10,000 or L15,000 amounts at tobacconists and news-stands. In smaller villages and islands, you can usually find *telefoni a scatti*, with a meter on them, in at least one bar (a small commission is generally charged). Try to avoid telephoning from hotels, which often add 25 per cent to the bill. Telephone numbers in Italy currently change with alarming regularity as the antiquated system is updated.

Phone centres in Naples are at the Stazione Centrale, at Via Depretis 40, and in the Galleria Umberto I. The code for Naples is 081.

Direct calls may be made by dialling the international prefix (for the UK 0044, Ireland 00353, USA and Canada 001, Australia 0061, New Zealand 0064). If you're calling Italy from abroad, dial 39 and then drop the first 0 from the telephone prefix.

Shopping

You'll find some of the lowest shopping prices in **Naples**, especially in its various markets (*see* p.86). **Amalfi**'s specialities are fine stationery (paper-making was already an art and an important industry here in the Middle Ages) and ceramics—mostly tourist bric-a-brac, but some of it very well done. Every conceivable luxury item Italy makes is sold in the shops of **Sorrento**—but make sure you come in the off-season (December and January are best) when you'll find some outstanding bargains in fashions, Murano glass and other trinkets. Sorrento's own speciality is *intarsia*, inlaid wood scenes on tables or trays, or simply framed for hanging. They are exquisite things, and prices are often reasonable. Prices for clothes in Italy are generally very high, and sizes are tailored for slim Italian builds. Shoes, in particular, tend to be narrower than in most Western countries.

Sports and Activities

Football

Soccer (*il calcio*) is a national obsession. For many Italians its importance far outweighs tedious issues like the state of the nation, the government of the day, or any momentous international event—not least because of the weekly chance (slim but real) of becoming an instant lira billionaire in the Lotteria Sportiva. The sport was actually introduced by the English, but a Renaissance game, something like a cross between football and rugby, has existed in Italy for centuries. Modern Italian teams are known for their grace, precision, and teamwork; rivalries are intense, scandals, especially bribery and cheating, are rife. The tempting rewards offered by such big-time entertainment attract all manner of corrupt practices, yet crowd violence is minimal compared with the havoc wreaked by other countries' lamentable fans. Serie A is the equivalent of the first division, comprising 18 teams. The big southern Serie A team is, of course, Napoli, whose most charismatic player's name still trips off the tongue of the least *sportif* foreigner. The legendary Maradona no longer plays for Naples after his fall from grace. But almost any weekend (matches are generally played on Sunday afternoons) you should find a good game somewhere in the region. Tickets aren't cheap for the top matches (L25,000–100,000). In Naples, the main ground is the Stadio di San Paolo in Fuorigrotta (a western suburb—take Ferrovia Cumana as far as Mostra and the stadium is directly outside), © 239 56 23.

Fishing

Many freshwater lakes and streams are stocked, and if you're more interested in fresh fish than the sport of it, there are innumerable trout farms where you can practically pick the fish up out of the water with your hands. Sea fishing, from the shore, from boats, or underwater (though not much with an aqualung) is possible almost everywhere without a permit; to fish in fresh water you need to purchase a year's membership card (currently L189,000) from the Federazione Italiana della Pesca Sportiva, which has an office in every province. In Naples it's in Piazza Santa Maria degli Angeli, © and @ (081) 7644921; they will inform you about local conditions and restrictions.

Watersports and Beaches

At most resorts it is possible to hire boats and equipment, and go windsurfing, waterskiing, or diving (in Naples contact the Subacquei Napoletani, Piazza Santa Maria degli Angeli 11, © 7641985). Capri is one of the best choices for such activities, with some of the cleanest waters in the Bay of Naples. You can also take submarine trips around the island. For scuba diving, waterskiing, canoeing and boat hire, contact the Sea Service Centre, Marina Piccola, Via Mulo 63 (© 8370221). Sorrento, Positano, Amalfi and Salerno also offer a range of watersports, and lots of cruises.

Many southern Italian beaches are disappointingly flat, and scarcely improved by regimented lines of parasols and sunbeds. Those around the Bay of Naples tend to be of grey volcanic sand and the free public ones are small, crowded and neglected with few facilities. Accept the fact, then, that to enjoy Italian beaches you will have to pay: most of the best stretches of sand (some of them artificial) are operated by private concessionaires. For the most attractive resort beaches, head for Positano, Minori or Maiori. Despite the appalling pollution immediately around Naples, the water off the islands of Ischia, Procida and Capri is generally clean and inviting. There's no denying that the Amalfi coast is scenically the most dazzling stretch of shoreline in the whole of Italy. Below the Gulf of Salerno, the Cilento coast is less spectacular, generally rocky rather than sandy, and popular for scuba diving. Good beaches do exist, however, and have the distinct advantage of more privacy and freedom from the crowds you find on the Amalfi coast.

Elsewhere in the south you'll never be far from an empty beach—there are hundreds of miles of them. Just don't expect them to be anything near clean (though the water is usually fine, save near the big industrial centres).

Sailing

Almost all the islands have some facilities for **yachts**, though they may not be equipped for a long stay. You can bring your own boat to Italy for six months without any paperwork if you bring it by car; if you arrive by sea you must report to the port authority. The harbourmaster (*capitaneria di porto*) at your first Italian port of call will give you a document called a *costituto*, which you will have to produce for subsequent harbour-masters; this permits the purchase of tax-free fuel. For further information, contact the Italian State Tourist Office or write to:

Mare Club d'Italia (MA.C.I), Via A Bargoni 8, 00153 Rome, ✆ (06) 5894046/5897084.

Other useful addresses are:

Federazione Italiana Vela (Italian Sailing Federation), Via Brigata Bisagno 2/17, Genoa.

Federazione Italiana Motonautica (Italian Motorboat Federation), VIa Piranesi 44/b, Milan.

The main Bay of Naples yacht harbours are Posillipo in Naples; Capri; Procida; and Porto, Casamicciola, Lacco Ameno and Forio d'Ischia on Ischia.

Tennis

Many of the more expensive hotels have courts, and non-residents may be able to use them by arrangement with the hotel or local tourist office. There are public courts in **Naples**, Via Giochi del Mediterraneo, ✆ (081) 7603912; **Benevento**, Viale Atlantici, ✆ (0824) 29920; and **Ischia Porto**, Lungomare Colombo, ✆ (081) 991013.

Time

Italy is one hour ahead of Greenwich Mean Time. From the last weekend of March to the end of September, Italian Summer Time (daylight saving time) is in effect.

Tourist Offices Abroad

UK: 1 Princes Street, London W1R 8AY, ✆ (0171) 408 1254.

US: 630 Fifth Avenue, Suite 1565, New York, NY 10111, ✆ (212) 245 4822, ✉ 586 9249; 12400 Wilshire Blvd, Suite 550, Los Angeles, CA 90025, ✆ (310) 820 0698, ✉ 820 6357.

Canada: 1 Place Ville Marie, Suite 1914, Montreal, Quebec H3B 3M9, ✆ (514) 866 7667, ✉ 592 1429.

Japanese: 2–7–14 Minami, Aoyama, Minato-ku, Tokyo 107, ✆ (813) 347 82 051, ✉ 34799356—also responsible for Australia and New Zealand.

Tourist and travel information may also be available from the offices of Alitalia (Italy's national airline) or CIT (Italy's state-run travel agency) in some countries.

Where to Stay

All accommodation in Italy is classified by the provincial tourist boards. Price control, however, has been deregulated since 1992. Hotels now set their own tariffs, which means that in some places prices have rocketed, even in the poorer south. After a period of rapid and erratic price fluctuation, tariffs are at last settling down again to more predictable levels under the influence of market forces. The quality of furnishings and facilities has generally improved in all categories in recent years. But you can still find plenty of older style hotels and *pensioni*, whose eccentricities of character and architecture (in some cases undeniably charming) may frequently be at odds with modern standards of comfort or even safety. In Naples, particularly, good accommodation is scarce and should be booked ahead. Campania's tariffs are generally lower than in the Grand Tour towns and cities further north, but Capri's ritziest establishments vie with any in Italy on price.

Hotels and Guesthouses

Italian *alberghi* come in all shapes and sizes. They are rated from one to five stars, depending on what facilities they offer (not their character, style or charm). The star ratings are some indication of price levels, but for tax reasons not all hotels choose to advertise themselves at the rating to which they are entitled, so you may find a modestly rated hotel just as comfortable (or more so) than a higher rated one. Conversely, you may find that a hotel offers few stars in hopes of attracting budget-conscious travellers, but charges just as much as a higher-rated neighbour. *Pensioni* are generally more modest establishments, though nowadays the distinction between these and ordinary hotels is becoming blurred. *Locande* are traditionally an even more basic form of hostelry, but these days the term may denote somewhere fairly chic. Other inexpensive accommodation is sometimes known as *alloggi* or *affittacamere*. There are usually plenty of cheap dives around railway stations; for somewhere more salubrious, head for the historic quarters. Whatever the shortcomings of the decor, furnishings and fittings, you can usually rely at least on having clean sheets.

Price lists, by law, must be posted on the door of every room, along with meal prices and any extra charges (such as air conditioning, or even a shower in cheap places). Many hotels display two or three different rates, depending on the season. Low-season rates may be about a third lower than peak-season tariffs. Some resort hotels close down altogether for several months a year. During high season you should always book ahead to be sure of a room (a fax reservation may be less frustrating to organize than one by post). If you have paid a deposit, your booking is valid under Italian law, but don't expect it to be refunded if you have to cancel. Tourist offices publish annual regional lists of hotels and pensions with current rates, but do not make reservations for visitors. Major railway stations generally have accommodation booking desks; inevitably, a fee is charged. Chain hotels or motels are generally the easiest hotels to book, but are often less interesting to stay in. If you arrive without a reservation, begin looking or phoning round for accommodation early in the day. If possible, inspect the room (and bathroom facilities) before you book, and check the tariff carefully. Italian hoteliers may legally alter their rates twice during the year, so printed tariffs or tourist board lists (and prices quoted in this book!) may be out of date. Hoteliers who wilfully overcharge should be reported to the local tourist office. You will be asked for your passport for registration purposes.

Price guide for double rooms

The price categories used in this guide are for a double room per night in high season:

Very expensive: L360,000 upwards

Expensive: L210,000–L359,000

Moderate: L105,000–L209,000

Inexpensive: L70,000–L104,000

Cheap: up to L70,000

You can expect to pay about two-thirds the rate for single occupancy, though in high season you may be charged the full double rate in a popular beach resort. Extra beds are usually charged at about a third of the room rate. Rooms without private bathrooms are generally 20–30 per cent less, and most establishments offer discounts for children sharing parents' rooms, or children's meals. A *camera singola* (single room) may cost anything from about L30,000 upwards. Double rooms are normally twin-bedded (*camera doppia*). If you want a double bed, specify a *camera matrimoniale*.

Breakfast is usually optional in hotels and *pensioni*. You can usually get better value by eating breakfast in a bar or café if you have any choice. In high season you may be expected to take half-board in resorts if the hotel has a restaurant, and one-night stays may be refused.

Youth Hostels

There aren't many of these in Italy (where they are known as *alberghi* or *ostelli per la gioventù*), but they are generally pleasant and sometimes located in historic buildings. The Associazione Italiana Alberghi per la Gioventù (Italian Youth Hostel Association, or AIG) is affiliated to the International Youth Hostel Federation. For a full list of hostels, contact AIG at Via Cavour 44, 00184 Roma, ✆ (06) 4871152, ✉ (06) 4880492. An international membership card will enable you to stay in any of them (cards can be purchased on the spot in many hostels if you don't already have one). Hostels around Naples include: Agerola-S. Lazzaro or Mergellina (Naples) and Irno (Salerno). Rates are usually somewhere between L12,000 and L18,000, including breakfast, for a place in a dormitory. Discounts are available for senior citizens, and some family rooms are available. You generally have to check in after 5pm, and pay for your room before 9am. Hostels usually close for most of the daytime, and many operate a curfew. During the spring, noisy school parties cram hostels for field trips. In the summer, it's advisable to book ahead. Contact the hostels directly.

Camping

Most of the official sites are near beach resorts, though there are a few inland in scenic areas or near major tourist centres such as Pompeii or Paestum. Camping is not the fanatical holiday activity it is in France, for example, nor necessarily any great bargain, but it is popular with many holiday-making families in August, when you can expect to find many sites at bursting point. Unofficial camping is generally frowned on and may attract a stern rebuke from the local police. Camper vans (and facilities for them) are increasingly popular. You can obtain a list of local sites from any regional tourist office. Camp site charges generally range from about L7000 per adult; tents and vehicles additionally cost about L7000 each. Small extra charges may also be levied for hot showers and electricity. A car-borne couple could therefore spend practically as much for a night at a well-equipped camp site as in a cheap hotel.

To obtain a camping carnet and book ahead, write to the **Centro Internazionale Prenotazioni Campeggio**, Casella Postale 23, 50041, Calenzano, Firenze, and request their list of camp sites as well as the booking form. The **Touring Club Italiano** (TCI) publishes a comprehensive annual guide to camp sites and tourist villages throughout Italy. Write to: TCI, Corso Italia 10, Milan, ✆ (02) 8526245. Note that camping is strictly forbidden on Capri (though there are several sites on Ischia and Procida). The closest site to Naples is near the bubbling, sulphurous, rotten-egg-smelling volcanic crater of Solfatara, in the Pozzuoli district west of the city. It's usually crowded.

Agriturismo

For a breath of rural seclusion, the normally gregarious Italians head for a spell on a working farm, in accommodation (usually self-catering) that often approximates to the French *gîte*. Often, however, the real pull of the place is a restaurant in which you can sample some home-grown produce (olives, wine, etc.). Outdoor activities may also be on tap (riding, fishing, and so forth). This branch of the Italian tourist industry has burgeoned in recent years, and every region now has several Agriturist offices. Prices of farmhouse accommodation, compared with the over-hyped 'Tuscan villa', are still reasonable (expect to pay around L40,000–60,000 for a cottage or double room). Agriturismo isn't as well established in Campania as in Tuscany or Umbria, but possibilities certainly exist. To make the most of your rural hosts, it's as well to have a little Italian under your belt before you bury yourself in an olive grove. Local tourist offices will have information on this type of accommodation in their areas; otherwise you can obtain complete listings compiled by the national organization Agriturist, Corso Vittorio Emanuele 101, 00186 Rome, ✆ (06) 6852342, or Turismo Verde, Via Mariano Fortuny 20, 00196 Rome, ✆ (06) 3669931. Both publications are available in Italian bookshops. The local office in Naples is at Via S. Lucia 90, 80132 Napoli, ✆ (081) 281397.

Self-catering Tour Operators

One of the most enjoyable, and best-value, ways of visiting Italy is to opt for self-catering accommodation, with the family or friends. Centralized booking agencies exist in many countries as well as Italy, and can organize holidays on the coast or in genuinely rural settings, sometimes offering discounted air or ferry fares and fly-drive schemes to egg you on. Watch for the small ads, or see the list below.

Apartment Service, 5–6 Francis Grove, London SW19 4DT, ✆ (0181) 944 1444, ✆ 944 6744: selected apartment accommodation for short or extended stays in different locations in several Italian cities.

Citalia, Marco Polo House, 3–5 Lansdowne Road, Croydon, CR9 1LL, ✆ (0181) 688 9989: tailor-made holidays and self-catering along the coast.

CV Travel, 43 Cadogan Street, London SW3 2PR, ✆ (0171) 581 0851: villa holidays.

Hometours International, PO Box 11503, Knoxville, TN 37938, ✆ (423) 690 8484/ (800) 367 4668

Interhome, 383 Richmond Road, Twickenham, Middx,TW1 2EF ✆ (0181) 891 1294.

Italian Chapters, 102 St John's Wood Terrace, London NW8 6PL, ✆ (0171) 722 9560: villa holidays in Naples, Amalfi, Sorrento, Cilento and Calabria.

Long Travel, The Steps, All Stretton, Shropshire, SY6 6HG, ✆ (01694) 722193, ✆ 724291: villas in southern Italy for those seeking authentic unspoilt Italy.

Sovereign Italia, First Choice House, London Rd, Betts Way, Crawley, W. Sussex RH10 2GX, ✆ (01293) 560777: villa-apartments in Ravello and Sorrento.

Vacanze in Italia, Bignor, Nr Pulborough, W. Sussex, RH20 1QD, ✆ (01798) 869433: individual villa holidays specialists.

History and Art

Masaniello

Some 50,000 years ago, when the Alps were covered by an ice cap and the low level of the Mediterranean made Italy a much wider peninsula than it is now, Neanderthal Man was gracing Italy with his low-browed presence. HIs successors, the much more talented and debonair Cro-Magnon Italians, turned up about 18,000 BC; they knew something about keeping animals and fishing, and as elsewhere in Europe they created some genuine art: female statuettes made from bone, and other bones carved with tidy geometric patterns. They were fond of shellfish, and used the shells for jewellery.

The transition from the Palaeolithic (old stone age) to the Mesolithic (middle stone age) occurred in the 9th millennium BC. The time of nomadic hunters had passed, and a settled and quite civilized agricultural society comes soon after with the Neolithic era, perhaps reaching Italy *c.* 7000 BC. The first Neolithic Italians may have come in an invasion or migration from the Balkans. These peoples installed themselves first on the plains around Fóggia, in Apulia; by 4000 they had spread across the peninsula. Never great builders (except in Apulia, which has almost all of the dolmens in Italy) these apparently peaceful folk proved easy marks for the various tribes of Indo-Europeans, who arrived about 3000.

800–358 BC: in which the South gets a heavy dose of Hellenic culture

When the first Greek colonists arrived, in the 8th century, they found the region inhabited by a number of powerful, distinct tribes with related languages. Chief among them were the powerful Samnites, who occupied much of inland Campania and the south, while the area around the Bay of Naples was inhabited by the Ausones, or Oscans, and the Opici. Further south were the Daunii in northern Apulia, the dolmen-building Messapians in southern Apulia and the Bruttians in Calabria. The Greeks, whose trading routes had long covered Italy's southern coasts, looked upon that 'underdeveloped' country as a New World for exploration and colonization. All over the south, there are tantalizing archaeological clues that the Greeks had begun settlements even earlier, in the Mycenaean age before the fall of Troy, but about these little is known.

In 775, Greeks founded a trading settlement at Pithecusa, on the island of Ischia, squarely in the middle of the important trade route that carried Tuscany's iron to the east. The first planned urban colony in Campania was Cumae, in 750, and after that new Greek cities started springing up all over the south and Sicily, including Elea in Campania, Rhegium (Reggio di Calabria) on the straits, and Taras (Táranto), Sybaris, Croton and Metapontum on the Ionian Sea. Another band of Greeks founded a city called Parthenope, on the hill called Pizzofalcone that now divides the old and new quarters of Naples, and on the nearby island where the Castel dell'Ovo is now. Centuries later, the poet Virgil, who loved this coast and spent much of his life on it, dressed up the city's origins with the story of a siren named Parthenope; according to Virgil, Odysseus visited here, and when he resisted all her attempts to seduce him into remaining with her, Parthenope threw herself off the cliff and drowned.

The city Parthenope didn't fare too well either. Throughout Greek Italy, neighbouring cities tended to fight like Kilkenny cats, and Cumae and Parthenope slugged it out until the latter succumbed. The Cumaeans may have destroyed their rival; in any case they founded a new city—*Neapolis*—right next to it. Like most Greek foundations, Neapolis was laid out in a rigid rectangular grid, like Manhattan or Chicago, a pattern that has survived with almost no changes in the Spacca district today.

The Greeks could never hope to have such a desirable land entirely to themselves. In the 6th century, the Etruscans arrived from the north. This powerful and talented nation, then at the height of its culture and expanding in all directions, colonized much of Campania's interior, founding the cities of Capua, Nola and Acerra (modern historians trace Etruscan expansion by their manic habit of surveying land into 700m squares; besides gladiatorial combats, portrait busts, rampant religious superstition and many other contributions, the Etruscans also taught their Roman neighbours how to make straight roads). Conflict with the Greeks, their greatest trade rivals, was inevitable, and serious. Warfare began in 524 with an unsuccessful Etruscan siege of Cumae. The Greeks got the better of it from then on, and finally defeated the Etruscans at sea in the decisive Battle of Cumae (474). Their southern colonies straggled on for a while, but the taking of Capua by the Samnites in 432 put an end to Etruscan hopes in the south forever.

Greek Campania by this time was only the northernmost province of a genuine New World—*Magna Graecia*, a land of rich culture and wealthy cities that included Sicily and all of southern Italy's coasts save the Adriatic. Greek Italy's painters and sculptors took their places among the greatest of Greece's golden age, but its most memorable contributions were in philosophy. The famous Elean School (from the city of Elea, in the Cilento) included some of the most important pre-Socratics: Parmenides, who invented the concept of atoms, and Zeno, with his pesky paradoxes. Down in Calabria and Sicily, the Greeks also distinguished themselves by a consistent bestiality towards each other—constant wars between cities and civil wars within them, with the losers usually massacred or sold off as slaves. Somehow the Campanian towns managed to avoid most of the unpleasantness, while playing an important role in teaching art and culture to their Italian neighbours. The Ausones, Samnites and other nations became more or less Hellenized, while a bellicose and rapidly growing little republic up north was proving a less gifted student—Rome.

358 BC–AD 406: a ride on the Roman rollercoaster

In the 6th century, Rome had chased out its Etruscan rulers and began terrorizing all the towns and tribes of central Italy. By the 4th century, she had gobbled up the lot, and the borders of the Roman state extended into Campania. About 358 the senators were able to turn their attention to the only power in Italy capable of competing with Rome on an equal basis: the Samnites. These rugged highlanders of the southern Apennines, with their capital at Benevento, had begun to seize parts of coastal Campania from the Greeks. The Romans drove them out in 341, but in the Second Samnite War the Samnites dealt them a severe defeat (Battle of the Caudine Forks, in 321). In the third war, feeling themselves surrounded by Roman allies, the Samnites formed an alliance with the northern Etruscans and Celts, leading to a general Italian commotion in which the Romans beat everybody, annexing almost all of Italy by 283.

After the Samnites, it was the turn of the Greeks. The frightened cities of Magna Graecia sent off for Pyrrhus of Epirus, a brilliant adventurer with a big army, to help keep the barbarians out. Pyrrhus won a string of inconclusive 'Pyrrhic' victories, but after finally losing a battle in 275, at Benevento, he quit and returned home, allowing the Romans to leisurely snatch up the deserted Greek cities one by one. Now the conquest was complete. All along the Romans had been diabolically clever in managing their new demesne, maintaining most of the tribes and cities as nominally independent states, while planting Latin colonies everywhere in or near the ruins of cities they had destroyed, such as Paestum, Puteoli (Pozzuoli), and Benevento.

Rome went on to fatten on even bigger prey—the Carthaginians in the 3rd century, the rest of the Mediterranean in the 2nd—while the south became thoroughly integrated into the Roman system. Wealthy senators and businessmen lined the Bay of Naples with their villas, while Puteoli grew up as the leading port of Italy, the terminus for the grain ships from Sicily and Africa. Campania was booming, largely from the manufacture of ceramics and luxury goods; its metropolis, Capua, was a city renowned for perfume and fair ladies, in population and wealth the second city of Italy.

But especially in the lands south of Naples, Roman rule had its darker side. The conquerors appropriated most of the good land and divided it among themselves, creating vast estates called *latifundiae* and a new society where a small class of fantastically wealthy landowners lorded it over an increasingly impoverished peasantry and middle class. Debt and Roman law pushed large numbers of the poor into slavery. In other parts of Italy the situation was just as bad; the 1st century BC witnessed a continuous political and social crisis, breaking out into a series of civil wars and rebellions that did not end until the accession of Augustus and the end of the Roman Republic. In the year 91, a coordinated revolt broke out among the southern peoples called the Social Wars, a genuine threat to Rome that was finally defeated by the campaigns of Marius and Sulla, and by an offer to extend Roman citizenship to all Italians. Both generals, the former a populist and the latter an arch-reactionary, later ruled as dictators in Rome. Under the tyrannous Sulla, an effective autocracy was created and all opponents either murdered or exiled. Italy careered into anarchy, with many rural districts reverting to bandit-ridden wastelands, a setting for the remarkable revolt in 73 of Spartacus, an escaped gladiator of Capua who led a motley army of dispossessed farmers and runaway slaves—some 70,000 of them—back and forth across the south until the legions finally defeated him in 71.

The later civil wars—Pompey vs. Caesar and Augustus vs. Antony—largely spared the south, though many of the plots were hatched in villas around the Bay of Naples. Under Augustus and his imperial successors, things settled down considerably, while the bay continued its career as the favoured resort of the emperors and the rich. In the economic decline of the late empire, troubles returned. The rural south sank deeper into decline, while even the commerce of Magna Graecia gradually began to fail, ruined by foreign competition, high taxes and bureaucracy. The great eruption of Vesuvius in AD 79 must have increased the economic disarray; three sizeable towns, Pompeii, Herculaneum and Stabiae, completely disappeared, and vast tracts of fertile land withered under volcanic ash. In northern Italy, meanwhile, a sounder, more stable economy led to the growth of new centres—Milan, Padua, Verona, Florence and others. The economic north–south divide, a problem for which no solution is in sight even today, was already beginning.

406–1139: Goths, Greeks, Lombards and Normans try on the Roman boot, and none find a good fit

The 5th-century barbarian invaders of Italy, Goths and Vandals, passed through Campania without any notable outrages, and after they passed the region and the rest of the peninsula got a half-century's breathing space under Theodoric's tolerant, well-run Gothic Kingdom of Italy. The real disaster began in 536, with the invasion of Italy by the Eastern Empire, part of the relentlessly expansionist policy of the great Justinian. The south, still largely Greek by race and sentiment, welcomed the Greek army from Constantinople, but much of the worst fighting of the Greek–Gothic War took place in the region; Neapolis, or Naples, by now the largest city in the south, was captured and sacked in turn by both sides. Justinian's brilliant generals, Belisarius and Narses, ultimately prevailed over the Goths in 563, but the damage to an already stricken society and economy was incalculable. Italy's total exhaustion was exposed only five years later, when the Lombards, a Germanic tribe who worked hard to earn the title of barbarian, overran northern Italy and parts of the south, establishing a kingdom at Pavia in the north and a separate duchy at Benevento (571). A new pattern of power appeared, with semi-independent Byzantine dukes defending much of the coastal areas, and Lombard chiefs ruling most of the interior. Byzantine control was always tenuous at best, and cities like Naples and Salerno gradually achieved a *de facto* independence.

No one usually bothered to write down what was going on in the south during the Dark Ages, but even if they had it would be a confusing story. The Lombard Duchy of Benevento reached its height in the 9th century, while enclaves around the coasts remained in the hands of the Byzantines, and for a short time in the 9th century much of Apulia was held by Arabs from Sicily as the 'Emirate of Bari'. Some of the coastal cities, at least, weren't doing too badly. Naples, which proclaimed its complete independence in 763 under its dukes, seemed to have been keeping itself afloat and carrying on at least a little trade, as were Sorrento and Salerno. And in this unpromising time a new city rose up to join them, and cut a surprising career for itself as a merchant republic: Amalfi. As early as the 7th century, Amalfi had its fleet. In the 900s, the city established its independence from Naples and elected a doge, like Venice's. Its trading stations extended across the eastern Mediterranean, and there was a large colony of Amalfitan merchants in Pera, across the Golden Horn from Constantinople.

The year 1000, the dawning of the millennium, makes a convenient date for the beginning of the Middle Ages, and the great economic and cultural upsurge that came with it. In southern Italy, the major event of this time was the arrival of the Normans. The first of these arrived in the 9th century, as mercenaries or pilgrims to Monte Sant'Angelo in the

Gargano. They liked the opportunities they saw for booty and conquest, and from about 1020 younger sons of Norman feudal families were moving into the south, first as mercenaries but gradually gaining large tracts of land for themselves in exchange for their services. Often allied with the popes, they soon controlled most of Apulia and Calabria. One of their greatest chiefs, Robert Guiscard came to control much of the south as Duke of Apulia. In 1084, he descended on Rome for a grisly sack that put the best efforts of the Goths and Vandals to shame. His less destructive brother, Roger de Hauteville, began the conquest of Sicily from the Arabs in 1060, six years before William the Conqueror sailed for England. Naples fell to the Norman armies in 1139.

1139–1494: in which, thanks to a despised Frenchman, Naples becomes a Kingdom

Roger de Hauteville eventually united all of the south into the 'Kingdom of Sicily', and by the 1140s, under Roger II, this strange Norman-Arab-Jewish-Italian-Greek state, with its glittering, half-oriental capital of Palermo, had become the cultural centre of the Mediterranean, a refuge of religious tolerance and serious scholarship. Under Roger and his successors (William the Bad, who wasn't bad at all, and William the Good, who was something of a weakling), it remained one of the strongest and best-organized states in Europe. The entire 12th century was a boom time for the south, as it was for most of Europe. Apulia in particular knew the greatest age in its history, and its trading towns began the Romanesque cathedrals that remain the south's greatest architectural treasure.

In 1194, the line of the Hautevilles became extinct and the Kingdom of Sicily fell to Holy Roman Emperor Henry IV of Hohenstaufen, who brought down an army from Germany to claim it. His son, the legendary Frederick II (1194–1250), the 'Wonder of the World', was at once Emperor and King of Sicily, though he preferred to spend most of his time in southern Italy, presiding over a court even more brilliant than that of Roger II, one in which some of the first Italian poetry was written. Frederick gave his lands a constitution, the *Constitutio Melfitani*, and founded Naples's University, the third in Italy and first in the south.

Frederick did not have an easy reign, largely thanks to his most dangerous political enemies, the popes; during his reign they excommunicated him twice. After his death, Pope Urban IV began a disastrous precedent by inviting in the French, in the person of Charles of Anjou, brother of the King of France, to seize the southern kingdom. Charles defeated Frederick's son Manfred (Battle of Benevento, 1266) and foully murdered the last of the Hohenstaufens, Conradin, in 1268. He held unchallenged sway over southern Italy until 1282, when the famous revolt of the Sicilian Vespers chased the hated French from Sicily and inaugurated a period of wars and anarchy throughout the south.

Despite its unity under the Normans and Hohenstaufens, the south was falling behind both politically and economically. The Normans ruled their domains fairly and intelligently, but they also deserve the blame for introducing feudalism into a country that had never known it—just as the mercantile states of the north were breaking loose from the feudal arrangements brought down by the Goths and Lombards. Now the 'Kingdom of

Naples', as the southern state had become known, to distinguish it from the now separate Kingdom of Sicily, was a tapestry of battling barons, each busily building or improving his castle and increasingly less inclined to listen to kings or popes or anyone. The trading cities, especially Naples, Amalfi and Bari, saw their woes increase with strong competition from the Venetians and Genoese. With little encouragement from king or barons, they could only continue to decline.

Robert the Wise (1309–43) was a good king, and patron of Giotto, Petrarch and Boccaccio. For a successor, he left only a granddaughter, Giovanna I, and under her unsteady hand the barons mightily increased both their power and their contentiousness. Her reign witnessed the Black Death (1347–8), in which Italy lost one third of its population, and also the beginnings of civil war between Angevin factions, something that would continue fitfully through a century of confusing intrigues and insurrections. It ended in the hands of yet another foreigner, Alfonso the Magnanimous, King of Aragon, who conquered Naples and tossed out the last Angevins in 1442 (Alfonso, a student of the classics, had been reading an account of how Belisarius took Naples in the Greek–Gothic Wars by sending men through the channel of a Roman aqueduct that breached the walls; he located the exact spot, with the ruined aqueduct still present, and sent his soldiers in the same way). Once more the Kingdom was reunited with Sicily, part of the Aragonese crown since the Sicilian Vespers. Alfonso and his successor, the cruel King Ferrante, ruled Naples with harshness and skill; both were typical Renaissance princes who, as leaders of the only kingdom in Italy, played major roles in the eternal petty wars and intrigues of the age.

1494–1713: the kingdom falls to the Spaniards, who make a mess of it

The Wars of Italy, that terrible series of conflicts that eventually rang down the curtain on the Renaissance and on Italian liberty, began in 1494 with a quarrel over Naples. Charles VIII, King of France, took advantage of Italian disunity to invade the peninsula, seeking to make good the claim to the kingdom he had inherited from the Angevins. The last Aragonese king, the ineffectual Alfonso II, fled the city rather than face him. Spain, at this time, was at the height of its powers after the union of Aragon and Castile in 1492, under Ferdinand and Isabella. The Spaniards sent *El Gran Capitan*, Gonsalvo di Córdoba, with a strong army, and he restored Naples to its Spanish king the following year. More fighting between Aragonese factions followed, and when the dust settled, in 1502, Naples and its kingdom were directly under the Spanish crown, and ruled by a viceroy.

In the decades to come, nearly all Italy would be beaten or bullied into the Spanish system, either through puppet rulers, alliances or outright control, but nowhere more than in Naples was the Spanish influence stronger. The Inquisition snuffed out the city's intellectual life, while the nobles of the realm learned to forsake their wonted gay colours and dress all in black; they came to affect the haughty manners of the grandees, and started calling each other *Don*, and they carried rapiers and poignards in the streets—in the atmosphere of the Wars of Italy, it had become an extremely violent age. The greatest of the viceroys, Don Pedro de Toledo, was a benefactor to Naples, and rebuilt much of it; he also built Castel Sant'Elmo on the highest hill to keep watch over the Neapolitans.

Spanish rule lasted over two centuries, and as Spain decayed into senile decadence its government in southern Italy grew ever more oppressive and useless. Times would have been bad enough, in the general Italian economic collapse of the 17th century, but Spanish misrule gradually turned the already-poor rural south into a nightmare of anarchic depravity, haunted by legions of bandits and beggars, and controlled more tightly than ever by its violent feudal barons. Peasants by the thousand gave up their lands and villages for a marginally safer life in Naples, and the city ballooned in population—an estimated half-million by 1700—to become the largest in Europe. To everyone's surprise, the south rose up and staged an epic rebellion. Beginning in Naples (Masaniello's Revolt, 1647), the disturbances soon spread all over the south and Sicily. For over a year peasant militias ruled some areas, and makeshift revolutionary councils defended the cities. But when the Spanish finally defeated them, they massacred some 18,000, and tightened the screws more then ever.

1713–1860: a mild case of Bourbonic Plague

In 1713, after the War of the Spanish Succession, the Habsburgs of Austria came into control of most of Spain's Italian possessions, including Naples. The Austrians made no impression on anyone, and Naples' hard luck continued when the Austrians were forced to transfer it to a branch of the House of Bourbon (1734); under them the kingdom was again independent, but just as poorly governed as before. For the next century and a quarter, the southern *Regno* enjoyed a colourful era of poverty, backwardness, bad art and intellectual torpor, in which the city of Naples perfected the peculiar charms and vices it displays today. An exception was the reign of Charles III (1734–59) who introduced many long overdue reforms. Charles also built the San Carlo Opera, the Archaeological Museum, and the palaces at Capodimonte and Caserta. His son, Ferdinand I, has gone down in history as the 'Lazzarone King' (*lazzarone*, a key Neapolitan word, refers to the crowds of gainfully unemployed men that lounged on every streetcorner of old Naples; it does not literally mean 'good-for-nothing', but that would be an accurate translation). The perfect king for the time, Ferdinand ruled with a light hand and spoke only Neapolitan dialect; state visitors found him generally surrounded by noise, food and children.

The French invasion of 1799, during the Napoleonic Wars, woke Naples up with a start from its Baroque slumbers; local patriots gaily joined the French cause—even the monks of San Martino, who sewed tricolour flags for the new 'Parthenopean Republic', and invited all the French officers up to the monastery for a banquet. In 1799, however, while Napoleon was off in Egypt, the advance through Italy by an Austro-Russian army, aided by Nelson's fleet, restored the status quo. This was often accompanied by bloody reprisals, as peasant mobs led by clerics, the 'Army of the Holy Faith' or *Sanfedisti*, marched across the south massacring liberals and French sympathizers.

In 1800, after Marengo, Napoleon returned, and crowned himself King of Italy; Joseph Bonaparte, and later Joachim Murat, ruled at Naples. For the second time, Admiral Nelson and his fleet had to remove the king and his family to Sicily for safety. Napoleonic rule lasted only until 1814, but in that time important public works were begun and laws, education and everything else reformed on the French model; immense church properties were expropriated, and medieval relics everywhere put to rest.

The 1815 Congress of Vienna put the clock back to 1798; indeed the Bourbons seemed to think they could pretend the Napoleonic upheavals had never happened, and the political reaction in their territories was fierce (from this time on, incidentally, the *Regno* was officially and confusingly called the 'Kingdom of the Two Sicilies'). But the experience had given Italians a taste of the opportunities offered by the modern world, as well as a sense of national feeling that had been suppressed for centuries. Almost immediately, revolutionary agitators and secret societies like the famous *Carbonari* kept Italy convulsed in plots and intrigues. A big revolt in Naples forced King Ferdinand, now a bitter old reactionary after his experiences with the French, to grant a constitution (1821), but when Austrian troops came down to crush the rebels he took it back.

The next king, Ferdinand II (1830–59), gets a bad press; his subjects gave him the nickname *Re Bomba* (King Bomb) after his army shelled Messina during the next popular revolt, in 1848–9. On the credit side, Ferdinand exerted himself mightily to bring his kingdom into the modern world, building the first railways, and laying the foundations for a modern industry and merchant fleet (he also built the Amalfi drive, a great feat of engineering). His autocratic, paternalistic rule was entirely out of step with the atmosphere of the Italian *Risorgimento*, however, and when the climactic events of national reunification took place in 1859–60, few were left even in Naples to support the Bourbon monarchy.

In 1860, when the entire north was in revolt, and ready to unite under the Piedmontese King Vittorio Emanuele, Giuseppe Garibaldi and his red-shirted 'Thousand' sailed from Genoa to Sicily, electrifying Europe by repeatedly beating the Bourbon forces in a quick march across the island. The Thousand had become 20,000, and they soon crossed the straits and marched towards the capital, meeting little resistance. Garibaldi entered Naples on 7 September (on Ferdinand's new railway), and though a few bitter-enders still held out in the Abruzzo, the Bourbon kingdom was finished.

1860–1944: in which the cure proves worse than the disease

The new Italy established a constitutional monarchy under Vittorio Emanuele, one in which the radical aspirations of Garibaldi and his followers were given little hearing. The new parliament almost immediately decomposed into cliques and political cartels representing powerful interests. Italy's finances started in disorder and stayed that way, while corruption was widespread. There were other problems. Naples's loss of capital status was a heavy blow to the city, both politically and culturally, and the new state's tariff policies, dictated by northern interests, caused a sharp decline first in the south's small industrial base, and then in its agriculture. Thus was the new Italy born with the 'problem of the south' as the biggest item on its agenda—and with a regime doing little or nothing about it.

In the disappointed south, agents of the displaced Bourbons and of the pope contributed to the continuing unrest, though conditions were such that most of the troubles began spontaneously. Through the 1860s over a hundred thousand troops were tied down pursuing the 'bandits' of the south. The guerrilla bands concentrated on killing landowners and officials of the new government, raiding town halls to burn the tax and property records; the army responded in kind, with the brutality of an occupying power, and the woes of the south found scant sympathy in the more developed regions of Italy. Ironically, southerners came to hold a disproportionate share of power and positions in the new regime. The *galantuomini*, the ignorant, parasitical class of local bosses and landlords, soon learned the possibilities offered them by Italy's limited democracy, and found it as easy to manipulate as the Bourbon kingdom had been. Their influence has contributed much to Italy's political troubles in all the years since. Meanwhile, southerners were solving the problem in their own way, by packing their suitcases. Some two and a half million Italians emigrated for the Americas and elsewhere between 1880 and 1914, most of them from the south.

For all the south's discontent, Fascism made very little headway in the region in the years after World War I. Mussolini choreographed his march on Rome in 1922, but even a year after that, his power in the south was negligible. The Fascist takeover here only occurred when it became clear that the Duce was dismantling the parliamentary state; southern Italians realized that they were to have a new master, and adjusted accordingly. While the most powerful party, the Socialists, dithered and fiddled uncomprehendingly, suddenly the local authorities began turning a blind eye to the terror tactics of the Fascist *squadri* (as their more willing northern counterparts had already been doing for three years). Fascist Party groups around the south, usually bankrupt and squabbling among themselves, just as suddenly found themselves swamped with new members and contributions; when the dust settled everyone who was anyone was in the party, and things went on as before, run by the same faces only in new uniforms.

Mussolini did well by the south, contributing plenty of impressive public works (the Apulian aqueduct, civic centres for cities like Bari and Táranto, and the beginnings of industrialization). The Fascists also waged a constant and relatively successful war against the Camorra—a rival gang, after all, was the last thing Mussolini would tolerate. It isn't commonly realized how much Naples suffered in '43 and '44. First came intensive Allied bombings, after the landings in Sicily; with the port area so close to the centre, many monuments were severely damaged, such as the church of Santa Chiara. After the Salerno landings, the successful short cut that put the Allies on Naples' doorstep, the city surprised everyone, perhaps surprised itself, by staging a tremendous and entirely spontaneous popular revolt, the 'Four Days in Naples' that drove the Germans from the city. Other parts of the south suffered too; Fóggia, Bari, Benevento and Reggio di Calabria in particular were bombed first by the Allies, and then by the Germans.

1944–Present: once again, Naples illustrates its talent for making the present look very much like the past

Neapolitans found liberation a sad disappointment, a nightmare of destitution and corruption brilliantly chronicled in Norman Lewis's book, *Naples '44*. The Allied government tried, but the problems of a region with no government or services and an economy in total collapse proved overwhelming. Cholera and malaria became widespread. Possibly a third of the female population in Naples was forced into prostitution to survive, and a third of all the supplies unloaded by the Allies disappeared, fuelling a gigantic black market in everything from flour to armoured vehicles. Robber bands appeared once more in the countryside, and the Camorra resurfaced and tightened its grip over Naples and its suburbs, as did the similar 'Ndrangheta in Calabria and smaller gangs elsewhere (the general Allied policy of emptying the jails wherever they went during the war helped to start this).

In the 1946 referendum that established the Italian Republic, the south was the only region that said no; in Naples, 80 per cent voted to keep the monarchy. Still, change came quickly in the post-war decades: a wave of building in the cities, much of it *abusivo* or illegal, and new industry, like the Alfa-Sud plant and Bagnoli steel works around Naples and the huge industrial area at Táranto, all financed by the government's southern recon-struction fund, the *Cassa per il Mezzogiorno*. It wasn't enough to enable the southern economy to keep even, let alone catch up with northern Italy, and tens of thousands of southerners flocked north to work in the factories of Turin, Milan and Germany. One positive advance in the post-war era was the reclaiming of huge coastal areas from the malaria mosquito by the use of DDT; regions that had been wastelands since Roman times became populated once more; in Calabria especially, it started a social and agricultural revolution that is only today beginning to show some fruits.

Post-war politics were turbulent, especially in Naples, where the era was dominated by 1950s mayor Achille Lauro, a shipping magnate who had been well connected with the Fascists under Mussolini, though he opposed the war. When the Christian Democrats didn't meet his terms, he founded his own rightist-populist movement, *Uomo Qualunque* ('everyman'). Amidst the usual claims of graft, most of them justified, this eventually fizzled out, to be replaced by a close Christian Democrat–Camorra machine that ran the city until 1993 under 'modern bosses' such as Antonio Gava.

So far this history has said little about one of the most prominent features of life in this region, the disasters—there would have been little room for anything else. But we could mention the Black Death of 1347–8, the plague of 1529 that carried off 50,000, the plague of 1656 that took 200,000 more, a dozen or so volcanic eruptions and as many earthquakes, especially the terrible one of 1688 that wrecked much of Naples, or the severe cholera epidemics of 1884, 1944 and 1973; and finally the earthquake of 1980, largely ignored in the press, that caused tremendous damage and suffering in rural Campania. More than anything else, these are the events that have made Naples and its region what they are. They help to explain the sombre, fatalistic side of the Neapolitan character, its philosophical seriousness—and the other side too, the frivolous, laugh-in-the-face-of-Vesuvius manner that animated the old Bourbon *Regno*, as well as the strong, often underestimated resilience of a city that has already recovered and rebuilt so many times.

Lately most of the catastrophes have been man-made: economic stagnation, widespread political corruption, the vampirism of the local mafias and an ever-increasing degradation of public services. Currently, the new leftist city administration in Naples has to deal with an urban crisis of the first order: hospitals, public transport and sanitation in scandalous condition, reports of contamination in the city's water and municipall -run dairies, chronic traffic gridlock; the list runs depressingly on and on. In the hinterlands, refugees from the 1980 earthquake still live in public buildings and hotels; in Benevento you can see ruins and bomb damage left from World War II. With Italy in the midst of its torturously slow political revolution—they're already calling it the 'Second Republic'—it's anybody's guess as to what will happen.

Art and Architecture

Greek and Roman

With the arrival of the Greeks and Etruscans in the mid-8th century BC, Italy joined the wider Mediterranean world, artistically as well as politically. The wealthy cities of Magna Graecia imported classical Greek art and artists wholesale, and even though many of the cities themselves have disappeared, the archaeological museums of Naples, Táranto, Bari and Reggio di Calabria have huge stores of sculpture, painted vases, architectural decoration, figurines and lovely terracotta ex-votos. Native artists also made endless copies of painted Greek ceramics, many of them excellent. For Greek architecture, there is the great Doric temple at Paestum (which also has an extremely rare Greek fresco in a tomb), and ruins at Cumae, Velia and Metapontum.

In Campania, the art and architecture of the Roman world is out on display, in Naples' museum and at the matchless sites of Pompeii and Herculaneum. There are plenty of other ruins of Roman buildings to see: at Pozzuoli, Baia, and other sites around the western bay, including some grandiose survivals of Roman engineering, such as the reservoirs and canals of the great naval base at Cape Misenum and the Fuorigrotta road tunnel, the longest ever built in antiquity, in Naples. What's left of the second- and third-largest amphitheatres of the Roman world can be seen at Capua and Pozzuoli; Capua also has a remarkable, well-preserved underground Mithraic temple.

Most of these spectacular works came in the confident, self-assured age of the Flavian and Antonine emperors (late 1st–2nd centuries), a time that also saw important progress in sculpture. Until then, Roman work had been closely bound to Hellenistic styles, or was expressed in outright copies of classical Greek sculpture. The new departure, a vivid, arresting style which some scholars have called 'impressionism' can be seen on the reliefs of Trajan's arch in Benevento.

Painting and mosaic work were both present from at least the 1st century BC, though Romans always considered them as little more than decoration, and only rarely entrusted to them any serious subjects. Both are a legacy from the Greeks, and both found their way to Rome by way of talented, half-Greek Campania. Painting, in the days of Caesar and Augustus, usually meant wall frescoes in the homes of the wealthy (*see* p.111), with large scenes of gardens in the form of window views, making small Roman rooms look brighter and bigger; also mythological scenes, paintings of battles and, occasionally, portraits (the best, courtesy of Vesuvius, are at Pompeii and Herculaneum, also in the museum of Naples and in the Mithraeum in Capua).

Mosaics, another import, had its greatest centre at Antioch, in Hellenized Syria, and only became a significant medium in Italy as painting was declining. As with the other arts, mosaics were done better in cultured Campania. If Rome too, had been buried under volcanic lava, at whatever period, it is unlikely that much would be found to surpass the 2nd- and 1st-century paintings and mosaics discovered at Pompeii.

Byzantine and Medieval

So much from every age has been lost due to earthquakes and neglect, it is not surprising that even the most rudimentary structure from the Dark Ages is a rarity. Two churches that survived are the small 5th-century S. Maria Maggiore, near Nocera Inferiore, and the 8th-century Santa Sofia, at Benevento, both central-plan temples more in keeping with the contemporary architecture of Byzantium than of Rome. Naples' cathedral retains its 5th-century baptistry. Further south, Byzantine influence predominated until the late Middle Ages, especially in areas that remained Greek in religion and culture; In Calabria, two small Byzantine churches survive at **Stilo**.

In the 10th–12th centuries, cultural revival was made possible by a number of factors: the trade and overseas contacts of Amalfi, Naples and the Apulian cities, not only creating wealth but bringing in influences from Byzantium and the Muslim world; the ascent of the Normans, bringing the blessings of political stability and a sophisticated court; and, artistically, the work of Abbot Desiderius at the great Abbey of Montecassino, between Naples and Rome, importing artists and architects from Constantinople, and helping to spread their advanced styles and techniques across the south—one good example being finely incised bronze church doors, a Greek speciality. Nearly a score of southern towns have them, beginning with the set made for **Amalfi** (1066). The fashion spread to many other cities, and it was not long before Italian artists were producing their own, notably those of Barisano da Trani at **Trani** and **Ravello**. Painting too, in this age, was largely a matter of importing styles and artists from Greece, and Byzantine art, so unfairly disparaged by the Renaissance, would continue to influence all of Italy, not only the south, until the fall of Constantinople. Byzantium's own medieval 'renaissance' shows up clearly in the exceptional 11th-century frescoes at S. Angelo in Formis in **Capua**, the 14th-century S. Maria del Casale in **Brindisi**, and in the cave churches of **Matera** and **Massafra** (along with scores of little-known works in caves all through southern Apulia and the Basilicata).

Because of religious and cultural prejudices, the role of Muslim influence in Italian medieval art has never been satisfactorily examined. In Campania it is often obvious, in the interlaced arches of **Amalfi** cathedral, and the exotic patterned decoration in its façade, and in the churches of **Salerno** and **Caserta Vecchia**. Another southern speciality to which Muslim art probably contributed is the decoration of pavements, pulpits, paschal candlesticks and tombs with geometric patterns in chips of coloured stone or glass, an art that reached a plateau of excellence at Amalfi, Ravello, and Salerno, spreading to many other towns and reaching as far north as Tuscany; this exotically precise work became the prime inspiration for the Roman decorative style called Cosmatesque.

Romanesque architecture, so important in northern Italy and the rest of Europe, does not seem to have made much of an impression in Campania. In Apulia, however, one of the most distinctive and sophisticated of all Romanesque styles appeared. Beginning with the construction of San Nicola in **Bari** in 1087, a wave of cathedral building swept over the region; some of the best are **Troia, Bitonto, Trani, Molfetta,** and **Matera**. These churches draw their inspiration from numerous sources; there are hints of Norman French work in many churches, not to mention Lombard and Pisan Romanesque. Some of the features of Apulian Romanesque are the profile of the sharp roof-line angle, and small rose windows, which combine to create the distinctive Apulian façade, along with blind arcading around cornices, galleries (both interior and exterior), elaborately carved portals and apses, and above all an emphasis on height that anticipates the Gothic. To match the architects, Apulia developed an equally talented group of sculptors; their intricately carved lions and other fantastical beasts make up the cathedrals' most important decoration, along with finely carved pulpits and especially bishops' thrones, as at Bari. Other medieval monuments of Apulian architecture include the exotic tomb of the crusader knight Bohemund, in **Canosa di Puglia**, and Frederick II's mystical castle, **Castel del Monte**.

Elsewhere in the south, one of the most ambitious buildings of the early Middle Ages was **Salerno** cathedral, begun by Robert Guiscard in 1085, an idiosyncratic work that shows a faithfulness to early Christian fashions (like the exterior *quadroporticus*). Gothic churches are more common than in most parts of Italy; the style was brought down by the French under the rule of Charles of Anjou after 1266 (San Domenico Maggiore in **Naples** is one of the best examples). Late Apulian cathedrals where Romanesque has evolved into Gothic are those at **Altamura** and **Ruvo di Puglia**, while Gothic churches also survive at **Cosenza** and **Altomonte** in Calabria. Survivals of painting and sculpture are sadly few. Giotto came down to Naples to work for Robert the Wise, and he painted a series of frescoes for the Castel dell'Ovo, now completely lost.

An Imported Renaissance

In the 15th and 16th centuries, while the rest of Italy made a revolution in western art and culture, the south unfortunately was not often able to take part. With the economic decline of the southern cities, there was little opportunity for artistic advance. Northern artists, especially Tuscans, still came to Naples in the 1400s, but like the Gothic masons and sculptors of 200 years before they must have found themselves acting as cultural missionaries. They left some fine works behind, but for reasons that are difficult to see clearly they never seemed to make a strong impression on the southern sensibility (notable visitors at Naples include Donatello and Michelozzo, tomb in S. Angelo a Nilo; Antonio Rossellino, tombs at Monteoliveto; Giuliano da Maiano, the Capua gate; many of the important early Renaissance painters are represented at Naples's Capodimonte museum).

There are a few exceptions, unexpected little candles in the prevailing gloom. In **Galatina**, a small town near Lecce, the church of Santa Caterina contains a remarkable fresco cycle, an attempt by southern artists to adapt the early Renaissance manner of Tuscany. Giovanni da Nola, a first-rate sculptor though little known, decorated many churches in **Naples**. That city also contributed some fine and original work, such as Romolo Balsimelli's Santa Caterina a Formiello. The most important Renaissance achievement in Naples was the Castel Nuovo (1454–67), and especially its triumphal arch. Built for Alfonso I, this was a Renaissance landmark, a mythological rendering of statesmanlike virtue entirely equal to the arches and columns of antiquity. Local talent, such as Tommaso Malvito's Cappella Carafa at the Duomo, tried to carry the trend onwards, but in Naples the ideals of the Renaissance would never really take hold.

Baroque and Neoclassicism

If the Baroque began in Rome, it soon found a warm welcome throughout the south. With its escapism, emotionalism and excess, the new style proved an inspiration to a troubled and long somnolent region, and the concentration of wealth in the hands of the court and the Church ensured a lavish patronage.

In Naples, the greatest exponent of the Baroque was a brilliant, tortured soul named Cosimo Fanzago (1591–1678), sculptor, architect and decorative artist who designed the great cloister of San Martino, the *guglia* in Piazza San Domenico and a little masterpiece of a church, Santa Maria Egiziaca at Pizzofalcone (a *guglia* is a tall, elaborately decorated religious monument for a piazza, a Neapolitan speciality). Fanzago is known for his love of *pietra dura* work, exquisite floral patterns in brightly coloured marble inlay (as in S. Domenico Maggiore), an art from late Renaissance Florence; it set the trend for the lush interiors of Neapolitan churches over the next century. Another Neapolitan worthy of mention is Ferdinando Sanfelice, a light-hearted pastry chef of churches (the Nunziatella) and palaces, famous for his fascinating, geometrically complex grand staircases (Palazzi Sanfelice, Bartolomeo di Maio, Serra di Cassano).

For all that, the most distinctive brands of southern Gothic appeared not in the capital, but in provincial centres such as Noto, Catania and Mazara del Vallo in Sicily, and best of all **Lecce** near the southern tip of Apulia. It was a remarkable achievement—an obscure little city, only a little more prosperous than its neighbours, and doing its best to uphold a threadbare but ardent heritage of cultural distinction, Lecce created and advanced its own style of architecture for almost two centuries. It began in the 1500s, with the surprisingly sophisticated Renaissance folly called the Sedile, and reached its height with architects Giuseppe and Antonio Zimbalo and sculptor Csare Penna in the mid-17th century (all three collaborated on Lecce's masterpiece, Santa Croce). Exotic, ornate decoration, more than any advances in building forms, is the hallmark of the Leccese style, and upon close examination this proves to be more influenced by the Renaissance and even Apulian Romanesque than anything from contemporary Naples or Rome. Reflections of the Lecce style can be seen in the churches and palaces of many towns in southern Apulia, notably **Ostuni, Manduria, Maglie** and **Nardò**.

In sculpture, the best Neapolitan works are the most eccentric—the spectacular virtuosity of Francesco Queirolo, Antonio Corradini and Giuseppe Sammartino in the Sansevero Chapel; art historians always damn these to the lowest circles of the inferno, but you might enjoy them. Almost all the Neapolitan sculptors devoted much effort to figures for *presepi*—Christmas cribs; the San Martino museum has a delightful collection. In painting, Naples and the south began the Baroque era under the spell of Caravaggio, who arrived in Naples in 1607 (paintings at Capodimonte). Among his followers, adapting the dark and dramatic realism of the master to different ends, were the Spaniard José Ribera (San Martino) and the Calabrian Mattia Preti, one of the most talented of all southern artists, who did much of his best work for the Knights of Malta (also Capodimonte, and at S. Pietro a Maiella in Naples, and the painter's home town of **Taverna**). Another important painter, at his best in unusual, highly original landscapes, was the native Neapolitan Salvator Rosa (1615–73).

Later Neapolitan painting, frivolous and colourful, with little to challenge the intellect or the imagination, was just right for the times and enjoyed a widespread influence. Luca Giordano, the mercurial and speedy *Luca fa presto* (1634–1705), painted all over Italy, spent ten years at the court in Madrid, and still found time to cover acres of Neapolitan ceilings with clouds and *putti*, tumbling horses and pastel-robed floating maidens (as at the Duomo and San Martino). His greatest follower, in his time perhaps the most popular painter in Italy, was Francesco Solimena (1657–1747; S. Paolo Maggiore, Gesù Nuovo).

A more modern, sober turn in Neapolitan art came with the reforming King Charles III, in 1750. That year saw the death of Fernando Sanfelice, and the arrival of two architects from the north who brought the neoclassical manner to Naples. Ferdinando Fuga was for a time court architect to the Bourbons (his work includes the *Albergo dei Poveri* on Via Foria, the biggest and fanciest poorhouse in the world). The 18th century, though, belonged to Luigi Vanvitelli (1700–73), son of the Italianized Dutch painter Gaspar van Wittel and favourite architect of King Charles, the most assiduous builder among the Bourbon kings. Most of Vanvitelli's energies were expended on the huge Royal Palace at **Caserta**, fully in line with the international neoclassicism of the time with its tastefully unimaginative façades, grand stairways and axis-planned gardens. Neoclassicism in Naples, a surprising reaction against the city's long-standing love affair with the Baroque and the bizarre, dominated the 1700s and indeed the remainder of the Bourbon period, as seen in such buildings as the Capodimonte palace and the San Carlo opera house (both by G. A. Medrano, in the 1730s) and the grandiose domed San Francesco di Paola (1817).

Topics

Coffee Culture

Some people like it straight, a short sharp shot of rich dark liquid, usually downed in one gulp while standing at the bar. Others temper their favourite brew with a dash of hot milk—a *caffè macchiato*, literally, a stained coffee. In Italy, there are almost as many ways of taking a *caffè* as there are of eating pasta, and Naples is generally regarded as the capital of the country's coffee culture.

There is also the *latte macchiato*—a long glass of hot milk with a dash of milk to give it colour and flavour, a wimp's drink by macho Neapolitan standards. The cappuccino, an espresso coffee topped with steam-whipped milk, is known to all, but it can be ordered in a myriad number of ways, *con schiuma* (with froth), *senza schiuma* (without froth), *freddo*, *tepido* or *bollente* (cold, warm or piping hot). It may be *scuro* or *chiaro*, depending on the amount of milk desired. And it will always be restricted to the first coffee of the day. The foreign tourists' habit of ordering a milky cappuccino after lunch or dinner is enough to make any Neapolitan stomach heave.

In Naples, more than anywhere else, the all-important act of going out to the bar for a fix of caffeine is a ritual that is repeated every few hours. For Neapolitans, coffee is a sacred thing, its preparation an art form. At the best bars in town, barmen in starched white jackets with gleaming brass buttons serve the dark syrupy brew with a glass of water, to prepare the palate for the treat in store. In Naples your coffee will usually be served already sugared. If you want it without, you must ask the barman for a *caffè amaro*.

Every Neapolitan has his favourite bar—and his favourite barman—but the 150-year-old Caffe Gambrinus on Piazza Trieste e Trento is widely recognised as the most venerable temple of them all. Also favoured are the Verdi in Via Verdi, the Caflish, in Via Toledo, and La Caffettiera in Piazza dei Martiri, a popular spot with well-dressed Neapolitan ladies after a busy morning's shopping.

On summer evenings, outside the bars along the seafront at Mergellina, you'll see Neapolitans indulging in the ultimate bliss, a cup of coffee served to them in the comfort of their own car, on trays which slot conveniently over the window of the driver's seat.

As any Neapolitan barman worth his salt will tell you, the perfect espresso is made with a blend of arabica coffees, with water passed through at a temperature of 90°C, for precisely 30 seconds. Connoisseurs can tell whether the coffee will be good or not before they even taste it. The foam is the give-away. It should be a uniform light brown colour, dappled with darker brown. Very dark brown or greyish foam is a clear warning sign that the barman is an amateur, or the coffee second rate. Most self-respecting Neapolitans would rather leave such a brew untouched on the counter and head for another bar. A bad cup of coffee can cast a blight over the entire day.

On Pleasure's Shore

If they had had postcards back in the Roman Empire, your Aunt Vulpecula would certainly have sent you one from Campania—*Having a Wonderful Time in Baiae on the Sinus*

Puteolanus. The photo on the front would show gaily painted pleasure-boats in the bay, with silken canopies and slaves waving golden fans over the languorous occupants; in the background would be a row of delicious villas, each with two or three levels of gleaming marble porticoes perched on the cliffs over the blue Tyrrhenian. This playground of the Roman world is the place where holidays as we know them were invented. The young world had never seen anything like it. Everyone in the Empire, from Londinium to Baalbek, had heard of the bay and its prodigies of beauty and luxury; no doubt everyone dreamed of actually going there.

The first mention of a villa on the bay comes from the early 2nd century BC. The Roman state, which had seized all the land in the area after conquering it, was now selling it off to help finance the Second Punic War, the bloody and expensive struggle against Hannibal and the Carthaginians. One of the first buyers was Scipio Africanus, the general who brought that war to a successful conclusion, and who became the richest man in Rome in the process. He built himself a villa near Liternum, overlooking the sea, and other members of the Roman elite soon followed. In the two centuries that followed, as Rome spread its rule over the Mediterranean world and the booty rolled in, the dour senators and knights found something they had never had before—*otium*, or leisure. Thanks to contact with the cultured Greek world, in Campania and in Greece itself, Rome was growing up, even becoming a tiny bit civilized in its awkward and bumptious way.

If they hadn't yet acquired many of the accomplishments of culture, at least the Romans knew how to tack up a good façade: the villas housed copies of Greek statues, frescoes, Greek cooks, poets and musicians. The nabobs affected Greek dress, the elegant *chlamys* worn by the locals, instead of their impractical togas. Some of them even learned the language, and impressed their friends at dinner parties by extemporizing a few lines of verse. In the 1st century BC, everyone who was anyone in Rome had a villa, and the Campanian coast entered its golden age of opulence. The populist dictator Marius had one, and the reactionary dictator Sulla who followed him built an even bigger model, which he shared with his family, a few hundred of his picked slaves, kept ladies, whichever of his clients and hangers-on were lucky enough to be invited, and plenty of entertainment—among others, 'Roscius the comedian, Sorex the mime, and Metrobius the female impersonator', as a historian of the time solemnly recorded. Julius Caesar owned a few villas, and his murderers plotted the deed at Cinna's place just up the coast.

These famous names of history, and the clique of politicians and speculators that went with them, had serious money; when Rome conquered the world a select few raked in the lion's share of the loot, amassing fortunes that make the greatest private hoards of our day seem pocket change in comparison. The honest Cicero often wrote disapprovingly of his fellows' ostentatious displays of wealth—but he had three villas on the bay himself, and a string of lodges all the way to Rome so he would always have somewhere cosy to sleep as he travelled back and forth; we can imagine how the folks in the fast lane must have been carrying on.

The holiday trip was called the *peregrinatio*, and everyone would come down in mid-April. In the heat of summer they would go back to Rome if there was money to be made or intrigues to be hatched, or else retire to a cooler villa up in the mountains. Most would be back on the bay in autumn, and stay as long as there was blessed *otium* left to enjoy. In whatever season, amusements were never lacking. There were the famous baths of Baiae, the most sumptuous such establishment in the ancient world, and above all the dinner parties, which would fill up nearly every evening. For the afternoon, lazy cruises on the bay were in favour, or rides in slave-born litters to Puteoli or Neapolis or the countryside. In Caesar's time pet fish were a craze among the bay set—bearded mullets decorated with jewels, trained to leap up and eat out of their masters' hands. Humbler citizens must have been as fascinated with the doings of the rich as they are today, and even if they had no patron to invite them to stay over, they must have come in great numbers to gawk and dream.

The bay, having invented holidays, can also probably take credit for the first secular souvenirs. Archaeologists have dug up plenty of examples: small items of Puteoli's famous glassware decorated with hand-painted scenes of the coastline and its villas. Almost incredibly, contemporaries describe the entire bay, from Misenum to Sorrentum, as being solidly lined with these palaces, giving the impression of a single, tremendous marble city. It must have been the grandest sight of the classical world, and it isn't certain that our own time has anything to match it.

The bay remained in fashion well into the imperial age. Augustus bought Capri from the city of Neapolis, and covered it with pavilions and terraced gardens; his house was decorated with whale bones and other marvels of the sea, and with relics of classical heroes. All the other early emperors spent much of their time there, notably Tiberius (*see* p.127). Some of the glamour wore off in greyer times, under Vespasian and after, when the wealth and glory of the emperors shamed everyone else's into the shade; later emperors would build their own pleasure palaces in places closer to the necessities of power or military leadership; some of these were huge cities in themselves, such as Trajan's, near Tivoli, or Diocletian's, which survives today as the city of Split, Croatia.

By the late 5th century, there were no more pleasure boats in the bay—only prowling Vandal pirate craft from Africa. The last mention of any of the villas in antiquity was when Romulus Augustulus, the last pathetic emperor of the west, was sent off to live under close guard in the Villa of Lucullus (now Naples' Castel dell'Ovo) by his Gothic conqueror, Odoacer. Many of the villas must have been destroyed in this era; earthquakes, Vesuvius, time and stone quarriers have done for the rest. So often, in and around Naples, the most affecting and unforgettable sights are the ones no longer present. Constant reminders of the impermanence of all our glories may be a major contributor to the melancholy many visitors to Naples have always felt. But there's no need to be melancholy; the Neapolitans, true heirs of antiquity, hardly ever are. Or as Martial put it, gazing at Caesar's tomb through the window of his Roman flat:

> *The great dead themselves, with jovial breath,*
> *Bid us be merry, and remember death.*

The Lady and the Dragon

The first Normans in southern Italy came as pilgrims to the great Mediterranean shrine of St Michael at Monte Sant'Angelo in Apulia. Obviously, they could have saved themselves a long and unpleasant trip by choosing instead to do whatever Michaelian pilgrims do at the saint's northern branch office: Mont Saint Michel, close at hand in Normandy. Monte Sant'Angelo must have had a reputation even then; visit it today, and it won't take you long to realize you are in one of the most uncanny holy sites in Christendom. The light and air, the austere, treeless landscape, and the dramatic mountaintop setting all conspire to strangeness, and the churches and shrines of the town only add to the effect.

Across Europe, the cult of St Michael was often associated with water, especially underground water. At Monte Sant'Angelo, the sanctuary is a cave that once had a flowing fountain in it. Souvenir stands outside peddle familiar images of the archangel spearing his dragon, or serpent, but it is likely that this tableau recalls something older and deeper than Christian legend—you won't find it anywhere in the Bible. Some mythologists speculate that before they were demonized by Christian theologians, western dragons were really more like the benign Chinese sort, representing underground streams and currents of energy in the earth. On some of the other weird old churches of Monte Sant'Angelo, you will encounter the serpent again—a pair of them, usually, whispering into the ear of a fork-tailed mermaid, or siren. Whoever this lady might be, she is figured in a quite alarming pose, with her tails spread wide to expose a part of mermaids seldom seen in churches.

Nearly every site dedicated to St Michael has something mysterious about it (at San Galgano in Tuscany they have a sword in the stone, like King Arthur's), but this one would be hard to beat. There is a suggestion of something ancient and a bit heretical, something that could be openly portrayed in the anarchically tolerant 12th century, but was later suppressed or just disappeared, leaving no trace; one Italian scholar suggests the mermaids were a symbol of a Dionysiac dancing cult that lasted until the Middle Ages—but your guess is probably as good as his.

The Church has any number of explanations for this lady: she is the Church itself, or personified wisdom, or personified vice, or else just meaningless decoration. Unfortunately, all of these explanations are utterly contrived and false. When you meet the local priests and monks you'll find they really don't want to talk about her at all. Mermaids do not only occur in Apulia. You can see them in medieval churches all over Italy and southern France, especially on churches dedicated to St Michael. In many small churches they are hidden–look hard and you'll find her peeking out from the back of a pier, or on a capital in a dimly lit corner.

Nevertheless, Apulia is the lady's special province. In Monte Sant'Angelo she seems to be the reigning deity, and she turns up in a conspicuous place in churches all over the region. If you follow her tracks as far as they lead, you'll see her in the mosaic floor of Otranto cathedral, at Apulia's Land's End on the Salentine peninsula. The smiling, spread-tailed mermaid here presides over the whole crazy Creation portrayed in this unique mosaic, seated next to King Solomon himself. There is an inscription around the figure that prob-ably explains everything—only it is in Arabic Kufic script, and nobody knows what it says.

The *Civitas Hippocratica*

As the industrial world struggles with its problems of health care—costs, ethical issues and disconcerting technology—it is refreshing to go back a thousand years to Salerno, where the first medical school of modern Europe was founded in the 11th century. Founded by the legendary 'Four Doctors'—an Italian, a Greek, a Jew and an Arab—it was for centuries the finest in Europe, the *Fons Medicinae* as Petrarch called it. Its doctors and teachers played an important role in the transmission of Greek and Arab science into Europe. Before the teachings of Salerno became widespread in Europe, what succour existed lay in the hands of monks and priests, who often blamed any illness on divine wrath. Salerno's school marked a definite improvement, by going back to Hippocrates and seeking natural causes. The school also marked the beginnings of medicine as a commercial enterprise, giving its students sound advice on collecting bills: 'When the patient is nearly well, address the head of the family, or the sick man's nearest relative, thus: "God Almighty having deigned by our aid to restore him whom you asked us to visit, we pray that He will maintain his health, and that you will now give us an honourable dismissal. Should any other member of your family desire our aid, we should, in grateful remembrance of our former dealings with you, leave all else and hurry to serve him."' At the same time, a natural sliding fee was the order of the day; a king was expected to pay a hundred times more for his cure than a small merchant.

Much of Salerno's teaching was based on numerology and astrology, following the science of the time, but there was a more practical side too. Medieval doctors sought to maintain a balance between the four humours of the body: phlegm (cold and moist), blood (hot and moist), bile (hot and dry) and black bile (cold and dry)—a poetic, metaphorical way of looking at things, but one that experience found instructive for centuries. To judge the soundness of this approach, consider the Health Rule of Salerno. Famous throughout the Middle Ages, the Rule was compiled by a certain Robert of Normandy, who was wounded during the First Crusade and convalesced in the city. Originally in Latin verse, its recom-mendations were translated into English by an Elizabethan, Sir John Harington:

> *A king that cannot rule him his diet*
> *Will hardly rule his realm in peace and quiet.*
>
> *For healthy men may cheese be wholesome food,*
> *But for the weak and sickly 'tis not good.*
>
> *Use three doctors still, first Dr Quiet,*
> *Next Dr Merry-man and Dr Diet...*
>
> *Wine, Women, Baths, by art of nature warme,*
> *Us'd or abus'd do men much good or harme.*
> *Some live to drinke new wine not fully fin'd.*

But for your health we wish that you drink none,
For such to dangerous fluxes are inclin'd,
Besides the lees of wine doe breed the stone.
But such by our consent shall drink alone.
For water and small biere we make no question
Are enemies to health and good digestion;
And Horace in a verse of his rehearses,
That water-drinkers never make good verses.

Oil for the Madonna

Sotto questo cielo non nascono sciocchi
(Under these skies no fools are born)

Neapolitan proverb

Camorra means a short jacket, of the kind the street toughs of Naples used to wear in the days of the Bourbon kings. But as with Sicily's Mafia, the origin of the Neapolitan Camorra is lost in legend. Some accounts put it in the slums of the *Quartiere Spagnuole*, under the rule of the Spanish viceroys of the 16th century. Spanish soldiers of that time lived the life of picaresque novels—or at least tried to—and the fathers and brothers of the district did their best to defend their girls from such picaresqueness, which usually meant a knife in the back in some dark alley.

There may be some truth to that, or it could all be romantic bosh. Criminals in southern Italy seem to always have been well organized, with a hierarchy, initiations, a set of rules, and a code of *omertà*. Foreign visitors to the city in the 1700s wrote that when something was stolen, they were able to get in touch with the 'King of Thieves' who would magically get it restored—stealing from guests, after all, was a discourtesy. It's doubtful they were ever so polite to their fellow citizens, for as long as there has been a Camorra it has lived mainly by extortion, with a fat finger in whatever rackets of the age looked most profitable. For a long time, the gang's biggest takings came from the prisons, which they controlled. In the old days, prisoners in Naples, as anywhere else, had to pay for their upkeep, and each new arrival would be met by the Camorristi with a subtle request for 'money for oil for the Madonna': that is, to keep the light burning at the shrine in the Camorra's favoured church, the Madonna del Carmine in the Piazza del Mercato; you can imagine that the Madonna required a lot of fuel.

Relations between the Camorra and the authorities have always been rather complex. In the last days of the *Regno*, Ferdinand II made use of them as a kind of anti-liberal secret police. In 1860, it was claimed that Garibaldi was forced to make a deal with them, handing over control of the city government in return for nobody shooting at him and his army when they entered the city. The new Italian state, run by northerners, could not see the logic in this, and tried to wipe out the Camorra by vigorous police action. The mob trumped that ploy easily by going into politics, setting the pattern of close alliance between organized crime and centre-rightist parties that continues in Italy to this day. In a typical irony of parliamentary democracy, the titled gentry of the ruling class and the thugs found that their interests coincided perfectly, and by 1900 the theory and practice of southern machine politics had been refined to an art. As people used to say: 'the government candidate always wins'. In another place that might seem a cliché; in Naples it was a proverb, a piece of the deepest folk wisdom.

Like the Mafia in Sicily, the Camorra took some hard knocks under Mussolini. If there was any cream to be skimmed, the Fascists wanted it all for themselves, and the ambience of the dictatorship proved wonderfully convenient for getting around the legal niceties of arrest and conviction. And like the Mafia, the Camorra was able to easily manipulate the Allied Military Government after 1944 to get back on its feet. Perhaps the Americans were sincerely convinced that the mobsters would be a useful ally in an impossible situation, or maybe they had got a message that a little cooperation would save their army a lot of trouble (accidents can happen...). In any case it seems always to have been Allied policy on the Italian front to throw open the prisons in every town they captured.

In 1944, top American mobster Lucky Luciano went to Sicily to arrange things. He was swindled royally by his supposed brothers; there has always been less of a connection between the native and foreign Mafias than one might suppose. One of his New York lieutenants, Vito Genovese, was from around Naples; he went back there, and had better luck than Lucky, insinuating his way into the confidences of the Allied High Command. From the old Camorra stronghold of the 'Triangle of Death', in the villages north of the city, and from the *bancarelle* of the Forcella market, Genovese oversaw an incredible orgy of black-market wheeling and dealing, largely over stolen army supplies, while the old Camorra hands revived the hallowed traditions of extortion.

Today, it is estimated that 60 per cent of all businesses in the Naples area pay protection money to the Camorra. The gang takes its cut from most sorts of common crime, and like the Mafia has become heavily involved in drugs—not so much exporting them as pushing them on their neighbours. If the old Camorra ever knew any bounds or limits, or had any sense of decency, the current model has forgotten it; even the youngest children are forced and tricked into crime. Unlike the Mafia, the Camorra has no recognized central authority; factions settle their differences with reciprocal assassinations, spectacles conducted out in the streets of the old quarters where all may enjoy them. The politicians in league with the Camorra have robbed and cheated Naples of fantastic amounts, enough to make the difference between the modern European metropolis it could be and the decomposing live body it is.

As late as 1992, your newspapers and Italy's newspapers managed to cover events in the south without ever daring to mention the obvious fact that government and organized crime were one and the same; it wasn't 'proved', and so even the most discreet insinuation might have been risky. Today, when Italy is in the midst of a revolution, things aren't so clear. The Camorra and the Mafia are undergoing a possibly serious crisis, thanks to the disgust of the electorate and the determined efforts of a few incorruptible policemen, prosecutors and judges. They are trying to make their arrangements with the new powers that be, wherever they can; meanwhile we all may wonder, as the Italians do, just what our newspapers aren't telling us now.

The New Science

> *It is the driest, obscurest, metaphysicalest book I ever got hold of. Confucius is a more lucid writer. Mortgages and remainders are pleasanter to peruse.*
>
> John Fiske, a Harvard scholar (1858)

Probably only a Neapolitan, living in the shadow of Vesuvius, could have written *La Nuova Scienza*, and Giambattista Vico was a true son of the city. Born in a little room over his father's bookshop on Via San Biagio dei Librai, he spent most of his life among the mouldering alleys of the *Spacca* and the University. Vico tells his very Neapolitan story in his *Autobiography*, a classic of unintentional hilarity. The fun starts on the first page; after getting his own birth date wrong by two years, Vico continues (writing in the third person):

> *He was a boy of high spirits and impatient of rest, but at the age of seven he fell head first from the top of a ladder to the floor below, and remained a good five hours without consciousness... The surgeon, indeed, observing the broken cranium and considering the period of unconsciousness, predicted that he would either die of it or grow up an idiot. However by God's grace neither part of his prediction came true, but as a result of this mischance he grew up with a melancholy and irritable temperament, such as belongs to men of ingenuity and depth, who thanks to the one, are quick as lightning in perception, and thanks to the other, take no pleasure in verbal cleverness or falsehood.*

The rest of the autobiography is pretty much in the same tone, with lofty, pompous phrasings befitting a man who held the chair of rhetoric at Naples University, and with a prickly defensiveness that came from a lifetime of being ignored or laughed at by his colleagues and nearly everyone else. Teaching rhetoric earned Vico a measly hundred ducats a year, and to get by he had to squander his talent writing fulsome eulogies and panegyrics for the king and the grandees of Naples. All the while, the poor philosopher was spending much of his time feeding and caring for his flock of children, a job his horrible, illiterate wife didn't much care for. A turning point in Vico's life came at the age of 55, when he tried to secure appointment to the much better-paying chair of law. For the occasion, he composed a brilliant treatise on the philosophical basis of law, and delivered it to the assembly blissfully unaware that almost all his fellows had been bribed to support one of the other candidates. The winner, best known as 'a notorious seducer of servant girls', eventually tried to publish a book and was found out as a plagiarist. The disgusted Vico gave up trying to get ahead, and devoted the rest of his life to his great work, the *New*

Science. To get it printed, in 1726, he had to sell his diamond ring, and even then he could only afford to do it in type so small it could barely be read.

Nevertheless, the work brought him some fame and respect in his last years, and the position of Official Historiographer to the King. Vico died in 1744; at the funeral, a quarrel broke out between his fellow professors and his religious confraternity over who would carry the coffin to the church; somehow this degenerated into a general neighbourhood brawl, and Vico's corpse was abandoned in the middle of Via dei Tribunali. Finally someone carted him off to the Girolamini Church, and fifty years later his last surviving son got around to putting up a marker on the tomb, where it can be seen today.

As James Joyce put it (writing of Finnegan, and maybe Vico): 'A good clap, a fore marriage, a bad wake, tell hell's well'. But Vico has had the last laugh. In our troubled times, when the airy certainties of Voltaire and Locke begin to look a bit superficial, Vico may well be the only thinker of the 18th century still worth a serious reading; his strange and utterly subversive book has increased its renown and influence with every generation since his death. Vico called the *New Science* an essay on the 'principles of Humanity'. His system is expressed in the language of myth, partly from Vico's own imaginative turn of mind, and possibly also from a desire to not arouse the Inquisition, still in business in 18th-century Naples. Vico has been called an 'Orphic voice', an oracle. He explains the development of language, for example, as beginning in a 'mute speech' of gestures and signs, a 'divine poetry'. The next stage is symbols—like heraldic arms; only then comes conventional speech. After a spin through the Wonderland of the *New Science*, this begins to make sense. The major theme of the book is an exploration of the origins of culture and society, and the circular 'course the nations run' through four stages: first a theocratic age, founded by giants out of barbarism; next comes the age of heroes, an aristocratic society, and then 'human' government, where equality is recognized, though this inevitably declines into monarchy (like Augustus's Rome). At last, through what Vico calls 'the barbarism of reflection', man's egotism causes disintegration and fall, and the stage is cleared for the whole cycle to start afresh.

Scholars today emphasize Vico's contributions to social thinking—somewhat primitive ones, in their view—and he has been called the 'first political scientist'. They do not get the point. James Joyce did, and he turned the *New Science* inside out and tickled and teased it to make an even stranger book: *Finnegans Wake*. As Norman O. Brown put it, 'Joyce wore his eyes out staring at Europe and seeing nothing'. Western civilization, for him, was over, simply biding time until the barbarians come (who could argue?), and he arranged his murky masterpiece in four parts, following Vico's four stages of history. Joyce's 'farced epistol to the hibruws' is just that—a farce, appropriate to our time of disarray, something to instruct and entertain us while we all wait for the Word, the divine thunderclap of Jove to sound and start civilization, by ' a commodious vicus of recirculation', back on its circle again. Why not take Joyce and Vico along on your trip? (along with Brown's *Closing Time*, and *A Skeleton Key to Finnegans Wake* by Joseph Campbell and H. M. Robinson)—a little light reading for the beach, a beach with a view of Vesuvius on the horizon.

Naples

Porto di Napoli

The most loathsome nest of human caterpillars I was ever forced to stay in—a hell with all the devils imbecile in it.

John Ruskin

...it reveals itself only to the simpatici.

Peter Gunn

For many, Naples is the true homeland of a particular Italian fantasy, the last bastion of singing waiters and red checked tablecloths, operatic passion and colourful poverty, balanced precariously between Love's own coastline and the menace of Vesuvius. But mention Naples or the Neapolitans to any modern, respectable north Italian, and as they gesticulate and roll their eyes to heaven you will get a first-hand lesson in the dynamics of Italy's 'Problem of the South'. Many Italians simply cannot accept that such an outlandish place can be in the same country with them, a sentiment that probably contains as much envy as contempt. Naples, the city that has given the world Enrico Caruso, Sophia Loren, pizza, and syphilis (the disease appeared here in 1495, and was immediately blamed on the French garrison), may also be the first city to make social disorder into an art form.

Degradation, Italian Style

On Naples' Piazza Garibaldi you can buy a boiled pigs' organ on a stick, served with a slice of lemon, and watch eight-year-old *scugnizzi*—street children—puff on contraband Marlboros while casually tossing firecrackers into traffic. Fireworks, along with slamming doors, impromptu arias, screams, ambulance sirens and howling cats, are an essential part of the Neapolitan ambience. This anarchic symphony is harder to catch these days, unfortunately, drowned as it is under the roar of Italy's worst traffic problem. In central Naples, three-quarters of a million rude drivers chase each other around a street plan that hasn't changed much since Roman times. Meanwhile, the nation's worst air pollution keeps the hospitals full, in spite of occasional half-hearted attempts to solve the problem by only allowing drivers to take their cars out on alternate days, and every few weeks some old lady on a back street burns to a crisp while the firemen, just down the block, gamely push illegally parked cars out of their way.

Another chronic problem is housing, enough of a nightmare even before the earthquake of 1980; on the outskirts of the city, you may see Napoletani living in stolen ship cargo containers, with windows cut in the sides, in shacks made of sheet metal and old doors, or in abandoned buses. In the city centre, thousands of earthquake refugees are still camping in hotels. One bizarre side-effect of this housing shortage—found all over Italy, but particularly visible here—is the 'quivering car' phenomenon. You'll see them everywhere, especially up on Posillipo hill, cars parked nose to tail, their windows blacked out with newspaper, turned into temporary bedrooms by courting couples or even married couples who have no privacy at home. A cruel but popular prank with Neapolitan kids is to sneak up on the cars and set fire to the newspaper.

Reform has been the buzz word in recent years but the city still has to deal with the spectre of the Camorra, a loose term for the crime syndicates that keep Naples as securely strung up as any mountain village in Sicily. Crime is so well organized here, to give one example, that seagoing smugglers have formed a trade union to protect their interests against the police.

In the 18th century, when the city and its spectacular setting were a highlight of the Grand Tour, the saying was 'See Naples and die...'. Nowadays you usually can't see much of anything through the smog, and you'll probably survive if you're careful crossing streets. Don't let Naples' current degradation spoil your visit, though; you haven't seen Italy—no, you haven't seen the Mediterranean—until you have spent some time in this fascinating metropolis. The only thing subtle about Naples is its charm, and the city will probably win your heart at the same time as it is deranging your senses.

On the Other Hand...

If Naples immediately repels you, however, it means you are probably a sticky sort, and will miss all the fun. The city has an incomparable setting, and much of it is still admittedly beautiful, but its real attraction is a priceless insight into humanity, at the hands of a population of 2.2 million dangerous anarchists. The Napoletani may be numbered among the few peoples of Europe who realize they are alive, and try to enjoy it as best they can. Their history being what it is, this manifests itself in diverse ways. The Napoletani do not stand in lines, or fill out forms, or stop for traffic signals; they will talk your ears off, run you over in their ancient Fiats, criticize the way you dress, whisper alarming propositions, give you sweets, try to pick your pockets with engaging artlessness, offer surprising kindnesses, and with a reassuring smile they will always, always give you the wrong directions. In an official capacity, they will either break the rules for you or invent new ones; in shops and restaurants, they will either charge you too much or too little. The former is much more common, though whichever it is, they will do it with a flourish.

If the accounts of long-ago travellers are to be believed, Naples has always been like this. Too much sunshine, and living under such a large and ill-mannered volcano, must contribute much to the effect. It would be somewhat harder to explain some of Naples' ancient distinctions. First and foremost, Naples is Italy's city of philosophers. Her greatest, Giambattista Vico, was a Neapolitan, and others, such as St Thomas Aquinas and Benedetto Croce, spent much of their time here. Naples can also claim to be first in music. Among native composers are Gesualdo, Scarlatti, and Leoncavallo, and the conservatory is claimed to be the oldest in Europe. Even today, members of the opera company at San Carlo look down on their colleagues at Milan's La Scala as a band of promising upstarts who could stand to take their jobs a little more seriously. Neapolitan popular song, expressive and intense, is an unchained Italian stereotype; the Napoletani maintain its traditions as jealously as they do their impenetrable dialect, one of the most widely spoken and robust in modern Italy

History

Naples' rise to become the metropolis of Campania was largely the result of the lucky elimination of her rivals over the centuries. Capua, Cumae, and Benevento rose and fell, and Pompeii and Herculaneum disappeared under volcanic ash, but fortune has always seemed to protect Naples from the really big disasters. As a Greek colony founded by Cumae in 750 BC, the city began with the name Neapolis, and prospered moderately throughout the periods of Greek, Samnite, and Roman rule. Belisarius, Justinian's famous general, seized the region for Byzantium in 536, after invasions of the Goths and Vandals, but a duke of Naples declared the city independent in 763, acknowledging only the authority of the pope.

The chronicles are understandably slim for this period; early medieval Naples offers us more fairy-tales than facts. Many of its early legends deal with none other than the poet Virgil; somehow, folklore in the dark ages had transformed the greatest Latin poet into Master Virgil, a mighty magician who was given credit for many of the unexplainable engineering feats of the ancient Romans. Naples claimed him for its founder, and its legends told of how he built the Castel dell'Ovo, balancing it on an egg at the bottom of the harbour. Master Virgil also built a talking statue that warned the city of enemies, earthquakes, or plagues, and medieval chroniclers mention the bronze horses and bronze fly he built over two of the city's gates, still to be seen in those days, and said to be magical charms on which the fortune of the city depended.

Naples lost its independence to the Normans in 1139, later passing under the rule of the Hohenstaufen emperors along with the rest of southern Italy. Charles of Anjou took over in 1266, and lopped off the head of the last Hohenstaufen, Conradin, in what is now Naples' Piazza del Mercato. Under the Angevins, Naples for the first time assumed the status and architectural embellishments of a capital. The Angevin kings of Naples, however, did little to develop their new realm, expending most of their energy in futile attempts to recapture Sicily, lost to them after the Sicilian Vespers revolution of 1282. After their line expired in 1435 with the death of Giovanni II, the kingdom fell to Alfonso V of Aragon—a fateful event, marking Spain's first foothold on the Italian mainland.

Habsburgs and Bourbons

Aragonese rule seemed promising at first, under the enlightened Alfonso. In later decades, though, it became clear that the Spaniards were mainly interested in milking Italy for taxes with which to finance further conquests. The city itself, as the seat of the viceregal court, prospered greatly; by 1600 its population of 280,000 made it perhaps the largest city on the Mediterranean. The long period of Spanish control did much to give Naples its distinct character, especially during the 17th and 18th centuries, when the city participated almost joyfully in the decadence and decay of the Spanish Empire. This period saw the construction of the scores of frilly, gloomy Baroque churches—now half-abandoned, with bushes growing out of the cornices—that add so much to the Neapolitan scene. In manners especially, the imperial Spanish influence was felt; 'Nothing', in the words of one observer, 'is cheaper here than human life'.

In 1707, during the War of the Spanish Succession, Naples passed under the rule of Archduke Charles of Austria. Prince Charles of Bourbon, however, snatched it away from him in 1734, and mouldering, picturesque Naples for the next century and a half made the perfect backdrop for the rococo shenanigans of the new Bourbon kingdom. The new rulers were little improvement over the Spaniards, but immigrants from all over the south poured into the city, chasing the thousands of ducats dropped by a free-spending court. Naples became the most densely populated city in Europe, a distinction it still holds today, and crime and epidemics became widespread.

Nevertheless, this was the Naples that became a major attraction for thousands of northern aesthetes doing the Grand Tour in the 18th and 19th centuries. Goethe flirted with contessas here, while the English poets were flirting with dread diseases and Lord Nelson was making eyes at Lady Hamilton. The Neapolitans are frank about it; Naples owed its prominence on the Grand Tour less to Vesuvius and the ruins of Pompeii than to good old-fashioned sex. Naples at the time was incontestably the easiest place in Europe to find some, and everyone knew it—saving Goethe and the rest the trouble of ever mentioning the subject in their travel accounts and letters home.

Garibaldi's army entered Naples in February 1861. As the new Italy's biggest basket case, the city has since received considerable assistance with its planning and social problems—though not nearly enough to make up for the centuries of neglect. World War II didn't help; for four days in late September 1944, the city staged a heroic though unsuccessful revolt against the Germans. Even more damage was done by Allied bombing, and the destruction of the city's port and utilities by the retreating Nazis.

While the post-war period saw considerable rebuilding, it also brought new calamities. Illegal and speculative building projects grabbed most of the already-crowded city's open space (you'll notice the almost total absence of parks), and turned the fringe areas and much of the once-beautiful Bay of Naples shore into a nightmare of human detritus, one of the eeriest industrial wastelands of Europe. At the moment, there seems to be a common realization that Naples has reached a point of no return. It has either to clean itself up or perish; discussions of the city's problems in the press are often conducted in alarmingly apocalyptic tones. Leave some room for exaggeration—the Napoletani probably couldn't enjoy life properly without a permanent state of crisis.

In the political turmoil that has taken over Italy since the beginning of the nineties, with the collapse of the old parties, Naples has become one of the major bases of support for the neo-Fascist MSI party, in yet another twist to the city's history. It has, however, marked up one genuine accomplishment in the books in the last few years, though not one that will have much effect on the most serious problems—the *Centro Direzionale*, a huge modernistic development on the lines of a Neapolitan Manhattan built over the wastelands around Corso Malta, north of the Central Station. In spite of a few hiccups, most notably when the new palace of justice was mysteriously burnt to the ground (no prizes for guessing by whom), the project is currently nearing completion, its aim being to provide a new centre for the regional economy.

Most recently the city has seen the arrival of a new mayor, Basolino, who beat Alessandra Mussolini, Benito's grand-daughter, in the 1994 elections. The worst of the ghettos around the port have gone, tourist trails across Spaccanapoli have been encouraged, and churches and sites long closed are reopening. Most spectacularly of all, the Piazza del Plebiscito, for a long time choked by traffic and fated to remain the city's parking lot, has been emptied and cleaned up. A lot remains to be done but, believe us, it's a start.

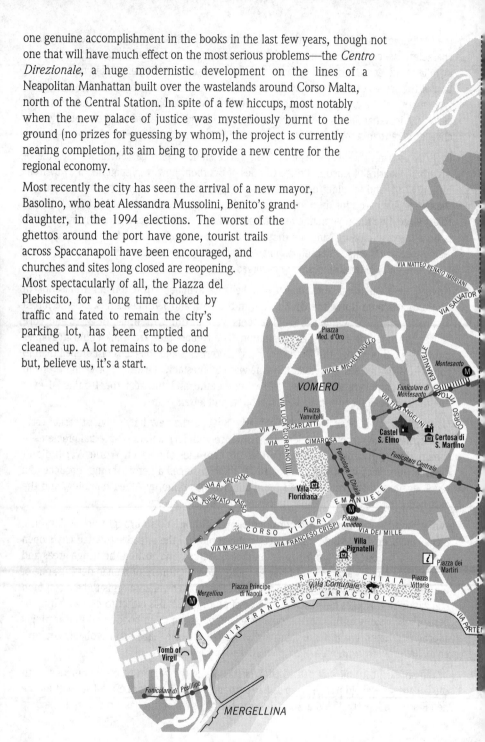

Naples

by air

Naples' **Capodichino airport** is on the north side of the city, relatively close to the centre. It has frequent direct services to and from all major Italian destinations and to many foreign cities, including London (several flights daily). For airport information, call ✆ 7896111. From 6am to midnight there is a bus service every 50 minutes (a blue bus run by Sepsa), between the airport and Piazza Municipio near the ferry harbour. For the Stazione Centrale there is the half-hourly city bus (no.14) which does not run as late. The journey takes 20–45mins, depending on the time of day. As on all city buses, tickets should be bought at a news-stand or ticket booth before boarding. Lastly, Curreri (✆ 8015420) runs a limited service to Sorrento departing from the stop outside the Arrivals hall (on the right).

If you opt for a taxi, remember that on top of the fare on the meter you will officially be charged extra supplements for the airport trip and for luggage—plus, very possibly, additional unexplained 'extras' as well (see below). If in doubt, ask to see the list of prices, which should be displayed in the cab, or try to agree on the fare to your destination before getting into the cab. If traffic is not too heavy—and this is a big if—the fare to the centre should not exceed L40,000.

by sea

Naples' port has more ship and hydrofoil connections than anywhere else in the Mediterranean, so you can choose to arrive by sea from—or flee to—a wide variety of places, among them the islands in the Bay of Naples, Sicily and the Aeolian Islands. Generally, ferries are cheaper than hydrofoils, but take approximately twice as long. One of the loveliest of the possible sea excursions is the night ferry to the Aeolian Islands, which arrives as the sun is rising over Vulcano.

Ferries and hydrofoils leave from three different points in Naples, but most longer-distance ferries operate from the **Stazione Marittima**, in the centre of the port near the Castel Nuovo. Consult the individual companies for timetables, or look in the daily newspaper *Il Mattino*. The main companies operating from the Stazione Marittima are **Tirrenia**, ✆ 7201111, for Palermo and Cagliari; and **Siremar**, ✆ 7201595, for the Aeolian Islands and Milazzo in Sicily. In addition, one company, **SNAV**, ✆ 7612348, operates a daily long-distance hydrofoil service from Mergellina quay to the Aeolian Islands.

For more information on all boat services from Naples and hydrofoil services to the islands and ports around the bay, *see* pp.8–9 and 122.

by rail

Most visitors arrive by train, at the modern **Stazione Centrale** (for information, call ✆ 1478 88088 between 7am and 9pm), on Piazza Garibaldi, which is convenient since this is also a junction for city buses and the local *Circumvesuviana* railway. Trains along the coast towards Rome or Reggio di Calabria pass through every half-hour on average. In addition, many trains also stop at **Napoli Mergellina** and **Napoli Campi Flegrei**, on the western side of the city, and at some other local stations. There are also good rail connections from Naples to Palermo (4–8 hours, depending on the train) via Messina.

As well as the state FS lines, there are three local railway lines serving the Bay of Naples area. One, the **Ferrovia Circumvesuviana** (information ✆ 7792444), runs trains to Herculaneum, Pompeii and Sorrento from the **Stazione Circumvesuviana** in Corso Garibaldi, and from the Stazione Centrale. Another separate line, the **Ferrovia Cumana**, ✆ 5513328, runs regular trains to the Campi Flegrei area, including Pozzuoli and Baia, from the station at Piazza Montesanto. A third line, the **Ferrovia Circumflegrea**, also ✆ 5513328, runs from the same station at Piazza Montesanto to points west, including Licola and Cuma. For more information on the regional rail lines *see* p.98.

by long-distance bus

Most services to destinations within the province and the Campania region operate from Piazza Garibaldi, in front of the FS Stazione Centrale. An exception is the bus service to Salerno along the coast, which runs from Via Pisanelli, near Piazza Municipio (*see* p.100).

by road

The A2 *autostrada* from Rome approaches Naples from due north, via Caserta, and in the outskirts of the city, just east of Capodichino airport, meets up with a series of massive road junctions: the A16 turns off east for Avellino, Bari and the Adriatic, and then two roads head off to the west, the P1 for the coast and the Naples inner ring road, the *tangenziale*, which leads around the back of the city towards Pozzuoli and the Campi Flegrei. Using the *tangenziale* makes it possible to reach most areas of the city without going through the centre. Traffic going further south should stay on the A2 until it meets the A3, so avoiding the city entirely.

Once you arrive at wherever you are staying in Naples, you are categorically advised to park your car in a safe place (such as a hotel garage) and not attempt to use it anywhere within the city (*see* p.70).

Tourist Information

The best place to go for information about Naples itself is the well-run and friendly information booth run by the city's **Azienda Autonoma di Soggiorno** on Piazza del Gesù Nuovo, ✆ 5523328/5512701, in the old town *(open Mon–Sat, 9–7; Sun 9–2)*. Their main office is in the Royal Palace, ✆ 418744, ✉ 418619. In summer they open offices in the Castel dell'Ovo, ✆ 764 5688. Information about excursions outside the city and so on is only available from the less helpful provincial **EPT**, Piazza dei Martiri 58,

© 405311. The EPT has another office at the Stazione Centrale, © 268779, which may be some help in finding a hotel. Two others are to be found at the airport, © 7805761, and the Stazione Mergellina, © 7612102.

Look out for the free monthly handbook *Qui Napoli*, available at tourist offices and some hotels, which carries a great deal of useful information, timetables, listings and calendars of events. The **EPT** produce good maps of the city centre and the bay itself (both free of charge).

As part of measures attracting visitors, walking trails through the old city centre have been established and sites of interest are now kept open for this purpose. Information on accompanied walks is available from the **AAST** at Piazza del Gesù Nuovo. For a fascinating trip around subterranean Naples, **Laes** (Libera Associazione Escursionisti sottosuolo, © 400256) operate guided tours from Piazza Trieste e Trento (next to Piazza del Plebiscito) at 10am, daily.

Getting Around

Transport around the city is a fascinating subject. Such is the state of most public transport and so impenetrable is the traffic that walking is often by far the most practical way of getting anywhere, apart from up to the heights by the *funicolari*.

Orientation is a little difficult. If you arrive by sea—the only proper way to do it—you'll get a good idea of the layout. Naples' dominant landmarks, visible from almost anywhere in town, are Castel Sant'Elmo and the huge, fortress-like monastery of San Martino. They are neighbours on the steep hill that slopes down to the sea near the port, neatly dividing the city into its old and new quarters.

Modern Naples is on the western side, the busy, pleasant districts of Mergellina, Vomero and Fuorigrotta, to which middle-class Napoletani escape from the city centre each night on their creaking old funicular railways. To the east, towards Vesuvius, lies the centre, along Via Toledo, and beyond it the oldest neighbourhoods, tall tenements jammed into a grid of narrow streets, reaching a climax in the oriental bazaar atmosphere of the Piazza Mercato and the Piazza Garibaldi.

One benefit of reforms aimed at cleaning up the city's image and attracting tourists is the introduction of the new-style 'Giranapoli' bus tickets (literally translated as 'Travel Naples'). There are two types, one lasting 90 minutes for L1200, and a day ticket for L4000. If you plan on staying in Naples for more than 9 days invest in a monthly pass (L35,000). These enable you to travel on buses, the funiculars and the Metropolitana throughout the city.

For more on travel by train or bus to destinations outside the city, around the Bay of Naples or further into Campania, *see* pp.9–10, 98, 100, 166 and 176.

Given the problems involved in using their own cars and even taxis in Naples, visitors often find themselves left with the local buses, which is small cheer, since the city indisputably has the worst bus system in Italy. Buses will be slow and usually indecently crowded. There are no schedules, no maps, and nowhere you can get accurate information; even the drivers usually do not have the faintest idea what is happening. The ultimate Neapolitan experience is waiting an hour for a bus after being misinformed by line employees, and then finding out that the right bus is the one marked 'out of service'. The confusion is compounded by the recent division of services run by the old bus company Atam under its successor ANM and other smaller companies. Most lines start at either Piazza Garibaldi or Piazza del Plebiscito. Some that might be useful are:

R2, from Piazza Garibaldi to Corso Umberto and Piazza Municipio.

R3, from Piazza Municipio to Riviera di Chiaia and Mergellina.

110, **127**, from Piazza Garibaldi to Piazza Cavour and Capodimonte.

152, from Piazza Garibaldi to Pozzuoli.

by Metro and funicolare

Naples also has a sort of underground. The **Metropolitana**, a single line from Piazza Garibaldi (basement of the Stazione Centrale) to Fuorigrotta, is really a part of the state railway, and uses the same underground tracks as the long-distance trains. The FS runs it as anarchically as the buses, but it will be helpful for reaching the station, the archaeological museum, and points in Vomero and Fuorigrotta. As on the buses, few people ever buy tickets.

A much more agreeable way to travel, though you can't go very far, is on the three **funicolari**, or inclined railways, up to Vomero. The longest—one of the longest in the world, in fact—is the **Funicolare Centrale**, from Via Toledo, just behind the Galleria, up to Via Cimarosa. The **Funicolare di Chiaia** also ends nearby in the same street, having started from Piazza Amedeo in Chiaia. Finally, the **Funicolare di Montesanto** travels up to Via Morghen from Montesanto Station, the start of the suburban Circumflegrea and Cumana rail lines. All three funicolari bring you out near the San Martino Museum and the Castel Sant'Elmo. All run until about 10pm daily.

by taxi

Neapolitan taxi drivers are uniformly dishonest, and try out any number of scams involving fixed meters, turning the meter on before you get in the car, imaginary 'surcharges' and so on. Also, the traffic is frequently so thick that relatively short journeys can take so long (and cost so much) that they're really not worth it. If you want to take a taxi to a specific destination, always try to agree on the fare in advance, whether there is a meter or not.

The first thing to get straight is simply—*leave your car elsewhere*. Cars disappear in Naples with alarming frequency, and foreign number plates are especially prized. Even if you get to keep your wheels, you'll be sorry. Driving in Naples is a unique experience. Motorists studiously disregard all traffic signals and warnings, and the city has given up trying to coerce them. There are no rules, except to get there first, and fatalities are common. Even if this sounds exciting, note that the novelty soon wears off, even for the most boorish motorhead. For scant sympathy about stolen cars, call the city police on ✆ 7941435.

Several **car hire** firms have offices in Naples, mainly on Via Partenope (near the port), at the airport, and/or at the Stazione Centrale. To find the office most convenient for you try: **Avis**, Via Partenope 32, ✆ 7645600; **Europcar**, Via Partenope 38, ✆ 7645859; **Hertz**, Via Sauro 21, ✆ 7645323; **IntalRent**, Via S. Lucia, ✆ 7645423. Be warned, however, that as car theft is rife in Naples some companies will not rent certain models in the city, so you may find your choice restricted. The most basic models start from L85,000 per day.

Check with hotels if they have secure parking (*parcheggio custodito*). If not you might want to use the private car parks. Overnight stays can cost L20,000 and more: Grilli, Via Galileo Ferrari 40, close to the Stazione Centrale, ✆ 264344; Mergellina, Via Mergellina 112, ✆ 7613470; Sannazaro, Piazza Sannazaro 142, ✆ 681437.

Piazza del Plebiscito

After years as a parking lot this immense and elegant square, the centre of modern Naples, has been rescued and restored to the city. Children now come here at sundown to kick a football, under the eyes of adoring parents. The recent shows staged here by the city for the benefit of national television have even forced some northern Italians to revise their opinions of Naples and admit to its attractions.

The huge domed church, embracing the piazza in its curving colonnades as does St Peter's in Rome, is **San Francesco di Paola**. King Ferdinand IV, after the British restored him to power in 1815, made a vow to construct it; the great dome and classical portico were modelled after the Pantheon in Rome. There's little to see in the austere interior, and anyone with a little understanding of Naples will not be surprised to find the colonnades given over to light manufacturing and warehouse space.

Across the square rises the equally imposing bulk of the **Royal Palace** (*Palazzo Reale*), begun by the Spanish viceroys in 1600, expanded by the Bourbons and finished by the kings of Italy *(open Tues–Sun, 9–1.30 and 4.30–7.30; adm)*. Umberto I, a good friend of the Neapolitans, added the eight giant figures on the façade, representing the eight houses that have ruled at Naples. It seems the 19th-century sculptors had trouble taking some of them seriously; note the preposterous figures of Charles of Anjou, whom the Neapolitans never liked, and Vittorio Emanuele II, the latter probably an accurate portrayal. There are

Ruritanian stone sentry boxes and stone peacocks in the courtyard to recall the Bourbons, and a number of rooms inside that can be visited—the ones that escaped the bombings in World War II, including a suitably grand staircase, a theatre, and several chambers in 18th-century style. The palace's theatre saw the premières of many of the works of Alessandro Scarlatti. The rear of the palace, now the home of Naples' important **Biblioteca Nazionale**, faces a pretty, little-visited garden across from the Castel Nuovo.

The Bourbons were great opera buffs, and they built Italy's largest opera house, the **San Carlo**, right next to their palace. Begun in 1737, making it older than La Scala, the theatre was sumptuously restored after a fire in 1816, during the period when Naples was the unquestioned capital of opera; so important was the theatre to the people of Naples that King Ferdinand made sure the the workmen got the job done in record time—300 days. Today the San Carlo is still among the most prestigious in the world (the Neapolitans of course would place it first), and its productions are certainly among the most polished and professional, and occasionally among the most adventurous. Each season at least one lesser-known Neapolitan opera is performed. Tickets are as expensive as anywhere (up to L500,000 on an opening night). Brief tours of the theatre for considerably less should be possible in 1996 after restoration *(© 7972111 for more information).*

Castel Nuovo

Opposite the San Carlo is the grandest interior of Southern Italy, the **Galleria Umberto I**. This great glass-roofed arcade, perhaps the largest in the world, was begun in 1887, nine years after the Galleria Vittorio Emanuele in Milan. The arcade is cross-shaped, with a mosaic of the zodiac on the floor at the centre, and its dome is 56m tall; surprisingly, the Neapolitans do not seem to like it as much as they once did; even at high noon, you are likely to find its vast spaces deserted but for a few small clouds of grey-suited men arguing politics around the entrances.

Castel Nuovo

The port of Naples has been protected by this odd, beautiful castle, looming over the harbour behind the Royal Palace and San Carlo, for some 700 years now. Charles of Anjou built it in 1279; many Napoletani still call it by the curious name of *Maschio* (male)

Angioino. Most of what you see today, however, including the eccentric, ponderous round towers, is the work of Guillermo Sagrera, the great Catalan architect who built the famous Exchange in Palma de Mallorca. Between two of these towers at the entrance, the conquering Aragonese hired the finest sculptors from all over Italy to build Alfonso's **Triumphal Arch**, a unique masterpiece of Renaissance sculpture and design inspired by the triumphal arches of the ancient Romans. The symbolism, as in the Roman arches, may be a little confusing. The figure at the top is Saint Michael; below him are a matched pair of sea gods, and further down, allegorical virtues and relief panels portraying Alfonso's victories and wise governance.

Inside, the castle currently houses parts of the Naples city administration and some cultural societies. If you come during office hours *(Mon–Fri, 8–1)*, someone will probably be around to show you the **Sala dei Baroni**, where the city council meets; it has a cupola with an unusual Moorish vaulting, an eight-pointed star made of interlocking arches. King Ferrante used this as his dining hall, and it takes its name from the evening when he invited a score of the kingdom's leading barons to a ball, and then arrested the lot. There are also two museums *(open Mon–Sat, 9–7; adm)*. One, housed in the Gothic **Cappella Palatina**, next to the council hall, contains 14th- and 15th-century frescoes; the other, in the south wing, has paintings, and a good collection of silver and bronzes, from the 15th century to the present day.

King Ferrante's Dungeons

Guillermo Sagrera was the Frank Lloyd Wright of the Renaissance, a brilliant, iconoclastic architect who dreamt up shapes and forms never seen before. In his rebuilding of the Castel Nuovo, with its arch and massive and eccentric towers, he and his intelligent patron, King Alfonso, must have been fully aware of the revolutionary design statement (as we might call it today) they were making—a castle meant to be not only a royal residence and stronghold, but a landmark and symbol for Naples.

Even before the arrival of the Spaniards and the rebuilding, the Castel Nuovo had witnessed a good deal of history. Here, when the castle was brand new, Charles of Anjou had received the news of the Sicilian Vespers, and reportedly cried out: 'Lord God, since it has pleased you to ruin me, let me only go down by small steps!' 1294 saw the visit of Pope Celestine V, who had been a simple and slow-witted hermit in the Abruzzo before his surprise election. The church bosses, who wanted a stronger hand on the papal throne, meant to get rid of him as soon as possible, and in this castle they tricked him into abdicating by whispering into his room through a hidden tube, claiming to be the voice of God and commanding him to quit. King Robert the Wise kept his great library here, and graciously received Petrarch and Boccaccio in his royal apartments.

Poor Sagrera would be quite sad to hear that the Castel Nuovo seems somewhat dark and sinister to many visitors today. It isn't his fault; perhaps it isn't even a matter of changing architectural tastes. Most of the credit must surely go to the ruler who stamped his own personality on the castle more than anyone else, the monstrous King Ferrante. Illegitimate son of Alfonso the Magnanimous (or just as likely, people whispered, of a certain Moor of Valencia), Ferrante took the throne of Naples in 1458; he was a devious and capable ruler, just the sort of man the state needed among the dangerous intrigues and ever-shifting political fortunes of Renaissance Italy. He is better remembered for his calculated cruelty. On one occasion, he invited an enemy back to Naples, professing great affection, and treated him to a month of parties before suddenly arresting him and sending him off to the torture room. A surprise invitation to the King's table for dinner was often as good as a death warrant. Ferrante was known to keep a 'museum of mummies' of executed foes and rebellious barons at the castle, each dressed in his own clothes. And stories went round that he kept a crocodile in the castle's dungeons, which was fed only on live prisoners.

Via Toledo

From the landward side of Piazza del Plebiscito and the Palace, Naples' most imposing street, the Via Toledo, runs northwards past the Galleria to Piazza Carita where it becomes Via Roma. Its name commemorates its builder, Don Pedro de Toledo, the Spanish viceroy at the beginning of the 16th century, and a great benefactor of Naples. Stendhal, in 1817, rightly called this 'the most populous and gayest street in the world', and it is still the city's main business and shopping street, leading up to Capodimonte and the northern suburbs. Don Pedro's elegant Renaissance tomb, among others, can be seen in the little church of **San Giacomo degli Spagnuoli**, now swallowed up by the 19th-century Palazzo Municipale complex, originally a home for the Bourbon royal bureaucracy.

Going north along Via Toledo, any street on your left can be the entrance to the dense, crumbling, slightly sinister inner sanctum of the Neapolitan soul, the vast slum called the *Quartiere Spagnuoli*. It can be a fascinating place to walk around, in daytime at least. Lately though, thanks to battling factions of the Camorra, the *Quartiere* has achieved even more than its accustomed share of notoriety; for a while the hoods were bumping each other off at a rate of one per week. Though the *Quartiere* covers almost all the area sloping up to San Martino and Vomero, the most populous and colourful part is that immediately adjoining Via Toledo, a strict grid of narrow streets laid out by Don Pedro de Toledo and now called the *Tavoliere*, or chessboard.

Four Days in Naples

The contempt that many northern Italians often show for this city and its accomplishments can look a bit silly when compared with the facts. Just for the record, we note that in September 1944 Naples did more than its part in redeeming Italian honour by becoming the first city to liberate itself, and the only one to do so until the German collapse at the end of the war.

At the time of the Allied landings in Salerno, the city was in a bad way. Rations of everything were short, sometimes nonexistent, and the Germans were preparing to dynamite all the important facilities in case the Allied advance should reach Naples.

Worst of all, SS units were combing every quarter for able-bodied males to ship off to forced labour in the north or in Germany. No one knows exactly what incident touched off the great revolt. In the excellent 1960s film account, *Quattro Giornate a Napoli*, a group of men who escaped from the Germans here in the *Quartiere Spagnuoli* is recaptured and lined up against a building to be shot. A basket on a string suddenly appears among them, of the type old women would send down from their windows in the tall tenements to buy tomatoes or chestnuts from the street vendors; this time, though, the basket contained a gun—unexpected aid from heaven has always been a common theme in Neapolitan mythology.

However it started, the uprising spread like a prairie fire through the city. Pistols and old rifles came out from their hiding places, and the police arsenals were broken into for more. *Scugnizzi* (street children) waited in doorways with stolen grenades, ready to try and tip one into a passing Nazi truck or tank. The prisons were thrown open, and while many of their inmates scuttered off into the shadows, plenty of others took what arms they could find and joined in the fight. Not long after, the rebels surrounded the heavily defended football stadium in Vomero, full of captured Neapolitans waiting to be sent to Germany; they took it, despite heavy casualties, and freed the lot.

At the beginning the rebels carried on without any leadership whatsoever—except of course among the Communists. The totally anarchic, overwhelming, totally spontaneous movement of the city's people was something that few cities but Naples could ever produce. The Germans found it the ultimate Neapolitan experience; it was as if they had kicked over a beehive. They responded with customary brutality—massacres of prisoners and tanks firing point-blank into apartment blocks—but stung and pestered on every side, they could not endure long. A hastily formed committee went to negotiate terms with the exasperated German commander, and a deal was cut: the troops would depart immediately, and attacks on them would cease. An eerie silence fell over the city and indifferent faces watched from their windows as the German columns filed out. And then Naples went back to being Naples.

To the right of Via Toledo, the confusion of Naples' half-crumbling, half-modern business centre conceals a few buildings worth a look. The **Palazzo Gravina**, on Via Monteoliveto, is a fine palace in the northern Renaissance style, built between 1513 and 1549. It now houses Naples University's Faculty of Architecture. Almost directly across the street, the church of **Monteoliveto** (*open Tues–Sat, 8.30–12.30*) is a little treasure house of late Renaissance sculpture and painting, with tombs and altars in the various chapels by southern artists like Giovanni da Nola and Antonio Rosellino, as well as some frescoes by Vasari.

Spaccanapoli

This street's familiar name means 'Split-Naples', and that is exactly what it has done for the last 2600 years. On the map, it changes its name with alarming frequency—Via Benedetto Croce and Via San Biagio dei Librai are two of the most prominent—but in Roman times you would have found it by asking for the *decumanus inferior*, the name for the second east–west street in any planned Roman city. No large city in all the lands conquered by Rome has maintained its ancient street plan as completely as Naples (the Greeks laid out these streets, of course, but the Romans learned their planning from them). It is easier to imagine the atmosphere of a big ancient city here than in Rome itself, or even in Pompeii. The narrow, straight streets and tall *insulae* cannot have changed much; only the forum and temples are missing.

This is the heart of old Naples—and what a street it is, lined with grocery barrows and scholarly bookshops, shops that sell old violins, plaster saints, pizza, or used clothes pegs. Drama is supplied by the arch-Neapolitan characters who live here, haunting the street-corners and entertaining wan hopes of dodging the manic motorists; the colour comes from the district's laundry—down any of the long alleys of impossibly tall tenements you may see as many as a hundred full clothes-lines, swelling bravely in the breeze and hoping for a glint of southern sun.

It has always been a poor neighbourhood, though even now it is not a desperate one. As always, its people live much of their life on the streets, carrying on whatever is their business from makeshift benches on the kerbs. The visitor will probably find that claustrophobia is right around the corner, but anyone born and raised here would never feel at home anywhere else.

Santa Chiara and the Gesù Nuovo

Your introduction to this world, just off Via Toledo, is the cramped, disorderly, most characteristic of Neapolitan squares: the **Piazza del Gesù Nuovo**, decorated by the gaudiest and most random of Neapolitan decorations, the **Guglia della Immacolata**. A *guglia* (pinnacle), in Naples, is a kind of Rococo obelisk, dripping with frills, saints and *putti*, of which there are three, all in this area. The unsightly, unfinished façade behind the Guglia, covered with pyramidal extrusions in dark basalt, belongs to the church of **Gesù Nuovo**. As strange as it is, the façade, originally part of a late 15th-century palace, has become one of the landmarks of Naples. The interior is typically lavish Neapolitan Baroque, gloriously overdone in acres of coloured marbles and frescoes, some by Solimena. One of his best works (dated 1725) is here above the main door inside, depicting three angels driving the Syrian minister Eliodorus out of the Temple of Jerusalem. In the second chapel on the right you will see a bronze statue of Naples' newest saint. Saint Giuseppe Moscati was a doctor who lectured at Naples University and otherwise devoted himself to caring for the poor. He died after a normal day of do-gooding on 12 April 1927.

Santa Chiara, just across the piazza, dates from the early 14th century, though it once had a Baroque interior as good as the Gesù; Allied bombers remodelled it to suit modern tastes in 1943, and only a few of the original Angevin tombs have survived. To get some idea of what the interior must have been like, stop in and see the adjacent **Majolica Cloister**, nothing less than the loveliest and most peaceful spot in Naples—especially in contrast to the neighbourhood outside (restoration on the cloister is due to finish mid-1996 during which time it can still be visited). So much in Naples shows the Spanish influence—like the use of the title 'Don', now largely limited to Camorra bosses—and here someone in the 1740s transplanted the Andalucian love of pictures done in painted *azulejo* tiles, turning a simple monkish cloister into a little fairyland of gaily coloured arbours, benches and columns, shaded by the only trees in the whole district.

Recently, during the restoration of a vestibule off the cloister, it was discovered that underneath the indifferent 17th-century frescoes (reached via the back of the church) there were some earlier, highly original paintings of the Last Judgement. They have since been uncovered and restored, revealing an inspired 16th-century vision of the event, in a style utterly unlike the slick virtuosity of the time, with plenty of novel tortures for the damned and angels welcoming some cute naked nuns among the elect.

The **Museo dell'Opera di S.Chiara** (*open Thurs–Tues, 9–1 and 4–6; Sat and Sun till 8.30pm; adm*) at the rear of the cloister, houses the church treasures, marbles and an area of archeological excavations on the Roman period.

The Sansevero Chapel

A few streets further down Via Benedetto Croce is tiny Piazza San Domenico, which has monuments from Naples' three most creative periods. **San Domenico Maggiore**, built between 1283 and 1324, was the Dominican church in Naples. St Thomas Aquinas lived in the adjacent monastery. Later this became the favourite church of the Spanish, and it contains some interesting Renaissance funerary monuments; a better one, though, is across the Piazza in the church of **Sant'Angelo a Nilo** (*open daily, 8–1 and 4–7.15*)— the tomb of Cardinal Brancaccio, designed by Michelozzo, with a relief of the *Assumption of the Virgin* by Donatello (the two artists had collaborated before on the Baptistery in Siena). The second of the Baroque pinnacles decorates the Piazza, the **Guglia di San Domenico**, begun after a plague in 1650. Best of all, just around the corner on Via F. De Sanctis, you can inspect Neapolitan Rococo at its very queerest in the **Sansevero Chapel** (*open Mon, Wed–Sat, 10–5; Tues, Sun 10–1.30; adm*).

Prince Raimondo di Sangro (b. 1701), who was responsible for the final form of this, his family's private chapel, was a strange bird, a sort of aristocratic dilettante mystic. Supposedly there is a grand allegorical scheme behind the arrangement of the sculptures and frescoes he commissioned, but a work like this, only 200 years old, seems as foreign to our sensibilities and understanding as some Mayan temple. The sculptures, by little-known Neapolitan artists like Giuseppe Sammartino and Antonio Corradini, are inscrutable allegories in themselves, often executed with a breathtakingly showy virtuosity. Francesco Queirolo's *Il Disinganno* (disillusion) is an extreme case; nobody else, perhaps, has ever tried to carve a fishing-net, or the turning pages of a book, out of marble. Others, such as Sammartino's *Cristo Velato*, display a remarkable illusion of figures under transparent veils.

There are a dozen or so of these large sculptural groups, all under a crazy heavenly vortex in the ceiling fresco, by Francesco Mario Russo. Down in the crypt are two complete human cardiovascular systems, removed from the bodies and preserved by Prince Raimondo in the course of his alchemical experiments. Ask to see them (if you care to).

Near San Domenico, a block south of the Spacca, is Naples' **University**, one of Europe's oldest and most distinguished. The Emperor Frederick founded it in 1224, as a 'Ghibelline' university to counter the pope's 'Guelph' university at Bologna, as well as to provide scholars and trained officials for the new state he was trying to build. It still occupies its ancient, woefully overcrowded quarters around Via Mezzocannone.

Around the Piazza del Duomo

Continuing down the Spaccanapoli (now Via San Biagio ai Librai), just around the corner on Via San Gregorio is the **San Gregorio Armeno** church, with another gaudy Baroque interior. If the gilding and the painting by Luca Giordano of the Arrival of Saint Basilio are not your cup of tea, try the **cloister** (*open daily 9.30–12.30*). This is another oasis of tranquillity and a step back to the 16th century. Since the 1500s the cloister has served the convent of Benedictine nuns. At the centre of the cloister there is a fountain sculpted in 1733 depicting Christ meeting the Samaritan woman. On the way out note the revolving drums for communicating with the outside world pre-1922, when the monastic order was totally closed off from the profane. A caustic note by the nuns on one of them dismisses the popular misconception that they were for abandoned newborn babies.

In December, this street and others around it become Naples' famous Christmas Market, where everyone comes to buy figurines of the Holy Family, the Three Kings and all the other accessories required for their Christmas *presepi*, or manger scenes, one of the most devotedly followed of local traditions. For several weeks, hundreds of stands fill up the neighbourhood's narrow streets.

The Presepi

It would not be easy to explain why the genius of Naples should have chosen Christmas cribs as a subject to elevate to an art form. After philosophy, pizza, and music, it's what this city does best. Churches and private homes have always had a little competitive edge on when they begin their displays (some time in November, if not earlier). The most extreme cases have been assembled inside the Museo Nazionale di San Martino. One is as big as a bus, and must have taken someone a lifetime; another is fitted inside an eggshell—still with over a hundred figures in it. The best parts are the large, finely carved individual wooden or ceramic figures. Most represent Neapolitans of two or three centuries ago, from every walk of life; with their painstakingly detailed and wonderfully expressive faces, each is a genuine portrait. To have them all here in one place is like old Bourbon Naples appearing before your eyes. For do-it-yourself, modern cribs, Via San Gregorio is the place to go. At Christmas time, the whole street is taken over by the stalls of artisans who make and sell figurines for the crib scene, as well as little trees, sheep, donkeys, amphorae, cooking pots, Turks, salamis, dogs, chickens, angels, cheese wheels, and all the other items without which no Neapolitan *presepe* would be complete.

Convention requires that, quite apart from the Holy Family, certain things be present in every crib. Besides the usual angels, shepherds, and animals, a *Roman ruin* is absolutely necessary, as are several *Turks* in Ottoman Empire dress (which come in handy if one of the Three Kings gets lost). A *band of musicians* is also expected, and all the better if they too are Turks. *Beggars and dwarfs* earn envy for the crib-maker—there is a whole display of figures called the 'deformities'—but above all there must be *tons of food* everywhere there is room for it. The best cribs have the busiest cooks and the most bulging pantries, with tiny wooden roast pigs, sausages, eggs, plates of macaroni, cheeses and fancy cakes—even a pizza or two. Look out for the giant *presepe* in the Galleria Umberto at Christmas time, and watch Neapolitans throw money at it to pay for its upkeep for another year.

A little further north up Via San Gregorio is **San Lorenzo Maggiore** (late 12th century), one of Naples' finest medieval churches; Petrarch lived for a while in the adjacent monastery. In addition, recent excavations have uncovered a considerable area of Greek and Roman remains on the site. Entering via the cloister where the base of a Roman *macellum* (market place) is being excavated, head down the stairs at the very back to see this fascinating piece of subterranean Naples. **San Paolo**, across the street, isn't much to see now, but before an earthquake wrecked it in the 17th century, its façade was the portico of an ancient Roman temple to Castor and Pollux. Andrea Palladio studied it closely, and it provided much of the inspiration for his classical palaces in the Veneto.

After Spaccanapoli, **Via dei Tribunali** (the *decumanus maximus*) is the busiest street of old Naples, and has been for a long time. The arcades that line the street in places, a sort of continuous covered market, are a thousand years old or more. Here, at the otherwise unremarkable **Girolamini Church** (*open daily 9–1*), you may see the modest tomb (at present unapproachable due to conservation) of Naples's greatest philosopher, Giambattista Vico (*see* **Topics**, p.57). Northwest of the Girolamini, around Via dell' Anticaglia, you'll find a few crooked streets, the only ones in old Naples that do not stick to the rectilinear Roman plan. These follow the outline of the **Roman Theatre**, much of which still survives, hidden among the tenements. A few arches are all that is visible from the street.

The Cathedral of San Gennaro

The wide **Via del Duomo** is a breath of fresh air in this crowded district—exactly what the city intended, when they ploughed it through Old Naples after the cholera epidemic of 1884. The **Duomo** itself is another fine medieval building, though it is hidden behind an awful pseudo-Gothic façade pasted on in 1905. The best things are inside: the Renaissance

Capella Minùtolo, the tomb of Charles of Anjou and the **Capella San Gennaro**, glittering with the gold and silver of the cathedral treasure, and with frescoes by Domenichino and Lanfranco, the latter a swirling *Paradiso* in the dome (1643). The **Basilica Santa Restituta**, a sizeable church in its own right, is tacked onto the side of the cathedral. Its columns are thought to be from the temple of Apollo that once occupied the site. Begun in 324, though often rebuilt, this is the oldest building in Naples. The ceiling frescoes are by Luca Giordano. Just off the basilica, the 5th-century **baptistry** contains a good Byzantine-style mosaic by the 14th-century artist Lello di Roma; the baptismal font itself probably comes from an ancient temple of Dionysus. Close by you can see a collection of archaeological remains dating from the Greeks to the Middle Ages *(open daily 9–12 and 4.30–7;adm)*. The last and most elaborate of the *guglie*, the **Guglia San Gennaro**, designed by Cosimo Fanzago, can be seen just outside the south transept.

If the sacristan is around, you can visit the **Crypt of San Gennaro**, patron of Naples, with elaborate marble decoration from the Renaissance, and the tomb of Pope Innocent IV.

The Legend of San Gennaro

San Gennaro (St Januarius) was a bishop from Benevento who was executed along with other martyrs at the Solfatara in Pozzuoli in AD 305 during the persecution of Christians under Diocletian. Initially he was sentenced to death by being torn apart by wild animals in the amphitheatre at Pozzuoli, but because the Roman governor was not present this was commuted to being beheaded at the Solfatara. After the execution, his body was taken to the Catacombs of S. Gennaro (*see* p.83). It was moved in the beginning of the 5th century, and from this date on he became identified as the patron of Naples, protecting it from destruction by Vesuvius and other disasters.

The saint's head is now kept upstairs in the chapel named after him, along with two phials of his blood that miraculously 'liquefy' three times each year—the first Sunday in May, 19 September, and 16 December—so as to prove that San Gennaro is still looking out for the Napoletani. The only time the miracle has ever failed, during the Napoleonic occupation, the people of the city became enormously excited and seemed ready to revolt. At this the French commander, a true son of the Enlightenment, announced that San Gennaro had 10 minutes to come through—or else he'd shoot the Archbishop. Somehow, just in time, the miracle occurred.

On a small piazza a block north of the Duomo, **Santa Maria Donnaregina** offers more overdone Baroque, but off to the side of this 17th-century work is the smaller, original church, built in 1307 by Queen Mary of Hungary (who was none other than the wife of Charles of Anjou; her title only reflects a claim to the throne). Her elaborate tomb, and some good contemporary frescoes, are the sights of the church. South of the cathedral in the Via del Duomo is the **Filangieri Museum**, housed in the 15th-century Palazzo Cuomo, a small collection of china, armour, and curiosities *(open Mon–Sat, 9–7; Sun 9–2; adm)*. Its picture collection includes works by some of Naples' favourite artists, Luca Giordano, Mattia Preti, Ribera and others. Almost all the collection was gathered in the last forty years. Count Filangieri's original collection was much larger, but the Nazis torched it before they left in 1944.

Piazza Garibaldi

In Italian, the word for a market stand is *bancarella*. In Naples they are as much a part of everyday life as they must have been in the Middle Ages; the city probably has as many of them as all the rest of Italy put together. The greatest concentration can be found in the Forcella market district, in the narrow streets east of the Via del Duomo, selling everything from stereos to light bulbs. According to the government's economists, at least one-third of Naples' economy is underground—outright illegal, or at the least not paying taxes or subject to any regulation.

Bootleg cassette tapes are one example; Naples is one of the world leaders in this thriving industry, and you'll have your choice of thousands of titles along these streets, though it might be a good idea to get them to play your tape before you part with any money. Hundreds of tired-looking folks sit in front of little tables, selling contraband American cigarettes. This is one of the easiest means for Naples' poor to make a living, and it is all controlled by the Camorra. As in New York, whenever it rains, shady characters crawl out of the woodwork selling umbrellas. You will see plenty of designer labels on the *bancarelle* —if they're real, don't ask where they came from.

Piazza Mercato, one of the nodes of the Neapolitan bazaar, has been a market square perhaps since Roman times. In the old days this was always the site of major executions, most notably that of 16-year-old Conradin, the rightful heir to the throne, by Charles of Anjou in 1268, an act that shocked all Europe. Charles ordered him buried underneath the Piazza—he couldn't be laid in consecrated ground, since he had just been excommunicated for political reasons by Charles's ally the pope. In 1647, Masaniello's Revolt started here, during the festival of Our Lady of Mount Carmel; Masaniello (Tommaso Aniello), a young fisherman of Amalfi, had been chosen by his fellow conspirators to step up in the middle of the ceremonies and proclaim to the people and the viceroy that the new tax the viceroy had introduced 'no longer existed'. As the plotters had hoped, a spontaneous rising followed, and for a week Masaniello ruled Naples while the frightened viceroy locked himself up in Castel Sant'Elmo. In Naples, unfortunately, such risings can burn out as quickly as a match; the viceroy's spies first secretly drugged Masaniello, so that he appeared drunk or mad to the people, and then in an unguarded moment they murdered him and sent his head to the viceroy. That was the end for Naples, but the incident touched off a wave of revolts across the south that took the Spaniards three years to stamp out.

The incredible **Piazza Garibaldi** is the other main centre of the Forcella area. For rail travellers, it is an unforgettable introduction to Naples; they walk out of the incongruously modern Stazione Centrale into the vast square, paved with asphalt that melts in the hot sun and sticks to their shoes, and enter a world unlike anything else in Italy—bums, addicts and crazies draped picturesquely along the pavement, solid ranks of *bancarelle* wherever there's room, eternal crowds of odd characters from every nation of the world,

Italy's worst hotels and its ugliest whores. Most of the piazza is really one gigantic parking lot; traffic whistles through it on lanes marked with yellow paint. Neapolitans don't mind the Piazza Garibaldi; tourists often come to like it. Sailors generally avoid it, as do the police.

The Capua Gate

Northwest of the Piazza Garibaldi, some of Naples' shabbiest streets lead towards the Piazza Enrico di Nicola, once the city's main gate. The **Porta Capuana**, built in 1484, seems a smaller version of the Castel Nuovo's triumphal arch, crowded in by the same squat round towers. The **Castel Capuano**, next to it, began its life as a castle-residence for the Hohenstaufen kings. Since its construction in the 13th century it has been reshaped so many times it doesn't even look like a castle any more; for four centuries it has served as Naples' law courts. If anything makes wandering into this unlikely district worthwhile, though, it is **Santa Caterina a Formiella**, facing the Porta Capuana, a church by the obscure architect Romolo Balsimelli that is one of the masterpieces of 16th-century Italian architecture. Completed in 1593, the church's bulky, squarish form was a Renaissance eccentricity, but an important stepping-stone towards the Baroque. Despite long neglect during which its dome seemed to tilt at a more precarious angle with each year, the church has now reopened to the public and further projects are under way for the conservation of its interior.

The Archaeological Museum

Back on the western side of the old city, Via Toledo, after passing Spaccanapoli and changing its name to Via Roma, continues northwards through the **Piazza Dante**, one of the most delightful and animated corners of the city; beyond this as Via Pessina, in an area of oversized tenements and busy streets, it opens to display the crumbling red palazzo that contains the **Museo Archeologico Nazionale** *(open Wed–Mon 9–7; adm)*.

Naples has the most important collection of Roman-era art and antiquities in the world, due partly to Vesuvius, for burying Pompeii and Herculaneum, and partly to the sharp eyes and deep pockets of the Farnese family—many of the best works here come from the collection they built up over 300 years. Unfortunately, the place is run by Neapolitans; at any given time, half of the collections will be closed for 'restorations' that never seem to happen, and what they condescend to let you see may well be the worst-exhibited and worst-labelled major museum in Europe.

On the first floor, room after room is filled with ancient sculpture. Many of the pieces on view are the best existing Roman-era copies of lost Greek statues, including some by Phidias and Praxiteles; some are masterpieces in their own right, such as the huge, dramatic ensemble called the *Farnese Bull*, the *Tyrannicides* (with other statues' heads stuck on them), and the truly heroic *Farnese Hercules* that once decorated the Baths of Caracalla. Several provocative Aphrodites compete for your attention, along with a platoon of formidable Athenas, the famous *Doryphorus* (spear-bearer), and enough Greek and Roman busts to populate a Colosseum.

Upstairs, most of the rooms are given over to finds from Pompeii. The collection of **Roman mosaics**, mostly from Pompeii and Herculaneum, is one of the two best anywhere (the other is in Antalya, Turkey); the insight it provides into the life and thought of the ancients is priceless. One feature it betrays clearly is a certain fond silliness—plenty of chickens, ducks and grinning cats, the famous *Cave canem* (beware of the dog) mosaic from the front of a house, comic scenes from the theatre, and especially one wonderful panel of crocodiles and hippopotami along the Nile. Some of the mosaics are very consciously 'art': a detailed scene of the Battle of Issus, where Alexander the Great defeated the Persian king Darius, and a view of the Academy of Athens that includes a portrait of Plato. A recently opened addition is a section devoted entirely to the Temple of Isis at Pompeii. Five rooms display sculptures, frescoes and paintings taken from the temple, which was first dicovered in 1765.

Toro Farnese

Besides the mosaics, nowhere in the world will you find a larger collection of **Roman mural painting** (*see* p.111), and much of it is fascinatingly modern in theme and execution. Many of the walls of Pompeiian villas were decorated with architectural fantasias that seem strangely like those of the Renaissance. Other works show an almost Baroque lack of respect for the gods—see the *Wedding of Zeus and Hera*. Scholars in fact do denote a period of 'Roman Baroque', beginning about the 2nd century. From it come paintings graced by genuine winged *putti*, called *amoretti* in Roman days. Among the most famous pictures are *The Astragal Players*—young girls shooting craps—and the beautiful *Portrait of an Unknown Woman*, a thoughtful lady holding her pen to her lips who has become one of the best-known images from Roman art.

Other attractions of the museum include large collections of jewellery, coins, fancy gladiators' armour, the famous *sezione pornografica* (closed for years and unlikely to reopen in the forseeable future), Greek vases, decorative bronzes and a highly detailed, room-sized **scale model** of all excavations up to the 1840s at Pompeii (lovingly restored since the memorable assault on it by the authors' baby boy, back in 1980). The Egyptian collection is not a large one, but it is fun, with a dog-headed Anubis in a Roman toga, some ancient feet under glass, and a mummified crocodile.

Capodimonte

North of the museum, the neighbourhoods along Via Toledo—briefly named Via Santa Teresa degli Scalzi—begin to lose some of their Neapolitan intensity as they climb to the suburban heights. On the way, after changing its name again to Corso Amedeo di Savoia, the street passes an area that was full of cemeteries in Roman times. Three Christian underground burial vaults have been discovered here, with a total area of over 100,000 square metres, only part of which has been completely explored. Two may be visited: the **Catacombe di San Gennaro** *(entrance through the courtyard of the Basilica dell'Incoronata a Capodimonte; look for the yellow signs. Tours daily, at 9.30, 10.15, 11.00, 11.45; adm)* is the more interesting, with extensive early Christian mosaics and frescoes, some as early as the 2nd century. The **Catacombe di San Gaudioso** *(tours Sun only, at 9.45, 11.45; adm)*, which include the 5th-century tomb of the saint of the same name, a martyred African bishop, were discovered under the Baroque church of **Santa Maria della Sanità**, on Via Sanità.

The **Parco di Capodimonte**, a well-kept and exotically tropical park, began as a hunting preserve of the Bourbons in the 18th century. Charles III built a Royal Palace here in 1738 that now houses Naples' picture gallery, the **Museo Nazionale di Capodimonte** *(open Tues–Sat 9–6; Sun 9–2; adm)*. The collection is the best in the south of Italy, and especially rich in works of the late Renaissance. Some of the works you shouldn't miss: an *Annunciation* by Filippino Lippi; a Botticelli *Madonna* ; the mystical portrait of the mathematician *Fra Luca Pacioli*, by an unknown quattrocento artist; two wry homilies by the elder Brueghel, *The Misanthrope* and *The Blind* ; works by Masaccio and Mantegna, and a hilarious picture of *St Peter Martyr* by Lotto, showing that famous anti-Semitic rabble-rouser conversing nonchalantly with the Virgin Mary—with a hatchet sticking out of his head.

Five big, beautifully restored Caravaggios take up one room; others are devoted to important works by Titian. One entire wing of the museum is filled with delightfully frivolous 18th-century **porcelain figurines**; the Bourbons maintained a royal factory for making such things at Capodimonte, which is still in operation today. In another hall, there are scores of 19th-century watercolour scenes of Naples and the Campanian countryside (the best of them by Giacinto Gigante). Here, for the first time, you will see the Naples that so struck the 18th-century travellers. Not much has changed, really; if only all the traffic could magically disappear, it would still be almost the same spectacular city today.

The museum's collections are mostly up on the second floor; the first, the old *piano nobile* (royal apartments), is still much the way the Bourbons left it. Persevere through the score of overdecorated chambers; the *Salotto di porcellana*, a little room entirely lined with Capodimonte porcelain, makes the whole thing worthwhile.

The Certosa di San Martino

Up on the highest point overlooking Naples, the 17th-century **Castel Sant'Elmo** *(open Tues–Sun 9–2; adm)* is an impressive enough Baroque fortification, partly built of the tufa rock on which it stands (the city now uses it to park the cars the police tow away). Next to it, hogging the best view in Naples, the Carthusians built their original, modest, monastery of **San Martino**, some time in the early 14th century. Two centuries later, like most Carthusian branch offices, they were rolling embarrassingly in lucre; building the poshest monastery in all Italy was the only thing to do. The rebuilt **Certosa** (charterhouse) is only marginally smaller than Fort St Elmo. Built on the slope of the mountain, it is supported by a gargantuan platform, visible for miles out to sea and probably containing enough stone to construct a small pyramid.

Nobody knows exactly what is in the **Museo Nazionale di San Martino** *(open Tues–Sat, 9–2; Sun 9–2; adm)*, which now occupies the monastery. Intended as a museum specifically of Naples, its history, art and traditions, San Martino suffers from the same mismanagement as the Archaeological Museum; only parts are ever open, and the Grand Cloister, at the time of writing, has become a wilderness of weeds and scaffolding. Not that this should discourage you from taking the long ride up the Montesanto Funicular. The views and the architecture are marvellous, and at least they always keep open the collection of *presepi*—what the Neapolitans come here to see (*see* p.77).

Upon entering the complex, the first attraction is the **church**, another of the glories of Neapolitan Baroque, with an excess of lovely coloured inlaid marble to complement the overabundance of painting. The work over the altar, the *Descent from the Cross*, is one of the finest of José Ribera. This tormented artist, often called *Lo Spagnuolo* in Italy, has paintings all over Naples. His popularity does not owe everything to his artistic talent; apparently he formed a little cartel with two local artists, and cornered the market by hiring a gang of thugs to harry all the other painters out of town.

The cloister, the **Chiostro Grande**, even in its present state, is a masterpiece of Baroque, elegantly proportioned and gloriously original in its decoration. Also, thanks to a sculptural scheme by a pious, mad artist named Cosimo Fanzago, it is the creepiest cloister east of Seville. Fanzago (who was also one of the architects of San Martino) gives us eight figures of saints that seem more like vampires in priestly robes and mitres, a perfect background for his little enclosed garden, its wall topped with rows of gleaming marble skulls. Most of the collections are in the halls surrounding the Chiostro Grande—costume, painting, ship models and every sort of curiosity; at the corners are **belvederes** from which to look over Naples (outside the complex, a series of lovely terraced gardens offer a similar view). The *presepi* take up a few large rooms near the entrance.

West of the Piazza del Plebiscito

The hill called Pizzofalcone rises directly behind the Piazza del Plebiscito; around it was the site of Parthenope, the Greek town that antedated Neapolis and was eventually swallowed up by it (though Neapolitans still like to refer to themselves as Parthenopeans). Parthenope had a little harbour, formed by an island that is now almost completely covered by the ancient, strangely-shaped fortress of the **Castel dell'Ovo** (*open Mon–Sat, 8.30–5; Sun, 9–12; adm)*—the one Master Virgil is said to have built balanced on an egg, hence the name. Most of it was really built by Frederick II, and expanded by the Angevins.

There isn't much to see today—though the chapel was once covered with murals by Giotto, of which nothing remains—and most of it is closed to the public, but the Egg Castle has been the scene of many unusual events in Italian history. Long before there was a castle, the island may have been part of the original Greek settlement of Parthenope. Later it contained the villa of the Roman general and philosopher Lucullus, victor over Mithridates in the Pontic Wars; Lucullus curried favour with the people by making his sumptuous gardens, and his famous library, open to the public. In the 5th century AD the villa became a home in exile for Romulus Augustulus, last of the western Roman emperors. The Goths spared him only because of his youth and simple-mindedness, and pensioned him off here. Columns from Lucullus' villa are still to be seen among the castle's famous dungeons.

Modern Naples: the Villa Comunale

Once past the Egg Castle, a handsome sweep of coastline opens up the districts of **Chiaia** and **Mergellina**, the most pleasant parts of the new city. Here the long, pretty **Villa Comunale**, central Naples' only park, follows the shore. In it, there is an **Aquarium** *(open Tues–Sat, 9–6; Sun 10–6; adm)*, built by the German naturalist Dr Anton Dohrn in the 1870s, and perhaps the oldest in the world. All the wide variety of fish, octopuses and other marine delicacies here are from the Bay of Naples; depending on the hour of day, you will find them fascinating, or else overwhelmingly appetizing. When the Allied armies marched into town in 1943, the Neapolitans put on a big party for the officers. There being practically nothing decent to eat anywhere in Naples, they cleaned out the aquarium and managed an all-seafood menu. General Mark Clark, the commander, is said to have got the aquarium's prize specimen, a baby manatee, though how they prepared it is not recorded.

Ask to see the murals and you will be led upstairs to see Dohrn, who was incidentally a friend and colleague of Charles Darwin, and other buddies depicted by the German artist Hans von Marees. The wall opposite has local boys frolicking naked under the orange groves. Recently restored after the 1980 earthquake, the murals are an insight into the secret life of aquariums.

Behind the park, on the Riviera di Chiaia, the **Museo Principe di Aragona Pignatelli Cortes** *(open Tues–Sat, 9–2; Sun, 9–2; adm)* will show you more of the same kind of decorative porcelain as at Capodimonte, along with a score of 18th- and 19th-century noble carriages, furniture and art.

If you're still not tired of little smiling figurines, you can plunge deeper into Chiaia to see the greatest collection of all at the Museo Nazionale della Ceramica, also known as the Duca di Martina Museum, but familiar to Neapolitans only as the **Villa Floridiana** *(open Tues–Sat, 9–2; Sun, 9–1; adm)*, after the tasteful 18th-century estate it occupies, with one of the loveliest gardens in Naples and one of Italy's great hoards of bric-a-brac. The museum is on Via Cimarosa, near the Funicolare di Chiaia.

Virgil's Tomb

Beginning a few streets beyond the western end of the Villa Comunale, **Mergellina** is one of the brightest and most popular quarters of Naples, a good place for dinner or a *passeggiata* around the busy Piazza Sannazzaro. Its centre is the **Marina**, where besides small craft there are hydrofoils to Sorrento and the islands in the summer months, and excursion boats which do daily tours of the shore between the Egg Castle and Point Posillipo. From the harbour, Mergellina rises steeply up the surrounding hills; there is a funicular up to the top (every 15 minutes). On the hillside, between the railway bridge and the tunnel that leads under the hill to Fuorigrotta, there is a Roman funerary monument that tradition has always held to be the **Tomb of Virgil** *(open daily, 9–1; free)*. The poet died in Brindisi in 19 BC, on his way back from a trip to Greece. Neapolis was a city dear to him—he wrote most of the *Aeneid* here—and Virgil was brought here for burial, though ancient authors attest that the tomb was closer to the Aquarium.

Just below it lies the entrance to one of the little-known wonders of the ancient world. The **Crypta Neapolitana**, unfortunately closed at present, is a 606m road tunnel built during the reign of Augustus, to connect Neapolis with Pozzuoli and Baiae, the longest such work the Romans ever attempted.

Shopping

Surprisingly, no one ever thinks of Naples as one of the prime shopping destinations of Italy; this is a mistake, as there are as many pretty and unusual things to be bought here as anywhere else, and usually at lower prices. The back streets around Spaccanapoli and other old sections are still full of artisan workshops of all kinds. The Royal Factory at Capodimonte, founded by the Bourbons, still makes what may be the most beautiful **porcelain and ceramic figures** in Europe, sold at the fancier shops in the city centre. Another old Naples tradition is the making of **cameos** from special seashells; you'll see them everywhere, but the shops outside the San Martino monastery have a good selection at relatively low prices.

Via San Biagio dei Librai, the middle of the Spaccanapoli, is as its name implies a street of **booksellers**—some of the best old book dealers in Italy, conveniently near the University—but the street is also full of many more odd surprises for shoppers as well. Many of the religious goods shops have surprisingly good works in terracotta; the **Doll Hospital** at No. 81, ℰ 203067, is one of the most charming shops in Naples.

All around the back streets near the Archaeological Museum, there are antique and junk shops that won't overcharge you unless you let them. The swankiest antique shops tend to be along Via Merelli off Piazza dei Martiri. The city also has an immense twice-monthly antiques market, the **Fiera dell'Antiquariato**, held on alternate Saturday and Sunday mornings in the gardens of the Villa Comunale.

You can buy lovely old prints of Naples and beyond at **Bowinkel**, at Piazza dei Martiri 24, ℰ 7644344, and beautiful candles, including some sculpted to depict well-known Italian political and showbusiness personalities, from the **Antica Cereria** at Via C. Doria 6–8, ℰ 5499745. For the once-in-a-lifetime souvenir, the 150-year-old **Fonderia Chiurazzi**, Via Ponti Rossi 271, ℰ 7512685, makes artistic bronzes, specializing in reproductions of works in the Museo Archeologico; if you have billions of lire to spare, they'll do them life-size, or even bigger.

For clothes and shoes the best area is again off Piazza dei Martiri, in particular along Via Chiaia. You can find its other end just to the right of the central Piazza del Plebiscito.

Last of all do not miss the *bancarelle* and open street markets around Piazza Garibaldi. The daily catch of fish, live squid and octopus is a must, just to the right off Corso Garibaldi. Here you can also find fruit stalls that sell lemons from the Sorrentine peninsula which are too big to cup with both hands.

Sports and Activities

The best sources of information on forthcoming events of all kinds are the local newspaper *Il Mattino* and the free multi-lingual monthly guide *Qui Napoli*. Many of the city's permanent attractions are concentrated in the Fuorigrotta district, west of Mergellina. **Edenlandia**, © 2391182, is the big amusement park there, on Viale Kennedy in the Mostra d'Oltremare, Naples' big trade fair site (take the Ferrovia Cumana to the station of the same name). There is also a **dog-racing** track and a small but fun **zoo** (*open daily, 9–5; adm*) in the same area (bus route 152 from the Stazione Centrale passes the gates).

Nearby on Via Fuorigrotta, just past the tunnel, there's **jai-alai** (Basque Pelota) every night at 8pm. Anything a Neapolitan can bet on flourishes here; the **race-track**, the *Ippodromo di Agnano*, with both thoroughbred and trotting races throughout most of the year, is out west in Agnano, 10km from the city centre along the *tangenziale*. And of course there's always **football**. With the help of Diego Armando Maradona, Napoli won its first-ever league title in 1987; since his departure the club has fallen on harder times, but every significant victory still calls forth a spontaneous celebration all over town that seems like Carnival in Rio de Janeiro, and any match is likely to prove an unforgettable experience with the Neapolitans to make up the crowd. Matches are played at the **Stadio San Paolo**, Piazzale Vincenzo Tecchio, © 2395623. To get there, take the Ferrovia Cumana to Mostra or the Metropolitana to Campi Flegrei.

However tempting the sea off Naples might look on a scorching summer day, it's worth waiting until you get to one of the islands before taking a plunge. There is a public **swimming pool**, the **Piscina Scandone**, also in the Fuorigrotta area of town, at Via Giochi del Mediterraneo, © 5709159. **Tennis** can be played at the **Tennis Club Napoli**, Viale Dohrn, © 7614656, in the Villa Comunale, the **Tennis Club Vomero**, Via Rossini 8, © 658912, and the **Sporting Club Virgilio**, Via Tito Lucrezio Caro 6, © 7695261.

Where to Stay

Naples can present real problems for the casual traveller who arrives expecting to pick up a reasonably priced room without difficulty. This will be compounded as Naples becomes more popular with so many new measures to attract visitors. There are many options at either extreme of the price range but few good choices in between.

The best area to stay is undoubtedly down on the waterfront where you have easy access to shopping, museums and good restaurants. It's less claustrophobic too. The area around the station offers thousands of cheap rooms, but many of them are in horrible dives. Sticking to those selected here you shouldn't go too wrong and at least you'll be safe.

very expensive

Naples does have less than its share of top-quality hotels; the Germans, inexplicably, blew up a few of them before their retreat in 1944. Three of the best are located in a row along Via Partenope, overlooking the Castel dell'Ovo, where the views over the bay more than compensate for the traffic noise below.

Visiting sheiks, kings and rock stars favour the ★★★★**Excelsior**, Via Partenope 48, ✆ 7640111, ✉ 7649743, Naples' finest, with beautiful suites and a tradition of perfect service ever since 1909. You pay for space; elegant lounges, a beautiful rooftop solarium and restaurant, rooms with large beds and antique style furniture. Above all, this is a place for those who think the hotel is the most important part of the holiday. Being on the right of the three, it faces Vesuvius. That's annoying for the ★★★★**Vesuvio**, Via Partenope 45, ✆ 7640044, ✉ also 4640044, which otherwise provides the same stuff. It also has a lovely roof garden for dining, important since none of these hotels' rooms have good balconies. The ★★★★**Santa Lucia**, Via Partenope 46, ✆ 7640666, ✉ 7648580, a beautifully restored 18th-century *palazzo*, is sandwiched between the others. Rooms are less grand with fussy floral curtains and a distinctly Laura Ashley feel. In face of the competition and its lack of roof garden, the management has clearly opted for the corporate crowd, offering extensive conference facilities.

expensive

Still on the seafront, the ★★★★**Miramare**, Via N. Sauro, ✆ 7647589, ✉ 7640775, is the find in this category. The manager Enzo Rosalino exudes the kind of old-world charm more often found outside cities. His infectious goodwill is apparent in the array of personal touches to each of his 31 rooms: a telephone, TV, video, safe, trouser press and tea/coffee maker to make you feel more at home. The atmosphere is intimate. Some rooms are too small but the old lift and rooftop solarium (where he plans to reopen his restaurant) more than make up. Rooms not facing the sea are quieter. Other good bets are the ★★★★**Paradiso**, Via Catullo 11, ✆ 7614161, ✉ 7613449, with stunning views over the bay—make sure you book a sea-facing room. For a more old-fashioned atmosphere, but further inland (near the Cumana stop Corso V.E), try the ★★★★**Parker's**, Corso Vittorio Emanuele 135, ✆ 7612474, ✉ 663527, which has ample charm, with plenty of polished wood, chandeliers and comfortable furniture. Lastly the ★★★★**Angioino**, Via De Pretis 123, ✆ 5529500, ✉ 5529509, owned by the French Mercure hotel chain, offers 86 good-sized rooms in a central location (a minute from Piazza Municipio), with efficient service that makes it popular with the business crowd. The views are unspectacular, the furnishings functional—you feel you could be in any city— but all rooms are comfortable and sound proofed. It is a good base.

moderate

Near the Stazione Centrale, the ★★★**Cavour**, Piazza Garibaldi 32, © 283122, ✆ 287488 is a well-run decent hotel in an otherwise desperate area. Book the top-floor suites for little more than a standard room. These enjoy ample terraces, good views over Vesuvius and are a respite from the bustle below. Rooms are nicely decorated in the omnipresent Liberty style. Bathrooms are good in an area where the plumbing hasn't been overhauled since the Greeks. The restaurant gets two Michelin fourchettes. Otherwise near the pretty Mergellina esplanade the good-value ★★★**Canada**, Via Mergellina 43, © 680952, ✆ 681594, offers 12 comfortable rooms where you won't want for TV, safe, minibar, hairdryer or ceiling fans. The hotel has no pretensions and a miserable excuse for a breakfast area. It is however well placed for the evening *passeggiata* here. Back in the central S.Lucia districts the ★★★**Rex**, Via Palepoli 12, © 7649389, ✆ 7649227, is slightly more expensive offering simple rooms with bare 70s-style furnishings. If you like lots of brown wood and breakfast in bed— there are no public areas in the hotel—then this is fine as a base in this good area. Lastly the ★★**Ausonia**, Via Caracciolo 11, © 682278, ✆ 664536 is a clean, comfortable *pensione*, with 20 rooms, all with bath, and a nautical character to its decoration. There are portholes around the numbers and nautical theme bedspreads. The owner is kind and cheerful. The rooms are well appointed, each with TV and video recorder (tapes are also available in English!). Located within a *palazzo*, looking onto an interior courtyard, this is the quiet option for the Mergellina area.

inexpensive

Naples has a dearth of reasonable inexpensive hotels. The ★★**Fontane al Mare**, Via N. Tommaseo 14, © 7643811, is definitely worth booking in advance. There are only 21 rooms located on the last two floors of an old palazzo next to the Chiaia gardens. To take the lift, you will need to bring L100 coins! Ask for rooms without bathroom since they enjoy the great sea view and are better value. Breakfast is available and costs extra. This hotel has character but bear in mind that it's well known and popular with the local *carabinieri* college!

cheap

As already mentioned, many of the cheap places are to be found around Piazza Garibaldi. It should be stressed that the hotels around here are invariably substandard. They are at best a place to sleep and certainly not a good holiday base. Elsewhere in Italy you can visit good one-star hotels and feel you have had a bargain but not here. A good night's sleep in this area depends pretty much on your neighbours. Best in the category is the ★**Zara**, Via Firenze 81, © 287125, with 10 rooms, two with baths. Here they operate a racist vetting procedure only admitting Poles and other Europeans in an area crowded with illegal immigrants from Africa. The Polish-Italian ★**Fiore**, Via Milano 109, ✆ 5538798—once rumoured to have Naples' fattest cat, now replaced by Lilly the dog— is barely acceptable, but good for the area (remember to bring L50 coins for the lift). Next to the Porta Nolana try the ★**Colombo**, Via G. Leopardi 115, ✆ 269254. This offers grubby-looking rooms, each with TV—hence the reinforced steel doors, but noisy hookers arriving back late in the small hours can make sleeping difficult.

Another place to look for cheap accommodation is Via Mezzocannone, south of Spaccanapoli. This street borders the university, and many of the most pleasant cheap lodgings in Naples can be found here—though with so many students it may be hard to find a vacancy. Naples' **youth hostel** is the **Ostello Mergellina**, Salita della Grotta 23, ✆ 7612346, ✇ 7612391, near the Mergellina Metropolitana station. IYHF cards are required.

Naples ✆ (081–)   ***Eating Out***

> Now, everyone thinks of China as a ponderous, elephantine
> country; Naples, on the other hand we think of as some-
> thing exciting, stimulating. Perhaps the Chinese invented
> slow, pacific fat macaronis, not the spaghetti that moves like
> the waves of the sea ...

Domenico Rea

This local savant, writing in the pages of *Qui Napoli*, is carrying on one of Naples' grand old causes. Forget those old legends about Marco Polo—just imagine anyone brazen enough to say spaghetti doesn't originally come from Naples! This capital of cooking, this citadel of *Italianità*, can already claim pizza, and probably many other Italian specialities as well. Neapolitans spend as much time worrying about what's for dinner as any people in the world, but like most other Italians they have a perfectly healthy attitude towards the subject. Neapolitan cuisine is simple—one of the most celebrated dishes is *spaghetti alle vongole*—and even in some of the more pretentious places you will see favourites of the Neapolitan *cucina povera* sneaking onto the menu, like *pasta e fagioli*. There are very few bad restaurants or tourist restaurants in the city, but an infinity of tiny, family-run trattorie or pizzerie; you will depart from most of them serene and satisfied.

For famous Neapolitan pizza, look for the genuine Neapolitan pizza oven, a built-in, bell-shaped affair made of stone with a broad, clean tile floor; the fire (only certain kinds of wood will do) is at the back, close to the pizza, not hidden underneath. Watch out in restaurants for the house wines; in cheaper places this is likely to be Gragnano from nearby Monte Faito—detestable rough stuff. On the other hand you can find some real surprises from Campania; a dry white called Greco di Tufo, and Taurasi, a distinguished red—as well as Falerno, the descendant of the far-famed ancient *Falernian* that Latin poets never tired of praising. Some restaurants in Naples, you will find, are the cheapest in all Italy—as they cheat on their taxes. Others can be alarmingly expensive, especially if you order fish.

Restaurants in all price ranges are spread pretty evenly around central Naples. For romantic harbour-side dinners, it's difficult to beat the Borgo Marinara besides the Castel Dell'Ovo where you will find the whole marina area set aside for dining. The Mergellina area also does pretty well. Up nearer the historic centre you will find character; poky streets with poky restaurants whose chefs pop over to the local street sellers for their fresh veg. For those in the know other less likely spots harbour one or two treats as well.

Many of the cheapest and homeliest places in Naples can be found on or around Via Speranzella, a block west of Via Toledo in the *Tavoliere*, where few tourists ever penetrate. As for the area around the railway station, restaurants here, more than elsewhere in Naples, have succumbed to opportunity and necessity; Piazza Garibaldi isn't nearly as much fun as it was a few years ago, and its hundreds of restaurants are neither keeping standards up nor prices down. But this area, and also Piazza Mercato, is an open bazaar, and you can get fat and happy just snacking from the bars and stands—slices of pizza, heavy *arancini*, and the flaky pastries called *sfogliatelle*, another Naples speciality.

expensive

La Cantinella, Via Nazario Sauro 23, © 404884, near the Castel dell'Ovo on the esplanade, is believed by many to be Naples' finest—also the place to be seen for the Parthenopeans, with a telephone on each table which they retain despite the invention of mobile telephones. Their *linguine Santa Lucia* made with home-made pasta, octopi, squid, prawns, clams and fresh baby tomatoes takes some beating. The risotto is also excellent. Though it certainly isn't cheap, you can easily spend more in other establishments nearby. The atmosphere is smart but relaxed and the service friendly. Close by in the Borgo Marinara beneath the Castel dell'Ovo lies **La Bersagliera**, Borgo Marinara 10, © 7646016. The location is excellent. The large 1900s restaurant cuts an elegant image despite the tacked-on 80s extension. The fish is excellent and the wine good too, especially the white Fiano de Avellino. *Closed Tues.* Closer to the civic centre is **Ciro**, Via Santa Brigida 71, © 5524072, near the Castel Nuovo. Go ahead and order *pasta e fagioli* or any other humble pasta dish; that's what the place is famous for, typical Naples cuisine at its best. They also do pizzas and are *numero uno* on the Vera Pizza trail. They have been around for decades but the restaurant is smartly refurbished and without the character that a place of its reputation might lead you to expect. *Closed Sun.* On the heights at Mergellina is **La Sacrestia**, Via Orazio 116, © 7611051, run for generations by the Ponsiglione family and another temple of Neapolitan gastronomy, in a superb location overlooking the Bay of Naples. Try the risotto with baby squid (*risotto con neonati di seppietta*). *Closed Mon.*

Giuseppone a Mare, Via Ferdinando Russo 13, © 7691384, overlooking Cape Posillipo since 1889, is one of Naples' institutions, especially popular with wedding parties. The fish is excellent, the setting memorable, and you probably won't forget the bill either. *Closed Mon.* On the Mergellina esplanade **Don Salvatore**, Via Mergellina 5, © 681817, has been around for more than 40 years, during which time it has built up a well-deserved reputation for turning out consistently fine Neapolitan dishes, accompanied by some of the area's best wines. There are set menus for those who want an introduction to Naples' best, and pizza for those who want to keep the bill down. *Closed Wed.* Lastly, a nice surprise in the area at the end of Piazza Garibaldi is **Mimi alla Ferrovia**, Via Alfonso d'Aragona 21, © 5538525. Again, you'll find no new-fangled concoctions, just honest-to-goodness dishes based on the freshest ingredients and recipes handed down for generations. The speciality here is *pasta e ceci*, a khaki green soup of flat pasta and chick peas to be savoured with closed eyes. Don't worry about the brusque service but concentrate on the seafood and excellent mozzarella. *Closed Sun.*

moderate

Off the Villa Communale approaching Piazza Sannazzaro, **La Cantina di Triunfo**, Riviera di Chiaia 64, © 668101, offers Neapolitan *cucina povera* raised to an art form—wintry soups of chestnuts and lentils, or lighter versions of broad beans and fresh peas in spring, *polpette di baccalà*—small balls of minced salt-cod, fried or served in a fresh tomato sauce—and mouth-watering pasta dishes, all of which change according to the season. Desserts are as good as everything else. The *crostata d'arance e mandorle* (an orange and almond tart) is excellent. The wine list is also exceptional, and many of the grappas—there are 80 types to choose from— home-made. Be sure to book, as space is very limited. *Closed Sun.* Back on the esplanade of Via Partenope beyond the Castel dell'Ovo but before the Villa Communale, track down the **Taverna e Zi Carmela**, Via Niccolò Tommaseo 11/12, © 7643581. Aunt Carmela runs a busy and well-kept ship, with excellent home cooking, much of it done by herself, and other members of the family waiting at table. The speciality here is once more seafood. *Closed Sun.* Up near the Mergellina end, **O Sole Mio**, Via Tommaso Campanella 7, © 7612323, is run by a fisherman's family, and though you will find some meat on the menu, you will be better advised to go straight for the seafood, in all its many forms. Try the wonderfully tasty *cassuola di pesce* (fish casserole) but tuck your napkin into your collar, Neapolitan-style, before you start! *Closed Tues.*

Pizza Paradise

Its origins are almost certainly Arab. Some people maintain the word may be derived from *pitta*, the unleavened bread eaten throughout Greece, Turkey and the Middle East. But wherever it hails from, pizza as we know it is an invention of Naples. Neapolitans are fiercely proud of this versatile dish, and haughtily disdainful of imitations and the variations made by others on the formula—the thin-crusted affair served in Roman *pizzerie* is enough to make a Neapolitan cry. And as for the deep-pan version invented in Chicago and served up in many British and American pizza parlours—the less said the better.

For Neapolitans, a real pizza must have an uneven base and be cooked in a real wood-fired oven. Some say the secret is in the flour, others in the water. But all agree the technique for flattening the dough is crucial. Not for the Neapolitans the pedantic practice of stretching out the dough with a rolling pin. In Naples, the *pizzaiolo* is a flamboyant character, flinging the dough up into the air, smashing it down on the marble table and swinging it round his head until it reaches the required shape and thickness. The best *pizzaioli* are much in demand, and take home very respectable salaries. As for the topping, the most authentic is *pomodoro fresco*—fresh tomatoes chopped over a bed of mozzarella, sprinkled with fresh basil and liberally doused with olive oil. Another Neapolitan favourite is the *ripieno*, a gut-buster of a pizza folded in two, and stuffed with fresh ricotta, mozzarella, pieces of salami and cooked ham.

However you order it, pizza should really be eaten with beer rather than wine. Many pizzerias only serve fizzy, bottled wine, which is much more expensive and best left alone. Pizza is usually eaten as a meal in itself, sometimes for lunch but more often in the evening, preceded by an antipasto of *bruschetta*—slices of thick toasted bread soused in olive oil and garlic and topped with tomatoes and basil, or fried bite-sized chunks of mozzarella and vegetables. For anyone on a tight budget—Neapolitans and tourists alike—the pizzeria is a lifeline. The bill for a pizza and a beer comes to about half that in a normal restaurant. In Naples, particularly good pizzerias are rewarded by a *vera pizza* (real pizza) emblem to hang up outside. Some of the best are the **Brandi**, the **Lombardi a Santa Chiara** and the exceptional **Da Pasqualino**, now in its fourth generation (for details *see* below).

inexpensive

Pizza is always the best friend of the budget-minded tourist (*see* above), and you can get two superb pizzas and lots of wine for the price of a plate of pasta in some smarter places at **Da Pasqualino**, Piazza Sannazzaro 78/9, ℭ 681524, in Mergellina. If you need cigarettes, shout 'Gennaro!' to the balconies above and they will appear. Don't miss the old granny in the corner, whose job it is to make the superb but calorie-laden *crocchette*—potato croquettes spiked with mozzarella cheese, with which the locals invariably start their meal. Sitting out in the piazza this is as simple as it gets but not to be missed. *Closed Tues.* In the historic centre the **Pizzeria Port'Alba**, Via Port'Alba 18, ℭ 459713, founded in 1830, will do excellent pizzas for both lunch and dinner. You can also get full dinners, including the house speciality, *linguine al cartoccio*—seafood pasta made into a foil parcel and baked in the oven, for a reasonable sum (it is vast so go easy on the antipasti). You can chose either to sit outside under the Port'Alba itself or inside, in which case the upstairs area is more snug. Just across the road at the **Bellini**, Via Santa Maria di Costantinopoli 80, ℭ 459774, you'll find more good pizza and pasta dishes, with a few outdoor tables for summer dining. Once more *linguine al cartoccio* are on offer or opt for *pesce all griglia. Closed Sun.*

Slightly more upmarket, but only slightly, the **Lombardi a Santa Chiara**, Via Benedetto Croce 59, ✆ 5520780, just off Piazza del Gesù Nuovo, offers memorable *antipasti* of fried courgettes, baby mozzarella and artichokes, before you ever get to eat your pizza, wonderfully cooked in the classic wood oven. Noisy but friendly, this place fills up quickly, so book ahead or be prepared to wait. *Closed Sun.* **Brandi**, Salita Sant'Anna di Palazzo 1/2, ✆ 416928, a pretty, lively pizzeria, claims to have invented the *margherita*, Naples' most famous pizza, with mozzarella, tomatoes and fresh basil, in honour of the 19th-century queen whose favourite dish it apparently was. She would pick up up her pizza on the way back from balls, to eat cold in the morning. They have two floors and a small terrace. The seafood pizza includes octopi cooked with their ink sacks intact!

Cheap and homely but occupying a million-dollar position down on the Borgo Marinara next to the Castel dell'Ovo, **Patrizia**, Via Luculliano 24 (no telephone) has barely seven tables and no menu. They serve you wine in plastic cups and tell you their daily fare as you relax next door to far more prestigious establishments. The food is delicious and the prices downright ridiculous. *Sphagetti alle cozze* made with fresh *pomodorini* is one of their staples. The grilled *scamorza* cheese and aubergine is likewise delectable.

Finally, we offer you an honest breakfast—bacon and eggs, if you like—at the **Ristorante California**, Via Santa Lucia 101, ✆ 7649752, Italy's greatest rendezvous for homesick Americans and a longtime Naples landmark. For dinner, the menu is split between Italian and Gringo dishes, and the roast turkey isn't bad.

cafés and gelaterie

As well as the inventors of the pizza, Neapolitans are, it is generally recognized, Italy's most dedicated and punctilious coffee consumers, and the city accordingly has its crop of elegant, ornate though now often faded 19th-century *gran caffè*, mostly not too far from the Galleria and the Piazza del Plebiscito (*see* above). The best location is occupied by **Gambrinus**, Piazza Trieste e Trento, ✆ 417582, overlooking the Teatro San Carlo and Piazza Plebiscito, but as you would expect it's not cheap. Other fine places to take coffee can be found along the waterfront, particularly out towards Mergellina. Naples also, naturally, produces some great ice cream and pastries. *Gelaterie* can be found all over town, but **Scimmia**, Piazza della Carità 4, just off the Via Toledo not far from Spaccanapoli, has for long been regarded as one of the city's best. Last of all, for *sfogliatelle* we recommend **La Bottega della Sfogliatella**, Via Cusanova 97, ✆ 5545364, close to Porta Capuana off Piazza Garibaldi.

For concerts, shows, and other cultural events—Naples always has plenty—the best information on programmes and times will be found in the newspaper *Il Mattino*, or in the free monthly guide *Qui Napoli*.

opera, classical music and theatre

For opera lovers one of the ultimate experiences is a night at the **San Carlo** (box office ✆ 7972370/7972111), but tickets are extremely hard to come by, and very pricey. Hotels may be able to get them most easily. Otherwise you must go to the box office in person. If you do manage to get a ticket, be sure to dress your best. You may have more luck catching a **concert** at the **Auditorium RAI-TV**, Via Guglielmo Marconi, ✆ 7251111, at the **Conservatorio di Musica**, Via San Pietro a Maiella, ✆ 459255, or at the **Associazione Alessandro Scarlatti**, Piazza dei Martiri 58, ✆ 406011, which holds concerts for jazz, chamber music and a bit of everything. Check with the tourist office or in *Qui Napoli* for programmes, and don't forget also that many, often free concerts are staged in the city's churches. Look out for street billboards with details of coming events. Tickets for major events may be obtainable at the ticket offices in the **Box Office**, Galleria Umberto, ✆ 5519188 and **Concerteria**, Via Schipa 23, ✆ 7611221.

Unless your Italian is fluent, **theatre** will probably be a frustrating experience, and if you go for one of the superbly executed dialect plays, you may not understand a word. If that doesn't put you off, the best theatres to try are the **Politeama**, Via Monte di Dio, ✆ 7645016, the **Cilea**, Via S. Domenico, ✆ 7141179, the **Bracco**, Via Tarsia, ✆ 5495904 and the **Sannazaro**, Via Chiaia 157, ✆ 411723.

clubs, bars and discos

Neapolitans are night-owls, probably thanks to their Spanish heritage, and many, especially in summer, don't even think about going out to dinner until 10pm. That doesn't leave too much time for partying, once the 2–3 hour eating ritual is over, but there are some reasonable clubs and late-night bars (as well as some terrible ones). The thing to remember is that some areas are best left alone after midnight, most notably the Piazza Garibaldi area near the station, and the so-called *quartiere*, the narrow side streets that run off the Via Toledo. And if the vampish hookers to be seen at every street corner after dark should take your fancy, remember to take a second look—those girls could well be boys. Naples is famous even in drag-obsessed Italy for its transvestites, and some of them are positively remarkable. The genuine female prostitutes tend to be the crones on the other side of the street.

It's worth checking with the locals where their most popular night spots are since the popularity of haunts can change with the current fads. Neapolitans tend to bop the weekends away, so very few open during the week. You will rarely pay over L30,000 to get in—the fairer sex often get in for less or even for free—which normally includes a drink. Remember that things never kick off until after midnight, so if you turn up before bring your own crowd.

A list of clubs can be found in *Qui Napoli* but for a start we include **La Mela**, Via dei Mille 41, ✆ 413881 which has good reports from the young and beautiful crowd. The **Kiss Kiss**, Via Sgambati 47, ✆ 5466566, Naples' biggest disco, is an institution, with different theme nights and an affluent young crowd. **My Way**, Via Cappella Vecchia 30/c, ✆ 7644735, is another popular nightspot, where Neapolitans have been dancing into the small hours for as long as anyone can remember.

At the **Otto Jazz Club**, Piazzetta Cariati 23, ✆ 5524373, you'll get **jazz** which looks for inspiration as much to the famous Neapolitan folk songs as to New Orleans. It also serves plates of pasta and light meals, and has a well-stocked bar serving 200 cocktails (their specials are beer based!). Don't take too much cash with you, as this otherwise very pleasant club is in a pretty hard area—when you leave it's best to get a taxi rather than walk around much outside. *Open Thurs–Sun.* The **Virgilio Sporting Club**, Via Tito Lucrezio Caro 6, ✆ 7695261, up on Posillipo hill, is a much more tranquil nightclub, set in its own parkland, with tables outside in fine weather. *Open Fri–Sun, midnight–4am.*

Around the Bay: from Baia to Sorrento

Naples' hinterlands share fully in the peculiarities and sharp contrasts of the big city. Creation left nothing half-done or poorly done; against any other part of the monotonous Italian coastline, the Campanian shore seems almost indecently blessed, possessing the kind of irresistibly distracting beauty that seduces history off the path of duty and virtue. Today, for all the troubles that come seeping out of Naples, this coast is still one of the capitals of Mediterranean languor.

In Roman days, it was nothing less than the California of the ancient world: fantastically prosperous, lined with glittering resort towns full of refugees from the Roman rat-race, as favoured by artists and poets as it was by rich patricians. Like California, though, the perfume was mixed with a little whiff of insecurity. Vesuvius would be enough, but even outside of the regularly scheduled eruptions and earthquakes, the region is Vulcan's own curiosity shop. West of Naples especially, there are eternally rising and sinking landscapes, sulphurous pools, thermal springs and even a baby volcano—altogether, perhaps the most unstable corner of the broad earth's crust.

Getting Around

Naples, of course, is the hub for all transport throughout the area; buses, ferries and local commuter rail lines lead out from the city to all points (*see* pp.66–7).

by rail

Regular FS trains aren't much help here, except for a fast trip between Naples and Salerno. Fortunately, there are the other, local, lines, of which the most important is the refreshingly efficient **Circumvesuviana**, the best way to reach Pompeii, Herculaneum and Sorrento. This line has its own ultramodern station, on Corso Garibaldi just south of the Piazza Garibaldi (© 7792444), but all of its trains also make a stop at the Stazione Centrale itself before proceeding east. At Centrale their station is underground, sharing space with that of the Naples Metropolitana; this can be confusing, since there are no schedules posted and the ticket windows aren't marked—you need to ask someone to make sure you are heading for the right train. The main lines run east through Ercolano (the stop for Herculaneum) and Torre del Greco, and then diverge near Torre Annunziata, one line heading for Sarno, out in the farm country east of Vesuvius, and the other for Sorrento. For the excavations at Pompei take the Sorrento line to the Scavi di Pompei/Villa dei Misteri stop. The Circumvesuviana terminal in Sorrento is two streets east from Piazza Tasso, the town centre. Circumvesuviana trains usually run every half-hour between 5am and 10.45pm. On a *direttissima*, of which there are several daily, the Naples–Sorrento trip takes 1 hour 10 minutes—locals are considerably slower. An additional Circumvesuviana line has infrequent trains north of Vesuvius to Nola and Baiano.

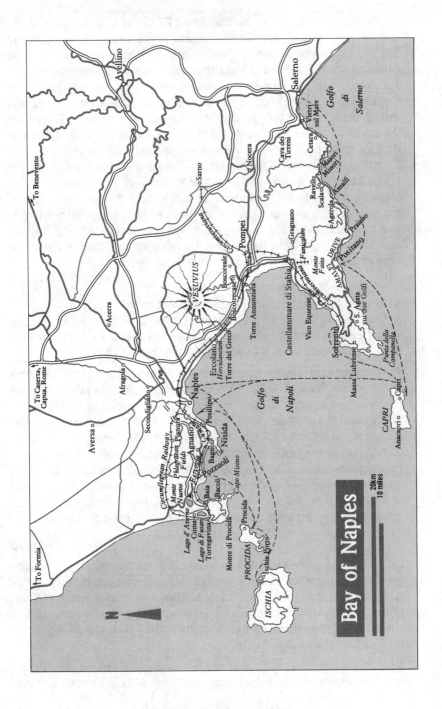

Bay of Naples

20km
10 miles

For the west bay, Naples' own **Metropolitana FS** goes as far as Pozzuoli-Solfatara (trains every 8 minutes). The two other regional lines both have trains about every half-hour from Piazza Montesanto Station, near the Piazza Dante. The **Ferrovia Cumana** (✆ 5513328) runs along the shore, through Fuorigrotta, Bagnoli, Pozzuoli, and Baia to Torregaveta (trains every 10 minutes). The remarkable **Circumflegrea** (also ✆ 5513328) also finishes at Torregaveta, after passing through plenty of places you probably won't want to visit (trains every 20 minutes) but usually only as far as Licola. For the stop at the archaeological site of Cumae it runs six trains daily, three in the morning and three in the afternoon. The Circumflegrea is easily the most macabre railway in the western world; the trip begins by passing a neon shrine to the Virgin Mary in the middle of the Montesanto Tunnel, and then passes through stations that are metal sheds or bombed-out ruins, with smashed and derailed cars lying alongside the tracks to give passengers something to think about. The station at Cumae is gutted and abandoned; those dodging the entrance fee can head up towards the acropolis through the thorn bushes and dense adder-haunted forests.

by bus

Naples city bus no.152, from Piazza Garibaldi and Via Mergellina, travels to Solfatara and Pozzuoli. There is a blue bus run by Sepsa departing Piazza Garibaldi and calling at Solfatara, Pozzuoli and Baia. From the bus stop in the centre of Baia, there are connecting buses to Cumae, Bacoli, and Cape Misenum.

The Circumvesuviana makes buses unnecessary for most of the east bay. Departing from the airport there is a bus to Sorrento three times a day. The express bus from Naples to Salerno, which usually runs every half-hour, leaves from the **SITA** office on Via Pisanelli, just off the Piazza Municipio, ✆ 5522176, and arrives in Salerno at the terminal at Corso Garibaldi 117, ✆ (089) 226604. SITA also runs the buses from Salerno for the Amalfi coast, with regular departures for Sorrento (in front of the Circumvesuviana station), or stopping short at Amalfi, Ravello or other towns along the route; they are usually so frequent that it is easy to see all the main coast towns on a day-trip, hopping from one to the next. Buses are definitely the best way to do it; driving yourself can be a hair-raising experience when it's busy.

by road

Drivers heading for the west bay area and wishing to arrive quite quickly should get onto the *tangenziale* out of Naples and stay on it until past Pozzuoli, before turning off onto the (by then) more tranquil SS7qu, which runs around the Miseno peninsula. Alternately, they can take the SS7qu all the way from the harbourside in Naples, via the Mergellina tunnel, or the pretty but slow coastal road—initially the Via Posillipo—around Cape Posillipo.

If you are heading towards Pompei and the east bay—where the distances are much greater, and so a car is much more useful—then, again, it's advisable to use the A3 *autostrada* to get out of Naples if you don't want to spend a long time on the SS18 coast road through the suburbs. Leave the A3 at the Ercolano exit for Herculaneum; south of here, though still pretty busy, the SS18 gradually becomes more attractive. At Pompei the SS145 road turns off to the right for the Sorrento peninsula; beyond Sorrento it becomes the famous, or infamous, **Amalfi drive**. This spectacular road—at its most extreme, no more than a winding ledge of hairpins halfway up a sheer cliff—is unquestionably worth seeing, but drivers should be aware of what is ahead of them, and avoid it in bad weather. The road was resurfaced and widened (!) as part of the works for the 1990 World Cup for football. For some idea of the difficulties of the road, consider that it takes the express bus almost 3 hours to navigate the 66km from Salerno to Sorrento.

West from Naples: Pozzuoli and the Phlegraean Fields

The very pretty coastal road leaving the city, with views of Vesuvius all through the suburb of Posillipo, passes the little island of Nisida; this was a favoured spot in ancient times, and legend has it that Brutus and Cassius planned Caesar's murder here in the villa of one of their fellow conspirators. Naples' suburbs continue through **Agnano**, a town of spas and hot springs set around a mile-wide extinct crater, and stretch as far as **Pozzuoli**.

Pozzuoli, Sophia Loren's home town, today is a modest little city, with only its ruins to remind it of the time when Roman Puteoli, and not Naples, was the metropolis of the bay. In the time of Caesar and Augustus, it was the main port of Italy; at one point the Senate actually considered the bizarre idea of digging a 160-mile-long canal to Rome to make shipping safer. The city's decline began in the 2nd century with the emperor Trajan's expansion of the port of Ostia, closer to Rome. During the 5th-century invasions, most of Puteoli's citizens took refuge in better-defended Naples.

The **Amphitheatre** (*open daily, 9am–one hour before sunset; adm*), on Via Domiziana, near the railway station, was the third-largest in the Roman world (after those in Rome itself and Capua), with 60 gates for letting the beasts in. It is remarkable for the preservation of its subterranean structure where the scenery, changing rooms and cells for storing wild animals prior to shows (*venationes*) were located. The long cavity in the centre was for hoisting up scenery. Unlike the chambers underneath, which were buried in mud and land slides, the stands were exposed and stripped of their masonry through the ages (visitors are not allowed onto them). The amphitheatre was built under Vespasian who renamed the city **Colonia Flavia Augusta Puteoli**, in thanks to Puteoli for its aid in the civil war that made him emperor. This was the second amphitheatre in Pozzuoli. Only a few broken arches of the older one survive 100m north. It was probably used for gladiatorial combats.

Pozzuoli's other important ruin is a little embarrassment to the town; for centuries people here were showing off the ancient **Serapeum**—temple to the popular Egyptian god Serapis—until some killjoy archaeologist proved the thing to be an unusually lavish *macellum*, or market. Only the foundations remain, in a park near Pozzuoli's small harbour.

For all ancient Puteoli's size and wealth, little else remains. There is a reason, and Pozzuoli would like to introduce a new word to your vocabulary to explain it: *bradyseism* is a rare seismic phenomenon that afflicts this town and other spots around the bay. It manifests itself in the form of 'slow' earthquakes. The level of the land fell 6m since Roman times only to begin rising in the 15th century. Most recently falling, all of Puteoli that hasn't been gently shaken to pieces over the centuries is now underwater. Roman moles and docks can still sometimes be made out beneath the surface.

Solfatara

What's troubling Pozzuoli can be seen more clearly just outside the town at **Solfatara**, the storm centre of what the Greeks called the Phlegraean (fiery) Fields, in Italian the *Campi Flegrei*. To the Romans, it was the *Forum Vulcani*, and a major attraction of the Campanian coast. It hasn't changed much since. Solfatara *(open daily, 8.30am–an hour beforesunset; adm)* is another crater of a collapsed volcano, but one that just can't be still; sulphur gas vents, bubbling mud pits and whistling superheated steam fumaroles decorate the eerie landscape. Guides are around to keep you away from the dangerous spots. Their favourite trick is to hold a smoking torch to one of the fumaroles—making a dozen others nearby go off at the same time. The effect is produced by the steam condensing around smoke particles. Solfatara is perfectly safe, even though the ground underneath feels hot and sounds strangely hollow. It is; scientists keep a close watch on the huge plug of cooled lava that underlies the whole of the area about Pozzuoli, and they say the pressure on it from below is only one-third as much as it was under Vesuvius in AD 79.

We promised you a baby volcano, and you'll see it near the coast west of Pozzuoli. **Monte Nuovo** has been quiet for some time (inexplicably passing up the opportunity to celebrate its 450th birthday, on 29 September 1988). The same earthquake in 1538 that wrecked much of Pozzuoli gave birth to this little cone. It's only about 140m tall, and an easy climb up to the crater (you can have a picnic inside it). Its percolation from the bowels of Campania filled up half of the **Lago di Lucrino**, separated from the sea by a narrow strip of land. Since antiquity, it has been renowned for its oysters. About 90 BC, a sharp Roman named C. Sergius Orata first had the idea of farming oysters here, and selling them to the rich owners of the villas around the bay; from this business he made one of the biggest killings of classical antiquity.

Cape Misenum

Baia, the next town along the coast, was nothing less than the greatest pleasure dome of classical antiquity (see **Topics**, p.50) Anybody who was anybody in the Roman world had a villa here, with a view of the sea, beach access, and a few hundred slaves to dust the statues and clean up after the orgies. You'll find little hint of that today; Goths, malaria and earthquakes have done a thorough job of wrecking the place. Most of ancient Baiae is now underwater, a victim of the same bradyseism that afflicts Pozzuoli. In summer, a glass-bottomed boat departs from Baia harbour to see this Roman Atlantis, ☎ 5265780 *(lasts 70 minutes; Sat, 12 and 4; Sun, 10.30, 12 and 4; L15000)*. Modern Baia is a pleasant small town, but its lovely bay has been consigned to use as a graveyard for dead freighters. Nevertheless, the extensive but humble remains of the imperial villa can be visited at the **Parco Archeologico** *(open daily, 9am–one hour before sunset; adm)*. Not much is labelled or explained, but the ruins include a part of the famous baths, a thermal spa for wealthy Romans that was probably the largest and poshest such establishment in the ancient world, and an inspiration for the great public baths of Rome and other cities.

At Baia, the coast curves southwards towards Bacoli and **Cape Misenum** (*Capo Miseno*), a beautiful spot that for centuries was the greatest naval base of the Roman Empire, home to 10,000 sailors (mostly Greeks and Syrians). As at Baia, foundations and bits of columns and cornices are everywhere, though nothing of any real interest has survived intact. Nearby Lake Miseno, also called the 'Dead Sea', was once a part of the base, joined to the sea by a canal dug by Augustus's right-hand man Cornelius Agrippa, in 37 BC. A memorable event of antiquity took place when Caligula ordered a double row of boats to be made across the bay, all the way from Bacoli to Pozzuoli. Suetonius wrote that the purpose was to fulfil a prophecy that Caligula would never become emperor until he rode across the bay on his horse (which he proceeded to do); it's more likely, though, that he did it to impress the Persian ambassador with the strength of the Roman navy.

That same distance was covered by the famous 'boy on a dolphin', a story that inspired many classical works of art. Many reliable witnesses attested to Pliny that they had seen it—a little boy of the peninsula who had befriended a dolphin, which gave him a ride every day to lessons with his tutor in Puteoli. Pliny records that the boy died after an illness, and that the dolphin, after waiting faithfully for his friend for several days, beached himself and died too. The two were burned together.

The pleasant village of **Bacoli**, nearby, has two sights: a covered Roman reservoir called the **Piscina Mirabile**, a vaulted chamber like the famous one in Istanbul; and the vast ruin of a villa that might have belonged to Julius Caesar, called by the locals **Cento Camarelle**, the 'hundred little rooms'.

Two other lakes, both created as a by-product of volcanic action, lie north of Cape Misenum; one, the **Lago di Fusaro**, is a large, shallow oyster farm, cut off from the sea by a sand bar near the woebegone fishing village of Torregaveta, the terminus of the Circumflegrea and Cumana railways. The decaying Rococo palace on an island in the centre is the Casino, built in 1782 by the Bourbon kings' favourite architect, Luigi Vanvitelli. **Lago d'Averno**—Lake Avernus—may ring a bell from your school days; it's the mouth of Hell, according to the ancient Greeks, who believed any passing bird would be suffocated by the infernal fumes rising from it. Cornelius Agrippa didn't have much respect for mythology, and he turned the lake into a part of the naval base by cutting another canal. Among the ruins that surround it are the remains of a domed building, perhaps a temple or a sort of spa, originally as big as the Pantheon in Rome. Emperor Nero was fond of this area, and he built a covered canal lined with colonnades from the lake all the way to Pozzuoli; no trace remains of this now.

Cumae

As the story has it, King Tarquin of Rome came here, to the most venerable and respected oracle in all the western Mediterranean, with the intention of purchasing nine prophetic books from the Cumaean Sibyl. Unwisely, he said they were too dear, whereupon the Sibyl threw three of the books into the fire and offered him the remaining six at the same price. Again he complained, and the Sibyl put three more in the flames; finally Tarquin gave up, and took the last three at the original price. It was a good bargain. The Sibylline Books guided Rome's destiny until they too were burned up in the great fire of 82 BC.

Cumae had other distinctions. As one of the first Greek foundations in Italy, the city was the mother colony for Naples and many other cities of Magna Graecia. In 421 BC, Cumae lost its independence to the Samnites, and declined steadily from then on; Arab raiders, who did so much damage everywhere else around Campania, finally wiped the city off the map in the 9th century AD. They did a good job of it, and there is little to see at the site *(open Tues–Sun, 9–7; adm)*, only the foundations of a few temples on the high **acropolis**, worth the climb for the views around Cape Misenum. One of the ruins was a famous Temple of Apollo, rebuilt by Augustus in thanks to the god after his victory at Actium.

Just below the summit, you may visit the **Cave of the Cumaean Sibyl** itself, discovered by accident in 1932. This was the setting of Aeneas' famous encounter with the Sibyl who leads him into the underworld, described in Book 6 of Virgil's *Aeneid*. It is a place of mystery, a long series of strange, trapezoidal galleries cut out of solid rock—impressive enough, even stripped of the sumptuous decoration they must once have had (all ancient oracles were marvellously profitable). Nobody has a clear idea how old it is. By classical times, it took the form of an oracle quite like the one at Delphi. At the far end of the cave, a plain alcove with two benches marks the spot where the Sibyls would inhale fumes over the sacred tripod, chew laurel leaves, and go into their trance. Serious stuff in Virgil's day, the cult was in decline by the 2nd century when Trimalchio, a character in Petronius' *Satyricon*, claims he saw the ancient Sibyl's remains preserved in a jar hanging in the cave.

West of Naples (© 081–)   ***Eating Out***

Nobody has made the western side of the bay a base for their holiday since the 4th century AD. If you are travelling in specially to visit the classical sites you may prefer to grab a sandwich. The mini-market in the Solfatara is a good place to pick up a *panino* for a picnic on the sunny acropolis at Cuma. At Baia also there is another mini-market opposite the station. If you're in need of proper sit-down, there are a few good places to have lunch.

Pozzuoli

The harbour area of modern Pozzuoli is not particularly scenic, but if you are fresh off the ferry from the islands of Ischia and Procida, or visiting the amphitheatre and

Serapeum there are two recommendations. On the harbour in Pozzuoli, the **Del Capitano**, Via Lungomare C. Colombo 10, ✆ 5262283 (*moderate*), is a good rendezvous for fish-lovers. *Closed Thursday in low season.* **Il Tempio**, Via Serapide 13, ✆ 8665179 (*moderate*), overlooking the ruined temple in Pozzuoli's main square, is justly famous for its antipasti. Leave it to the waiter and he will bring you plate after plate, mostly fish-based, including octopus, fried squid, baby red mullet, clams and giant prawns, until you tell him to stop. Many people call it a day after this, and few ever get beyond the *primi*. *Closed Wed.*

On the way out of Pozzuoli along the coastal road is **La Granzeola**, Via Cupa Fasane, ✆ 5243430 (*expensive*), where owner-chef Carmine Russo turns fish bought directly off the local boats into a dazzling array of unusual and tasty dishes, especially with pasta. Try the *rigatoni con ragu di cozze*—short pasta with a delicious mussel sauce. *Closed Sun.*

Baia to Cuma

At Baia's **L'Altro Cucchiaro**, Via Lucullo 13, ✆ 8687196 (*expensive*), you can dine on divine concoctions of seafood and pasta, and superb fish. The restaurant is opposite the railway station and very convenient for the archaeological park. *Closed Sun evenings, Mon, 3 weeks Aug.* Back along the road to Pozzuoli at **La Ninfea**, Via Lago Lucrino, ✆ 8661326 (*expensive*), you can bask on the lakeside terrace as you dine on fish and grilled meats.

Along the road from Fusaro to Cuma, there are several decent restaurants whose speciality is fish. Leaving Fusaro on the road to Cuma there is the **Villa Chiara**, Via Torre di Cappella 10, ✆ 8687139 (*moderate*). Near the archaeological site at Cuma are the **Giardino degli Aranci**, Via Cuma 75, ✆ 8543120 (*moderate*) and the **Anfiteatro Cumano**, ✆ 8543119 (*inexpensive*), also on Via Cuma. *Closed Tues.*

Torregaveta

Restaurants in shabbyish Torregaveta are cheaper than in the towns inside the bay. The **Ristorante Al Pontile**, Via Spiaggia Torregaveta, ✆ 8689180 (*inexpensive*), has full dinners for reasonable prices.

East of Naples: Mount Vesuvius and Pompeii

Tourist Information

There is a well-organized tourist office in Pompei town, at Via Sacra 1, 80045, ✆ (081) 8507255, ✉ 8632401, which has a branch office near the Porta Marina entrance to the old Pompeii site.

Despite its fearsome reputation, and its formidable appearance looming over Naples, **Mount Vesuvius** is a midget as volcanoes go—only 1281m. No one suspected it even was a volcano, in fact, until it surprised the people of Pompeii, Herculaneum, and Stabiae on 24 August AD 79. That titanic eruption did not include much lava, but it buried

IL Vesuvio

Herculaneum under mud and the other two cities under cinders and ash, while coating most of Italy with a thin layer of dust. After that explosion, Roman writers noted that the plume of smoke and ash over the volcano looked exactly like a young pine tree; observers have noted the same sinister tree-shape in many eruptions since.

Over a hundred eruptions since have destroyed various towns and villages, some more than once. But like at Mount Etna in Sicily, people just can't stay away from Vesuvius' slopes. Volcanic soil grows grapes and olives in abundance, though the novelty of it often makes the Italians exaggerate their quality. The AD 79 explosion hasn't been equalled since; it blew the top of the mountain clean off, leaving two peaks, with the main fissure in between. The lower one is called Monte Somma, or *nasone* ('big nose') by the Neapolitans; the higher, parallel peak is Vesuvius proper.

Vesuvius was last heard from in 1944. The final eruption left the lava flows you'll see on the upper slopes; it also sealed the main fissure, putting an end to the permanent plume of smoke that once was such a familiar landmark. You can bet the scientists are watching Vesuvius. Despite the long hiatus, they say there is no reason to expect another eruption soon, though if it were to explode now, they warn, it would cause a catastrophe—the area around the volcano has become one of the most densely populated in all Italy.

To visit the main crater (between the two peaks), take the Vesuvius bus from the Circumvesuviana stop in Ercolano; then you have a stiff half-hour climb up the ash path. Dismiss all hopes of an easy ascent to the top singing 'Funiculi, funicula' from the legendary Thomas Cook cable railway, long since defunct. The white scar up the side of the crater, left by a second funicular which was due to replace the seventies' chairlift, continues a running saga. Work halted after argument for control over it between the two communes of Torre del Greco and Ercolano. Whilst they argued the money 'disappeared'. Now the environmentalists have got a headache campaigning for colouring the concrete back Vesuvius style (*open daily, 9am–one hour before sunset; adm*).

Herculaneum

Naples' discouraging industrial sprawl spreads eastwards as far as Torre del Greco without a break. The drab suburb of **Ercolano** is a part of it, built over the mass of rock that imprisons ancient **Herculaneum**, a smaller and less famous sight than Pompeii but just as much worth visiting *(open daily, 9am–one hour before sunset; adm)*. Some people like it even better than its more famous sister site.

Unlike Pompeii, an important commercial centre, Herculaneum seems to have been a wealthy resort, only about one-third the size. Also, Vesuvius destroyed them in different ways. Pompeii was buried under layers of ash, while Herculaneum, much closer to the volcano, drowned under a sea of mud. Over time the mud hardened to a soft stone, preserving the city and nearly everything in it as a sort of fossil—furniture, clothing and even some of the goods in the shops have survived.

Like Pompeii, Herculaneum was discovered by accident. In the early 1700s, an Austrian officer named Prince Elbeuf had a well dug here; not too far down, the workmen struck a stone pavement—the stage of the city's theatre. The Bourbon government began some old-fashioned destructive excavation, but serious archaeological work began only under Mussolini. Only about eight blocks of shops and villas, some quite fashionable, have been excavated. The rest is covered not only by tens of metres of rock, but also by a dense modern neighbourhood; bringing more of Herculaneum to light is a fantastically slow and expensive operation, but new digs are still going on.

At any given time, most of the buildings will be locked, but the guards wandering about have all the keys and will show you almost any of them upon request (they are not supposed to accept tips, though you'll find they often seem to expect them). Many of the most interesting houses can be found along Cardo IV, the street in the centre of the exca-vated area; on the corner of the Decumanus Inferior, the **House of the Wooden Partition** may be the best example we have of the façade of a Roman house. Inside there is an amazingly preserved wooden screen (from which the house gets its name) used for separating the *tablinum*—the master's study—from the atrium. Next door, the **Trellis House** was a much more modest dwelling, with a built-in workshop; the **House of the Mosaic Atrium**, down the street, is another luxurious villa built with a mind to the sea view from the bedrooms upstairs. On the other side of the Decumanus, Cardo IV passes the **Samnite House** (so named because of its early-style atrium), and further up a column with police notices painted on it stands near the **House of the Neptune**, with a lovely mythological mosaic in the atrium.

Other buildings worth a visit are the **House of the Deer**, with its infamous statue of a drunken Hercules relieving himself picturesquely; the well-preserved **Baths**; and the **Palaestra**, or gym, with its unusual serpent fountain and elegant, cross-shaped swimming pool (much of which is under the ramp you enter over, but due for clearance).

Beyond Ercolano, the coastal road passes through the unattractive industrial sprawl and modern housing blocks thrown up to rehouse the homeless after the earthquake in 1980. The men of **Torre del Greco** have long been famous for gathering and working coral, a business now threatened by pollution. These days, much of the coral is imported from Asia, though it is still worked locally. Torre del Greco has recently become more famous for organized crime and gangland killings, though the population still turn out en masse to express their devotion to the Madonna in the procession for the Immaculate Conception, on 8 December, when the town gives thanks for having been spared in one of the last century's eruptions of Vesuvius.

The Roman Villa at Oplontis

Torre Annunziata, the next town, is another sorry place with a serious drug problem and a penchant for pasta production. The Roman villa excavated here, known as the **Villa Poppaea at Oplontis** (*open daily, 9am–one hour before sunset; free*) is well worth a detour. If you are arriving on the Circumvesuviana exit the station, walk downhill over the crossroads and it's the open area on the left opposite the military zone. Two-thirds of the villa have been fully excavated, revealing an extremely opulent pad with its own private bath complex, servants' quarters, monumental reception rooms and ornamental pool. There are beautiful wall paintings (*see* p.111), depicting rich scenes of monumental halls hung with military arms, a magnificent tripod set between a receding colonnade, bowls of figs and fresh fruit, vignettes of pastoral idylls and one with Hercules under a tree with the apples of the Hesperides which he persuaded Atlas to retrieve for him during his penultimate labour.

The part of the villa near the road is dominated by the great atrium hall and the family quarters. The wing further from the road seems to have been the servants' quarters. Here you can still see amphorae stacked up in a store room. Outside the latrines, partitioned for each sex, it may have been one of the slaves who left his name, scrawled in Greek, 'Remember Beryllos'.

An amphora marked with the name Poppaea has given rise to the suggestion that the villa may have belonged to the wealthy Roman family, the gens Poppaea, who also owned the House of Menander at Pompeii. The most infamous member of this family was Sabina Poppaea, a woman with everything but virtue. She used her charms to captivate the emperor Nero, leaving her second husband Otho—another future emperor—who was dispatched to Lusitania. Spurred on by her, Nero killed off his mother Agrippina and his first wife. Nero eventually killed Sabina by mistake in a fit of rage in AD 65, kicking her in the abdomen while she was pregnant.

Pompeii

Herculaneum may have been better preserved, but to see an entire ancient city come to life, the only place on earth you can go is this magic time capsule, left to us by the good graces of Mount Vesuvius. Pompeii is no mere ruin; walking down the old Roman high street, you can peek into the shops, read the graffiti on the walls, then wander off down the back streets to explore the homes of the inhabitants and appraise their taste in painting—they won't mind a bit if you do. Almost everything we know for sure concerning the daily life of the ancients was learned here, and the huge mass of artefacts and art dug up over 200 years is still helping scholars to re-evaluate the Roman world.

Though a fair-sized city by Roman standards, with a population of some 20,000, Pompeii was probably only the third or fourth city of Campania, a trading and manufacturing

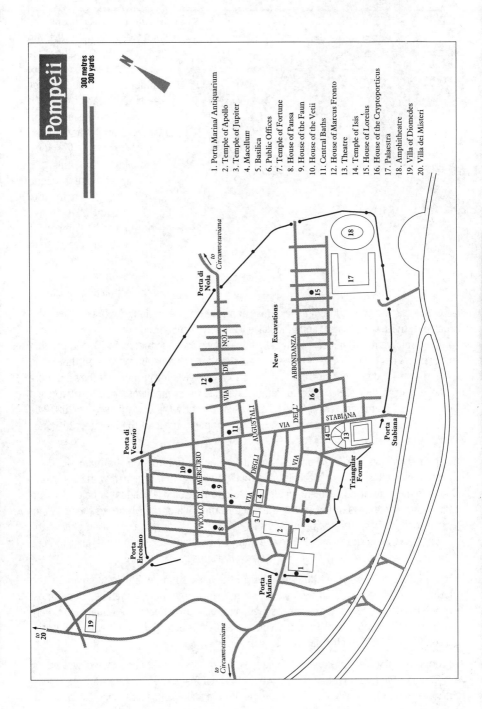

Pompeii

300 metres
300 yards

N

1. Porta Marina/ Antiquarium
2. Temple of Apollo
3. Temple of Jupiter
4. Macellum
5. Basilica
6. Public Offices
7. Temple of Fortune
8. House of Pansa
9. House of the Faun
10. House of the Vetii
11. Central Baths
12. House of Marcus Fronto
13. Theatre
14. Temple of Isis
15. House of Loreius
16. House of the Cryptoporticus
17. Palaestra
18. Amphitheatre
19. Villa of Diomedes
20. Villa dei Misteri

Porta di Nola
to Circumvesuviana

Porta di Vesuvio

New Excavations

VIA DI NOLA

VIA DELL' ABBONDANZA

VIA DELL' AUGUSTALI

VIA DEGLI

VIA

VIA STABIANA

VICOLO DI MERCURIO

Porta Ercolano

Triangular Forum

Porta Stabiana

Porta Marina

to Circumvesuviana

to Circumvesuviana

to 20

109

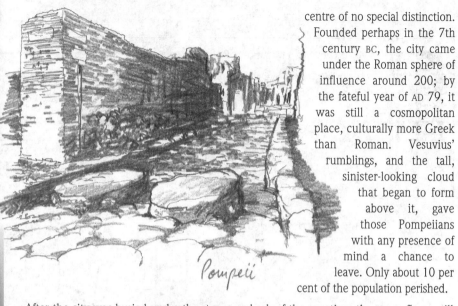

Pompeii

centre of no special distinction. Founded perhaps in the 7th century BC, the city came under the Roman sphere of influence around 200; by the fateful year of AD 79, it was still a cosmopolitan place, culturally more Greek than Roman. Vesuvius' rumblings, and the tall, sinister-looking cloud that began to form above it, gave those Pompeiians with any presence of mind a chance to leave. Only about 10 per cent of the population perished.

After the city was buried under the stones and ash of the eruption, the upper floors still stuck out; these were looted, and gradually cleared by farmers, and eventually the city was forgotten altogether. Engineers found it while digging an aqueduct in 1600, and the first excavations began in 1748—a four-star attraction for northern Europeans on the Grand Tour. The early digs were far from scientific; archaeologists today sniff that they did more damage than Vesuvius. Resurrected Pompeii has had other problems: theft of artworks, a good dose of bombs in World War II, and most recently the earthquake of 1980. The damage from that is still being repaired today, though almost all the buildings are once more open to visitors.

There are two ways to see Pompeii; spend two or three hours on the main sights, or devote the day to scrutinizing details, for a total immersion in the ancient world you won't find anywhere else (the detailed guidebooks sold in the stands outside will help you with this). Your ticket also entitles you to entrance to the Villa of the Mysteries (*see* p. 111). This is located 5 minutes' walk up the Viale Villa dei Misteri, to the left on exiting the Circumvesuviana. This is best left to the end of your sightseeing but remember to keep your ticket *(site open daily, 9am–one hour before sunset; adm)*.

Pompeii isn't quite a perfect time capsule; a little background will help to complete the picture. The site today is all too serene, with a small-town air. Remember that almost every building was two or three storeys high, and that most streets of a Roman town were permanent market-places. When the volcano struck, much of the town was still in the process of being rebuilt after earthquake damage in AD 62.

As long as daylight lasted, Pompeii would have been crowded with improvised *bancarelle*; any wagon driver who wished to pass would need all manner of creative cursing. At least the streets are well-paved—better than Rome itself in fact; Campania's cities, the richest in western Europe, could well afford such luxuries. All the pavements were much more smooth and even than you see them now. The purpose of the flat stones laid across the streets should not be hard to guess. They were places to cross when it rained—streets here were also drains—and the slots in them allowed wagon wheels to pass through.

The shops, open to the street in the day, would be sealed up behind shutters at night, just as they are in the old parts of Mediterranean cities today. Houses, on the other hand, turn a completely blank wall to the street; they got their light and air from skylights in the *atrium*, the roofed court around which the rooms were arranged. Later, fancier villas have a second, open court directly behind the first, designed after the Greek *peristyle*. As in Rome, no part of town was necessarily the fashionable district; elegant villas will be found anywhere, often between two simple workmen's flats. And don't take the street names too seriously. They were bestowed by the archaeologists, often, as with the Via di Mercurio (Mercury Street), after mythological subjects depicted on the street fountains.

Roman Frescoes

Not surprisingly, Pompeii and Herculaneum have been of prime importance in the study of Roman painting. It is imposible to know how much of this art was borrowed from the Greeks or the Etruscans, although by the time of Augustus it appears that Rome and Campania were in the vanguard. New fashions set in the palaces of the Palatine Hill were quickly copied in the villas of the Roman California. Or perhaps it was vice versa.

Wealthy Romans tended to regard their homes as domestic shrines rather than a place to kick off their *caligae* and relax after a hard day at the Forum (the public baths served that role—the ancient Italians behaved much like the modern ones, who do everything in groups of ten and can't bear being alone); at home they used as many mosaics and wall paintings as they could afford to lend the place the necessary dignity. In Pompeii and Herculaneum, four styles of painting have been defined by art historians, although as you roam the ruins you'll find that they often overlap. Style I (2nd century BC) was heavily influenced by Hellenistic models, especially from Alexandria: walls are divided into three sections, often by bands of stucco, with a cornice and frieze along the top and square panels (dados) on the bottom, while the middle sections are skilfully painted to resemble rich marble slabs. The prediliction for deep colours, combined with the lack of windows, often makes these small rooms seem claustrophobic to us (see Herculaneum's Samnite House).

Later Romans must have felt the same lack of air and space, for about 90 BC they moved on to the 'architectonic' Style II. Columns and architraves were painted around the edges of the wall, an architectural screen designed to provide an illusion of depth and space on the large central panels. At first the centres were more pseudo-marble, but landscapes and mythological scenes soon became more popular. The Villa of the Mysteries near Pompeii is a prime example; it is also one of the oldest to have portraits of real people, or at least local character types.

Vitruvius, the celebrated writer on architecture, sternly disapproved of Style III, which abandoned the pretence and architectural dissimulation in favour of more playful compositions in perspective, still always done with a strict regard for symmetry. A favourite motif was patterns of foliage, fountains and candelabras, decorated with delicate, imaginative figures; these would be called 'grotesques' in the Renaissance, when Raphael and his friends rediscovered some in a Roman 'grotto' that was really a part of Nero's Golden House. The middle panels are often done in solid colours, with small scenes at the centre to resemble framed paintings. In Pompeii, examples include the Houses of Lucretius Fronto and the Priest Amandus, the latter done by a remarkable artist who comes close to scientific perspective, albeit with several vanishing points.

The last fashion to hit Pompeii before Vesuvius did, Style IV, combines the architectural elements of Style II and the framed picture effects of Style III, but with a greater degree of elaboration and decoration. Additional small scenes are placed on the sides—landscapes, still lifes, genre scenes from everyday life, and architectural *trompe l'oeil* windows done with a much more refined use of perspective (see the House of the Vettii). Sometimes an entire stage would be painted, with the curtain pulled aside to show a scene from a play; borders are decorated with flowers, satyrs, grotesques and frolicking Cupids (Italians call these *amoretti*). Humourous vignettes of the gods and incidents from Virgil's *Aeneid* were popular, along with images of Pompeii's divine patroness, Venus. She also inspired the subject matter of the frescoes you have to bribe the guards to see.

Around the Forum

Past the throng of hawkers and refreshment stands, the main entrance to the site takes you through the walls at the **Porta Marina**. Just inside the gate, the **Antiquarium** displays some of the artworks that haven't been spirited off to the Naples museum, as well as some truly gruesome casts of fossilized victims of the eruption, caught in their death poses.

Two blocks beyond the Antiquarium and you're in the **Forum**, oriented towards a view of Vesuvius. Unfortunately this is the worst-preserved part of town. Here you can see the tribune from which orators addressed public meetings, and the pedestals that held statues of heroes and civic benefactors, as well as the once-imposing **Basilica** (the law courts), temples to Apollo and Jupiter, and, among other buildings, a public latrine and a **Macellum**, or market, decorated with frescoes.

Down Mercury Street

Heading for Pompeii's old East End, there are several interesting houses along the Via di Mercurio, and the **Temple of Fortuna Augusta** on the corner of Via di Nola. The real attractions in this part of town, though, are a few lavish villas off on the side streets: the enormous **House of Pansa**; the **House of the Faun**, with the oldest-known welcome mat (set in the pavement, really); and the wonderful **House of the Vettii**, owned by a pair of wealthy brothers who were oil and wine merchants. Here are several rooms of excellent, well-preserved paintings of mythological scenes, but the guards will be whispering in your ear (if you are male) to show you the little niche off the entrance with the picture of Priapus. This over-endowed sport, in legend the son of Venus and Adonis, together with a couple of wall paintings along the lines of the Kamasutra, has managed to make Pompeii something more than a respectable tourist trap. There are quite a few paintings of Priapus showing it off in the houses of Pompeii, besides the phallic images that adorn bakers' ovens, wine shops, and almost every other establishment in town.

The Pompeiians would be terribly embarrassed, however, if they knew what you are thinking. They were a libidinous lot, like anyone else fortunate enough to live on the Campanian coast during recorded history, but the omnipresent phalluses were never meant as decoration. Almost always they are found close to the entrances, where their job was to ward off the evil eye. This use of phallic symbols against evil probably dates from the earliest times in southern Italy; the horn-shaped amulets that millions of people wear around their necks today are their direct descendants. Even so, not so long ago, women visiting Pompeii were not allowed to set eyes on the various erotic images around the site, and were obliged by the guides to wait chastely outside while their spouses or male companions went in for a peek.

The nearby Via di Nola, one of Pompeii's main streets, leads to the north. It passes the **Central Baths**, a new construction that was not yet completed when Vesuvius went off, and the **House of Marcus Fronto**, with more good paintings and a reconstructed roof.

The 'New Excavations'

Beginning in 1911, the archaeologists cleared a vast area of western Pompeii, around what was probably the most important thoroughfare of the city, now called the Via dell'Abbondanza. Three blocks west of the Forum, this street leads to the Via dei Teatri and the **Triangular Forum**, bordering the southern walls. Two **Theatres** here are worth a visit, a large open one seating 5000, and a smaller, covered one that was used for concerts.

The big quadrangle, originally a lobby for the theatres, seems to have been converted at one point into gladiators' barracks. This is only one of the disconcerting things you will find on the streets of Pompeii. The ruined temple in the Triangular Forum was already long ruined in AD 79, and scholars who study the art of the city find the last (fourth) period to betray a growing lack of skill and coarseness of spirit—altogether, there are plenty of clues that 1st-century Pompeii had its share of urban problems and cultural malaise.

The Via dell'Abbondanza

Next to the theatres, a small **Temple of Isis** testifies to the religious diversity of Pompeii; elsewhere around town there is graffiti satirizing that new and troublesome cult, the Christians. Three blocks north, there is a stretch of Via dell'Abbondanza that is one of the most fascinating corners of Pompeii. Among its shops are a smith's, a grocer's, a weaver's, a laundry, and a typical Roman tavern with its modest walk-up brothel. The most common are those with built-in tubs facing the street—shops that sold wine, and oil for cooking and for lamps. Notices painted on the walls announce coming games at the amphitheatre, or recommend candidates for public office.

Some of the best-decorated villas in this neighbourhood are to be found along the side streets: the **House of Loreius**, the **House of Amandus**, and an odd underground chamber called the **Cryptoporticus**. Pompeii's two most impressive structures occupy a corner just within the walls: the **Palaestra**, a big colonnaded exercise yard, and the **Amphitheatre**, the best-preserved in Italy, with seating for about 20,000. Tacitus records that a fight broke out here between the Pompeiians and rival supporters from Nocera in a match staged in AD 59. Nero exiled those responsible for the games and forbade further spectacles for ten years.

Not all of Pompeii's attractions are within the walls. If you have the time, it would be worth visiting the tombs around the **Via delle Tombe**. The Romans buried their dead outside their cities. The manner of burial naturally depended on wealth and status, but here you can see several of the more impressive funerary monuments to local dignitaries and their families.

Finally, the famous **Villa dei Misteri**, a surburban villa located close to the same road out of Pompeii, is thought to have been used as a place of initiation in the forbidden Bacchic (or Dionysiac) Mysteries, one of the cults most feared by the Roman Senate, and later by the emperors. Scenes from the myth of Dionysus and of the rituals themselves are painted on the walls.

Modern Pompei

The town of Pompei (the modern town has one 'i'), an important pilgrimage centre, is also worth a visit, if nothing else for a look at the wonderfully overdone church, dedicated to the **Madonna di Pompei** *(open daily, 6–2 and 3–6.30)*. For a good view over the town and the excavations take the lift up the tower *(open daily, 9–1 and 3–5; adm)*. The Madonna of the church holds a special place in the affections of Neapolitan women. You'll probably see some of them, busily saying their rosaries, asking for the Madonna's intercession to help sort out their problems. If they have bare feet, this is not poverty, but devotion—usually the fulfilment of a personal pledge to the Madonna in thanks for a favour received. Neapolitans who ask for the Madonna's help often promise to walk there barefoot from Naples (26km) if their prayers are answered.

It is only justice that Pompei should play host to the **Vesuvian Museum** on Via Colle San Bartolomeo *(open 8–2; closed Sun)*, a couple of minutes' walk from Piazza B. Longo in front of the the church. This has more than enough to satisfy most basic volcano questions: prints of the volcano erupting, exhibits on the various materials produced in eruptions and much more that is explosive, if you like that kind of thing.

On leaving Pompei the road leads to the beginning of the Sorrentine peninsula. At the foot of the peninsula lies **Castellammare di Stabia** which little suggests the beauty further on. Roman *Stabiae* was the port of Pompeii, and the other big town destroyed by Vesuvius. Most famously it was where Pliny the Elder, who was in command of the fleet at Misenum during the AD 79 eruption, met his death as he tried to bring help to those fleeing the catastrophe. The description of the eruption and these events are recorded for posterity in his nephew's letter to Tacitus. Here, beneath a 12th-century Hohenstaufen castle, are the modern shipyards of the Italian navy. From Castellammare, you can take a short ride in the cable car up to **Monte Faito**, a broad, heavily forested mountain that may well be the last really tranquil spot on the bay—though a few hotels have already appeared—and a pleasant place for walks.

Ercolano/Pompei © *(081–)* **Eating Out**

The proximity of the picturesque Sorrentine peninsula with its excellent selection of hotels between Vico Equense and Sorrento means you would be unwise to base yourself in this built-up semi-industrial area. Sorrento itself is only 40 minutes away on the Circumvesuviana in one direction. Naples is about the same in the other.

At Ercolano there are no on-site facilities apart from toilets. The **Bar degli Amorini** opposite the entrance has a deceptively small front but upstairs is a reasonable dining area if you are hunting for a snack or pizza. If you are spending the whole day in Pompeii (which is only too easy) there is a restaurant on site just beyond the ancient forum area through the Arch of Tiberius. The food from the self-service is nothing special, but if you wish to escape the crowds opt for the waiter service and sit out under the colonnade adjoining the ancient baths.

moderate

Otherwise, restaurants in modern Pompei have a captive market in visitors to the ruins, and it is true that some of them see the tourists as easy marks. You can choose for yourself among the ubiquitous multilingual menus, or try one of the following if you're in the mood for a treat. **Zi Caterina**, Via Roma 20, © 8507447, with live lobsters in the tank and other noteworthy seafood dishes, is also a good place to try Lacrima Cristi wine from the nearby slopes of Vesuvius. At **Al Gamberone**, Via Piave 36, © 8638322, close to Pompei's main church, you can feast on prawns doused in cognac and other good fish dishes. In summer you may dine outside under the lemon and oranges. If you do not want fish there is an array of other dishes including a good cannelloni. *Closed Fri.* Immediately outside the excavations' exit next to the amphitheatre is **Anfiteatro**, Via Plinio 9, © 8631245. Here the seafood is more modest—it's one of the few places in Pompei you'll see *baccalà*, salt cod, on the menu, along with truly good *spaghetti alle vongole. Closed Friday.*

Getting About

In addition to the modes of transport listed earlier (*see* pp.98–100), Sorrento is well connected in summer by ferries and hydrofoils which ply from the Marina Piccola to Capri, Amalfi, Positano and Naples. This is only an option during daylight hours since few crossings run later than 7.30pm. In winter only reduced services to Capri and Naples operate.

Caremar, ✆ 8073077, run five ferries daily to Capri and back that take 45 minutes. **Linea Jet**, ✆ 8781861, run hydrofoils to Capri eight times a day, lasting 20 minutes. **Alilauro**, ✆ 5522838, run eight hydrofoil crossings to Capri. In addition they offer a fast alternative to the Circumvesuviana to Naples, a hydrofoil service which takes only 30 minutes. These run to both Molo Beverello near the Castel Nuovo and to the berths at Mergellina. For the return trip to Sorrento it is important to check from which station the hydrofoil is leaving.

The same company operate four services daily to Positano which continue to Amalfi, as well as a single daily service from Sorrento to Ischia departing at 9.30am and returning at 5.20pm.

As Sorrento is so well connected by ferries, coach and the Circumvesuviana, car hire is hardly essential. **Avis** have an office on Viale Nizza 53, ✆ 8782459/ 8071143. Do not be tempted into hiring a moped. The small roads are always busy with tour coaches and natives impatient to pass ahead.

Tourist Information

There are tourist offices in Sorrento itself, at Via L. de Maio 35, 80067, ✆ (081) 8074033, ✉ 8773397, and in Vico Equense, at Via S. Ciro 16, 80069, ✆ (081) 8798826, ✉ 8799351. The Sorrento office is a little difficult to find. From Piazza Tasso walk towards the sea into Piazza S. Antonino. Their office is just off the road from here down to the ferry port (and signposted). They are very helpful if you have yet to find accommodation.

After Pompei, the coastline swings outwards to meet Capri. At first, there is little intimation that you are entering one of the most beautiful corners of all Italy. The first clue comes when the coast road begins to climb into a corniche at **Vico Equense**, a pretty village that is becoming a small resort, absorbing some of the overflow from Sorrento; there is a nice beach under the cliffs at the back of the town.

Sorrento began its career as a resort in the early 19th century, when Naples began to grow too piquant for English tastes. The English, especially, have never forsaken it; Sorrento's secret is a certain perfect cosiness, comfortable like old shoes. Visitors get the reassuring sense that nothing distressing is going to happen to them, and sure enough, nothing ever does. It helps that Sorrento is a lovely, civilized old town. Not many resorts can trace their ancestry back to the Etruscans, or claim a native son like the poet Torquato Tasso. (Today, the Sorrentines are more proud of a songwriter named De Curtio, whose *Come Back to Sorrento*, according to a local brochure, ranks with *O Sole Mio* as one of the 'two most familiar songs in the world'. There's a bust of him in front of the Circumvesuviana station.)

Sorrento doesn't flagrantly chase after your money, like many places in Italy, and it lacks the high-density garishness of, say, Rimini. If Sorrento has one big drawback, it is its lack of a decent beach—though at some of the fancier hotels you may enjoy taking a lift down to the sea. There are also several *stabilimenti*—piers jutting out into the sea, kitted out with loungers and beach umbrellas, for which you pay a hire charge. Sorrento is built on a long cliff that follows the shore. A narrow ravine cuts the town in half, between a suburban area of quiet, mostly expensive hotels around Via Correale, and the old town itself, which still preserves its grid of narrow Roman streets. There isn't much of artistic or historical interest; Sorrento was never a large town, though in the Middle Ages it was for a while an important trading post. The Sorrentini recall with pride that their fleet once beat Amalfi in a sea battle (897). Even today the population is only 15,000.

Sorrento comes alive at dusk. Its major draw is the pleasant walk through the old streets, the *passeggiata*, which goes on till late in the evening. The old town around the tiny Via San Cesareo draws Italians and visitors alike. The sizeable community of ex-pats call it 'The Drain'. Half the shop windows seem to be displaying *intarsia*—surprisingly fine pictures done in inlaid woods, a local craft for centuries. Look out too for the laboratories, open to the street, producing perfume and *limoncello*, the distinctive lemon liqueur made from the lemons grown throughout the peninsula.

In Piazza S. Francesco stands the church of the same name adjoining a small 14th-century arched cloister with arabesques. In summer there are frequent art exhibits (free) and impromptu concerts. Near by, the Public Gardens offers the classic Sorrentine view along the cliff tops, with the sea and Vesuvius in the distance. You can get down to the *stabilimenti* by taking the lift from here. If you are stuck on a rainy day, you can visit the **Correale Museum,** on Via Correale, a grab-bag of Neapolitan bric-a-brac, art and curiosities *(open Mon, Wed–Fri, 9.30–12.30, 3–5; Sat, Sun, 9.30–12.30; closed Tues; adm).*

Around Sorrento, as far as the mountains permit, stretches one of the great garden spots of Campania, a lush plain full of vines and lemon groves. Among the excursions that can be made from the town are the visit to the scanty ruins of the Roman **Villa di Pollio**, in a beautiful setting on the cape to the west, and the short trip to **Massa Lubrense**, an uncrowded fishing village with more fine views as far as Campanella Point, the tip of the peninsula, opposite the rugged outline of Capri. In the old days, a permanent watch was kept on Campanella Point, and it takes its name from the big bell that was hung here and rung to warn the towns around the bay when pirates were sighted.

Beyond Vico Equense to Sorrento you can easily find hotels of most categories in which to base yourself and launch your explorations into surrounding Campania, even if you are without a car. The excellent Circumvesuviana connects you to the entire Bay of Naples. The Amalfi coast is serviced by an efficient bus network linking Sorrento and Salerno. In Sorrento alone there are some 90 hotels competing for your attention, the best of which are converted villas by the sea—almost indecently elegant, even when they're a bit frayed about the edges.

very expensive

In Sorrento Sant'Angelo at the top of the list is the ★★★★★**Grand Hotel Cocumella**, Via Cocumella 7, ☎ 8782933, ✆ 8783712, set in its own park with a beautiful swimming pool and external terraces for dining. It has two restaurants, one of which is in a converted cloister. Rooms are furnished as you imagine Renaissance villas should be. Before 1822 the hotel was a Jesuit monastery. Its Roman cistern reputedly supplied Tiberius with water for his Capri villa. It even has a private boat, the *Vera*, for excursions to Capri and the Amalfi coast.

expensive

Sorrento isn't the status resort it once was, but it still seems to have more four-star places than anywhere in Italy; most of them are good bargains too, compared to equivalent spots in the north. The Manniello family chain offer good-value quality hotels, in particular at the ★★★★**Grand Hotel Ambasciatori**, Via Califano 18, ☎ 8782025, ✆ 8071021, a bit removed from the centre, but with a palatial interior, pool, sea-bathing platform and gardens overlooking the sea. In the same area they also own the beautifully remodelled ★★★★**Grand Hotel Royal**, ☎ 8073434, ✆ 8772905, also with a pool and beach access. Both hotels perch atop the the cliffs above the Riviera Massa, west of the old centre. Most rooms have good balconies, so opt for the the sea view. In a more central location, set in incredible tropical gardens on Via Vittorio Veneto, the ★★★★**Imperial Tramontana**, ☎ 8781940, ✆ 8072344, is one of the places long favoured by British travellers, as is evident from the club-like décor. There is an elevator down to the private beach, and also a pool. Another villa-hotel, just around the corner on Via Marina Grande, is the ★★★★**Bellevue-Syrene**, ☎ 8781024, ✆ 8783963. This one has lush gardens, beautifully restored rooms and a lift to the beach. The cliff-top colonnade is a lovely spot for a drink even if you are not staying at the hotel. Do not be put off by the pompous staff.

If you have a car, beyond Sorrento where the dark cliff rises above the town you can follow the coastal road past the Marina Grande, turning left up SS145 until you reach the ★★★★**President**, Via Nastro Verde, Colle Parise, ☎ 8782262, ✆ 8785411. It is set in its own park, with lovely views and a good-sized pool.

In Vico Equense, the best places are a little outside the town centre, notably the **★★★★Capo La Gala**, ✆ 8015758, 🖨 8798747 (*moderate*), on the beach at nearby Scrajo (where there are sulphur springs)—a beautiful modern resort hotel where every room has a private terrace overlooking the beach. There's plenty of sea, and a pool too, but note that full board is usually required.

moderate

Not all the hotels in Sorrento are luxury villas; one of the charms of the place is that it caters to every budget. A real bargain, in a villa with a private beach and a good restaurant, is the **★★Pensione La Tonnarella**, Via Capo 31, ✆ 8781153, 🖨 8782169; it's advisable to make reservations here early. Another *pensione* with lovely sea views is the **★★Loreley et Londres**, Via Califano 2, ✆ 8073187. The high rooms with white walls, old wooden beds and chests of drawers, and long white cotton curtains that billow in the draughts make this the choice for romantics. In summer you must stay on half-board if you want one of the lovely rooms overlooking the sea. There is also a lift down to a private sea-bathing platform.

On the road east out of Sorrento the **★★★Minerva**, Via Capo 30, ✆ 8781011, 🖨 8781949, has 50 nice rooms, some with stunning views over the sea. *Closed Nov–Mar.*

inexpensive

There are several simple hotels around the town centre, of which the **★City**, Corso d'Italia 217, ✆ 877221, 🖨 8772210, is one of the nicest, close to the centre but not too noisy. The **★Nice**, Corso Italia 257, ✆ 8072530, 🖨 8071154, on the corner of the main road just in front of the Circumvesuviana station, is also a surprisingly good find, again close to the centre. Rooms are clean and have small but good bathrooms. They will give you a key if you plan to stay out late in the bars and clubs or return from Naples on the last train.

Sorrento ✆ (081–)

Eating Out

expensive

At Nerano, on the road from Sorrento to Massa Lubrense, **Da Pappone**, ✆ 8081209, specializes in fish fresh out of the sea, and elaborate (but pricey!) antipasto surprises.

Sorrento has every kind of restaurant, including the grand and gloriously decorated **O' Parrucchiano**, Corso Italia 67, ✆ 8781321, by tradition one of Italy's best, with a choice of anything you could imagine. If you are celebrating a social occasion, though, or just in the mood for a very unusual experience, the place to go nowadays is **Don Alfonso**, Piazza Sant'Agata, ✆ 8780026 (*very expensive*), in Sant'Agata sui Due Golfi, a Michelin-starred restaurant that some food critics reckon to be the best in southern Italy. Food here is an art form, beautifully cooked, and presented on fine china with wine served in delicate crystal glasses. The restaurant, run by husband-and-wife team Alfonso and Livia Iaccarino, is actually 9km outside Sorrento, but the trip is well worth it (*Sept–May closed Sun evenings and all year Mon*).

moderate/inexpensive

New in Sorrento is **Il Buco**, Il Rampe Marina Piccola 5, ✆ 8782354 (*moderate*), off Piazza S. Antonino in an underground cantina where the fresh pasta and excellent meat dishes also complement delectable seafood. *Open 7pm–1am; closed Sun*. For one of the best deals in town, try the **Trattoria da Emilia**, Via Marina Grande 62, ✆ 8781489, a family-run trattoria with tables on a terrace overlooking the sea, and an excellent-value fixed menu based on fresh local ingredients and classic Sorrento recipes. Up a side road parallel to Corso Italia, near the cathedral, **Gatto Nero**, Via S.M. della Pieta, ✆ 8781582, is a homely, pretty trattoria with checked table cloths. You need a good couple of hours here since the owner, Miniero Maria, takes pride in individually overseeing each guest. There's a good range of pasta, meat and fish. The *spaghetti alle vongole* is superb and so is the *mozzarella in carozza*. The prices are a treat too. *Closed Mon*.

bars and ice cream

There is no shortage of variety in Sorrento as far as bars are concerned, like the honestly named **Boozer Pub**, Via P.R Giuliani 65, ✆ 8783617, with light dinners, English beer and music. The place to be seen, though, is most definitely the **Fauno Bar**, Piazza Tasso 1, ✆ 8781021, where you can watch young and old alike gather in the piazza in the evening.

In a land where ice cream is culture you can hardly go wrong, but **Davide**, Via P.R. Giuliani 39, ✆ 8781337, is exceptional. At least fifty flavours are on offer at any one time, usually supplemented by others from yet another fifty-long list 'elaborated in about 40 years of ice cream tradition'!

Capri

The Islands of the Bay of Naples

Without a doubt, the islands in the Bay of Naples—Capri, Ischia, and to a far lesser extent Procida—are the holiday queens of the Italian islands. Every schoolchild has heard of Capri, made so notorious by the antics of Emperor Tiberius and Norman Douglas' 'gentlemanly freaks'.

Ischia, fifty years ago, was the favourite island of jet-setters jaded by Capri. Renowned in ancient times for its mud baths, it has become a home-from-home for the German bourgeoisie. If anyone tries to tell you it's still 'unspoiled', take this into consideration: Ischia is Italy's biggest buyer of spaghetti-flavoured ice cream. Still, the smart set can't get there fast enough; both Ischia and Capri are connected to Naples' Capodichino Airport by helicopter.

Procida, on the other hand, has hardly been developed at all, though not through any lack of charm. For many Italians, the very name of the island conjures up the same associations that Alcatraz does for Americans, which has managed to keep the developers away until very recently.

Despite their location, the three islands are of very different geological origins. Ischia and Procida are a part of the enormous submerged volcano of Campano, which stretches from Ventotene in the Pontine Islands down to Strómboli and the Aeolian Islands. In not too ancient times, the two islands were connected to each other and, if the Greek geographer Strabo is to be believed, also to the Phlegraean Fields on the mainland. Phlegraean means 'fiery' in Greek, and Strabo records how, during an eruption of the now dormant volcano Epomeo on Ischia, an earthquake split Ischia–Procida from the mainland, then, in another upheaval, jolted the once united island in twain. In this same geological cataclysm, Capri broke off from the Sorrentine peninsula, a blow that shattered its coasts to form the island's famous cliffs.

Getting There

In summer, there are as many as six ferries and 20 hydrofoils a day from Naples to Capri, and as many to Ischia. There are also regular departures to Procida. In addition, there are a frequent ferries and hydrofoils daily from Sorrento to Capri, from Pozzuoli to Procida and between the islands of Ischia and Procida. All are very short rides. For more information on long-distance ferry services from Naples, *see* pp.8 and 66.

Local and longer-distance ferries and hydrofoils from Naples leave from three different points along the harbourside—**Molo Beverello** and the **Stazione Marittima**, both in the centre of the port, and **Mergellina**, further to the west. Be sure to check you know the right dock for your ticket and destination. Listed here are the principal ferry and hydrofoil operators; check with them for timetables, or look in the daily newspaper *Il Mattino*.

From **Molo Beverello**: **Caremar** (ferries and hydrofoils), ✆ 5513882, for Capri, Ischia and Procida; **Navigazione Libera del Golfo** (hydrofoils), ✆ 5527209, for Capri; **Linee Lauro** (ferries and hydrofoils), ✆ 5513236, for Ischia; and **Alilauro** (hydrofoils), ✆ 5522838, for Sorrento and Capri.

From the **Stazione Marittima**: **Tirrenia** (ferries), ✆ 7201111, for Palermo and Cagliari; **Siremar** (ferries), ✆ 7201595, for the Aeolian Islands and Milazzo; and **Ustica Lines** (hydrofoils), ✆ 7612565, for the Egadi Islands and Trapani, Sicily.

From **Mergellina** (hydrofoils only): **Alilauro**, ✆ 7611004, for Ischia (Forio) and Sorrento; and **SNAV**, ✆ 7612348, for Capri, Ischia (Casamicciola), Procida, and the Aeolian Islands.

In addition, from Salerno there is a boat called the *Faraglione* that offers a different way of seeing the Amalfi coast, a daily ferry that hugs the shore to Capri, stopping at Amalfi and Positano along the way. It leaves Salerno at 7.30pm each day from Molo Manfredi, at the western end of town, and does not run between 15 October and 6 January.

Capri

Capri is pure enchantment, and can lay fair claim to being the most beautiful island in the Mediterranean; it is also the most overrun and exploited to the hilt. With more than 800 species of plant, it is very much a garden perched on a rugged chunk of limestone. Unlike Ischia and other, more recent, tourist haunts, Capri has the relaxed air of having seen it all. No room remains for property speculators. Everything has been built and planted; the tourists come and go every day and night, and they seem to be invisible to the Capriots and other residents who have learned to turn a blind eye to them, since the space they occupy will be filled next day by other anonymous camera-clutching tourists. Between June and September you begin to understand why the word 'trash' is inscribed on the bins in 30 different languages. However, if you don't mind all the trendy shops being closed, try going in November or February, when you may be lucky to arrive for a few brilliant days between the rains, and have this Garden of Eden practically to yourself. It's worth the risk of a soaking or two.

There are various schools of thought on the etymology of the island's name. The belief that it came from the Latin word for goat (*capra*) is now in disfavour; those who think it derived from the Greek *kapros* (boar) have fossils to back them up. Yet another group maintains that it comes from an ancient Tyrrhenian (Etruscan) word meaning 'rocky' (*capr—*) as evidenced by the many other places that begin with this suffix, such as Caprera (an island off Sardinia), Cabrera (off Majorca) and Caprara in the Tremiti Islands, to name just a few. It is the first syllable that is emphasized in the pronunciation of Capri—CAPri, not CapRI, like the Ford.

History

Some time in the Quaternary period Capri broke away from the Sorrentine peninsula, taking with it elephants and tigers, as we have learnt from the remains discovered by Ignazio Cerio at the beginning of this century. Other finds have dated the first inhabitants back to the Palaeolithic era. A strong tradition associates the island with the sirens of the *Odyssey*, and with the mysterious Teleboeans from the Greek island of Kephalonia, led by their king Telon. Neolithic ceramic-ware decorated with red bands, first found on the island, has since been designated the 'Capri style'.

Little is known of Capri at the time when Augustus arrived, except that it was still very Greek and that a dying ilex (holm oak) suddenly revived and sprouted new leaves. The emperor thought this was a good portent, and he traded Ischia to Naples for Capri and made the island one of his retreats. Life must have been good on Capri; at one point Augustus called it *Apragopolis*, or 'Lubberland', as Robert Graves translates Suetonius' 'land of layabouts'.

Augustus was succeeded by his stepson Tiberius, whose exploits reported by the same Suetonius gave Capri much of its early notoriety. The Roman writer turned the island into a dirty old man's dream come true, with Tiberius hurling his victims off the cliffs to add a touch of reality. Although scholars have now discredited much of Suetonius' yellow journalism, that imaginative writer's images of sexual acrobats dressing up as nymphs and frolicking in Tiberius' gardens, along with the anthropophagous Sirens singing seductive songs on the seashore, have permeated the Capri legends.

In reality, Tiberius made Capri the capital of the Roman Empire between AD 27 and 37. The sheer cliffs made it into a natural citadel, from where the ageing emperor could conduct (or neglect) the affairs of state as he pleased. Here he nurtured the future Emperor Caligula.

After the death of Tiberius, Capri is occasionally mentioned as a place of exile. Then the Benedictine friars arrived and built chapels on the island, and of course it suffered the usual ravages of Saracens and pirates. In 1371 a Carthusian monastery (La Certosa) was founded on Capri, on land granted by the Angevins, whom the Capriots favoured over the Aragonese until 1442 when they rather capriciously changed sides. A plague in 1656 left the island all but abandoned; only the Carthusians stayed behind, safe inside the walls of La Certosa, picking up the titles to land that had no owners and becoming quite wealthy (and unpopular) in the process.

In 1806, Hudson Lowe was commander of the English garrison on Capri. The life of Napoleon was full of strange coincidences. Lowe, for example, was quartered in Napoleon's house in Ajaccio when the English occupied Corsica, and he later became Napoleon's jailer on St Helena. He took his job on Capri seriously indeed, fortifying the island until it became 'a little Gibraltar', but for all that still managed to lose it to the French in 1808—a 'discreditable Lowe business' according to Norman Douglas, longtime resident and writer on things Capricious.

The last chapter of the island's history began with the 'discovery' of the Blue Grotto by a German artist called Kopisch in 1826; he swam into it 'by accident'. Perhaps it was just a coincidence that Kopisch's discovery followed the landslide that had covered the entrance of another, even lovelier cave. Anyway, the magic of the name, Blue Grotto of Capri, proved irresistible, and the Capriots converted their fishing boats into excursion boats to take tourists to the cave while farmers sold their land and built hotels.

Arriving in Marina Grande, you can ascend to either Capri or Anacapri by **bus**. They run every 15 minutes 8am–10pm, and every half-hour 10pm–midnight, daily. There is also a **funicular** that runs up to Capri town every 15 minutes 6.30am–12.30am, in summer (and until 9pm, Oct–April). The **chairlift** from Anacapri to Monte Solaro (a 12-minute ride) runs continuously from 9.30am to sunset in summer (and 10.30am–3pm, Nov–Feb, closed Tues). Buses run from Capri town to Anacapri, Marina Piccola and Damecuta. There are also buses from Anacapri to the Blue Grotto, Faro and Marina Piccola. From June until September, there are daily **tours** of Capri by motor launch, which leave from Marina Grande, beginning at 9am. Otherwise you can walk to most places. Indeed the series of beautiful trails across the island's hills is one of its major attractions though you would be wise to pack a mack out of season.

The island has tourist offices in Capri town, at Piazza Umberto 1, 80073, ✆ (081) 8370686, Marina Grande, at Banchina del Porto, ✆ (081) 8370634, and in Anacapri, at Via G. Orlandi 59/a, 80071, ✆ (089) 8371524. The tourist office in Marina Grande will help to find accommodation. Maps of the island are available from all the offices for L1000.

Marina Grande and the Grotta Azzurra

All the ferries and hydrofoils from the mainland call at **Marina Grande** (most pleasure boats anchor in the Marina Piccola on the other side of the island). Here, Capri's dependence on tourism is at its most evident. Marina Grande is little more than a commercialized station platform, but as such does its best to get you off to your destination: the *funicolare* (cable railway) will lift you to the town of Capri every 15 minutes, buses will wind you up to Anacapri, glorious old bath-tub convertible taxis hope to trundle you off to your hotel, boats for the Grotta Azzurra and other excursions around the island bob up and down at their landings. If you wish, a genuine yellow submarine will take you for underwater sightseeing around the island.

The **Blue Grotto** is well named if nothing else—its shimmering, iridescent blueness is caused by the reflection of light on the water in the morning. Similar caverns are fairly common in the Mediterranean, but Capri's is the yardstick by which they are measured. In summer (*1 June–30 Sept*), boats for the Blue Grotto leave at 9am—when the sea is calm. The entrance to the cave is quite low, and if there's any swell on the sea at all someone is sure to get a nasty knock on the head.

The **sea excursion around the island** is a rare experience, but again possible only in good weather. Besides visiting other lovely grottoes, such as the **Grotta Bianca** and the **Grotta Verde** (the White Cave and the Green Cave), it provides breathtaking views of the cliffs and Capri's uncanny rock formations.

Capri Town

Haunted by the smiling shade of Gracie Fields, the charming white town of Capri is daily worn down by the tread of thousands of her less ectoplasmic followers. The **megalithic walls** supporting some of the houses have seen at least 3000 years of similar comings and goings, although certainly on a much smaller scale than what you'll find here in August. Its architecture complements the island's natural beauty—much of what is typical and 'home-made' in Mediterranean architecture can be seen here in the older quarters: the moulded arches and domes, the narrow streets and stairways crossed by buttresses supporting the buildings, the ubiquitous whitewash, the play of light and shadow, and sudden little squares, just large enough for a few children to improvise a game of football. Most of the island's hotels are scattered throughout the town, generally very tasteful and surrounded by gardens. The supreme example is the famous Quisisana, a hotel whose register over the years is like a veritable *Who's Who* of the famous and pampered.

If you go up to Capri by *funicolare*, you'll surface right next to the Piazza Umberto and the much photographed **cathedral**, with its joyful campanile and clock. Built in the 17th century in the local Baroque style, the cathedral has a charming buttressed roof. In a little square in the church's shadow, known as **La Piazzetta**, are the outdoor cafés frequented by such a variety of past eccentrics, dilettantes and celebrities that each chair should have a historical plaque on it. The other side of the piazza is a sheer drop down to Marina Grande.

Walks from the Town

For the post office and for buses to Anacapri, take the Via Roma from the piazza; for the exclusive boutiques, head towards the Via Vittoria Emanuele to Via Camarelle and Via Tragara. The latter street eventually leads to the **Faraglioni**, the three enormous sheer-sided limestone pinnacles towering straight up in the ever blue-green sea. These rocks are home to the rare blue lizard (*Lacerta caerulea Faraglionensis*) and a rare species of seagull that supposedly guffaws. From Via Tragara a stairway descends to the point and the **Porto di Tragara**, where you can take a swim from the platforms beneath the vertical rocks.

Nearby is the **Tragara Terrace**, with magnifient views, and the tall skinny rock called **Pizzolungo**. Still following the main track along the coast and up the stairway, you will come upon the **Grotta di Matromania** (*always open*). The Romans worshipped the goddess Cybele, or *Mater Magna*, in this cave. Part of Capri's reputation as an island of orgies may derive from this ancient eastern cult's noisy hypnotic rituals, which culminated rather abruptly with the self-castration of the priest-for-a-day. Only vestiges now remain of the once elaborate decor inside the cave.

From the Grotta di Matromania a stepped path leads down to yet another famous eroded rock: the **Arco Naturale**, where dark pines—as everywhere else on Capri—cling to every tiny ledge they can sink their roots into. On the way back to town you'll pass some of the island's vineyards that produce the rare and famous *Lacrimae Tiberii*, and, in the Piazza Cerio next to the cathedral, the **Centro Caprense Ignazio Cerio**, with fossils and archaeological finds from Capri *(open Mon–Fri, 10–12)*. Ignazio Cerio was not the first person on the island to take an interest in such things. Emperor Augustus had founded a museum for the 'weapons of ancient heroes' and the collection of what he called his old 'Big Bones', then popularly believed to be the remains of monsters.

The Old Goat of Capri

London has its tabloids, and ancient Rome had Gaius Suetonius Tranquillus, born *c.* AD 60. All of Suetonius's other books are lost, including such titles as the *Lives of Famous Whores* and the *Physical Defects of Mankind*, but enough copies of his celebrated scandalmongering classic, *The Twelve Caesars*, were written out to ensure that the whole juicy text has survived. Modern historians have always argued over Suetonius's reliability, but the nature of his subjects has been confirmed by enough other sources to suggest that Suetonius couldn't have exaggerated that much. And his book was written with full access to the imperial archives; the author was chief secretary to Emperor Trajan.

One of the most entertaining chapters deals with the man who put Capri on the map, the Emperor Tiberius, adopted son of Augustus. A good general and, at first, a capable ruler, Tiberius had an unusual habit of declining honours and titles. Suetonius hints that the Emperor knew, or suspected that he would eventually go a bit mad, and wanted no pointless flattery left behind for his enemies to mock later. Mad or not, Tiberius did have a mania for privacy. He left Rome in AD 26 for Capri, which he admired for its beauty and for the fact that it had only one landing port, and he never went back to the capital again. The entire island became his pleasure garden, and while imperial decrees went out prohibiting 'promiscuous kissing' and ordering a clampdown on loose women, the Emperor himself was whooping it up. According to Suetonius:

> Bevies of young girls and men, whom he had collected from all over the Empire as adepts in unnatural practices, and known as spintriae, would perform before him in groups of three, to excite his waning passions. A number of small rooms were furnished with the most indecent pictures and statuary imaginable, also certain erotic manuals from Elephantis in Egypt; the inmates of the establishment would know from these exactly what was expected of them.

Once aroused, apparently, the imperial pervert would bore in on anything that caught his fancy, and the smaller the better. Suetonius pictures him rushing through a religious sacrifice to get at the little boy who was carrying the incense casket, and training other little boys, his 'minnows', to 'chase him while he went swimming and get between his legs to lick and and nibble him...such a filthy old man he had become!' Even Suetonius is shocked. Distracted by such pleasures, Tiberius let the Empire go to pot; the Persians invaded from the east, while Germanic bands roamed unchecked in Gaul. The generals and the civil service managed to see that no serious harm was done, but they could not stop the ageing Tiberius, in his island isolation, from turning into a murderous paranoid, torturing and killing anyone who opposed him, or seemed to. Suetonius names all the names and tells all the tales; nobody was ever better at capturing the essential vileness of imperial Rome.

One of the stories related of Tiberius' time on Capri by Suetonius is that of a fisherman who decided to surprise Tiberius, bringing him the gift of an enormous mullet. Tiberius was so scared that he ordered his guards to rub the poor man's face raw with it. In agony the fisherman shrieked, 'Thank Heavens I didn't bring that huge crab I caught!' Tiberius sent for the crab and had it used the same way.

La Certosa and Gardens of Augustus

A shorter but equally enjoyable walk starting from the Piazza Umberto (take Via Vittorio Emanuele, which becomes Via F. Serena, then Via Matteotti) leads you to **La Certosa** (*open daily, 9–2; closed Mon*), the Carthusian charterhouse founded in 1371 by Giacomo Arcucci (a member of a famous Capri family) and suppressed in 1808. Built over one of Tiberius' villas and topped by a Baroque tower added in the 17th century, the golden-hued church and cloisters are very pleasing, with a collection of paintings from the 17th to 19th centuries.

A few minutes away from La Certosa are the **Gardens of Augustus**, founded by Caesar himself. A wide variety of trees and plants grow on the fertile terraces and belvederes over-looking one of the most striking views in the world. A narrow road (Via Krupp, built by the arms manufacturer, who spent his leisure hours studying lamprey larvae off the Salto di Tiberio) takes you down the cliffs in a hundred hairpin turns to the **Marina Piccola**, the charming little port with most of Capri's bathing establishments—Da Maria, La Canzione del Mare, Le Sirene and Internazionale (all but the last connected to restaurants). On one side are the ruins of a Saracen tower; on the other is the **Scoglio delle Sirene** (Sirens' Rock); if you read the books of Norman Douglas and Edwin Cerio, son of Ignazio Cerio the archaeologist, they will convince you that this really was the home of the Sirens. There is a bus, fortunately, that makes the steep climb back up the cliffs to Capri town.

A much longer but equally rewarding walk (Via Botteghe to Via Tiberio) is to the **Villa Jovis** (*open 9am–one hour before sunset; adm*) passing the church of **Monte San Michele**, a fine example of local architecture, built in the 14th century. The Villa Jovis on Punta Lo Capo (310m) was the most important of the twelve villas on Capri: from here Tiberius governed the Roman Empire for his last ten years. Although much has been sacked through the centuries, the extent of the remaining walls and foundations gives a fair idea of the grandeur of the former imperial palace. The centre of the villa was occupied by vast cisterns for supplying the private baths of the villa. Close by, the **Faro**, or light-house, was believed to have been part of a system for sending messages to the mainland. The great sheer cliff beside the villa, the **Salto di Tiberio**, is always pointed out as the precipice from which the emperor hurled his victims. It had already become a tourist attraction in Suetonius' day. Certainly the view of both the Bay of Salerno and Naples is as spectacular as any.

Towards Anacapri

On the north coast between Capri and Anacapri, the only other town of the island, are the so-called **Baths of Tiberius** and the meagre remains of Augustus' sea palace, the **Palazzo a Mare**. You can swim here at the establishment of Bagni di Tiberio. Above here, carved into the escarpment of Anacapri, is the **Scala Fenicia**, in truth Greco-Roman in origin and for thousands of years the only way to reach the upper part of the island. Originally 800 in number, these steps have crumbled over the years and are impassable today. Near here, on the road from Marina Grande to Anacapri, lies the first Christian church on the island, dedicated to patron saint **San Costanzo**. According to legend Costanzo was a bishop of Constantinople whose body, packed in a barrel, floated to Capri during the Iconoclasm in Greece. A church, with a reputation for defending the island from Saracens, was built for him over one of the Roman villas. Four ancient columns support the Byzantine dome of this 11th-century church, designed in the form of a Greek cross.

Anacapri

On top of the green plateau spreads the town of Anacapri, once a fierce rival to Capri below, but since the building of the roads connecting them in 1874, the two towns have learned to reconcile their differences. Although it has its share of hotels, Anacapri retains a rustic air, with its many olive trees and vineyards surrounding it on all sides, and its simple style of architecture, rather Moorish in style with cubic, flat-roofed houses.

In Anacapri's Piazza San Nicola, the 18th-century church of **San Michele** *(open April–Oct, 9–7; Nov–Mar, 10–3)* contains a magnificent mosaic floor of majolica tiles, by the Abruzzese artist Leonardo Chiaiese. The design itself, showing Adam and Eve in the Garden of Eden, and their expulsion, is by D. A. Vaccano. The church of **Santa Sofia** very near it, on the Piazza Diaz, was built in the Middle Ages, but later Baroqued.

From Piazza Vittoria a chairlift travels to the summit of **Monte Solaro**, the highest point on the island at 585m. Also from Piazza Vittoria, take Via Orlandi to Via Capodimonte and the **Villa San Michele** of Axel Munthe (1857–1949), one of the greatest physicians of his day, and a leader in the field of psychiatry. Extremely generous, donating his services to the victims of plagues, earthquakes and World War I, he also found time to establish bird sanctuaries on Capri and elsewhere; in 1929 he wrote his best-selling autobiography *The Story of San Michele* to which his villa owes most of its fame. The house contains Roman artefacts discovered on Capri *(open daily, 9am until sunset; adm)*. Near here is the so-called **Castello di Barbarossa**, after the pirate captain who plagued the Mediterranean for so many years. These ruins date from the 8th and 9th centuries. Via Capodimonte continues through the valley of **Santa Maria a Cetrella**, another white church of local design. From the church the road goes to the top of Monte Solaro.

Another path from Piazza Vittoria (Via Caposcuro to Via Maigliara) skirts Monte Solaro, passing through the vineyards to the **Belvedere della Migliara**, from where you can see the Faraglioni and the entrance of the **Green Grotto**. A bus leaves Anacapri every hour in the summer for Punta Carena and its lighthouse at the southernmost tip of the island. The unusual arched doorways on the left belonged to the **Torre di Materita**; further on, overlooking the **Cala del Tombosiello**, is a ruined watchtower. **Punta Carena** is the most out-of-the-way place on the island for a quiet swim.

Another bus leaves from the piazza for the Grotta Azzurra and the bathing area adjacent to it, passing by way of the old windmill and the **Villa Imperiale**, another of the summer residences built by Augustus, known also as the 'Damecuta', from the tower next to it. After the Villa Jovis, this villa is the best preserved, and has recently been further excavated *(open from 9am until one hour before sunset; closed Mon)*.

Capri ☏ (081–)   **Where to Stay**

As one might expect, hotel prices on Capri are well above average for the surrounding area on-shore, and rooms for the summer months are often booked up months in advance. When looking for a Hotel on Capri, there are certain factors to consider. Exclusivity, space, a central position, the view and the extent of facilities available count for most here.

very expensive

If money is no object, the ★★★★★**Grand Hotel Quisisana**, Via Camerelle 2, ☏ 8370788, 🖷 8376080, is the place to stay in Capri town, a luxurious palace of a hotel set in its own grounds and equipped with pool, gym, tennis courts and just about everything else needed for a smart holiday on the island. The building was originally a sanatorium built by an Englishman, George Clark. With acres of white tiled floors, plush white sofas and lamps born by carved ebony figures, it is not merely the luxury but the sheer size that impresses (especially on an island where space is at a premium). For more of the same but with the focus on privacy ★★★★**La Scalinatella**, Via Tragara 8, ☏ 8370633, 🖷 8378291, is a jewel of a hotel, with 31 beautifully decorated rooms and stunning views. There is a pool and good restaurant but there are no large public areas, nor does the hotel take tour groups. Outside Capri town at Punta Tragara, the ★★★★**Hotel Punta Tragara**, Via Tragara 57, ☏ 8370844, 🖷 8377790, is a de luxe resort hotel, offering pool, gym, restaurants and more in a building designed by Le Corbusier. The architect's distinctive modern style and the predominance of strong reds, oranges and dark wood fittings come at a price but then the views from the rooms are spectacular.

expensive

★★★★**La Palma**, Via V. Emanuele, ☏ 8370133, 🖷 8376966, is good value by Capri standards. Just above the Quisisana in Capri town, it is set in its own gardens, with lovely majolica-tiled floors in the rooms and a pleasant airy feel. Established as a hotel in 1822, it's older than the Quisisana; the staff are charming and the whole atmosphere more comfortable than many of the more expensive hotels. Further up on the way to the panoramic Punta Tragara, the ★★★★**Villa Brunella**, Via Tragara 24, ☏ 8370122, 🖷 8370430, is a pretty hotel with rooms on terraces that overlook Monte Solaro. There is a good restaurant and pool for lazing away hot afternoons. The emphasis is on villa-style accommodation and privacy, suiting those who are looking for a retreat. Open all year round, the

★★★**Floridiana**, Via Campo di Teste, ✆ 8370101, ✉ 8370434, in Capri town, also has fine panoramas of the sea. Below the Quisisana and thus a little outside the limelight, the management are upgrading many of its rooms in unashamed pursuit of another star from the tourist board. Until prices go up this is a fair value hotel. Single travellers do not pay outrageous supplements, but merely half the cost of a double room. The views will be temporarily marred until they have finished turning a dark mud work into a new and pristine pool (scheduled for the summer of '97).

moderate

Book well ahead if you want to stay at the ★★**Villa Krupp**, Viale Matteotti 12, ✆ 8370362, ✉ 8376489, one of the loveliest, and most historic, lower-priced hotels in Capri. Situated above the path up to the Gardens of Augustus, the hotel has enviable views, antique furniture and a relaxed, welcoming ambience where one can sit and compose letters all day. Trotsky stayed here and even left a samovar.

inexpensive

Clean and well-run, the centrally located ★**Stella Maris**, Via Roma 10–19, ✆ 8370452, ✉ 8378662, close to the bus station, is a cosy family-run affair. They have been here for generations and are proud of their hospitality, so you will not want for towels. Most rooms are en suite and look down to the Marina Grande below and distant Ischia. ★**La Tosca**, Via D. Birago, ✆ and ✉ 8370989, still in Capri town but overlooking the opposite coast, has just reopened with new management. The owner is married to an American woman and together they hope to bring new life to the decent but no-frills establishment. Rooms are clean, tiled and with high ceilings. Ask for those with the view.

Capri ✆ *(081–)*

Eating Out
expensive

Capri's best restaurant has long been **La Capannina**, Via delle Botteghe 12–14, ✆ 8370732, set in a secluded garden in Capri town, with delicately prepared shellfish, pasta and fish, and good desserts. A close rival is a relative newcomer, **Al Geranio**, Viale Matteotti 8, ✆ 8370616, just above the path to the Gardens of Augustus, where the chef has a magic touch with fish, in particular. Tables overlook the classic Capri panorama from a terrace ideal for lounging away the afternoon. If you need an excuse this is a good place for tasting the *torta di Capri*, an island speciality, best with an espresso. **I Faraglioni**, Via Camerelle 75, ✆ 8370320, has delectable house specialities like *crêpes al formaggio*, paper-thin pancakes filled with cheese, and *risotto ai frutti di mare*, risotto with all sorts of shellfish.

moderate

On the way down from Capri town to Marina Grande at **Da Paolino**, on Via Palazzo a Mare 11, ✆ 8376102, you'll eat in an arbour of lemon trees, tasting dishes mainly inspired by the fruit—as in the pasta, fish and dessert courses, all heavily lemon-influenced. Up the stairs past the cathedral and down the tunnel to the right in Capri town, is another island institution, **Da Gemma**, Via Madre Serafina, ℂ 8370461. It's as nice in winter as it is in summer, a welcoming trattoria with walls decked with brass pans and ceramic plates, and superbly cooked local dishes including a fine *risotto alle pescatore* and a delicious mozzarella grilled on a lemon leaf. It also serves very good pizza.

In Anacapri about a half-hour's walk from the Piazzetta, **Da Gelsomina la Migliara**, on Via La Migliara 72, ℂ 8371499, offers not only home-made wine, but true home-cooked island specialities, including mushrooms collected on Monte Solaro. The risotto here is a real treat in all its forms.

Ischia

Ischia is a remarkably lovely island, able to hold its own even with Capri. The sea of vineyards encircling the island's highest peak, volcanic Monte Epomeo (793m), produces the excellent wine named after the mountain, and the villages high on its slopes, like Fontana and Buonapane, remain untouched by the international onslaught of tourists at the resorts of Casamicciola, Forio, Lacco Ameno and Ischia town.

Unlike Capri, Ischia has many long, first-class beaches, on one of which, Maronti, the volcanic nature of the island is very evident. The hot mineral springs that gush all year round have attracted cure-seekers since Roman times, and are still recommended today for people suffering from rheumatism, arthritis, neuralgia and obesity. Because many of the springs are radioactive, a doctor's permission is often required before you take a soak (there are physicians on the island who specialize in prescribing such treatments, and they charge a pretty penny). The hottest spring on the island is Terme Rita, at Casamicciola, which belches from the earth at around 180°F. For a lark, try the Terme Comunali at the port, or the unique baths at Cavascura above Sant'Angelo.

History

Inhabited by 2000 BC, Ischia became an important stop along one of the earliest trade routes in the Mediterranean, from Mycenean Greece to the Etruscans of northern Italy and the mineral wealth of Elba. The prevailing currents and winds made it natural for the Greek ships sailing west to circumvent Sicily and land in the Bay of Naples—as did that most famous sailor, Odysseus himself. As an island along the sea lane, Ischia was the perfect place to found an outpost to secure the route and trade, and here in 756 BC Chalcidians and Eretrians from the Greek island of Euboea settled the first Greek colony in western Europe.

They called the island *Pithekoussai*, referring to its abundant pottery clay (*pithos*). However, when Montagnone (a now-extinct volcano on Ischia) erupted, the colonists fled to the mainland, establishing themselves at Cumae, where they prospered. Roman writers later refer to the island as *Eneria*, deriving from Aeneas' supposed stop on the island to repair his ships, or *Inarime*, a name of unknown origin. The name Ischia is believed to be a corruption of *insula*, or just plain island.

In the year AD 6, Augustus traded the larger, more fertile island of Ischia for Capri, which then belonged to Naples. For most of its history Ischia and its famous castle remained attached to that great city, sheltering many of its nobles from political adversity; but during one period, in the early 16th century, the island outshone Naples as a cultural centre. This was due to one woman, Vittoria Colonna, who lived much of her childhood in the castle of Ischia, when her father's estates were confiscated by Pope Alexander VI. She was betrothed in the castle at the age of 6 to another leading personage of the era, Francesco Ferrante, nephew of Constanza d'Avolas, the duchess who ruled Ischia for 50 years. On 27 December 1509, Vittoria and Francesco were married at the castle of Ischia in the celebrity wedding of the decade, but two years later Francesco was drawn away by the wars in the north and only once returned to Vittoria and Ischia before he died.

Vittoria was one of the greatest poets of her day, and is particularly known through her spiritual friendship with Michelangelo, who wrote sonnets to her. Few poets of the time were untouched by her graciousness. She was on close terms with the most brilliant men of Rome, her opinions were sought after, and her behaviour was always perfectly proper amidst the intrigues that surrounded her belligerent family. The contrast between the elegant court that surrounded her during her years on Ischia and the ravages and slave-taking wrought on the island by the corsairs Barbarossa and Dragut, a few years after her departure for Rome, illustrate the extremities of the period.

Another writer of far-reaching influence to find inspiration on Ischia was Giambattista Vico. In the mid-17th century he was offered an easy tutoring job on the island, giving him the leisure to formulate his murky and celebrated *New Science*, a work that had a profound influence on James Joyce. George Bishop Berkeley, the Irish philosopher, visited the island at the beginning of the 18th century and wrote of it extensively in his journals; Henrik Ibsen spent the summer of 1867 at Casamicciola and wrote much of the play *Peer Gynt* during his stay.

In the 19th century, Ischia, like so many islands, was a political prison. During the Napoleonic Wars it suffered in the battles between French and English, and for a brief period was Nelson's base.

Getting Around

Ischia is considerably larger than Capri, divided into six self-contained communities. Buses (and taxis) to the various towns on the island depart from the square next to Santa Maria di Portosalvo in Ischia Porto, near the beginning of the SS270, which circles the island. An entire circuit of the island takes about 2½hrs. If you're planning a day trip round the island, your best bet is to buy a ticket valid for 24hrs for L4000, otherwise a standard ticket (valid for 1hr) will cost L1200. A weekly bus pass will set you back L15,000. Buses marked CD run clockwise, while those marked CS run anti-clockwise. Cars can be hired relatively cheaply here. At Forio, try **Davidauto**, Via G. Mazzella 104,

© (081) 998043, owned by the pleasant and reliable Davide Calise who's been in the business for 25 years, or in Ischia Porto the **Autonoleggio Balestrieri**, Via dello Stadio 16, © (081) 981055, inside a bar on the harbour front. Car hire will cost L40–70,000 per day. Or you may prefer to rent a *motorino* (moped) as traffic is less threatening than on the mainland (L30–40,000 per day).

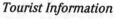

Tourist Information

There is one office in Ischia Porto, at Via Iasolino, 80077, © (081) 991146, near the ferry landing.

Ischia Porto

The first hint of Ischia's volcanic origins comes when you enter the almost perfectly round harbour of Ischia Porto, formed by a sister crater of Monte Epomeo. Only in 1854 was it connected to the sea, the narrow strip of land carved out by the engineers of Ferdinand II. Full of yachts, lined with restaurants, and a step away from the tourist information office, it is everything a Mediterranean port should be. Note that ships dock to the left (as you look out to sea), while hydrofoils dock to the right, near the newly modernized **Terme Comunali**.

Via Roma, the main shopping street of Porto, with cafés and boutiques, passes the **Chiesa dell'Assunta**, built in 1300 and since remodelled in the Baroque style. Further on, when Via Roma becomes the more fashionable Corso Vittoria Colonna, turn down Via V. F. d'Avalos for the numerous seaside hotels and *pensioni*, or in the other direction, Via V. E. Cortese for the **Pineta** (pinewood)—the lovely shady divider between Ischia Porto and Ischia Ponte.

Ischia

Ischia Ponte

Ischia Ponte, once a separate fishing village, is slowly being gobbled up by tourist sprawl. 'Ponte' refers to the causeway built by Alfonso (il Magnifico) of Aragon in 1438 to the **Castello d'Ischia** on its offshore rock. With the large dome of its abandoned church in the centre, the fortress where Vittoria Colonna spent so many years looks like a fairytale illustration from the distance. As King Alfonso also financed most of the walls around the islet, which can be visited, it is sometimes called the Castello Aragonese, and can be visited. Not only are the narrow streets and 500-year-old houses interesting; the views from the walls are superb. During the festival of Sant' Anna (end July), near the castle, you can see the island's traditional dance, the *'ndrezzata*, a ritualistic dagger dance dating from the time of Vittoria Colonna, accompanied by clarinets and tambours.

Even better views can be had from the summit of the extinct volcano, **Montagnone** (255m). Views from the top take in the Phlegraean Fields on the mainland, Ischia's little sister island Procida, and the rest of Ischia as well.

Popular beaches line much of the town's shore. Some are organized, like Ciro, Medusa, Lauro and Starace; others, like the Spiaggia degli Inglesi (named after the English occupation at the beginning of the 18th century) and Dei Pini, are free. The public tennis courts are on the Via C. Colombo, ✆ (081) 993416. And for those interested in diving, the Ischia Diving Centre is located at Via Jasolino, 106, ✆ (081) 985008, 🖷 985009.

Around Ischia: Casamicciola

Besides the state highway (SS270) there are many scenic secondary roads zigzagging across the island that you will be able to enjoy if you have a car or a sturdy constitution and a good pair of shoes. A few miles west of Ischia Porto (bus every half-hour) is the popular resort of **Casamicciola Terme**, the oldest spa on the island and the probable location of a Greek settlement. All remains of this, however, were obliterated in the 1883 earthquake in which 2300 people were killed, including 600 British tourists. Henrik Ibsen spent a summer in a nearby villa (a medallion minted in his honour can be seen in the Piazza). The mineral springs of Casamicciola are particularly potent—Rita and Gurgitello rate as the hottest—and contain large quantities of iodine.

Largely rebuilt, the resort of Casamicciola is more a conglomeration of hotels than a proper town, although there is a centre around the shady square at the **Piazza Marina** with shops, car-hire firms and banks. The rest of the town sprawls across the Gurgitello and Sentinella hills. Be prepared for some steep walks uphill if you can't wait for the bus which departs from the main square. Besides the Lido, there are beaches at Suorangela and Castagna. The heliport lies just west of the town. From Piazza Marina, an hour's walk will take you to the **Geophysical Observatory**, built in 1891. You can't go inside, but there are good views over the town.

Lacco Ameno

A half-hour's walk along the coast from Casamicciola leads you to the more fashionable **Lacco Ameno**, another large resort, where the local landmark is the **Fungho**, a mushroom-shaped rock that dominates the harbour. In the centre of town you can pay your respects at the pale pink **Sanctuary of Santa Restituta**, patron saint of Ischia. Martyred in the 3rd century, her body was thrown into the sea, then floated ashore at Lacco Ameno. The oldest part of the Sanctuary dates from 1036, and was constructed on the site of an early Christian basilica. Excavations in the church crypt have produced evidence of Roman baths. Greek and Roman tools and vases have also been discovered west of Lacco Ameno at Monte Vico and behind the town on Fundera plain. Some of these may be seen in the local **Museum** *(open Mon–Sat, 9.30–12.30 and 5–7; Sun, 9.30–12)* next door to the church and the neo-Pompeian **Terme Regina Isabella**, connected to the luxury hotel in Piazza Santa Restituta.

For the hardy, there is a charming country path, the **Calata Sant'Antonio**, leading from Lacco Ameno (off Via Roma) to the Chiesa dell'Immacolata in Casamicciola; the local milkmen, after delivering their wares udder-fresh from door to door, would herd their goats home along this path every evening.

Forio

Forio, the wine-producing centre of Ischia and a growing resort, is one of the prettiest towns on the island and supports a small art colony. Forio has four sites to include in a stroll through its centre, the first of which is the squat tower known as the **Torrione**, built by King Ferrante in 1480 on the site of an even older tower. It did little, however, to defend the island from pirate raids and was later converted to a prison and, nowadays, a gallery of local art. Near it lies the church of **Santa Maria di Loreto**, a fine Baroque church built in the 14th century; the two towers are decorated with majolica tiles. Off Corso Umberto, a crumbling portal and dusty courtyard mark the entrance to **Santa Maria Visitapoveri**, a tiny church built at the turn of the 17th century. Here poor children collected coins outside the customs house to buy lantern oil for a small street alcove to the Madonna. Faded majolica floor tiles and late 18th-century oval-framed paintings by Alfonso di Spigna are among the hidden treasures found in this atmospheric church. On the point furthest west, right on the sea, stands the pretty white sanctuary of **San Soccorso**, to whom the local fishermen pray for help. Inside little wooden ships float atop each pillar, carved by fisherman as votive offerings.

Behind Forio there are several paths leading up into the hills, towards Monterone, Sant'Antonio Abate and Santa Maria del Monte, below Monte Epomeo. There are beaches on either side of Forio, along with the very popular Citara and Cava dell'Isola to the south, and at Ghiaia and San Francesco to the north. Near Citara are the **Gardens of Poseidon**, a recently built complex of swimming pools set in a Mediterranean formal garden. More of an outdoor shopping mall, this ritzy establishment comes at a price. Entrance per person is L40,000 and parking an additional L5,000. Don't forget to pack your sequinned swimsuit—you have been warned!

Sant'Angelo

From Forio, still heading counterclockwise, the SS270 passes through the hill village of **Oanza** and on to **Serrara Fontana**, both of which have roads leading down to

Sant'Angelo. The buses to this lovely fishing port stop at the top of the hill because there isn't enough room for them to turn around in Sant'Angelo itself. The walk down at the edge of the cliff is quite lovely, with numerous views of the **Punta Sant'Angelo**, a small islet connected to Ischia by a narrow isthmus of sand. Only a stump remains of the **Torre Sant'Angelo** which once stood on top. If the wall-to-wall tourists start to get on your nerves, this is the ideal place to take to the high seas with plenty of boats to hire in the port.

East of the village stretches the lovely beach of **Maronti**, which you can reach either by taking the path or by hiring a boat. The path runs past numerous fumaroles, hissing and steaming, and the beach itself has patches of scalding hot sand where you can wrap your picnic lunch in foil and cook it, if you so wish. Above the beach are the hot springs of **Cavascura** *(adm.)*, at the mouth of an old river canyon; the sheer sides of the canyon, the little wooden bridges and the individual baths carved in the rock—each named after a mythological deity—make it an unusual place. Indeed, even the Romans are thought to have bathed here.

Monte Epomeo

From Serrara Fontana the road towards Barano is most picturesque, winding its way around the inner valleys of Monte Epomeo (790m). If you're going by bus, stop off at Fontana, where you can start your climb up to the old volcano—it hasn't erupted since 1302. Mules may be hired if you're not up to the climb (one gruelling hour), and there's a hermitage where you can spend the night, located in the very crater itself. Watching the sun rise or set from such vantage points is always memorable, but with the entire Bay of Naples spread out below you, it is sublime.

The next village along the route is **Buonopane** (the name means 'good bread'), followed by **Barano**, an oasis of tranquillity on exuberant Ischia. In the Piazza San Rocco, in the centre of town, the church of the same name has a characteristic campanile. The road from here to Ischia Ponte passes scattered homes and summer villas, half-hidden in the lush vegetation and pine trees.

Ischia © (081–)

Where to Stay

very expensive

The swankiest hotel on Ischia is the ★★★★★**Regina Isabella**, Piazza Santa Restituta, Lacco Ameno, © (081) 994322, ✆ 900190, right on the waterfront in Lacco Ameno, with a private beach and every kind of spa and gym facility imaginable. Typical of luxury resort hotels in Italy, this is a grandiose establishment straight out of the pages of *Hello!* Expect impeccable service and expansive style, but not warmth or intimacy. Another pricey choice, but with a very different style, is the ★★★★★**Grand Albergo Mezza Torre**, Via Mezza Torre, © 986111, ✆ 987892, up a long road just off the SS270 outside Lacco Ameno. This 60-room hotel is housed in a small castle that used to belong to the film director Visconti. Set in its own grounds, it lacks the facilities of the Regina Isabella, but for good old-fashioned luxury and a country-house atmosphere, it can't be beaten.

The finest hotel in Ischia Porto is the ★★★★**Excelsior Belvedere** at Via Gianturco 19, ℂ 991522, ✆ 984100. Situated down a side street off Corso Vittoria Colonna, it is quieter than most and guests can enjoy the fine pool and garden. Tastefully decorated with antique furniture and discreetly managed, its central location makes this a stylish choice for those looking to explore the island. *Closed Nov–Mar.* At the bottom end of this price range you can still indulge in a spot of luxury at the ★★★★**Mare Blu**, Via Pontano 40, ℂ 982555, ✆ 982938. This sleek hotel sits in a charming position right on the waterfront and a short walk from the centre of town. There's a private beach just over the road, two swimming pools and a memorable view of the Aragonese castle. *Open all year.*

For those who want to try Ischia's famous thermal treatments, without spending the kind of sums charged in the smarter hotels, the ★★★**Parco Verde**, Via Mazzella 29, Ischia Porto, ℂ 992282, ✆ 992773, is a good bet. Set in an attractive park amid shady pines, this hotel offers full thermal facilities and trained staff. If you prefer to do without mudbaths, there's a pool in the grounds and it's just a short walk to the beach. Also in Ischia Porto is the ★★★★**Villarosa**, Via G Gigante 5, ℂ 991316, ✆ 992425. Just off Via Roma, this elegant hotel is screened from the outside world by a leafy forecourt. Leave behind the heat and bustle of the streets for this cool inner sanctum, tastefully furnished with a minimum of fuss and surprisingly well-priced for a hotel of such finesse. Small pool, garden and thermal treatments available.

In pretty Sant'Angelo, on the south side of the island, the ★★★★**Miramare**, Via Comandante Maddalena 29, ℂ 999219, ✆ 999325, is a lovely hotel, with panoramic views over the small harbour. Further west at Forio is the ★★★★**Punta del Sole**, Piazza Maltese, ℂ 989156, ✆ 998209, tucked away in a lovely flower-filled garden in the heart of the town. This cool and restful hideaway stands like an oasis among the abundant bougainvillea. Leafy walks, helpful management and attractive balconies combine to make this one of the most likeable hotels on the island. Also in Forio, try ★★**Umberto a Mare**, Via Soccorso 2, ℂ and ✆ 997171, right by the church of San Soccorso overlooking the sea. Old-fashioned and defiantly lacking in swanky accessories, it houses an attractive restaurant which serves good food. You can swim from the rocks below.

In Lacco Ameno, the ★★★**San Montano**, Via Monte Vico, ℂ 994033, ✆ 980242, offers a pool, tennis courts and many other comforts, in addition to thermal baths.

Prices tend to be a bit lower in Casamicciola. One bargain that has special reductions for families is the ★★**Pensione Monti**, Calata S Antonio 7, ℂ 994074. Situated high up on the hill behind the main town, it's a lively spot with good views, a swimming pool and private parking. Given the position a car is essential and half-board is obligatory—though no one complains! In Ischia Ponte, one of the least expensive places to stay is within the Castello Aragonese itself. Open all year, ★Il Monastero, Via Castello Aragonese, ✆ 992435, has 14 clean and simple en suite rooms, housed in the cells where monks once slept. It's a bit of a climb, but the view is unforgettable. Also a bargain, two steps from the harbour front in Ischia Porto, is ★★Antonio Macri, Via Jasolino 96, ✆ 992603. Clean and well-run, Antonio's is a convenient and relaxed venue which should prove popular with the younger, independent traveller. Ask for a room on the first floor. *Open all year.* In Lacco Ameno, the ★★Bristol, Via Fundera 72, ✆ 994566, with a small garden and swimming pool, is your best bet if you can't afford the plusher hotels.

Ischia ✆ (081–) ***Eating Out***

In Ischia, fish features prominently on the menu, but you will also find meat here, and specifically rabbit. For some reason, Ischia is fairly hopping with rabbits, and the locals have dreamed up endless ways of eating them, in stews, roast, or even with pasta.

expensive

In Ischia Ponte for fantastic views and excellent seafood, the loveliest place to eat is **Da Ugo Giardini Eden**, Via Nuova Cartaromana 50, ✆ 993909, set right on the sea. It's a bit of a hike if you're staying in Ischia Porto, but there is a regular bus service between the two towns, and you're guaranteed to dine on the freshest fish, since it's as good as plucked out of the water in front of you. Leaving Ischia Porto and heading out towards Casamicciola, those with transport might like to check out **Il Damiano**, on the SS270, ✆ 983032. This pleasant restaurant offers diners superb views over the sea, plus beautifully cooked seafood and fish dishes—best of all the *linguine all'aragosta*, long pasta with a lobster sauce. *Open evenings only.*

moderate

In Ischia Porto, **Gennaro**, Via Porto 66, ✆ 992917, ✆ 983636, serves superb giant prawns and many other delicious Ischian specialities. Gennaro Rumore is a charismatic and convivial host and probably the best-known restauranteur on the island. In the past he has entertained the likes of Tom Cruise, his wife Nicole Kidman, and Andrew Lloyd Webber, who incidentally gave him a superb write-up in the *Telegraph*. The food is a perfectionist's dream, carefully prepared and guaranteed to leave your tastebuds tingling. Just before you reach the causeway, on the seafront at Ischia Porto, you can enjoy traditional food in unpretentious surroundings at **Coco**, Piazzale Aragonese, ✆ 981823. Run by Salvatore di Meglio, a retired fisherman who claims to be 'in love with the sea', this relaxed eaterie comes highy recommended by the locals who cram into the noisy and friendly dining area. Still in Ischia Porto, **Zi Nannina a Mare**, Via Cristoforo Colombo, ✆ 991350, is a delightful family-run trattoria with an outdoor terrace offering traditional, well-cooked specialities of the region, based on either fish or meat. For a good pizza or a lighter meal try **Pirozzi**, Via Seminario 47, ✆ 991121, a popular and bustling pizzeria where the smell of freshly cooked dough hangs in the air and the doors are flung open to the humming streets.

In the open countryside near Forio, en route to Santa Maria del Monte, the **Cavé Gran Diavolo**, Via Bocca 88, ✆ 989282, serves more meat than fish, with pride of place going to the famous dish of Forio, *bucatini con sugo di coniglio*—fat spaghetti served in rabbit sauce. The rustic feel and good local wine make this a very pleasant place for lunch or dinner.*Closed Wed.* Right on the water's edge in Forio, the **Cava dell'Isola**, Via G. Mazzella, ✆ 997830, is especially enjoyable at lunchtime. The relaxed ambience is popular with hungry young people in search of a bite to eat after a morning spent on the nearby beach. Good local specialities are the mainstay.

At Lacco Ameno, right on the harbour front, head for **Al Delfino**, Corso A Rizzoli, ✆ 900252. Steaming plates are carried from the kitchen across the street to the chattering clientele in the glass-fronted restaurant. *Spaghetti alle vongole* (with clams) is the house speciality, but whatever you choose, the management promises you will eat well and pay fairly.

At Sant'Angelo the **Conchiglia**, Via Sant'Angelo, ✆ 999270, offers al fresco dining on a tiny but charming terrace, overlooking the harbour. There is also a handful of nice, inexpensive rooms to let above the restaurant.

Procida

Lovely, uncomplicated and tiny, Procida is in many ways the archetypal image of all that an 'Italian island' evokes in any holiday dreamer's mind. Scented by lemon groves, said to produce the finest lemons in Italy (the lemon granita served in almost every local bar is a treat worth savouring), embellished with colourful houses as original as they are beautiful, a setting for two famous love stories, Procida is an island where most people still earn a living from the sea, as fishermen or sailors, and also from carving exquisite models of historic ships. Its very proximity to the glamour, chaos and more celebrated charms of Naples, Capri and Ischia has saved it from the worst ravages of touristic excess. Procida was most recently given an international outing when it was used as the setting for the Oscar-winning film, *Il Postino*. The pace of life is delightfully slow: when there was talk of closing the penitentiary and converting it into a Grand Hotel, the locals shuddered—they preferred the cons to any Capri-like transformation of their idyllic life. Connected to Procida by a modern bridge is the minute islet of Vivara—officially, though it sounds bizarre, a natural park of Naples. It teems with wild rabbits, an important ingredient in Procida's cuisine along with the more obvious fruits of the sea.

History

Only a few miles from the mainland and Monte Procida itself, Procida the island was near enough to Naples to have a minor, or at least a spectator's role in many of the turbulent events that transpired there, but far enough away to stay out of trouble. Like Ischia, to which it was once connected, Procida (ancient *Prochyta*, or 'deep') was inhabited in the Neolithic period. The Romans used the island as a hunting reserve, and there was at least an agricultural settlement there in the Dark Ages—Pope Gregory the Great wrote a letter in the 6th century praising the wine of Procida. Shortly thereafter the first chapel of San Michele Arcangelo was erected on Punta Lingua, on the site where a statue of the saint stood; according to legend, during a pirate attack the people prayed fervently to the statue for deliverance, and the saint responded and saved his beloved Procida at least this once.

In the 11th century a Benedictine abbey was founded by the chapel, and the fortifications of the Terra Murata ('the walled land') were begun. These proved insufficient against the ravages of first Barbarossa (1544), then Dragut (1562) and Bolla (1572). After Barbarossa burned the church, the fishermen had to donate a third of their income to reconstruct it— Pope Julius III generously decreed they could fish on Sundays and holidays as well for 10 years to make ends meet, permission which was extended for 15 more years after Dragut. By then, however, the Benedictines had long abandoned Procida.

The Bourbon kings, like the Romans before them, often came to Procida to hunt; Fernando IV made the island and its town a royal domain, but turned its fortress into a prison. Procida prefers to recall another event of the period: the visit in 1811–12 by the wandering French poet Alphonse Lamartine. A beautiful daughter of a fisherman fell in love with him and gave up an advantageous marriage for his sake, only to be jilted by the fickle Frenchman. Inconsolate, she died two months later, and at least received the dubious compensation of immortality in his novel *Graziella*, a spectacular bestseller in its day. Procida, for its part, pays homage to her memory with an annual end-of-summer Miss Graziella beauty pageant.

Another famous personage connected with the island was so fond of it that he incorporated it in his name, becoming Giovanni da Procida. Born in 1210 in Salerno, this nobleman, a good friend of Emperor Frederick '*Stupor Mundi*' and his son Manfred, had a castle on the island which he visited often on tours of his domains. When Charles of Anjou, a Guelph, took Naples, he confiscated all the property of Ghibellines like those of Giovanni da Procida, and the latter was forced to flee to Spain. Here Constance, the last of the Swabians and wife of King Peter of Aragon, received him well and made him Baron of Valencia.

But Giovanni got his revenge on Charles of Anjou. When the proud Sicilians began to chafe under the harsh rule of the French, Giovanni acted as a middleman to assure them that should they rise up in arms, Peter of Aragon would support their cause and be their king. The Sicilian Vespers resulted, and some 8000 Frenchmen died in that island's spontaneous combustion. The French were then symbolically revenged on Giovanni da Procida. When they occupied Procida in 1806 during the Napoleonic Wars—about 650 years after the Sicilian Vespers—they destroyed his marble coat of arms, the last reminder of his presence on the island.

Readers of Boccaccio may recognize Giovanni's nephew, Gianni da Procida, from the Sixth Tale of the Fifth Day of the *Decameron*. Gianni so loved a girl of Ischia named Restituta that he sailed over daily, to look at the walls of her house if nothing else. One foul day a band of Sicilians pounced upon her and carried her off to Palermo, determined to give such a lovely prize to their king, Frederick of Aragon, who stowed Restituta in his garden villa, La Cuba, for future pleasures. Meanwhile Gianni in despair went in search of his sweetheart and finally discovered her whereabouts; he contrived to enter La Cuba with the aid of Restituta to plot an escape and make love; the king caught them *in flagrante* and was about to burn them publicly at the stake when a courtier recognized Gianni, and informed the king he was about to execute the nephew of the man who gave him the throne of Sicily, and there's a happy ending.

Getting Around

There are frequent ferry and hydrofoil services from both Naples and Ischia to Procida. The harbour itself is tiny, and if you want to explore further afield, jump on one of the colourful diesel-powered buggies that serve as taxis. Alternately, there is a bus service about every half-hour between the harbour and the other end of the island at Chiaiolella, stopping more or less at every point in between.

Tourist Information

The tourist office is at Via Roma 92, © (081) 8101968, ⊜ 981904, in the Marina Grande (the only substantial town), near the ferry departure point.

The Port and Corricella

Ships and hydrofoils call at the port, the **Marina Grande**, also called Sancio Cattolico, or known locally as Sent'Co. The church near the landing, **Santa Maria della Pietà** (1760), immediately gives you a taste of Procida's delightful architecture—wide arches in random rhythms and exterior rampant stairs crisscrossing the façades, all in softly moulded lines and faded pastels of pinks, blues and yellows. The style reaches its epiphany over the hill at **Corricella,** the oldest village on the island, built on a protected cove by fishermen, under the citadel of the Terra Murata. Steep stone stairways cascade down amongst the rounded arches; from the little port they're like a hundred watchful eyes, scanning the sea for the return. Some have been so remodelled over the centuries according to the needs of their inhabitants as to give immediate proof of an old island saying, that 'a house isn't only a house. A house is a story.'

The same could be said of Corricella's simple church, **San Rocco**, restored numerous times throughout the centuries. From here Via San Rocco leads to the Piazza dei Martiri where twelve Procidanese were executed in 1799 by the Bourbons for plotting a revolt. Near the Piazza is the domed **Madonna delle Grazie** (1700), containing a much-loved statue of the Virgin.

The Terra Murata

Via Madonna delle Grazie leads to the Terra Murata (91m, Procida's highest point), passing on the right the romantic if roofless ruins of **Santa Margherita Nuova**, built in

1586 at the edge of the Punta dei Monaci. The fortifications of the citadel belong to different dates, the latest portions from 1521; the oldest section of the medieval walls can be seen near the Porta Mezz'Olmo, at the beginning of the Via San Michele. Rising above the walls, houses and the now-abandoned prison of Terra Murata are the three domes of **San Michele Arcangelo**, which, despite its exotic, almost Saracen appearance from a distance, wears a simple unadorned façade, rebuilt after the various pirates' depredations. The domes are untiled—Procida receives so little rain that tiles aren't strictly necessary, or at least worth the cost. Of the original pre-16th-century structure, only part of the ceiling in the Sala del Capitolo remains. Many rich works of art in the three-naved church itself attest to the former splendour of the monastery; the painted wooden ceiling dates from the 17th century, as do the apse paintings by Nicola Rosso, the most interesting of which shows the God's aide-de-camp Michael and his troop of *putti* swooping down to save Procida from the Turks. Pride of place goes to a splashy canvas by Neapolitan Luca Giordano.

In the Piazza d'Armi is the Cardinal of Aragon's 1563 **Castello d'Aragona** (once upon a time the local clink); here, too, you can see parts of the walls, in which are crammed tortuous alleyways and steep narrow houses. Other old palaces may be seen along the escarpment over **Chiaia beach**—including the **Palazzo Minichini**, on Via Marcello Scotti, adjacent to the fine old church of **San Tommaso d'Aquino**. Over the south side of the beach is the so-called 'Casa di Graziella'.

Across Procida

North of Marina Grande is the quarter known as Annunziata, after the old **Chiesa dell'Annunziata**, reconstructed in 1600 and containing a miraculous Madonna, to whom are given the many, varied votive offerings that adorn the interior of the church. There are pretty views from here of Punta Pioppeto and the **faro**, or lighthouse, where people often come for a swim. Nearby stands the only remaining watchtower of the original three constructed in the 16th century. From Punta Cottimo you can see the island of Ventotene, halfway to Rome though geologically related to Procida.

The rest of the island has many rural beauty spots, shaded walkways and narrow roads, old farmhouses and crumbling small palazzi, such as that of Giovanni da Procida on Via Giovanni da Procida. The areas around **Centane**, especially Punta Solchiaro, is most typical, and has the most striking belvedere, with views over the entire east coast of the island.

On the west end of the island, the long stretch of sand between Punta Serra and the peninsula of Santa Margherita Vecchia has been divided into three beaches—**Spiaggia Ciraccio**, where two Roman tombs were discovered; **Spiaggia Ciraciello**, on the other side of the pyramid-shaped rock, Il Faraglione di Procida; and towards the peninsula, the **Lido**. The hillock on the peninsula is capped by the tower-like ruin of the church of **Santa Margherita Vecchia**, once a Benedictine abbey abandoned in 1586; on the other side of it lies the small fishing port and beach **Marina di Chiaiolella**, on a rounded cove that long ago was a volcanic crater.

From here you can cross the new pedestrian-only bridge to the islet of **Vivara**, where the birds are protected these days but the rabbits are fair game. Here were discovered the Neolithic implements (at Capitello and Punta de Mezzodi) now in Ischia's museum. A narrow road leads towards the summit of Vivara, through the crumbling arch of an old hunting lodge, to the Belvedere, with fine panoramas of Procida and Pozzuoli on the mainland.

Procida ✆ (081–)   **Where to Stay and Eating Out**

There are very few places to stay on Procida. However, it's an ideal spot for relaxing in the sunshine away from the crowds. There are enough ferries not to feel isolated, but your evenings will be quiet as nightlife is minimal.

moderate

There are several good restaurants along the port at Marina Grande, like the Michelin-recommended **La Medusa**, Via Roma 116, ✆ 8967481, serving excellent seafood—including the house speciality *spaghetti ai ricci di mare* (spaghetti with sea urchins)—and good local wine literally 'on tap'. Definitely worth making the trip for.

inexpensive

Further along the Marina Grande, **Il Cantinone**, Via Roma 55, ✆ 8101932, is a low-key eaterie serving homely dishes and a very good *fritto misto di pesce* .

Right on the harbour front in Chiaiolella and a short walk to the beach, the ★★★**Crescenzo**, Via Marina Chiaiolella, ✆ 8967255, ✆ 8101260, is a landmark in Procida. Its rooms are simply but pleasantly furnished, and the restaurant, which serves local specialities and pizza in the evening, is worth a try even if you are not staying here. Most rooms come with showers and the sunroof offers a great view. *Open all year.*

On the main bus route through the centre of the island, and about 10 minutes walk outside Chiaiolella is the ★★**Riviera**, Via Giovanni da Procida 36, ✆ 896 7197.This is a pretty hotel with 23 rooms all with showers and a relaxed sunny environment, where the owner will welcome you with open arms and force his daughter to practise her English.

Amalfi Coast

The Amalfi Coast

...the only delectable part of Italy, which the inhabitants there dwelling do call the coast of Malfie, full of towns, gardens, springs and wealthy men.

Boccaccio

When confronted with something generally acclaimed to be the most beautiful stretch of scenery in the entire Mediterranean, the honest writer is at a loss. Few who have been there would argue the point, but describing it properly is another matter. Along this coast, where one mountain after another plunges sheer into the sea, there is a string of towns that not long ago were accessible only by boat. Today, a spectacular corniche road of 'a thousand bends' covers the route, climbing in places to a thousand feet above the sea; necessity makes it so narrow that every oncoming vehicle is an adventure, but everyone except the driver will have the treat of a lifetime. Nature here has created an amazing vertical landscape, a mix of sharp crags and deep green forests; in doing so she inspired the Italians to add three of their most beautiful towns.

This coast has always attracted foreigners, but only relatively recently has it become a major resort area. Places like Positano have become reserves for the wealthy, and swarms of day trippers are likely to descend at any moment. Rumour has it that the boutiques here are so fashionable that the Romans come to Positano to shop for their summer wardrobe (though you would never guess it from the baskets of frilly bikinis piled up in the street). But tourism will never spoil this area; all the engineers in Italy couldn't widen the Amalfi road, and the impossible terrain leaves no room at all for new development. For a map, *see* p.99.

Tourist Information

There are tourist offices along the peninsula in **Positano**, at Via Saracino 4, 84017, ℂ (089) 875067, ℮ 875760; **Amalfi**, at Corso Roma 19, 84011, ℂ (089) 871107, ℮ 872619; **Ravello**, Piazza Vescovado 1, 84010, ℂ (089) 857096, ℮ 857977; and **Maiori**, at Corso Regina, 84010, ℂ (089) 877452, ℮ (089) 853672. In **Salerno** the helpful EPT is at Piazza V. Veneto (outside the railway station), 84109, ℂ and ℮ (089) 231432. Their excellent *Annuario Alberghi* has, besides a list of hotels throughout the province (which includes the Amalfi coast), a map and just about everything else you may need to know.

Getting Around

Buses are the only form of public transport on the Amalfi coast. SITA services travel between Sorrento and Salerno about every 50min (*see* p.10).

Positano

To complement the vertical landscape, here is Italy's most nearly vertical town. Positano spills down from the corniche like a waterfall of pink, cream and yellow villas. The day trippers may walk down to the sea; only the alpinists among them make it back up (fortunately, there is a regular bus service along the one main street). After World War II, Positano became a well-known hideaway for artists and writers—many of them American, following the lead given by John Steinbeck —and fashion was not slow to follow. Now, even though infested with coach parties, Positano reverts to the Positanesi in the off-season, and quietens down considerably. However, do be aware that parking here, as with most of the Amalfi coast, is extremely tricky and you may be forced to hand over a fat wad of lira if you bring your car. Off the main thoroughfare, the road spirals down to the town centre—avoid bringing your car this far if you can. There are usually more spaces as you approach along the drive, and even when it looks to be a fair hike into town, steps often provide a short cut down the hillside. When you get to the bottom, there is a soft, grey beach and the town's church, decorated with a pretty tiled dome like so many others along this coast. A highlight of the town's year is its spectacular *festa* on the Feast of the Assumption, 15 August—the main holiday of the summer throughout Italy—when the local people take their town back in order to stage a performance recreating the Amalfi coast's centuries-long battles with the Saracens (*see* 'Festivals', p.18).

If you have time, take a trip further up to **Montepertuso**, a village perched 3km above Positano, and which takes its name (meaning 'hole in the mountain') from an old legend—the devil challenged the Virgin Mary to blow a hole in the mountain, saying the winner could have control of the village. The devil tried, but failed miserably, while the Virgin coolly walked through the mountainside, leaving a hole still visible today. The locals re-enact the scene each 2 July, with much merriment and fireworks. On the last Saturday in August, the village stages another of the best festas in all Italy, the *sagra del fagiolo*—the feast of the bean. The streets are decked out with stalls selling beans cooked in every possible way, plus a great many other home-cooked dishes, washed down with local wine served from oak barrels by waiters dressed in traditional costume.

The next town east along the drive from Positano, **Praiano**,

Positano

could be Positano's little sister: with a similar beach and church, but not quite as scenic and perpendicular, and not quite as beleaguered by tourism. Her natural attractions, however, leave her ripe for creeping exploitation. After Praiano, keep an eye out for the most impressive natural feature along the drive, the steep, impenetrable **Furore Gorge**. On either side are tiny isolated villages along the shore, with beaches—if only you can find a way to get to them. Further down the road you'll notice the lift leading down to the **Grotta Smeralda** *(open April–Oct, daily, 9.00–5; Nov–Mar, daily, 10–6; adm)*. The strange green light that is diffused throughout this sea-level cavern gives it its name. Beyond this, **Conca dei Marini** is another vertical village, with a beach and a Norman lookout tower to climb.

Positano ℂ (089–)

Where to Stay

luxury

With Positano's new-found status has come some of the highest hotel prices in Italy. If you're feeling self-indulgent—and very rich—you may care to stay at a place many believe to be the finest resort hotel in the country. The ★★★★★**San Pietro**, ℂ 875455, ✆ 811449, lies 1½km outside Positano en route to Amalfi. The entrance is hidden behind an old chapel, with only a discreet sign to alert you to the intimate paradise which spills down the cliff face beneath you. It's all part of the management's plan to maintain the privacy and tranquillity of its celebrity clientele. Amid the richly coloured gardens, 58 individual rooms are immaculately maintained, each offering a private terrace and spectacular views round every corner—even when you're soaking in a hot tub. It also offers a private beach, tennis courts and its own excursion boat. Given its position outside Positano, it's worth bearing in mind that a car is vital if you wish to explore further afield– unless you bring your helicopter that is, for which there is a landing pad. Still, shopping *is* available in the form of branded T-shirts and towels, and given the extraordinary range of facilities, you may never want to leave. *Closed Nov–Mar.*

very expensive

★★★★★**Le Sirenuse**, Via Cristoforo Colombo 30, ℂ 875066, ✆ 811798, is the former home of a noble Neapolitan family to whom it still belongs. It became a hotel in 1951 and takes its name from the islands of the Sirens which it overlooks. Everything is done with style, from the beautifully decorated drawing room to the swimming pool with its mosaic tiles. Cool and sophisticated, it lies close to the shops and restaurant, and offers a private pool, jacuzzi and fitness area.

expensive

The ★★★★**Palazzo Murat**, Via dei Mulini 23, ℂ 875177, ✆ 811419, in the heart of Positano, is an 18th-century palazzo which once belonged to Napoleon's brother-in-law Joachim Murat, briefly King of Naples. It has plenty of old-world charm, with antiques in many rooms and a beautiful courtyard shaded by lofty palm trees, where classical concerts are sometimes staged in summer. An elegant hotel with oodles of atmosphere.

On a more modest level, the ★★★**Casa Albertina**, Via Favolozza 4, ✆ 811149, ✉ 875540, is furnished in a lovely, understated manner, the better to accentuate the views over Positano and the sea. It's a family-run place, with a nice restaurant on the rooftop terrace, a few minutes from the beach, and in the busy season its quietness can be an advantage. Be aware that half-board is compulsory during high season. A little closer to the water is the ★★★**Ancora**, on Via Columbo, ✆ 875318, ✉ 811784. A small and professionally run place, it offers sea views and much-needed parking in the centre of town.

If you have a car, you can expand your horizons to include some of the more secluded spots along the coast. Tourism has yet to infiltrate the heart of Praiano and if you climb up behind the road, you will find a sleepy fishing village, undisturbed by the whirr of cameras or the rumble of coaches. Still, there is some pleasant accommodation running along the coast, much of it just outside the village at Vettica Maggiore—a little way back towards Positano along the Amalfi drive. One exceptional bargain here is the ★★★**Tramonto d'Oro**, ✆ 874008, ✉ 874670, which offers tennis courts, a pool, beach access, and great views. The management is friendly and helpful. Forty recently renovated rooms, most with showers, are tastefully decorated with attractive tiling and bright materials. The regular clientele reinforces the high opinion this hotel has earned. Further towards Amalfi at Conca dei Marini, the ★★★★**Belvedere**, ✆ 831282, ✉ 831439, is an airy and modern resort hotel in a delightful setting, with a nice beach and an old Norman tower in the grounds. The sea-water pool offers a refreshing dip to those not adverse to salt.

In Positano, a good bargain is the ★★**California**, Via Colombo 141, ✆ 875382, with 15 very pleasant rooms, all with bath, and a lovely terrace for breakfast and other meals. Set slightly back from the sea, it is nonetheless well located and charmingly run, but there is no parking. Still in Positano, the ★**Maria Luisa**, Via Fornillo 40, ✆ 875023, has 10 rooms, all with baths, and a friendly family atmosphere. A few very inexpensive *pensioni* can also be found along Via Fornillo and on the other streets leading down to the beach. In Praiano, similarly, there are some cheaper old pensions by the port, but they are usually full to bursting in the summer. For a clean and reliable option, look out for ★★★**Le Terrazze**, ✆ 831290, under the same management as Tramonto D'Oro and situated right on the sea. A more individual choice, also in Praiano, is ★★**La Tranquillita**, ✆ 874084, a holiday village offering small wooden bungalows complete with bathroom, a window onto the sea and a private terrace for that evening tipple. Steps built out of the rocks offer access to the water and plenty of opportunity to tone your calf muscles on the way back up. Breakfast can be taken on the restaurant terrace and evening meals are also available. Not luxurious, but clean, thoughtfully managed and a cheap alternative for the more independent traveller. For young groovers, it is so close to the Amalfi coast's hottest dance floor, the Africana nightclub, you can dance to the music in your own bedroom.

In the high season at least, most of the resort hotels along the coast will expect you to take half-board, which means having either lunch or dinner in the hotel restaurant. Not that that's always bad—some of the better hotels have well-known gourmet restaurants and it is often extremely good value. However, there are also some equally good places elsewhere to enjoy—if you can escape! Like many of the restaurants on the Costiera, a good number of Positano's eateries close from November till Easter.

expensive

La Cambusa, Spiaggia Grande, ℗ 875432, in a lovely position with a terrace looking out onto the beach, is a Positano favourite. The chef serves excellently cooked fresh fish and seafood in as many ways as you can think of, and more. A house speciality is *penne con gamberetti, rucola e pomodoro*—penne with prawns, rocket and fresh tomatoes. Across the road, the **Buca di Bacco**, Via Rampa Teglia 8, ℗ 875699, is another Positano institution and *the* place to stop off for a drink on the way back from the beach. The fish is always well cooked here, and you'd be crazy to go for anything else. Accommodation is also available here during high season—ask at the restaurant. Down on Positano's beach, the centre of the action in the summer is **Chez Black**, Via Brigantino, ℗ 875036, a slick and sophisticated joint run by local entrepreneur Salvatore Russo. As with all the restaurants along the Spiaggia Grande, it's not what you eat, but who sees you eating, that matters. And those privileged enough to be seated in a director's chair, close to the water's edge, will know they have really arrived. However, good Neapolitan favourites like *spaghetti alle vongole* (with clams) are done well here, and maybe a banana split with *liquore Strega* for dessert.

moderate

O'Caporale, just off the beach on Via Regina Giovanna, ℗ 811188, offers simple and well-cooked seafood. The swordfish and *zuppa di pesce* are particularly good.

Lo Guarracino, Via Positanesi d'America 12, ℗ 875794, is situated in one of Positano's most lovely spots, on a terrace perched over the sea, reached by a short walk along the cliff path towards Fornillo beach. This pizzeria-cum-trattoria is pleasantly informal after the fashionable Spiaggia Grande, and as such it is a favourite with the Positanesi. Further uptown, the **Grottino Azzurro**, Via Chiesa Nuova, ℗ 875466, is a family-run trattoria, where the *signora* comes to the table to advise you on the catch of the day, and how best you should sample it.

In summer, for a memorable experience, watch out for boats marked **Da Laurito** leaving the jetty at Positano beach. This is a free ferry service to a delightful trattoria (℗ 875022) around the next bay, set on a small beach, with makeshift tables

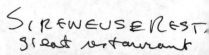
SIREWEUSEREST great restaurant

under a straw canopy. The speciality here is good old-fashioned recipes such as *totani con patate*—squid cooked with potatoes in a wonderful sauce of oil and garlic, all washed down with white wine spiked with fresh peaches. At the end of your meal, they'll ferry you back again as part of the service.

Just east of Praiano, a sharp turn down to the beach brings you to the **Petit Ristorante**, Via Praia 15, ✆ 874706, tucked away in a tiny bay at the foot of Il Furore. This is an informal eaterie whose tempting smells beckon in the hungry bather. Diners eat at tables outside, surrounded by gaily painted fishing boats, choosing from a menu that features mainly simple dishes such as fresh grilled fish and salad. *Closed Oct–Easter.*

inexpensive

Given Positano's fashionable standing, genuinely cheap places to eat are hard to find, though there are some pizzerias around Via Fornillo, and some of the restaurants listed above, such as Chez Black provide pizzas at less than their main-menu prices. Those with a car could try **Taverna del Leone**, Via Laurito 43, ✆ 875474, just outside Positano heading towards Amalfi. This busy pizzeria, bustling with young Positanesi, serves tasty nosh in relaxed surroundings and at very reasonable prices. For those looking for something more sophisticated, the adjoining restaurant is more formal, though equally popular. At Montepertuso, above Positano, **Il Ritrovo**, Via Monte 53, ✆ 811336, is a pretty trattoria, with tomatoes strung from beams and good local dishes including, a rarity in these parts, grilled meats. A pleasantly rustic experience for anyone wishing to escape the crowds (if only for a night).

Nightclubs

If you fancy a night on the town, two bright firmaments stand out along the Amalfi coast. **The Africana**, Via Torre a Mare, Praiano, ✆ 874042 is *the* place to be seen. It is built into a man-made cave at sea level, so you can dance with the fish as they swim in brightly lit pools beneath your feet, or strut like a tribal chief amid the African bric-a-brac. Watch out for the parrot, he's vicious! For those looking to arrive in style, there is a boat service available from Positano. Or you can park your car at the tiny bay at Furore and walk along the cliff path (about 5 mins). *Open May–Oct.* For cabaret-style entertainment, try the recently opened **Music on the Rocks**, Grotte dell'Incanto 51, ✆ 875874, owned by the proprietor of Chez Black and a short stroll to the left of the Spiaggia Grande.

Amalfi

Sometimes history seems to be kidding us. Can it be true, can this miniscule village once have had a population of 80,000? There is no room among these jagged rocks for even a fraction of that—but then we remember that in Campania anything is possible, and we read how most of the old town simply slid into the sea during a storm and earthquake in 1343. The history is a glorious one. Amalfi was the first Italian city to regain its balance after the Dark Ages, the first to recreate its civic pride and its mercantile daring. As such, she showed the way to Venice, Pisa and Genoa, though she would get to keep few of the prizes for herself.

History

It is only natural that the Amalfitani would try to embroider their history a bit to match such an exquisite setting. Legends tell of a nymph named Amalphi who haunted this shore and became the lover of Hercules. As for their city's founding, they'll tell you about a party of Roman noblemen, fleeing the barbarians after the fall of the Empire, who found the site a safe haven to carry on the old Roman spirit and culture. Amalfi first appears in the 6th century; by the 9th it had achieved its independence from the dukes of Naples, and was probably the most important trading port of southern Italy, with a large colony of merchants at Constantinople and connections with all the Muslim lands. In 849, the chroniclers record the Amalfitano fleet chasing off an Arab raid on Rome. At the beginning, the Amalfitano Republic was ruled by officers called *giudici*, or judges; the year 958 brought a change in constitutions, and Amalfi elected its first doge, in imitation of Venice. At about the same time, the city's merchants developed the famous *Tavola Amalfitana*, a book of maritime laws that was widely adopted around the Mediterranean.

All of this came at a time for which historical records are scarce, but Amalfi's merchant adventurers must have had as romantically exciting a time as those of Venice. Their luck turned sour in the 11th century. The first disaster was a sacking by Robert Guiscard in 1073. Amalfi regained its freedom with a revolt in 1096, but the Normans of the new Kingdom of Sicily came back to stay in 1131. These, unfortunately, proved unable to protect it against two more terrible sackings at the hands of its arch-enemy Pisa, in 1135 and 1137. Today, Amalfi only gets a chance to recapture its glory days once every four years, when it hosts the Pisans, Genoese and Venetians in the antique boat race of the Four Maritime Republics. Amalfi next hosts the race on the first Sunday in June 1997.

The Cathedral and the Cloister of Paradise

The disaster of 1343 ensured that Amalfi's decline would be complete, but what's left of the place today—with its 5000 or so people—is beautiful almost to excess. Over the little square around the harbour, a conspicuous inscription brags: 'The Judgement Day, when the Amalfitani go to heaven, will be a day like any other day.' The square is called **Piazza Flavio Gioia**, after Amalfi's most famous merchant adventurer (his statue looks as if he's offering you a cup of tea); he's probably another fictitious character—more Amalfitano embroidery—but they claim he invented the compass in the 12th century.

From here, an arch under the buildings leads to the centre of the town, the **Piazza del Duomo**, with a long flight of steps up to what may be the loveliest **cathedral** in all the south of Italy (9th–12th centuries). Not even in Sicily was the Arab-Norman style ever carried to such a flight of fancy as in this delicate façade, with four levels of interlaced arches in stripes of different-coloured stone (much restored a century ago). The lace-like open arches on the porch are unique in Italy, though common enough in Muslim Spain,

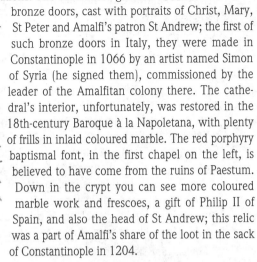

Duomo di Amalfi

one of the countries with which Amalfi had regular trade relations. The cathedral's greatest treasure is its set of bronze doors, cast with portraits of Christ, Mary, St Peter and Amalfi's patron St Andrew; the first of such bronze doors in Italy, they were made in Constantinople in 1066 by an artist named Simon of Syria (he signed them), commissioned by the leader of the Amalfitan colony there. The cathedral's interior, unfortunately, was restored in the 18th-century Baroque à la Napoletana, with plenty of frills in inlaid coloured marble. The red porphyry baptismal font, in the first chapel on the left, is believed to have come from the ruins of Paestum. Down in the crypt you can see more coloured marble work and frescoes, a gift of Philip II of Spain, and also the head of St Andrew; this relic was a part of Amalfi's share of the loot in the sack of Constantinople in 1204.

One of the oldest parts of the cathedral to survive is the **Chiostro del Paradiso** *(adm)*, a whitewashed quadrangle of interlaced arches with a decidedly African air. Many of the bits and pieces of old Amalfi that have survived its calamities have been assembled here: there are classical sarcophagi, medieval sculptures and coats of arms. Best of all are the fragments of Cosmatesque work, brightly coloured geometric mosaics that once were parts of pulpits and pillars, a speciality of this part of Campania.

From the centre of Amalfi, you can walk in a few minutes out to the northern edge of the city, the narrow 'Valley of the Mills', set along a stream bed between steep cliffs; some of the mills that made medieval Amalfi famous for paper-making are still in operation, and there is a small **Paper Museum** *(open 9–1; closed Mon and Fri; adm)* in the town. You can also watch paper being made and buy paper products at **Armatruda**, Via Fiume, ✆ (089) 871315, in central Amalfi, near the museum. If you'll be staying some time in this area, one of the best ways to spend it is walking the many lovely paths that navigate the steep hills into the interior of the peninsula, passing through groves of chestnut and ash; these, such as they are, were the main roads in the days of the Republic. One particularly nice one is the Amalfi–Pontone path, passing the ruins of the old monastery of Sant'Eustacchio, and there are many others around Ravello and Scala; ask the locals to point them out.

Amalfi ✆ (089–) **Where to Stay**

Unlike Positano, Amalfi has been a resort for a long time, and some of its older establishments are among the most distinctive on the Mediterranean.

The ★★★★★**Santa Caterina**, ✆ 871012, 🖷 871351, just outside Amalfi, has perhaps the loveliest gardens of all. A converted villa, with wonderful sea views from most rooms, its atmosphere is cool and elegant, and its staff courteous and discreet.

expensive

To really get away from it at all, your best bet is the 12th-century ★★★★**Cappuccini Convento**, Via Annunziatella, ✆ 871877, 🖷 871886, built by Emperor Frederick II on a mountainside over the town, with a suitably ancient lift running down through the cliffs to the beach. The converted cells, now hotel bedrooms, are dark and unsophisticated, in keeping with the closed monastic order that once prevailed here. You eat in the original refectory and there is a chapel and cloister (now enclosed and dismally converted into a conference centre) which seems to ensure a spiritual hush throughout. Set high above the tourist-infested streets, its colonnade bedecked with flowers offers the best view in Amalfi. Meals, like the rest of the hotel, are a treat to be savoured. Indulge!

St Francis himself is said to have founded the ★★★★**Luna**, ✆ 871002, 🖷 871333, though the lifts and Hollywood-style pool are a little more recent. This former monastery, above the drive on Amalfi's eastern edge, was already a hotel in the waning days of the Grand Tour—Wagner stayed here while searching for his Garden of Klingsor, and they can show you the room where Ibsen wrote *A Doll's House*. Among other famous guests, the owners claim the Luna to have been a favourite of both Mussolini and Otto von Bismarck. Deftly modernized, it provides comfortable rooms and attentive service.

moderate

Not all of Amalfi's accommodation offers such heights of luxury. For hotels in this category, it might be better to select a hotel along the drive between Amalfi and Positano (*see* above). However, two reliable hotels conveniently located close to Amalfi and the beach are the efficient ★★★★**Miramalfi**, ✆ 871247 and 🖷 871287, a sixties-style hotel with pool, beach and private parking; and right in the centre of town, through a series of warren-like streets, the ★★★**Amalfi** on Via dei Pastai, ✆ 872440, 🖷 872250. Popular with package tours, both are valuable alternatives for those without transport. Further along the Corso Roma, the ★★**Sole,** Largo della Zecca, ✆ 871147, is located in a quiet piazza, behind the beach front and next to the Highland Pub—should you be in need of a spot of eclectic refreshment. It's clean and airy, with private parking.

inexpensive

There is also a fair collection of inexpensive places around the cathedral. Two of the best are the tiny and elaborately furnished ★★**Sant'Andrea**, Via Santolo Camera 1, ✆ 871145, with angled views of the cathedral and an effusive welcome from your proprietress; and the ★★**Fontana**, Piazza Duomo 7,

© 871530, which has 16 spotless rooms offering plenty of space and a prime location at bargain prices. Both hotels are recommended to night owls only, being situated off the main piazza which hums until the early hours. There's no need to bring an alarm clock either: the cathedral bells should do the job nicely.

| *Amalfi* © *(089–)* | **Eating Out** |

Amalfi has several fine restaurants, including those in the luxury hotels mentioned above. But for a sense of this exuberant little city, try one of the many attractive restaurants listed below. Amalfi lacks the pretensions of her sister, Positano, but what you lose in finery, you make up for in the fundamentals—good, honest grub!

expensive

Da Gemma, Via Fra Gerardo Sasso 9, © 871345, established in 1872, is one of Amalfi's oldest restaurants, with an attractive terrace for outdoor dining and an excellent fish-based menu. Their *zuppa di pesce* (fish soup) is a wonderfully rich mixture of all sorts of different fish and seafood, although at L100,000 for two, this is no poor man's gruel. *Closed Wed.* **La Caravella**, Via Matteo Camera 12, © 871029, near the tunnel by the beach, is a busy restaurant which serves generous helpings of pasta, including a delicious ravioli stuffed with seafood, and a good range of home-made desserts. *Closed Tues or Thurs out of season—whenever the cook feels like it, one assumes.*

moderate

Almost directly under the cathedral is the cosy **Taverna degli Apostoli**, Via Sant'Anna 5, © 872991, with a warm and informal atmosphere which, when we last visited, echoed with the ribald laughter of local festivities. Highly recommended. *Closed Tues.* At ***Lo Smeraldino**, Piazzale dei Protontini 1, © 871070, at the far end of the port on the water's edge, you'll be offered the house speciality, *scialatiello*—fresh pasta with mixed seafood—and a range of good *secondi*, most notably an excellent *fritto misto*—mixed fried fish. Good food and bustling waiters are the order of the day in this popular eaterie. Heading up the main street towards the Valley of the Mills, you could do worse than stop at **La Taverna del Duca**, Largo Spirito Santo 26, © 872755. Tables lie scattered around a small piazza and diners eat off hand-painted plates. A relaxing midday stop, offering pizza, pasta and traditional Amalfi cooking. *Closed Thurs.*

inexpensive

North of the cathedral, the **Tarì**, Via P. Capuano, © 871832, is a pretty, welcoming trattoria with traditional checked tablecloths and service with a smile. It's cool, cavernous surroundings beckon in the hot and weary traveller and there are no unpleasant surprises when it's time for the bill. **Da Barracca**, Piazza dei Dogi, © 871285, is everything an Italian trattoria should be. Tables and chairs spill out onto this tranquil piazza just west of the cathedral, where diners are shielded from the midday sun by a shady awning and leafy plants. Friendly waiters proffer tasty snacks and plates of steaming pasta—and there are no hidden costs to leave you with a sour taste in your mouth.

At the **San Giuseppe**, Via Ruggiero II, 4, © 872640, a family-run hostelry, the pizza is sublime—it should be, as the owner is a baker. Homely bowls of pasta are also available, brought to you by a trio of portly brothers, and consumed amid the noise of television and shrieking Italian children. *Closed Thurs.* In the centre of town, **Da Maria**, Via Lorenzo d'Amalfi 14, © 871880, displays a highly embellished—and multi-lingual—menu to entice the traveller off the streets and into this lively trattoria and pizzeria. Allow yourselves to be tempted: the waiters are cheerful and helpful, and the food a cut above some of the other less expensive places.

Villages Inland: Ravello and Scala

As important as it was in its day, the Amalfitan Republic never grew very big. At its greatest extent, it could only claim a small part of this coast, including these two towns up in the mountains; like Amalfi they were once much larger and more prosperous than you see them today. **Ravello** is another beauty, a balcony overlooking the Amalfi coast and a treasure house of exotic medieval art and tropical botany. The sinuous climb can be made by bus or car, but be aware that parking here is a nightmare—and expect to pay through the nose if you bring your car. Ravello seems to have been a resort even in Roman times; numerous remains of villas have been found. As the second city of the Amalfitan Republic, medieval Ravello had a population of 30,000 (at least that's what they claim); now it provides an example of that typically Italian phenomenon—a village of 2000 with a first-rate cathedral.

Ravello's chief glories are two wonderful gardens. The **Villa Cimbrone** *(open daily, 9–7; adm)* was laid out by Lord Grimthorpe, the Englishman responsible for the design of Big Ben. The priceless view over the Amalfi coast is now owned by the Swiss Vuillemier family who run the Hotel Palumbo *(see* below) and it is, without doubt, one of the most beautiful properties in all Italy. The **Villa Rùfolo** *(open daily, 9–8 ; adm)*, as fans of Wagner will be interested to know, is none other than Klingsor's magic garden. Wagner says so himself, in a note scribbled in the villa's guest book. He came here looking for the proper setting in which to imagine the worldly, Faustian enchanter of *Parsifal,* and thus his imagination was fired. The villa itself is a remarkable 11th-century pleasure palace, a temporary abode of Charles of Anjou, various Norman kings, and Adrian IV, the only English pope (1154–9), who came here when fleeing a rebellion in Rome. Even in its present, half-ruined state, it is worth a visit; inside there is a small collection of architectural fragments, including a Moorish cloister and two crumbling towers, one of which can still be climbed. The garden, with yet more fine views, is a semi-tropical paradise; in summer it reverberates with 'sounds and sweet airs' as the setting for various open-air concerts.

The **cathedral** is named after Ravello's patron San Pantaleone, an obscure early martyr; they have a phial of his blood in one of the side chapels, and it 'boils' like the blood of San

Gennaro in Naples whenever the saint is in the mood. Lately he hasn't been, which makes the Ravellans worry. The cathedral has two particular treasures: a pair of bronze doors by Barisano of Trani (1179), inspired by the Greek ones at Amalfi, and an exquisite pair of marble *ambones*, or pulpits, that rank among the outstanding examples of 12th–13th-century sculptural and mosaic work; the more elaborate one, its columns resting on six curious lions, dates from 1272. The sacristy contains two paintings by the southern Renaissance artist Andrea da Salerno, including an unusual subject, the *Assumption of the Magdalen*. In this cathedral in 1149, the English pope, Adrian IV, crowned William the Bad King of Sicily. Two other Ravello churches where you can see decorative work similar to the cathedral's are **Santa Maria a Gradello** and **San Giovanni del Toro**.

From Ravello, it is only a lovely 1½km walk to **Scala**, smallest and oldest of the three Amalfitan towns and a genteel option for the traveller seeking peace and parsimony in the refreshing mountain air. Perched on the hillside across from Ravello, this is a timeless gem of a town which offers a rural escape, unfettered by the glitz of other resorts. Scala has another interesting old cathedral, **San Lorenzo**; inside, over the main altar is a 13th-century wooden crucifix.

Gerardo da Sasso, a citizen of Scala, started out running a small hostel for pilgrims in Jerusalem and ended up founding the Knights Hospitallers, or Knights of St John (1118); his family's ruined palace can be seen near the village. After the fall of Jerusalem, the order moved to Rhodes and subsequently Malta. The Sovereign Order of the Knights of Malta still share the distinctive swallow-tail cross which you see throughout Amalfi. Above Scala, the chapel of **San Pietro in Campoleone** has medieval carvings of St Michael and St Catherine inside, if you can find someone with the key.

Between Amalfi and Ravello, before reaching the turn-off inland, the Amalfi drive passes through **Atrani**, an old village whose church of San Salvatore has another tiled dome, and yet another set of bronze doors from Constantinople; inside it, note the lovely Byzantine relief of a pair of peacocks (peacock flesh was believed to be incorruptible back then, and therefore a symbol of immortality; but why the birds are standing, respectively, on a man and a rabbit is anybody's guess). In the days of the Republic this church was called San Salvatore della Biretta; the Amalfitan doges wore cloth caps like those of Venice, and they would come here for their ceremonies of investiture. Atrani and Amalfi don't much

Atrani

care for each other. Such Lilliputian rivalries are common on this coast (it's the same with Ravello and Scala); in Amalfi they'll tell you how Atrani was ruined after the Pisan raids, and how Emperor Manfred repopulated it with Muslims from Sicily. Such neighbours!

Beyond the Ravello turn, next along the way towards Salerno come **Minori** and **Maiori**. Minori is a typical *Costiera* hill-town, which despite encroaching tourism maintains considerable charm. The **Maritime Roman Villa** (*free*) excavated here may have belonged to the Vettii brothers of Pompeii according to the archaeologists on the site. The evidence is based on an amphora, inscribed with the name Vettius Montanus, discovered among reused material in the construction of the local church. If the villa and area really were dominated by this powerful merchant family, it could explain the origin of the town's little-used first name, Vettica.

Its bigger sister is somewhat less enticing, mainly due to a major flood in 1954, which washed away most of the seafront; today, most of the buildings and hotels along the shore are depressingly modern. **Erchie**, a tiny hamlet on the shore far below the road, seems a lovely spot—if you can figure out a way to get down to it. Then, near the end of the drive, the real world comes back into view as the busy port of Salerno stretches before you. Here you find the tiny resort of **Cetara**, with a fine beach behind a newly constructed fishing port, and, just before Salerno, **Vietri sul Mare**, another steep and pretty town, famous throughout Italy for its beautiful *maiolica* ware. There are ceramics shops everywhere, where you can watch craftsmen hand-painting jugs, vases and tiles, and pick up souvenirs at surprisingly good prices.

Around Ravello ⓒ *(089–)* **Where to Stay**

Ravello also has its share of dream hotels, offering no beaches, but unforgettable gardens and views down over the coast. In the shadow of Amalfi and Ravello, the two thoroughly pleasant beach lidos of Minori and Maiori may seem a little dull, but they can be useful bases, especially if hotels in the better-known resorts are full.

very expensive

Ravello's finest, with an incredible guest book full of the names of the famous over the last 120 years, is the ★★★★★**Palumbo**, Via S. Giovanni del Toro 28, ⓒ 857244, 🖮 858133. The entrance opens onto an elegant Arabic-style courtyard which only hints at the 12 rooms, each individually decorated with antiques. The restaurant is highly renowned, and the excellent Episcopio wine really is house wine—made on the premises. It's certainly elitist and your absolute privacy is guaranteed—but if you are searching for a taste of the real Italy, the smart, international atmosphere might just disappoint. There is also a simpler *dipendenza*, with 7 rooms for slightly lower prices. Courtesy buses, pool share (with Hotel Giordano), and private parking all available.

expensive

In Ravello, the ★★★★**Caruso Belvedere**, Via S. Giovanni del Toro, ⓒ 857111, 🖮 857372, was once popular with the Bloomsbury set and with Greta Garbo (she had room 21). Behind its sun-bleached facade, this hotel encapsulates the quiet elegance of the old patrician villa it once was—even the laundry room holds a fading fresco. The present owner's grandfather, a cousin of the famous Neapolitan tenor Enrico Caruso, opened it as a hotel 100 years ago. In the beautifully laid out gardens, there is a belvedere over the sea and mountains, and the well-tended vegetable garden and vineyard on another level provide fresh produce and the hotel's own wine. Guests are encouraged to take half-board, which is no real hardship since the food is superb, and meals are taken on one of the loveliest terraces in Ravello.

With the lushest gardens on the coast, the ★★★**Villa Cimbrone**, Via Santa Chiara 26, ✆ 857459, ✉ 858072, is a very special place to stay: another elegant old villa, once the property of an English duke, set in its own parkland perched dizzyingly high on the cliffs. The 10 rooms are beautifully decorated (half with sea views) and the view from the terrace where breakfast is served is a feast all on its own. There are drawbacks, however, such as the lack of a restaurant and the 10 minute walk needed to get there (cars have to be parked further down in the village). Nonetheless, it does have a swimming pool.

One of the prettiest hotels and perhaps the most welcoming place to stay in Ravello is the delightful ★★★**Villa Maria**, Via Santa Chiara 2, ✆ 857255, ✉ 857071. A light, airy charm prevails in this gracious and tastefully converted villa. First choice among such leading lights as Rudolf Nureyev, Tim Robbins and Susan Sarandon, and the disgraced Andreotti (whose visit is barely acknowledged!), it is made all the more attractive by the helpful and friendly owner, Vincenzo Palumbo, known to everyone as *Il Professore* or 'Prof'. The vast suite (more expensive than the normal rooms) has one of the most breathtaking terraces in Ravello and there is a beautiful eating area in the garden, sheltered by vines and graced with yet another astonishing view. Even if you don't stay here, it's worth coming to eat. The restaurant recently won an award in the highly reputed '*gambero rosso*' scheme, and is acknowledged throughout the region.

Further along the coast in the small suburb of Raito, just outside Vietri sul Mare is the ★★★★★**Raito**, ✆ 210033, ✉ 211434, a grandiose hotel, occupying a formidable position and recently restored from top to bottom. It is popular with business conferences, as is apparent from the smart, functional interiors and impeccable service.

moderate

Under the same obliging ownership as the Villa Maria, and only a few minutes walk away, is the ★★★**Hotel Giordano** (same address and phone numbers as the Villa Maria). A modern sister hotel, with the added advantage of a heated outdoor swimming pool and solarium, the Giordano is a comfortable alternative, reasonably priced and well stocked up with useful information on the area. Villa Maria guests have equal access to the facilities and parking for both hotels is available here.

Along the coast in Minori, certainly the best of the hotels in the less elegant resorts of Maori and Minori is the ★★★★**Villa Romana**, ✆ 877237, ✉ 877302, a stylish and comfortable, modern hotel. The management is eager to please, and the hotel well situated in the heart of the town (but not on the sea). The rooftop pool is well away from crowds and car fumes, and the rooms are clean and pleasant. Parking, however, is difficult. In Maiori the ★★★★**San Pietro**, ℂ 877220, ✆ 877025, is a modern hotel popular with Italian holidaymakers. Don't expect a beauty spot. Besides being situated at the far end of town, and well away from the beach, it's square, grey and characterless. However, for a longer stay on the coast, its sports facilities are good, and there are private family-sized bungalows in the grounds. Heading out to Salerno, the tiny resort of Cetara is based around a fine sandy bay and ancient village. The newly renovated ★★★★**Cetus**, ℂ and ✆ 261388, clings precariously to the cliffs between the devilish drive and the deep blue sea. Attractively redecorated with a hint of art-deco, its isolated position and undisturbed bay make the Cetus a rising star among the many hotels on this coastline, the only disadvantage being the long journeys when travelling back and forth along the often packed Amalfi drive. Parking available.

Should you find yourself in Vietri sul Mare, or prefer to stay here instead of Salerno, you could try the ★★★**Hotel Bristol**, Via C. Colombo 2, ℂ 210216, ✆ 761170, just above the beach. It's clean and characterless, but useful for a stopover. A swimming pool and beach are available, but if you're planning a night on the town, it's a long walk uphill!

inexpensive

For a five star view at a third of the price in Ravello, why not check into the ★★**Villa Amore,** ℂ 857135, a delightful small hotel with 12 clean simple rooms, and a lovely terrace where you can take cappuccino with the canaries. It retains a warm, homely atmosphere not common to most of the larger hotels in this area.

Another gem in this price category can be found in unspoilt Scala. The newly built **Villa Giuseppina**, ℂ and ✆ 857106, offers comfort and charm at affordable prices. Good food and great views from the swimming pool make this a tranquil spot to wile away those hazy days of summer. If you prefer you can stay at the older-style **Margherita** which shares the facilities. Parking is easy and you can enjoy some lovely walks down to Amalfi. Just be sure to catch the bus back.

In Maiori, there are several simple hotels near the beaches, such as the ★★**Baia Verde**, ℂ 877276, and the ★★**Vittoria**, ℂ 877652, that offer some of the most convenient budget accommodation on the Amalfi coast. These clean, but unglamorous *pensione* will suit those hoping to explore the Amalfi coastline without paying the price. Typically, both are situated at the top of modern blocks of flats and **Baia Verde** in particular offers a great view from its terrace. If you can cope with the cranky lifts and strict noise restrictions ('no clogs!'), this might be the place for you. Parking available.

Located on one of the main roads in Minori, the ★★★**Santa Lucia**, ℂ and ✆ 877142, is a convenient and inexpensive option, not far from the beach and almost next door to the archaeological park, though just why it was awarded three stars is difficult to imagine. The nylon furnishings will delight anyone with fond memories of the sixties.

Unusually, most of the best dining in Ravello is in the hotels, most notably at Villa Maria · and at the Caruso (*see* above); non-residents are welcome at any of them, either for lunch or dinner. By comparison the rest of the restaurants pale into insignificance, but one exception is **Cumpà Cosimo**, Via Roma 44–46, ✆ 857156 *(moderate)*, where owner-cook Signora Netta Bottone is always happy to advise diners on her latest concoctions and try out her school English on visitors. She's something of an earth mother, and swears by the fresh produce grown on the family farm in Scala. Framed recommendations, lovingly cut from both national and international papers, line the walls enthusing over recipes handed down by Grandma and the warm, homely atmosphere of this traditional restaurant. A holiday high spot, where any meal feels like a family affair. If you make the trip up to Scala, alongside Ravello, try **Zi'Ntonio**, ✆ 857118 *(moderate)*, which serves well-cooked local dishes out on a beautiful covered terrace.

At Maiori, you'll get good fresh fish at **Mammato**, Via Arsenale 6, ✆ 877036 *(Closed Wednesday)*. A glass-fronted restaurant appropriately located overlooking the sea, Mammato is a popular and relaxed venue for beach bums and locals alike *(moderate)*. On a side street in sleepy Minori, is the pretty and floral **Il Giardinello**, Corso V. Emanuele, 17 ✆ 877050. Pass under the leafy archway, and you find yourself in an elegant restaurant, humming with appreciative diners. The menu is varied and interesting, with plenty of fish, but also pasta and the house speciality —pizza for four! *(inexpensive)*.

Even if it's not on the agenda, one delightful reason for stopping in Vietri sul Mare is **Ristorante La Locanda**, Corso Umberto 1, ✆ 761070 *(inexpensive)*. Despite the electronic doorbell, the atmosphere is mellow and welcoming. Guests eat upstairs in a stone-walled dining room that flickers with candlelight, so it's probably more suited to dinner *à deux* than a rowdy party. The food is inventive, tasty and plentiful, and served on the attractive hand-painted plates which have made the town famous. Finishing touches, rarely found in an area now consumed by tourism, make this a truly memorable experience— and if you're really good, you might even take home some pottery of your own. *Closed Mon.*

Salerno

Anywhere else in the south of Italy, a city like Salerno would be an attraction in itself; here it gets lost among the wonders of the Campanian coast—just the big town at the end of the Amalfi drive—and few people ever stop for more than a very brief visit. Nevertheless, Salerno has its modest charms, not least of which is that it is a clean and orderly place; that should endear it to people who hate Naples. Its setting under a backdrop of mountains is memorable. The Italian highway engineers, showing off as usual, have brought a highway to Salerno on a chain of viaducts, one lofty span after another, an unusual and pleasing ornament for the city; at night the road lights hang on the mountain slopes like strings of fairy lights on a Christmas tree.

Salerno's ancient distinction was its medical school, the oldest and finest of medieval Europe. Traditionally founded by the legendary 'Four Doctors'—an Italian, a Greek, a Jew and an Arab—the school was of the greatest importance in the transmission of Greek and Muslim science into Europe. Most of us, however, may recognize Salerno better as the site of the Allied invasion in September 1943, one of the biggest and most successful such operations of World War II.

Salerno's port is on the outskirts of town, and the shore all through the city centre is graced with a pretty park, the Lungomare Trieste. Parallel with it, and two streets back, the Corso Vittorio Emanuele leads into the old town. Here it changes its name to Via dei Mercanti, most colourful of Salerno's old streets. The **cathedral**, a block to the north on Via del Duomo, is set with its façade behind a courtyard, or *quadroporticos*, with a fountain at the centre, and a detached campanile—as if it were not a church at all, but a mosque. The Corinthian columns around it come from the ancient city of Paestum, not far down the coast. The cathedral's treasures are of the same order as those of the Amalfi coast: another pair of bronze doors from Constantinople, and another beautiful pair of Cosmatesque pulpits. The building itself has been much restored, and many of the best original details have been preserved in the adjacent **Museo del Duomo** *(open daily, 9–7)*.

Robert the Cunning and his Blushing Bride

On the inscription across the cathedral façade, you can read how the cathedral was built by 'Duke Robert, greatest of conquerors, with his own money'. This was Robert Guiscard, 'the Cunning', one of the first and greatest of the Norman warriors who came to plunder southern Italy in the 11th century. Robert de Hauteville came to Italy in 1046, one of the younger brothers of that remarkable Norman family that would one day found a dynasty in Sicily. His elder brother Drogo, chief of the clan, had no lands to give him, so Robert was on his own, hiring his sword out first to the Lombard Count Pandulf of Capua, later to his brothers or anyone else who could pay for it.

Contemporary accounts describe Robert as a fair-haired, blue-eyed giant. The Byzantine Anna Comnena wrote of him as 'in temper tyrannical, in mind most clever, brave in action, very clever in attacking the wealth and substance of magnates...' He earned his sobriquet Guiscard for tricks like the taking of Malvita, a fortified monastery in Calabria. One day a party of unarmed Normans came up to the gate with a coffin, and asked to have a funeral Mass said for one of their comrades. The monks let them in, and once inside, the coffin burst open to reveal a very live knight lying on a pile of swords. Combined with cleverness like this, Robert's formidable strength and skill in battle soon earned him an important position in the south. In 1058 he found a fitting bride, Princess Sichelgaita of the ruling Lombard house of Salerno. Nearly as tall and as strong as Robert himself, she loved nothing better than accompanying him into battle, her long blond hair pouring out from her helmet. The pair went from success to success, and capped it all with Robert's papal investiture as Duke of Apulia and Calabria.

But Robert's greatest exploit would not come until 1084, a year before his death. That year there were two popes in Rome, a common occurrence, one supported by the German emperor Henry and the other, Gregory VII, by Robert. When the Normans brought up a big army to force the issue, Rome resisted, and Robert's men (along with Saracen mercenaries from Sicily) took the city and treated it to the worst sacking in its history, far more destructive than anything the 5th-century barbarians ever dared. Gregory, the great reformer Hildebrand before becoming pope, had worked unceasingly for decades to build the power of the papacy; now he had his victory, but the Romans hated him so thoroughly he could not stay in the city. He was forced to accompany Robert to Salerno, where he died soon after. Robert buried him in this cathedral, which he had begun, perhaps in expiation, the same year.

From Salerno you can make an easy excursion up into the mountains to the town of **Cava de' Tirreni**. Near it, perched precariously on the slopes of the Val di Bonea, is a little-visited Benedictine monastery called **La Trinità di Cava**—rebuilt, as usual, in tiresome Baroque, but preserving a wealth of 12th–14th-century frescoes, stone-carving and Cosmati work.

Salerno ✆ (089–) **Where to Stay**

Salerno's hotels are fairly modest and utilitarian. Though the cathedral is well worth a visit, this is not a good base for a holiday. The beach is popular in the summer with the locals and covered with litter. For these reasons it is better to head up to Paestum where beaches are cleaner and less crowded. If you just want to stay a couple of nights, the hotels and restaurants should satisfy most explorers' needs.

expensive

At the top end the ★★★★**Jolly Hotel delle Palme**, Lungomare Trieste 1, ✆ 225222, ✉ 237571, is pleasant and reliable, and right on the seafront.

moderate

More than acceptable for an overnight stay is the ★★★**Plaza**, Piazza Ferrovia 42, ✆ and ✉ 224477, right across from the station offering modern and comfortable rooms. Close by, in the pedestrian area, is the recently refurbished ★★★**Montestella**, Corso Vittorio Emanuele 156, ✆ 225122, ✉ 229167. All rooms have showers. Convenient for the beach is the ★★★**Fiorenza**, Via Trento 145, ✆ and ✉ 338800, a clean, well-run hotel with 30 bedrooms.

Several cheaper hotels are to be found on or around the Corso Vittorio Emanuele. Try the **★★Salerno**, Via G. Vicinanza 42, ✆ 224211, @ 224432—simple but comfortable. Lastly Salerno also has a youth hostel, **Ostello per Gioventu' Irno**, Via Luigi Guercio 112, ✆ 790251 and @ 252649 *(closed daily 10.30am–5pm; curfew 1am)*.

Salerno ✆ (089–)   **Eating Out**

expensive

Nicola dei Principati, Corso Garibaldi 201, ✆ 225435, in the old centre of Salerno, serves mainly fish dishes, including an excellent *linguine con astice*, long pasta with lobster. At **Il Timone**, Via Generale Clark 29, ✆ 335111, the speciality is *tubetti alla pescatrice*, short pasta served with a delicious fish sauce. The second courses, almost all fish, are equally good. *Closed Mon.*

moderate

One of the liveliest restaurants in town, right in the *centro storico*, is the **Vicolo della Neve**, Vicolo della Neve 24, ✆ 225705, an attractive place decorated with wall paintings by some of the many artists who have established it as their local. The chef turns out good Campanian favourites such as *melanzane alla parmigiana*, aubergines cooked in layers with mozzarella, parmesan, tomato and basil, and the classic *pasta e fagioli*. You can also order excellent pizza. *Open evenings only; closed Wed* At **Alla Brace**, Lungomare Trieste 11–13, ✆ 225159, as well as the usual fish dishes, you will be offered a host of delicious local specialities such as stuffed peppers, ravioli filled with ricotta, and a remarkable potato soufflé. There is also a wide range of home-made desserts. **Al Cenacolo**, Piazza Alfano I, ✆ 238818, in front of the cathedral, serves excellent seafood and is recommended by the locals.

inexpensive

Da Sasa at Via Diaz 42, ✆ 220330, is a good inexpensive trattoria, with traditional home-cooking and especially tasty pasta courses at very accessible prices. For good pizza and seafood, **Ristorante Pinocchio**, Lungomare Trieste 56–58, ✆ 229964, is also great value. Head here to dine shoulder to shoulder with Salernitani. *Closed Fri.*

Paestum

Campania

There's more to the region than just the Bay of Naples. However, the coast and its endless attractions draw off most of the tourists, and it's a rare soul indeed who ever makes it up to old Capua, or the excellent little city of Benevento.

Getting Around

The interior of Campania makes up a rather large piece of territory—the three main towns are all provincial capitals. None are on the main **railway** lines, however, and you will have to scrutinize the schedules in Naples carefully to find your way around. For Capua take the Piedimonte Matese train from Naples to Santa Maria Capua Vetere. Trains to Caserta are rather more frequent and very convenient for the Royal Palace–the Reggia–which is just in front of it.

Buses for Caserta, Capua, Avellino, and Benevento leave Naples from Piazza Garibaldi, in front of the Stazione Centrale. The **CTP** (Consorzio trasporti pubblici), © (081) 7001111, runs regular buses to Caserta (1hr) stopping at the station. From here you can also take buses to S.M. Capua Vetere.

By far the fastest way to get to the interior of Campania is **by car**, along the A2, which passes between Caserta and Capua, or the A16 Bari *autostrada*, which runs past Avellino. A slower but slightly quieter route to Caserta is along the old SS87 road. To get to it, take the Viale Maddalena to the left of Capodichino airport, and then follow the signs for Caserta.

Tourist Information

The provincial EPT tourist office is at Caserta, right in the Royal Palace, 81100, © (0823) 322170.

Capua

This is a double city, consisting of the modern town, founded in the 9th century, and the ancient one, once the second city of Italy, but deserted in the Dark Ages and now modestly reborn as **Santa Maria Capua Vetere**.

Capua can trace its founding to the Oscans, blithe folk of ancient Italy who introduced farce to the theatre, and who probably give us the word *obscene*. It is believed that the Oscan farces, banned by all decent Roman emperors, created the prototypes of the *commedia dell'arte* stock characters, including Naples' favourite Pulcinello—Punch. All that should give you some idea of the spirit of old Capua, a city best known for beautiful women and the manufacture of perfume, and as renowned for loose morals in its day as Sybaris. Everyone but the jealous Roman historians liked to give Capua credit for defeating the great Hannibal. The Capuans had always hated those dreary dour Romans, and they eagerly took the Carthaginians' part. Hannibal's men enjoyed Capuan hospitality in the

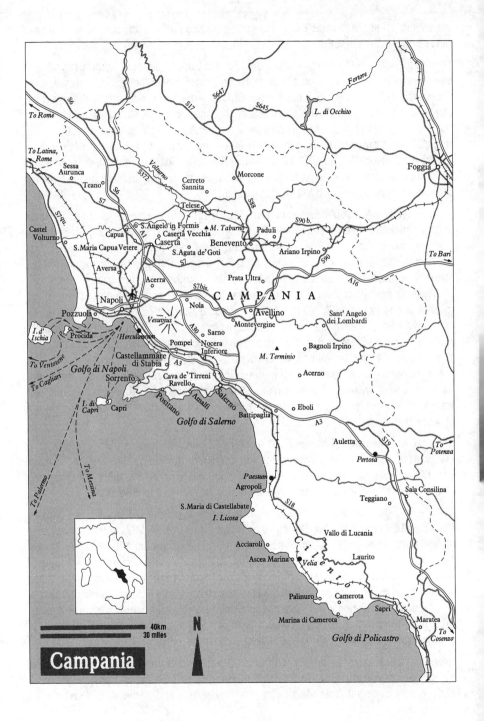

winter of 216 BC; they came out in the spring so dreamy-eyed and dissipated that they never beat the Romans again.

Of course there was hell to pay when the Romans came back, but Capua survived, and even flourished for several centuries more as the greatest city of the region. Finally though, some even worse drudges than the Romans arrived—the Arabs, who utterly destroyed the city in about 830. The survivors then refounded Capua on a new site, a few kilometres to the north. Of old Capua, at Santa Maria Capua Vetere, you can see the remains of the second-largest **amphitheatre** *(open 9–6 in summer, till 4 in winter; adm)* in Italy—largest of all before Rome built its Colosseum. Here Spartacus began his gladiators' revolt in 73 BC. Few sections of the stands are still intact, but there is an underground network of tunnels and trap doors much like the Colosseum.

A short walk away you'll find something much more interesting— perhaps the best example of a **Mithraeum** *(open 9–4.30, closed Mon; free)* discovered anywhere in the Mediterranean. The cult of the god Mithras, imported from Persia by the legionaries, was for a while the most widespread of the cults that tried to fill the religious vacuum of the imperial centuries. Some scholars see in it much in common with Christianity. The resemblance isn't readily apparent; Mithraism was an archaic, gut-level cult, with mystery initiations and lots of bull's blood splashing about. Though it originally took hold in the army, and always remained a men-only affair, as late as the 3rd century AD it could probably claim more adherents than Christianity. The upper classes were never too impressed with it; that is why it lost out to the Christians, and why such well-executed frescoes as these are rare. The *mithraeum* is an underground hall, used in the initiations, and dominated by a large scene of Mithras, a typical Mediterranean solar hero, slaying a white bull with a serpent under its feet; the complementary fresco representing the moon on the opposite wall is less well-preserved.

The new **Archaeological Museum of Ancient Capua**, Via Roberto D'Angio *(open 9–7, closed Mon; free)* provides a convenient introduction to the site complementing the more important Museo Campano at new Capua. Also around Santa Maria, there is a crumbling triumphal arch, and some elaborate Roman tombs, off the road to Caserta.

The new Capua has all the most interesting finds from the old one at the **Museo Provinciale Campano**, Via Principi Longobardi 1/3 *(open 9–2, closed Mon; free)* though most people will probably make do with the new museum at S.M Capua Vetere. Just north of the town, on the slopes of Mount Tifata, a site once occupied by a temple of Diana now contains the 11th-century basilica of **Sant'Angelo in Formis**. The 12th-century frescoes here are some of the best in the south, oddly archaic figures that would seem much more at home in Constantinople than in Italy. And, more than mere artistry, there is an intense spiritual vision about these paintings—note especially the unearthly, unforgettable face of the enthroned St Michael above the portal.

North of Capua, near the border with Lazio, the last town in Campania along the Via Appia is **Sessa Aurunca**, with a Roman bridge and some other scanty ruins, as well as a 12th-century cathedral, interesting for its surviving ancient and medieval sections.

In one shot, you can see the biggest palace in Italy, and also the most wearisome; both distinctions belong uncontestably to the **Reggia**, or Royal Palace, built here by the Bourbon King of Naples, Charles III *(the Royal Apartments open Mon–Sat, 9–2, Sun til 1; adm)*. His architect, Luigi Vanvitelli (really a Dutchman named Van Wittel) spared no expense; like the Spanish Bourbons, those of Naples were greenly jealous of Versailles, and wanted to show the big Louies back home that they, too, deserved a little respect. The Reggia, begun in 1752, has some 1200 rooms, not much compared to the 2800 of the Bourbon palace in Madrid, but larger than its Spanish cousin just the same (it's also larger than Versailles); the façade is 245m across. Inside, as in Madrid, everything is tasteful, ornate and soberingly expensive; the only good touches from Vanvitelli's heavy hand are the elegant grand staircases. Only the **Park** *(open 9–one hour before sunset; adm)* makes the trip worthwhile, an amazingly long axis of pools and cascades climbing up to the famous **Diana fountain**, with a lifelike sculptural group of the goddess and her attendants catching Actaeon in the act. There is also an **English garden**, of the sort fashionable in the 18th century. The Reggia was commandeered for use as Allied military headquarters in Italy in 1943, and it was here that the final surrender of the German armies in Italy was accepted two years later.

The village of **San Leucio**, nearly 3km north of Caserta, was founded by the Bourbon kings as a paternalistic utopian experiment, and also an establishment for the manufacture of silk. Ferdinand IV, for most of his life, personally saw to every detail of its operation, even christening the children of the workers. The successor of his *Real Fabbrica* is still a centre for silk. Some 9km to the east there is the half-deserted town of **Casertavecchia**. The building of the Reggia drew most of the population down to modern Caserta, but the old town still has the

Reggia di Caserta

12th-century **Cathedral**, *(open 3–4)* with a great octagonal *ciborium* (a cylindrical or prismatic dome) that is one of the glories of Arab-Norman architecture.

Caserta ✆ (0823–)   ***Eating Out***

Neither Capua nor Caserta makes a very attractive base for an overnight stay. The environs of Caserta, though, do have some good restaurants. There are three good spots at Casertavecchia and one offering in Caserta close to the Reggia.

moderate

Outside Casertavecchia, at the **Ritrovo dei Patriarchi**, Via Conte Landolfo 14, Località Sommana, ✆ 371510, you'll find game in abundance, including pheasant, venison, partridge and wild boar, depending on the time of year. There are also good hearty soups and vegetable dishes. *Closed Thurs.*

In the centre of Casertavecchia, **Rocca di Sant'Andrea**, Via Torre 8, ✆ 371140, offers delicious pasta dishes and a variety of *secondi*, many of which are based on meat grilled on the open fire in front of you. There is also a good selection of home-made desserts. *Closed Mon.*

inexpensive

At **La Castellana**, Via Torre 4, ✆ 371230, near Rocca di Sant'Andrea, you can feast on wild boar or venison, when available, as well as a wonderfully innovative selection of soup and pasta openers. *Closed Thurs.* Lastly, back at Caserta itself, **La Massa**, on Via Mazzini 55, ✆ 444096, is a simple and convenient place for lunch near the Reggia. *Closed Fri.*

Benevento

Getting Around

Remote Benevento is not well connected with any of Italy's main transport systems. It is on the Naples–Foggia **railway** line, but be careful about Naples–Benevento trains, as some but not all of them are operated by a private railway, and you will need to find out which—ask at the information booth in Naples' Stazione Centrale—to buy the right ticket. The private line is faster.

The most frequent public transport connections are by **bus**. The **Consorzio Trasporti Irpini**, ✆ (081) 5534677, has regular services to Avellino (50min) and Benevento (1½hrs) from Piazza Garibaldi in Naples. In Benevento, buses to Naples and a surprising variety of other places (including one daily to Rome) leave from Piazza Pacca, on Corso Dante just west of the cathedral. There are several companies; check at the Benevento EPT for schedules.

To get to Benevento **by road** from Naples take the A2 north and then south of Caserta look for the SS265 eastwards, which joins up with the SS7, the Via Appia, for Benevento. This road is quite slow. An alternative is to take the A16 *autostrada* to Avellino, and then the SS88 north from there to Benevento.

Tourist Information

Benevento's EPT is east of the city centre at Via Nicola Sala 31, 82100, © (0824) 319903, 🖂 312309. Its information office is in Palazzo Bosco at Piazza Roma 11, 82100, © (0824) 319930.

The Duchy of Benevento

Ever since the Middle Ages, the land around Caserta and Capua has been called the *Terra del Lavoro*—cultivated land, a broad garden plain that is one of the most fertile corners of Italy. Today its lush landscapes have suffered a bit from creeping industrialism, though it's in the stretch to the south, between Caserta and Naples, where the worst modern depredations can be seen. Nowadays, the Napoletani call the towns around Afragola, Acerra and Secondigliano the 'Triangle of Death', an industrial wasteland of shanties and power lines ruled by the Camorra that has Italy's worst unemployment, and some of its worst social problems.

Go east instead, up into the foothills of the Apennines towards **Benevento**, yet another smallish city that has often played a big role in Italian history. On an old tower in the centre of town, the city fathers have put up maps of southern Italy, showing the boundaries of the two important states of which Benevento was the capital.

At first, as *Malies* or *Maloenton*, it was the leading town of the Samnites, the warlike mountain people who resisted Roman imperialism for so long. The Romans were later to make a big city of it, an important stop along the Appian Way. They Latinized the name to *Maleventum*—ill wind—but after a lucky defeat of Pyrrhus of Epirus here in 275 BC, they thought it might just be a *Beneventum* after all. In 571, the city was captured by the bloodthirsty Lombards, becoming their southern capital. After the Lombards of the north fell to Charlemagne, the Duchy of Benevento carried on as an independent state; at its greatest extent, under relatively enlightened princes like Arechi II (*c.* 800), it ruled almost all of southern Italy. The Normans put an end to it in the 1060s.

Coming to Benevento in the winter, you're bound to think the Romans were crazy to change the name. When people in Salerno are ready to hit the beaches, you'll find the Beneventani shivering on street corners like Muscovites in their fur caps, victims of traditionally the worst weather in southern Italy. It is often claimed this makes them more serious and introspective than people on the coast—certainly coming here from Naples seems metaphorically like a trip of a thousand miles. Benevento has often been the scene of earthquakes, and the city took plenty of hard shots during the battles of 1943, but there are still enough attractions around to make a stop worthwhile.

Benevento's **cathedral** (under restoration in 1996) is in the lower town, the part that suffered the most in the bombings. The cathedral itself was almost a total loss; only the odd 13th-century façade remains, built of miscellaneous bits of Roman buildings—inscriptions, reliefs, friezes and pillars—arranged every which way. In the old streets behind the cathedral, you can see a well-preserved **Roman Theatre** *(open daily, 9am–sunset)*—not an amphitheatre, but a place for classical drama, something rare this far north. By the time the Romans conquered them, the culture of the Samnites was almost completely Hellenized. This theatre, built under Hadrian, originally seated 20,000. All through this quarter, called the **Triggio**, you will see bits of Roman brick and medieval masonry—something ancient built into the walls of every house. There is half a Roman bridge over the Sabato (one of Benevento's two rivers), ruins of the baths, remains of a triumphal arch, and plenty of gates and stretches of wall from the fortifications built by the Lombards. On Via Posillipo, a Baroque monument houses the **Bue Apis**, a sacred Egyptian bull sculpture found in Benevento's Temple of Isis.

Trajan's Arch

Some people claim Benevento's triumphal arch to be better than those of Rome itself; built in AD 117, it is a serious piece of work—over 15m of expensive Parian marble from Greece—and certainly better preserved than the ones in the capital. It marks the spot where the Appian Way entered Beneventum, (now Via Traiana on the northern edge of the old town) and the skilfully carved reliefs on both faces record significant events in the career of the emperor.

Trajan (AD 98–117), the conqueror of Dacia (modern-day Romania) and Mesopotamia, ranks among the greatest of the emperors, and a little commemoration would not seem out of hand; nevertheless cynics will enjoy the transparent and sometimes heavy-handed political propaganda of ornaments like this. In one of the panels, Trajan (the handsome fellow with the curly beard) is shown distributing gifts to children; in another he presides over the *institutio alimentaria*—the dole. Most of the scenes are about victories: Trajan announcing military reforms, Trajan celebrating a triumph, Jove handing Trajan one of his thunderbolts, and finally the Apotheosis, where the late emperor is received among the gods while the goddess Roma escorts Hadrian to coronation as his divinely ordained successor.

The Museo Sannio

Corso Garibaldi is Benevento's main street, just south of Trajan's Arch. Near its eastern end stands the city's oldest church, **Santa Sofia**, built in the late 8th century. It is unusual for its plan, an irregular six-pointed star, and was built for the Lombard Prince Arechi II by an architect thoroughly grounded in the mystic geometry of the early Middle Ages. The vaulting is supported by recycled Roman columns, and other columns have been hollowed out for use as holy water fonts.

The church cloister contains one of the south's more interesting provincial museums, the **Museo Sannio** *(open 9–1, closed Mon; free)*. *Sannio* refers to Samnium, as Benevento's province is still officially called. The 12th-century cloister is itself well worth a look, with a variety of strange twisted columns under pulvins carved with even stranger scenes: monster-hunting, dancing, fantastical animals, bunnies, and a camel or two. The best things in the museum are in the archaeological section. Almost all the classic vases are Campanian copies of Greek ware—the production of ceramics was the engine that drove *Campania Felix*'s economy in its glory days.

Some Samnite Curiosities

Two rooms in the museum are filled with objects from the Temple of Isis. Anyone who has read Apuleius' *The Golden Ass* will remember just how important the cult of the transcendent goddess Isis was throughout the Roman world. This Egyptian import certainly seems to have found a home in Beneventum; nowhere in Europe has so much fine Egyptian statuary been retrieved. The temple had imperial backing. One of the statues is of the founder, Emperor Domitian himself, in Egyptian dress. Other works portray priestesses, sacred boats and sphinxes, another Apis bull, and a porphyry '*cista mistica*', carved with a snake. The image of Isis is also there, formidably impressive, even without a head.

Somehow this leads naturally to Benevento's more famous piece of exotica—the witches. In the days of the Lombards, women by the hundreds would dance around a sacred walnut tree on the banks of the River Sabato ('sabbath'). Even after the official conversion to Christianity in 663, the older religion persisted, and Benevento is full of every sort of 'witch' story as a result. The best piece of modern sculpture in the Museo Sannio is a representation of the witches' dance. Of course the city has found ways to put the legend to use. In any bar in Italy, you can pick up a bottle of 'liquore Strega' (*strega* means witch) and read on the label the proud device: 'Made next to the train station in Benevento, Italy'.

Just a few streets west of the museum on Corso Garibaldi, the dedicatory **obelisk** from the Isis temple stands in front of the town hall. East of the museum, the Corso takes you to the **Rocca de' Rettori**, a fortress built by the popes in the 14th century; for centuries Benevento was a papal enclave surrounded by the Kingdom of Naples. The fortress is now a part of the Museo Sannio. Behind it is a lovely park, the Villa Comunale.

Benevento ℰ (0824–)   **Where to Stay**

Benevento sees few tourists and accommodation is therefore limited. This is one of the reasons why it is even more attractive to those chancing upon it. There are several good restaurants and prices, in general, are markedly lower than the well-visited coast and Naples. It is an ideal base for making forays into inland Campania, as well as Caserta and Capua.

moderate

The ★★★★**Gran Hotel Italiano**, Viale Principe di Napoli 137, ℰ 24111, ✉ 21758, is located just a block from the Stazione Centrale. The building and interior decor are 70s, but the hotel's simple policy of providing a decent standard coupled with the courtesy of the staff, all at provincial prices, makes this good value. The 20-minute walk into the historic centre is its drawback.

inexpensive/cheap

It is hard to beat the ★★**Della Corte**, Piazza Piano di Corte, ℰ 54819, both for charm and for its location right in the heart of the historic quarter. The rooms are clean and quiet, the bathrooms modern and the place and proprietor have character. The hotel only has 7 rooms and as yet remains fairly undiscovered.

Benevento ⓒ (0824–) **Eating Out**

Dining in Benevento can be interesting; it's another world from the Campanian coast, with seafood replaced on the menu by rabbit, duck, lamb and veal. Samnium makes some good but little-known wines; you might ask for a bottle of stout-hearted Solopaca red with your Samnite repast.

moderate/inexpensive

Benevento's favourite restaurant is probably the **Antica Taverna**, at Via Annunziata 41, ⓒ 54840, which you can find by walking through Piazza Roma in the centre down Via O. Pupillo. You eat off long wooden tables covered with paper tablecloths in this popular trattoria. The roast kid is one of the more unusual items on the menu. *Open Mon–Sat; Sun until 3pm.* In the piazza in front of Trajan's Arch the fun **Ristorante Teatro Gastronomico**, Via Traiano–Palazzo L. Andreotti, ⓒ 54605, serves up a truly gastronomic menu of local specialities under a barrel vault painted with architectural backdrops lined with real balconies.

cheap

At the **Ristorante–Pizzeria Traiano**, Via Manciotti 48/50, ⓒ 25013, again opposite Trajan's Arch, you can help yourself to a huge plate of antipasti and then move on to excellent pizza in this popular pizzeria. In summer there are also tables outside.

If you are basing yourself in Benevento to explore inland Campania, the **Pizzeria Romana**, a stand-up *tavola calda* on the corner of Corso Dante and Corso Vittorio Emanuele, a block west of the cathedral, provides an excellent selection of very affordable delicacies for perfect picnics in the gardens of the Reggia at Caserta and other sites.

Samnium

Samnium is one of Italy's smallest provinces, but there are a few towns and villages of interest; the countryside, full of oak and walnut forests, is often reminiscent of some corner of Umbria. **Morcone**, to the north, has a memorable setting, draped on the curving slope of a hill like a Roman theatre. **Telese**, to the west on the road towards Lazio, lies near a small but pretty lake of the same name, with a popular spa establishment. The nearby ruins of the Samnite-Roman town of *Telesia* are remarkable for their perfectly octagonal walls, with gates at the cardinal points.

Best of all, perhaps, is the town of **Sant'Agata dei Goti**, some kilometres north of the Via Appia between Benevento and Caserta, with its long line of buildings like a man-made cliff overhanging a little ravine. Sant'Agata takes its name from the Goths who founded it in the 6th century; it was badly damaged in the 1980 earthquake, and its modest monuments, the **Castello** and the 12th-century **Church of Santa Menna**, are still undergoing restoration.

Tourist Information

Avellino's tourist office is at Via Due Principati 5, 83100, ✆ (0825) 74695.

Continuing this broad arc around Naples, south and east of Benevento there are few attractions, but some attractive mountain scenery in a region called **Irpinia**, consisting of most of the province of Avellino. In places, the mountains bear fine forests of oaks and chestnuts, as well as plantations of hazelnut trees; other parts are grim and bare, an introduction to the 19th-century deforestation that ruined so much of southern Italy. Irpinia was the region worst affected by the 1980 earthquake.

The main highway south from Caserta, around the back side of Vesuvius, isn't that much more promising. **Nola**, the biggest town on the route, began as another Oscan foundation. It had a famous early bishop, St Paulinus, a friend of St Augustine and also, it is claimed, the inventor of the bell (bells are *campane* in Italian, from their Campanian origin). To celebrate the anniversary of St Paulinus' return from imprisonment at the hands of the Vandals, every 27 June the people of Nola put on one of the more spectacular festivals of the south, the 'Dance of the Lilies', a procession of 15m wooden steeples, elaborately decorated and carried by the men of the town (*see* 'Festivals', p.17). Further south, in the hills above the city of **Nocera Inferiore**, an ancient hamlet called **Nocera Superiore** has somehow kept intact its 4th-century church, an unusual round building with a cupola that may have been converted from a pagan sanctuary.

The road into the mountains of Irpinia begins at Nola, leading towards **Avellino**. This little provincial capital, important in Norman times, has been wrecked so many times by invaders and earthquakes that little remains to be seen. In the centre, the 17th-century Palazzo della Dogana has a façade of ancient statues and a big clock tower; nearby stands a Baroque fountain with Bellerophon dispatching the Chimaera. Archaeological finds, ancient and medieval, from around Irpinia are kept in the modern Museo Irpino on Corso Europa.

Northwest of Avellino, **Montevergine** has been the most important pilgrimage site of this region since the arrival of a miraculous 'Black Madonna' in 1310—a Byzantine icon of the Virgin, stolen from Constantinople by the Crusaders in the sack of 1204; like the others across Europe, the oxidation of its yellow paint has turned it black over the centuries. Montevergine can be reached either by a long and tortuous road, or by a cable railway from the village of Mercogliano. The 12th-century church, built over a sanctuary of Ceres and many times reconstructed, has two fine tombs of the 1300s.

North of Avellino, separate roads lead to Taurasi, the centre of a wine region, and **Prata di Principato Ultra**, a tiny village with one of the oldest Christian monuments in the south. The Basilica dell'Annunziata was probably begun in the 3rd century; there are fragments of paintings and two small catacombs. Eastern Irpinia is a wild and mountainous area where villages are few and far between. **Monte Terminio**, lately become a modest skiing area, has extensive woods and rushing mountain streams, along with plenty of pheasants, stags and boars, wild mushrooms and chestnuts—and a few truffles, perhaps the southern-most truffles found anywhere. **Sant'Angelo dei Lombardi**, further east, was an important medieval monastic centre; the earthquakes have spared bits of two simple churches (12th and 13th centuries).

Paestum and the Cilento

After the Bay and the Amalfi coast—two heavy courses for a holiday banquet—we can offer the Cilento peninsula, as a light, refreshing dessert. The Cilento is a squarish low massif jutting out from the coast between the Gulf of Salerno and the Gulf of Policastro. Its mountain scenery may not be quite as breathtaking as the Amalfi drive, but the Cilento makes up for it by being delightfully wild and unspoilt, and altogether one of the most beguiling out-of-the-way places to spend your time in southern Italy. The interior of the Cilento is not traversed by any easy roads, and the traveller heading south from Salerno will have a choice of two routes: a long, leisurely drive along the coast, past the remark-able ruins of ancient Paestum and a number of small, very casual resorts, or along the present main road, the A3 *Autostrada del Sole*, over the mountains and skirting the eastern edge of the Cilento, a route of often beautiful, wild scenery down the valley of the Tanagro River.

Getting Around

Paestum has a station on the main **railway** line between Naples and Reggio di Calabria, but only local trains stop there. More conve-niently, there are frequent **buses** from the Piazza Concordia in Salerno (on the shore, by the Porto Turistico). They are run by several companies; some follow the coast route, while others go through Battipaglia. Some of these continue on to various resort towns on the Cilento coast.

All the Cilento towns are connected by **bus** to Salerno's Piazza Concordia; there is a bewildering list of companies, towns and schedules, but fortunately the EPT in Salerno publishes a full list of them in the front of their annual hotel book. The **railway** line only touches the Cilento coast at two points—Ascea and Pisciotta—and, as at Paestum, not too many trains stop.

As we have mentioned, there are only two main **road** routes, the SS18 coast road and the A3 and parallel SS19 further inland. At Agropoli the SS267 leaves the SS18 and runs round the Cilento coast. North of Paestum there is also another turn off the SS18, the SS166 to the east, a long and winding road across the Cilento interior that eventually connects up with the A3.

Tourist Information

The tourist office, close by the main station, in Piazza V. Veneto, ✆ (089) 231432, has the most complete information on transport and accommodation in Paestum and the Cilento. There is also the

AAST, in the central Piazza Amendola, 84100, ℂ (089) 224744, ✆ 752839.

There are information offices in Paestum, Via Magna Grecia (near the archaeological zone), ℂ (0828) 811016, ✆ 722322, and Palinuro, in Piazza Virgilio, ℂ (0974) 938144.

Paestum: A Lost City

Along the coast, the route begins in a fertile plain that meets the Cilento near the ruins of **Paestum**, site of the only well-preserved Greek temples north of Sicily *(site open Tues–Sun, 9am–one hour before sunset; closed first and third Mon of every month for restoration work; museum open Tues–Sun, 9–2 only; joint adm for both)*. And there is another important player on the Mediterranean stage who needs to be introduced. The anopheles mosquito, as fate would have it, gets the credit for preserving Paestum's ruins so well. By the 9th century or so, this once-great city was breathing its last, a victim of economic decline and Arab raiders. As its people gradually abandoned it for safer settlements in the hills, Paestum was swallowed up by the thick forests of this subtropical corner of Italy.

As usual on a Mediterranean coastal plain, when the people leave the malaria mosquitoes take over. By the Middle Ages, the site of Paestum became utterly uninhabitable—it meant certain death to stay there overnight—and after a while the city's very existence was forgotten. After being hidden away, like the Mayan temples in the Mexican jungle, for almost a thousand years, the city was rediscovered in the 18th century; a crew of Charles III's road builders stumbled onto the huge temples in the midst of the forest.

Originally *Poseidonia*, the city was founded in the 7th century BC by the Sybarites, as a station on the all-important trade route up Italy's west coast. The Romans took over in 273 BC, and the name became Latinized to Paestum. As a steadfast supporter of the Roman cause throughout the Punic Wars, Paestum was a favoured city. Famous around the Mediterranean for its flowers, especially roses, it prospered until the end of the Roman era. Today the forests have been cleared, and the ruins of the city stand in the open on the green and quiet plain. Not only the celebrated temples have survived; much of the 4km circuit of **walls** still stands to some height, along with some of the towers and gates.

Most of Paestum's important buildings were grouped along an axis between the Porta Aurea and the Porta Giustizia, with the forum at its centre. The two grand temples that everyone comes to see are at the southern end: the **Basilica** and the **Temple of Neptune**, two Doric edifices in the finest classical style. The names were just guesses on the part of the early archaeologists. The 'Neptune' temple, the best preserved, was built about 450 BC. It is about 60m long, and all of the structure survives except the roof and the internal walls. Similarities to another temple at Tarentum may suggest it was dedicated to Apollo but Hera and Zeus are possible contenders. The **Basilica** was divided to house two cults, most probably connected with Hera, the tutelary goddess of the city. It is a century older, and a little smaller. Missing its Doric frieze and pediment the first archaeologists did not recognize the building for a temple, hence the name **Basilica**.

The aesthetic may not be quite what you expected—dimensions squat and strong rather than graceful and tall. Still, this is the classic austerity of Greek architecture at its best.

There is more to it than meets the eye. If you look closely along the rows of columns, or the lines of the base, you may notice that nothing in either of them is perfectly straight. The edges bulge outwards, as they do in the Parthenon and every other Greek building; this is an architectural trick called *entasis* ; it creates an optical illusion, making the lines seem straight at a distance. Greek temples like this are the most sober and serious build-ings in western architecture, based on a simple system of perfect proportion. The form may seem austere and academic, but with some imagination you can picture them in their original beauty—covered in a sort of enamel made of gleaming ground marble, setting off the brilliant colours of the polychromed sculptural reliefs on the pediments and frieze.

To the west, some of the streets of the city have been excavated, though very little is left to see. To the north, around the broad Forum—really a simple rectangular space in the manner of a Greek *agora*—are the remains of an ampitheatre, a round *bouleterion*, or council house, and other buildings. Still further north is the third and smallest of the surviving temples, the **Temple of Ceres**.

Paestum's **Museum** holds most of the sculptural fragments and finds from the town. Some of the best reliefs are not from Paestum at all, but from the recently discovered sanc-tuary of Hera, a few kilometres north at the mouth of the river Sele. This temple, mentioned by many ancient writers, is said to have been founded by Jason and the Argonauts during their wanderings. From tombs excavated just outside the city come some examples of Greek fresco painting—nothing special in themselves, but probably the only ones in existence. Look out for the most famous fresco, *The Diver*, which you have probably seen reproduced innumerable times elsewhere. Even though the Greeks took painting as seriously as they did sculpture, you will not find any similar surviving examples in Greece, or anywhere else.

While you are exploring Paestum, keep an eye out too for the wild flowers. More than one 19th-century traveller claimed to have found descendants of Paestum's famous roses (*bifera rosaria Paestum*) growing wild, and some may still be around.

The Cilento Coast

For many, one of the best attractions of Paestum will be the fine, long beaches that line this part of the coast. South of the ruins, the shore becomes jagged and mountainous, passing groves of pines alternating with rugged cliffs and pocket-sized beaches. Most of the villages along it have become quiet, cosy resorts that cater mostly to Italians. One is usually close to the next, and if you care to stay over, you can keep going until you find one that suits your fancy.

Agropoli comes first, then **Santa Maria di Castellabate**, **San Marco**, and **Punta Licosa,** on the westernmost point of the Cilento, named after the siren, Leucosia. Legend has it that she threw herself into the sea after her failure to entice Ulysses on to the rocks.. From here, you can take a small boat out to an uninhabited islet, also called Licosa, where there are some unidentified ancient ruins. Further down the coast, **Acciaroli** and **Pioppi** are among the nicer resort towns of the Cilento. South of the latter, and just inland from the village of Ascea Marina, you can visit the ruins of another Greek city, **Velia**.

Don't expect any spectacular ruins of the order of Paestum. Velia disappeared gradually, and most of its buildings were carried off for building stone long ago. *Elea*, as it was known back then, was a colony of the Ionian city of Phocaea, and a sister city of another important Phocaean foundation—Marseille, in France. Elea was never large or important, but its name lives on gloriously in philosophy; the Elean school of philosophers produced some of the most brilliant minds of the ancient world: logical grinds like Parmenides, who proposed the first theory of atoms, and wiseacres like Zeno with his pesky paradoxes. Some of the fortifications survive, including one well-preserved gate—the Porta Rosa, and just enough of the *agora*, baths, and streets are left to enable us to guess at how the city may have looked.

Sta. Maria Castellabate

Both **Ascea Marina** and its neighbouring locality of **Casalvelino** have pretty beaches, but the best ones of all, perhaps, can be found in the rugged terrain around **Palinuro**. This town, which has a small museum of archaeological finds, takes its name from Aeneas' pilot Palinurus, who is supposedly buried here—Virgil made the whole story up for the *Aeneid*, but that hasn't stopped it from sticking fast in local legend. Beyond Palinuro, the sandy coast curves back north into the Gulf of Policastro; here two more pleasant beach villages, **Scario** and **Sapri**, mark the southern boundary of Campania.

The Inland Route: Around the Cilento

South from Salerno, the *autostrada* skirts the back edge of the Cilento on its way to Calabria. Christ may have stopped at **Eboli**, as a local saying goes, but there's no reason why you should—and that goes for **Battipaglia** and **Polla** too. The true delights of this region are subterranean, two first-rate caves on opposite slopes of the Monti Alburni. **Pertosa** *(open Tues–Sun, 9–5.30; adm)*, near the highway, is the easier and probably the better choice; the pot-holers (spelunkers) suspect it is connected to the other one, at **Castelcivita**, near the village of Controne, which now forms part of the National Park of Cilento, a conservation project established by local inhabitants as part of the new measures to attract tourists to the area.

At **Teggiano**, there is a 13th-century castle and cathedral, as well as a little museum. **Padula**, just off the highway, is the unlikely location of the **Certosa di San Lorenzo**, after San Martino in Naples probably the biggest and richest monastery in the south. The Certosa has been closed for over a century, but in its heyday it would have held hundreds of Carthusians, in a complex laid out in the form of a gridiron (recalling the martyrdom of St Lawrence, the same plan used in El Escorial in Spain, also dedicated to the saint). Though it was continuously expanded and rebuilt over 400 years, the best parts are

Baroque: an enormous, elegant cloister, some wonderfully garish frescoes and stucco figures in and around the chapel, and eccentric but well-executed decorative details throughout. A small archaeological museum is part of the complex.

Where to Stay

Most people think of Paestum as a day trip, but there are enough hotels around the site, and on the nearby beaches, to make an overnight stay possible—and very convenient, if you have a car. Some of the best accommodation is at Laura beach, about 5km north of Paestum.

Hotels on the Cilento are on the whole modern and unremarkable, though there are some exceptions. For a stay of three days or more, an alternative to a hotel may be a *villaggio turistico*, of which there are dozens (look out for signs along the coast, or consult the rear section of the hotel guide-book distributed free by the Salerno tourist office). These are Italian-style holiday camps, but are much nicer than they sound, often with small bungalows set in well-landscaped grounds overlooking the sea, and with excellent sports and recreation facilities usually included in the all-in price.

expensive

The ★★★★**Ariston**, ✆ (0828) 851333, ✆ 851596, is situated on the main road as you enter Paestum from Salerno. A modern hotel with a businesslike atmosphere, it offers large comfortable rooms and full amenities. Still in Paestum, the elegant ★★★★**Schumann**, ✆ (0828) 851151, ✆ 851183, is set in its own lush gardens and faces directly onto the sea. All rooms come with balconies and air conditioning.

Further south, located high on the point above the small towns of San Marco and Santa Maria di Castellabate, stands the ★★★★**Castelsandra**, ✆ and ✆ (0974) 966021, with a pretty setting and outstanding views back towards the Amalfi coast. The hotel proffers a club-med style complex of landscaped villas and innumerable sports facilities, as well as evening entertainment. Popular with foreign package holiday operators. On the approach to Castelsandra, the ★★★★**Hotel Hermitage**, ✆ (0974) 966618, ✆ 966619, is perfect for a short stay while exploring the Cilento. Bedecked with flowers, and retaining its traditional rustic facade, the hotel has been completely renovated inside to ensure a comfortable and relaxing visit. Traditional Cilentan cooking is served in the well-situated restaurant and open-air terrace.

Towards the southern end of the Cilento coast, Ascea has a small collection of hotels around its marina, but Palinuro has developed into a fully fledged holiday town. Try the ★★★★**Gabbiano**, ✆ (0974) 931155, ✆ 931948, a well-maintained and crisply furnished hotel situated on the seafront at a short distance from the centre of town. The modern design incorporates a sheltered swimming pool and fine, sandy beach. Outside Palinuro, the ★★★★**King's Residence**, ✆ (0974) 931324, ✆ 931418, is in a stunning setting, perched in a crow's nest position high on the cliffs and overlooking the *Buondormire* (sleep well) bay. Every room comes with a terrace or balcony. A pathway runs down to the pretty little private beach, kitted out with a small bar for drinks and light meals. Sleek and well-run.

moderate

Set back from Laura beach in Paestum, ★★★★**Le Palme**, ✆ (0828) 851025, ✉ 851507, is a recently renovated hotel popular with German tourists. It offers good sports facilities and the private beach is a short walk away. Just north of here, the ★★**Laura**, ✆ (0828) 851068, is a good family hotel, pretty and relaxed, with helpful management. It offers its own private beach and 13 rooms, all with showers. Close by the Porta Giustizia entrance to the ruins, the ★★★**Villa Rita**, ✆ (0828) 811081, ✉ 722555, under the same management as the **Nettuno** restaurant, is a modern hotel set in attractive countryside and just 1km from the sea. Convenient for an overnight visit to the temples.

A couple of kilometres beyond Acciaroli is the village of Pioppi. For a touch of kitsch, traditional cooking and buckets of local enthusiasm, try the maritime-themed ★★★**La Vela**, ✆ (0974) 905025, ✉ 905140. Portholes, boat-shaped tables, ropes and rafters are gregariously strewn to conjure of the notion of being at sea. There is an outdoor terrace hung with *pomodorini* and an open-fire for cooking. Despite the drawback of a grubby, pebbly beach and wild open sea, La Vela is a treat for the adventurous traveller.

In Palinuro ★★★**La Torre**, ✆ (0974) 931264, is an attractive hotel, a short distance from both the town and beach. Tastefully redecorated, it is marred only by the extremely unhelpful management. Self-catering appartments also available. In the town of Palinuro, the ★★★ **Conchiglia**, ✆ (0974) 931018, ✉ 931030, like so many Cilentan hotels, is a remnant from the sixties. It offers 25 clean and pleasant rooms, simple hospitality and friendly management. However, parking nearby is a non-national's nightmare.

Camerota, near the southeastern point of the Cilento, has a fairly uninspiring bunch of hotels. The ★★★**America**, ✆ (0974) 932131, ✉ 932177, is modern, clean and acceptable, though without any particular charm.

inexpensive

Most of the less expensive hotels around the Castellabate area of the Cilento are found in the quaint resort of Santa Maria and the holiday beaches at Ogliastro. At Santa Maria, the ★★★**Sonia**, ✆ (0974) 961172, is an authentic Cilentan hotel. Well-placed on the seafront, it offers pleasant rooms and courteous management. ★★**Da Carmine** at the Ogliastro Marina, ✆ (0974) 963023, is a clean and sunny hotel, very reasonably priced and popular with Italian families.

Most hotels in the quiet village of Acciaroli are similarly modest, and good bargains too; the best is ★★**La Scogliera**, ✆ (0974) 904014, a 'nautical' hotel with a popular local restaurant situated on the tiny harbour front. A pleasant and convenient stop-over midway along the Cilento coast.

Further south in Camerota, the ★**Pinguino**, ✆ (0974) 932115, is typical of the no-fuss, no-frills accommodation in the region. Tucked away in a shady corner of town, its charms include an in-house pizzeria offering speciality penguin pizza. On the road going up to Camerota Alta, **★San Giorgio**, ✆ (0974) 932468, is a simple, family-run pension with parking and a strong local feel. It has 13 rooms, all with showers.

Eating Out

In the Cilento, most of the restaurants are in the hotels, and in summer the chances are you'll be stuck on full or at least half-board. There is some consolation to be had from the fact that such arrangements are often an excellent deal. Nevertheless, there are some good restaurants to look out for.

moderate

At Paestum there are two good and typical restaurants specializing in seafood in the archaeological zone itself: the excellent **Nettuno**, ✆ (0828) 811028, under the city walls near Porta Giustizia, a family-run restaurant for over 70 years, offering freshly prepared food at lunchtime only; and the **Museo**, ✆ (0828) 811135, next door to the museum with an informal dining room and outdoor terrace. Both are well worth their moderate-range prices. Alternatively if you are just seeking a tasty snack close to the museum, **Bar Anna**, ✆ 811196, run by the kindly Signora Pia, offers a good selection of cold antipasti, as well as the local buffalo mozzarella in a tomato salad (*insalata alla caprese*).

Just outside Palinuro, **Da Carmelo**, ✆ (0974) 931138, 1km along the road towards Camerota, is a lively trattoria where guests dine well on dishes prepared according to old traditional recipes, often to the strains of Neapolitan songs belted out by a strolling minstrel with a guitar. Seafood comes highly recommended by the throng of participating locals. Self-catering appartments are also available above the restaurant.

Camerota has one first-class restaurant, the attractive **Da Valentone** on Piazza San Domenico, ✆ (0974) 932004, which specializes in freshly caught seafood, and first courses including such local specialities as *spaghetti alla valentone* (tuna, capers and olives).

moderate/inexpensive

Two good places to eat near the beach in Palinuro (no phones, no reservations needed) are the two-tiered **Taverna del Porto**, where lunch is served at tables a stone's throw from the water's edge and dinner in the more formal upper level; and **O' Guarracino**, a pretty cafe-cum-trattoria with tables under a pleasantly shady canopy.

inexpensive

If you don't mind the wait, the tiny **Reganata e Vasulara**, localita S. Vito (no phone), in Camerota Alta, is a delightful spot, one of a kind fast disappearing in Italy. Guests eat cheek by jowl, choosing from a limited but excellent menu based on Neapolitan *cucina povera*—home-made *pizzette*, stuffed tomatoes, aubergines and all sorts of pasta. There is often a queue outside, and once all the food has been eaten, the kitchen closes up. *Summer only; closes end of Aug.*

Calabria and the Basilicata

Italy may be a country unusually blessed by fortune, but her favours are by no means evenly spread. To balance regions like the Veneto or Campania, with their manifold delights, nature has given Italy its own empty quarter, the adjacent regions of Calabria and the Basilicata. Calabria is the toe of the Italian boot, a gnarled, knobby toe, amply endowed with corns and bunions and pointed accusingly at neighbouring Sicily. Almost all of it is ruggedly mountainous, leaving just enough room at the edges for the longest, broadest, emptiest beaches in Italy. It can claim three natural attractions: a scenic western coast, the beautifully forested highland regions of *Aspromonte*, at the toe, and the *Sila*, in the centre of the region. Most man-made attractions have been shaken to bits by the earthquakes, Calabria's eternal plague, and consequently there are plenty of ruins and ghost towns.

The Basilicata, still better known to many people under its old name of *Lucania*, takes on all comers for the title of Italy's most obscure region. It offers plenty of lonely, wild-west landscapes and two increasingly popular destinations, the resort of Maratea and the strange city of Matera where people used to live in caves.

Magna Graecia

It was not always this way. Starting in about 750 BC, the Greeks extensively colonized southern Italy. *Rhegium*, today's Reggio di Calabria, came first, followed in short order by Sybaris, Croton and Locris, among others. These towns, happily situated along the major trade route of the Mediterranean, rapidly became as cultured as those of Greece itself—and far wealthier. It was a brilliant hour, and a brief one. After a time, blessed with a lack of external enemies, the cities of 'greater Greece' took to fighting among themselves, in a series of ghastly, cruel wars over the most trivial of causes, often resulting in the total destruction of a city and the massacre of its inhabitants. Weakened by their own barbarous behaviour, the Greek cities then became pawns between Rome and Carthage in the Punic Wars; the victorious Romans took a terrible vengeance on those such as Taras (Táranto, in modern Apulia) that supported the wrong side. Roman rule meant a slow decline for the survivors, and by the 6th century the beautiful cities of Magna Graecia were abandoned to the mosquitoes.

Don't, however, come to Calabria looking for classical ruins. The great museum at Reggio gives a hint of what these cities were, but at the sites themselves almost nothing remains. Golden Sybaris has only just been found by the archaeologists, and only at Metapontum will you see so much as a few standing columns. Some may call the emptiness a monument to Greek hubris, or perhaps somehow these cities were doomed from the start. Considering Magna Graecia can be profoundly disconcerting; even in the ancient Mediterranean it is strange and rare for so many big cities to disappear so completely.

Nor has this corner of Italy been any more hospitable to civilization in the centuries since. Calabria in particular has suffered more at the hands of history than any region deserves.

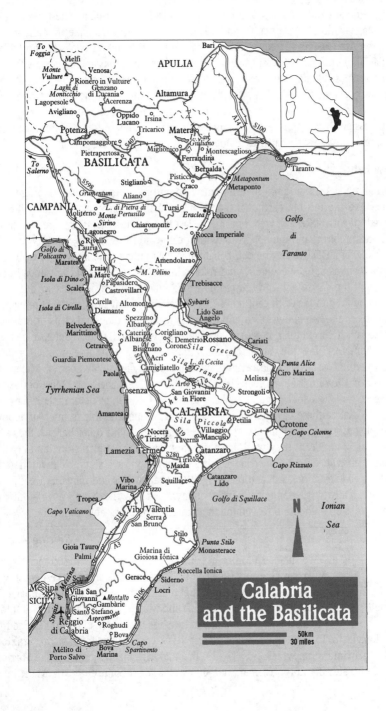

Calabria
and the Basilicata

50km
30 miles

After the Romans and the malaria mosquito put an end to the brilliant, short-lived civilization of Magna Graecia, Calabria has endured one wrenching earthquake after another, not to mention Arab raiders and Norman bully-boys, Spaniards and Bourbons, the most vicious of feudal landlords and the most backward and ignorant of monks and priests. By the 18th century, all these elements had combined to effect one of the most complete social breakdowns ever seen in modern Europe. Calabria staggered into anarchy, its mountains given over to bands of cut-throats while the country people endured almost subhuman poverty and oppression. Not surprisingly, everyone who was able chose to emigrate; today there are several times as many Calabresi living in the Americas as in Calabria itself.

A New Land

While famine, disease and misgovernment were putting an end to old Calabria, natural disasters like the terrible earthquake of 1783, and the even worse one in 1908 that destroyed the city of Reggio, were erasing the last traces of it. Calabria's stage was cleared for a modest rebirth, and the opportunity for it came after the Second World War, when Mr Rockefeller's DDT made the coasts habitable for the first time in over a millennium. Within a few years, a government land reform improved the lives of thousands in both regions, and the *Cassa per il Mezzogiorno*'s roads and industrial projects set out to pull their economies into the 20th century. Today, despite the many problems that remain, it's possible to see the beginnings of an entirely new Calabria. A thousand years or more ago, the Calabrians deserted their once-great port cities for wretched, though defensible villages in the mountains. Now they are finally moving back, and everywhere around Calabria's long and fertile coasts you will see new towns and cities; some, like Locri or Metaponto, are built over the ruins of the Greek cities that are their direct ancestors. Most of this new Calabria isn't much to look at yet; the bigger towns, in fact, can be determinedly ugly (like Crotone). Calabria these days, for all its history, has an unmistakable frontier air about it. The people are simple, straightforward, and a little rough. Unlike other Italians, they seem to have lots of children; they work hard, fix their own cars and tractors, and lay their concrete everywhere. So far, the changes have amounted to such a humble revolution that few people have even noticed, and the emigration rate remains enormous. But both these regions are, if anything, a land of survivors, and who is to say they aren't now taking their first baby steps on the road to reclaiming their ancient prosperity and distinction?

Getting Around

Two major **rail** lines pass through these regions: the Rome–Naples–Villa San Giovanni/Reggio di Calabria route along the west coast, with 15 trains a day, and the branch that runs from Battipaglia in Campania through Potenza and Metaponto on its way to Táranto (6 trains a day). A third line follows the long shore of the Ionian Sea from Reggio to Táranto. Reggio di Calabria has two railway stations: the **Stazione Marittima**, from which crossings are made to Messina in Sicily, and the **Stazione Centrale**; if you're just making a quick stop for the museum, the Marittima is closer.

Rail connections to anywhere in the interior are chancy at best: a few trains go through to Cosenza, but you'll usually have to change at Paola or Sibari. There are also regular **buses** from Paola to Cosenza. At Catanzaro it is the same; most trains stop only at Catanzaro Lido, 9km away (though there is a regular local bus to the city centre). In Cosenza, buses leave from Piazza L. Fera, at the northern end of Corso Mazzini, for Catanzaro (several daily) and points around the province, including towns in the Sila. A pleasant way to see the Sila itself is on the old private FCL **narrow-gauge railway** that runs three trains each day between Cosenza and San Giovanni in Fiore. The FCL station in Cosenza is hard to find, as it's behind the now disused FS station in the town. Near the tip of Calabria there is another attractive local rail line, around the Tropea peninsula between Pizzo and Rosarno.

Matera is served only by another FCL private rail line, which runs 12 trains a day from Bari in Apulia—in fact, a day trip from Bari, only 46km, may be a convenient way to see Matera. The station there is on Via Nazionale on the western edge of town. There is also a very slow FCL line between Potenza and Bari, via Altamura. FCL and other companies also operate daily bus services from Matera's Piazza Matteotti to Ferrandina, Potenza, Naples and Metaponto.

Airports in Calabria are at Lamezia-Terme (the main regional airport) on the Plain of Santa Eufemia near the SS280 Catanzaro turn-off from the SS18, which has scheduled flights to most of the major Italian cities, and at Reggio di Calabria, just south of the city, with regular services only to Rome and Milan. Car and passenger **ferries** to Sicily leave from Villa San Giovanni—the quickest route, with the most frequent services—and Reggio di Calabria. There are three companies: the FS (℡ 758241), Caronte (℡ 756725) and Tourist Ferry (℡ 751413). Don't worry; the service is very frequent, and whenever you arrive you'll be directed to the ferry leaving next.

Road routes around Calabria are simple—the SS18 runs down the western side of the peninsula to Reggio, and the also scenic SS106 goes up the eastern side, both hugging the coast, while the *Autostrada del Sole*, the A3, runs for much of the way through the middle. The main routes across the peninsula are the slow but spectacular SS107 between Paola and Crotone via Cosenza, and the faster SS280 through Catanzaro. Other minor roads across are slower. The main road to the Basilicata for drivers coming from the north is the SS407 *superstrada* (currently being upgraded), the Táranto road, which leaves the A3 near Zuppino 25km east of Eboli, and passes Potenza and Metapontum. An interesting route to Matera is the old Roman Via Appia (SS7), which is now only a minor road for most of the stretch from Potenza.

Roads aren't that bad, though you'll be skirting lakes, or crossing them, on those rare occasions when it rains. Service and petrol are never a problem anywhere on the coasts, but fill up before venturing into the mountains.

Tourist Information

Maratea (AAST), Piazza del Gesù 32, ℘ (0973) 876908

Cosenza, Piaza Rossi 70, ℘ (0984) 390595

Vibo Valentia, Via Forgiari 20, ℘ (0963) 42008

Villa San Giovanni, in the Piazza Stazione, ℘ (0965) 751160

Reggio di Calabria, Via Tripepi 72, near the museum, ℘ (0965) 858496. In Reggio there are also offices at the Stazione Centrale and the airport.

Gambarie, Piaza Mangeruco, ℘ (0965) 743 295

Maratea and the Coast

Just south of Campania's Cilento peninsula, a little corner of the Basilicata stretches out to touch the Tyrrhenian Sea. The scenery here differs little from the steep cliffs and green slopes of the Cilento; after Sapri, the coastal route 18 becomes a spectacular and rugged corniche road, passing over cliffs covered with scrubby *macchia*, and soft grey beaches on hidden coves—not so hidden any more, since a few hotels have been springing up on them, as at **Acquafredda**, just over the border. The centre of the Basilicata's coast is **Maratea**, a pretty hill village of tiny alleys and steps, with more modern additions tucked between the cliffs by the sea far below it. Maratea has in the last few years become quite sophisticated and expensive, though the atmosphere is still pretty laid-back. Besides some of the best coastal scenery in the deep south, you can enjoy relatively uncrowded beaches and modest hotels at Acquafredda, Maratea Marina (where trains on the main Rome–Reggio rail line stop), and several other points along the coast. The town itself, all tiny old alleys and steps, lies under what must be the queerest hilltop Jesus in Italy; all marble, and 20 metres tall. Designed by Bruno Innocenti in 1963 at the start of Maratea's push to become a resort, from a distance it looks more like a perfume bottle with wings. There is little reason to leave the coast at this point. Some of the twistiest roads in the Basilicata will take you up to the A3 *autostrada*, or to the sleepy Baroque villages of **Lagonegro**, with its Baroque churches, and **Lauria**. The most interesting of them is **Rivello**, a charming, isolated hilltop village with some distinguished buildings; well worth exploring, though on its steep alleys you'll be doing more climbing than walking.

Some 10 kilometres further down the coast and you're in Calabria, on the outskirts of another resort on a less dramatic stretch of coast: **Práia a Mare**, where there is a 14th-century castle. From the beach you can rent a boat to visit the 'Blue Grotto' on the **Isola di Dino**, an uninhabited islet just off the shore. Further south along the road is the now pretty much overdeveloped **Scalea**, a resort with a good early Renaissance tomb in its church of San Nicola and bits of Byzantine frescoes in another, the Spedale. In the hills above Scalea is a place called the Mercurion, once a centre of Greek monasticism; only the ruins of a church remain. Further into the mountains, near **Papasidero**, is a cave decorated with Paleolithic bulls (not currently open to the public).

Beyond Scalea is **Cirella**; from here you can take a boat excursion to another uninhabited islet, the Isola di Cirella, or climb up to visit the overgrown remains of **Cirella Vecchia**, a village founded by the Greeks that survived until a battle and a French bombardment in the Napoleonic Wars; bits of a Greek mausoleum remain along with streets of half-ruined homes and churches. **Guardia Piemontese**, a small thermal spa on a balcony over the coast, is still partially inhabited by descendants of the Waldenses, religious dissenters from 13th-century Piedmont and Liguria; Frederick II granted them refuge here from Church pogroms, but most of them were massacred by the Spanish in 1561.

Diamante comes next, a pretty village of narrow streets, stacked on a rock above the sea. **Páola**, where the road from Cosenza meets the coast, is a larger, somewhat dishevelled resort, a fitting introduction to the towns of the 'Calabrian Riviera' to the south. Above it stands the 15th-century **Santuario di San Francesco di Pola**, dedicated to the town's most famous son, Calabria's patron saint—not the same Francis as the Saint of Assisi—and the object of pilgrimages from all over southern Italy. The sanctuary is also the focus for the town's lavish annual *festa*, which reaches its climax on the saint's day, 4 May.

Where to Stay and Eating Out

Seldom in Calabria or the Basilicata will you see a hotel older than the 1960s—a comment both on how much the regions have changed since the Second World War, and how little they had ever had to do with tourism beforehand. In the sixties, there were thoughts of a tourist boom—Calabria as the new Riviera—but problems with bureaucracy, bad planning and a lack of good sites for hotels has prevented this from taking off as much as had been expected. Still, you will find acceptable hotels almost everywhere; if you are just passing through, there are plenty along the coastal route 18. One thing you'll hardly ever see is a swimming pool—there isn't a lot of water in Calabria.

Maratea (© 0973)

Maratea has become a mature enough resort to have some excellent accommodation. At the top of the tree is the ★★★★★**Santavenere**, Via Santavenere, © 876910, ✆ 877654 (*very expensive*), 1½km north of Porto di Maratea at Fiumicello-Santa Venere. A modern building, though furnished with unusual elegance, in a fine setting on cliffs above the sea, it has a pool and tennis courts, and all rooms are air-conditioned. Less expensive choices are many, with some of the best being a little up the coast at Acquafredda—such as the ★★★★**Villa del Mare**, © 878007, ✆ 878102 (*moderate*), just off the SS18 coastal highway and located up on the cliffs, with a lift down to its private beach. A good cheaper hotel at Maratea-Fiumicello is the ★★**Villa degli Aranci**, Via Profitti 7, © 876344 (*inexpensive*).

In Maratea Porto, at Via Grotte 2, **Za Mariuccia**, © 876163 (*expensive*), is a practically perfect seafood trattoria, with tables overlooking the sea, excellent risottos and pasta dishes that use scampi, lobster and other delights, and the very best of whatever Maratea's fishermen have come up with on that particular day. *Closed Fri.* Another treasure is the **Rovita**, Via Rovita 13, ℂ 876588 (*expensive*). Here excellent fish is matched with equally good pastas and meat dishes, all making the most of local Basilicata produce—rocket, aubergines and so on. *Open Sept–April; closed Tues.*

Práia a Mare (ℂ 0985)

Here the beach hotels are generally simple places; the **★★Calabria** on Via Roma, ℂ 72350 (*inexpensive*), is near the sea, and has its own stretch of beach. Práia makes a good place to look for a cheap room, as there are at least ten other places just like this one. The **Vecchio Frantoio**, on Corso da Viscigliosa (*inexpensive*), has a wide selection of grilled fish and seafood served with *porcini* mushrooms or rocket.

Scalea (ℂ 0985)

Prices tend to be higher here. The best part of the beach is occupied by the **★★★★De Rose**, Lungo Mare Mediterraneo, ℂ 20273, 🖳 920194 (*expensive*), a typical modern Mediterranean hotel, with air-conditioning and TV—both considerations around these parts, where it's always hot, and there can be little to do. You can get many of the same amenities at a slightly better rate at the **★★★Talao**, Corso Mediterraneo 66, ℂ 20444 (*moderate*), also near the beaches.

Cetraro (ℂ 0982)

Here you'll find an exception to the no pre-1950s rule—a pretty old villa, converted into a hotel to provide a rare island of elegance in homespun Calabria. The **★★★★★Grand Hotel San Michele**, ℂ 91012, 🖳 91430 (*expensive/very expensive, depending on room*), is near Cetraro in a location called Bosco—which is no deception, as there are plenty of trees around for shade, as well as a golf course, a beach, and a good restaurant that turns simple local specialities into gourmet treats. The house wine is made in the hotel's own vineyards.

For something less grand, try the **★★★Park Hotel** on the SS18 at Fuscaldo Marina, south of Cetraro, ℂ 610945, 🖳 610910 (*moderate*). This too is a distinctive establishment; not the usual concrete resort hotel, but a collection of attractive cottages under the trees.

Cosenza

So far, there hasn't been much reason to leave the coast. **Cosenza** may not be a stellar attraction, but as cities go it's the best Calabria can do. Cosenza has been one of Calabria's chief towns throughout most of recorded history; it began as the capital of the Bruttians, the aboriginal nation from whom today's Calabrians are descended. Medieval Cosenza was a busy place: the Arabs took it twice, Norman freebooters fought over it, and at least one king of France passed through on his way to the Crusades. Today, its most obvious attraction for visitors may be as the chief hub for bus services to the surrounding area.

The River Busento divides Cosenza neatly, between the flat modern town and the old citadel on the hill. The river is famous, if only because buried somewhere beneath it is no less a personage than Alaric the Goth. Alaric—no drooling barbarian, but just another scheming Roman general with a Teutonic accent—came to Cosenza in 410, fresh from his sack of Rome and on his way to conquer Africa. He died of a fever here, and his men temporarily diverted the Busento and buried him under it, probably along with a fair share of the Roman loot. Archaeologists are still looking for it.

Cosenza gained some unexpected notoriety in the 16th century, as one of Counter-Reformation Italy's last bastions of tolerance and free thought, under the influence of the Waldenses and and of an important humanist philosopher named Bernardino Telesio (1509–88), one of the first theorists of science. His student, the radical monk Tommaso Campanella, became a fully fledged utopian mystic, writing a splendidly crazy book called *The City of the Sun* and leading an astrologically ordained revolt against the Spanish in 1599. Campanella later helped defend Galileo in his Inquisition trial—by letter, since he himself spent 27 years in their jails.

For all its history, Cosenza has little to show; even in Calabria, no place is more prone to earthquakes—four big ones in the last 200 years, with added destruction by Allied bombers in 1943. The **cathedral** has survived, a simple Gothic structure built in 1222, during the reign of Frederick II. A museum will, it is officially stated, one day be opened alongside the cathedral in order to display the cathedral treasure, but in the meantime, if you want to see the collection, it's necessary to ring at the door of the nearby Archbishop's Palace or the marriage office. This little extra effort is worth it, as the real treasure is a little-known masterpiece of medieval art, a Byzantine-style gold and enamel crucifix, made in Sicily in the 12th century and given by Frederick himself on the occasion of the cathedral's consecration. A few blocks south of the cathedral, on Piazza XV Marzo, there is a small **Museo Civico** (*open daily except Sun, 9–1; adm*), with paintings and archaeological finds, and from there you can also climb up to the well-preserved **castle** overlooking the city (*open April–Sept, 9–1 and 3.30–sunset; Oct–Mar, 9–1 only*); most of that was built by Frederick too. Just west of Cosenza, the big village of **Rende** has a Museo Civico with a very good collection of exhibits on every aspect of Calabrian country life and folklore (*open daily, 9–1; adm*).

Albanian Villages

North of Cosenza, the valley of the Crati flows towards the Ionian Sea. With it runs the A3 motorway; if you are passing this way there are a few chances for detours. A stretch of Albanian villages ocupies the mountains west of the river, all connected by a tortuous mountain road, from San Benedetto Ullano north to Santa Caterina Albanese. Further north is a small spa, **Spezzano Albanese**, and **Altomonte**. This unpromising village, remote even by Calabrian standards before the building of the motorway, contains one of the most unusual churches in the south; **Santa Maria della Consolazione** is genuine 14th-century Gothic, with a big rose window. Most likely it is the work of architects from Siena. Inside, works of art include a painting by the Tuscan master Simone Martini, and the fine tomb of Duke Filippo Sangineto, by a follower of Tino di Camaino. Sangineto was a local boy who made good fighting for Charles of Anjou. Besides becoming a duke down here, Sangineto was also Seneschal of Provence; his descendants, occupying a cultural sphere wider than most Calabrians, financed this church.

Further north, near the border with the Basilicata, **Castrovíllari** has an Aragonese castle, a small archaeological museum, and the church of Santa Maria del Castello, interesting for the odd bits of art from many centuries inside (there is a small museum in the sacristy), and for the view over the mountains. **Civita**, just to the east, has a small museum dedicated to the life and history of the Albanians in Calabria, the **Museo Etnografico Arbërësh** (ring ✆ (0981) 73043 if you want to see it). From Castrovíllari, you have the choice of either retreating eastwards to the coast, near Sybaris (*see* below), or west with the motorway for Naples. You can't go any further north, for in your way stands **Monte Pollino,** a huge, largely forested massif that is one of the most unspoiled natural areas of the south—the difficult terrain and lack of roads see to that.

The Sila

Cosenza is the northern gateway to this region, a lovely, peaceful plateau between mountains that offers an unusual experience of Alpine scenery near the southern tip of Italy. Much of the Sila is still covered with trees—beeches, oaks and *laricio* pines. In summer you can find wild strawberries, and in winter—well, maybe—wolves. Some of Italy's last specimens make their stand in the Sila's wilder corners, and there is currently an attempt to repopulate them in the two small areas called the Parco Nazionale della Calabria (the third part of the park is on Aspromonte). The Sila is the best place in Calabria for motoring or hiking, and canoeing—from Cosenza you can float down the River Crati all the way to the Ionian Sea. Maps and information are available from the Cosenza tourist office. Most likely you will see only the largest and prettiest section, the *Sila Grande* in the middle, though more adventurous souls can press on to the barely accessible *Sila Greca* to the north, or south to the *Sila Piccola*, around the little mountain resort of Villaggio Mancuso.

Despite the name, the **Sila Greca** is inhabited not by Greeks, but by Albanians of the Greek Orthodox faith, called the *arbërësh* in Calabria. They came to Calabria and Sicily as refugees from the Turks in the 15th century, and today constitute one of Italy's largest ethnic minorities. Albanians can be found all over Calabria, especially here and in the north around Castrovíllari; you'll know you've stumbled on one of their villages if you see a Byzantine-domed church or a statue of Skanderbeg, the Albanian national hero. Acri is the biggest village of the region, but the real Albanian villages are further north over Monte Crista d'Acri, strung out along a difficult mountain road. These include Santa Sofia d'Epiro, Vaccarizzo Albanese and **San Demetrio Corone**, where there has been an Albanian college since 1791.

Sila Grande

Artificial lakes, built since the war as part of Calabria's hydroelectric schemes, add to the scenery here in the **Sila Grande**, notably **Lago Arvo** and **Lago di Cecita**, between Cosenza and the town of San Giovanni in Fiore. Lago di Cecita borders one part of the Parco Nazionale della Calabria, the heavily forested Bosco di Gallopani. **San Giovanni in Fiore**, the biggest village, owes its founding to another celebrated Calabrian mystic, the 12th-century monk and devotional writer Joachim of Fiore. Emperor Henry IV granted the privileges of Joachim's new abbey in 1195, and throughout the Middle Ages it was one of the most important communities of the south. The austere abbey complex has been restored, and now contains a deadly serious endeavour with the bizarre title of **Demographic Museum of the Economy, Labour and Social History** (*open daily July–Sept, 9–1, 3–7; adm*). Much of the economy and labour in this town has to do with handmade carpets and fabrics, a longtime speciality.

On the eastern edge of the Sila, the forests in many places give way to *calanchi*, weird sculpted hillsides created by deforestation and subsequent erosion. On the way to Crotone and the coast, **Santa Severina**, population now about 2500, used to be a much more important place. The village's skyline makes a striking sight, dominated by a lovely **Norman castle**, currently under restoration. The castle is connected to the rest of the village by a tall bridge; underneath this is the charming 11th-century church of Santa Filomena, with a dainty cupola on sixteen slender columns and carved floral arabesques around the windows. The **cathedral** was begun in Norman times too, but it has metamorphosed into an elegant Baroque building with a façade of 1705 and a quirky Rococo altar. The real surprise is found through a secret door built into the left aisle: a 7th–9th century **baptistry,** one of the oldest in Italy (no mystery, really; it seems as if the Baroque refurbishers made the door invisible simply to keep the symmetry of their decoration). Like nearly all ancient baptistries, this one is octagonal, after the model of the one Constantine built at the Lateran in Rome. It is furnished with eight granite columns, a font that may be the original, and bits of frescoes.

Sila Piccola

This part of the plateau is even wilder and more remote. Its main centre is a resort, **Villaggio Mancuso**, surrounded by forests and embellished with wood-frame buildings and wood fences that give it a strangely New Englandish air. Just south of the village is the **visitors' centre** of the Calabria National Park, a new complex laid out with loving care by the men of the *Corpo Forestale*. Besides information, you can see exhibits on the flora and fauna of the Sila, a 'didactic nature path' (and another one for the disabled), a herb garden and a reproduction of a *carbonaia*, an old-fashioned charcoal works.

On the southern edge of the Sila, on the road to Catanzaro, **Taverna** was the birthplace of the only notable artist ever to come out of Calabria, Mattia Preti. The best work of this 17th-century follower of Caravaggio can be seen in Naples and on Malta, but he left a number of paintings here; recently these have been restored, and collected from the village's churches into the **Museo Civico**, in the cloister next to San Domenico (*open daily 9–12, 4–7; adm*).

Cosenza (© 0984)

One place to stay that's comfortable and well-run is the ★★★**Centrale**, Via dei Tigrai, © 73681 (*expensive*), with a very good restaurant called **Il Cantuccio** (*moderate*). The only budget hotel is also in the centre, the very inexpensive and basic ★**Bruno**, Corso Mazzini 27, © 73889. You'll find a wider choice at Spezzano della Sila/Camigliatello, just east of Cosenza, where there is a number of moderate hotels on or near the E846.

Castrovíllari (© 0981)

The only place to stay here is at nearby Frascineto, near the motorway exit: ★★**Skanderbeg**, Via Arcuri 24, © 32117 (*moderate*). But Castrovíllari is worth a stop for one of Calabria's best restaurants, the hotel ★★★★**La Locanda di Alia**, Via Jetticelle 69, © 46370. The menu includes inventive seafood dishes as well as traditional Calabrian favourites with the best fresh ingredients—and plenty of wild mushrooms (*expensive*, though there is a L40,000 *degustazione*).

The Sila (© 0984)

In Villaggio Mancuso, the ★★★**Grande Albergo Parco della Fate**, © 922057 (*moderate*), allows you to see the Sila in style; the same management also runs an inexpensive alternative (Italians call this a *dipendenza*) nearby, the ★★**Della Posta**, © 922033, one of a half-dozen or so budget alternatives in and around Villagio Mancuso, all modern and pretty much the same. There is also a pleasant campground under the trees at Villagio Racise, 4km to the north, the **Racise**, © 922009.

San Giovanni in Fiore makes another possible base; ★★★**Dino's**, just outside the town in Pirainella, at Viale della Repubblica 166, © 992090, @ 970732 (*moderate*, though there are inexpensive rooms without baths) is a comfortable enough overnighter; Dino's also has the best restaurant in the area, specializing in roast kid, trout and other delights of the uplands (L25–30,000, and a good bargain). Elsewhere around the Sila, there is very modest accommodation available at Bocchigliero and Longobucco, to the north in the Sila Greca. Around the Albanian villages, accommodation is mostly in Spezzano Albanese, including the ★★★**San Francesco Terme**, Loc. Bagni, © 953068 (*moderate*), which caters to the spa customers, and the cheap and cheerful ★★**Due Torri**, © 953613, on the SS19.

Alternatively, you could find a good base for visiting the Sila at **Tiriolo**, on the southern end near Catanzaro (*see* below).

The spirit of *campanilismo* (the familiar Italian vanity of local patriotism) is in the air in Italy, and not only among Umberto Bossi and the malcontents of the north. New provinces are appearing across the land; in Calabria, a little pocket along the coast from Pizzo to Nicótera has decided to secede from Reggio di Calabria and go it alone as the province of Vibo Valentia—that's VV on the car licence tags, and on the the signs put up everywhere by the new provincial tourist promoters, lest we fail to notice that this is a province of Vim and Vigour.

Heading down the coast from Cosenza, and just a few kilometres from the main road up in the hills, is the town of **Nocera Terinese**, famous for only one thing—its festival every Easter, when processions of flagellants go around the town, fervently beating themselves into a bloody mess with thorn bushes, in one of the local events that is most regularly deployed to demonstrate Calabria's distance from the modern world. If you miss it, the flagellants' paraphernalia can be seen in the village's new museum (ask at the Pro Loco). Further south again, the road descends to the Plain of Santa Eufemia, one of the new agricultural areas reclaimed from the mosquito. Calabrians make good gardeners when given the chance; the orchards and nurseries that fill the plain are impressively lush. The town of **Maida**, site of one of the first French defeats during the Napoleonic Wars, gave its name to London's Maida Vale.

Pizzo, a larger town on a cliff over the sea, also has its Napoleonic association. The emperor's great cavalry commander Marshal Murat, whom Bonaparte had made King of Naples, tried after Waterloo to regain his throne by beginning a new revolution in Calabria. When his boat landed here in 1815, instead of the welcome he expected, the crowd almost tore him to pieces. The Bourbons executed him a few days later in the **castle**, built in the 1480s by Ferdinand of Aragon. By the port in Pizzo, there is a small **Museo del Mare** dedicated to the village's fishermen (*open daily in summer, 8pm–midnight*).

The best part of Calabria's coast begins near Cape Vaticano. **Vibo Valentia**, proud capital, has views overlooking the coast, a 12th-century Norman castle, remains of the fortifications of the ancient Greek city of Hipponion, and a number of overwrought Baroque churches. Finds from the excavations of Hipponion are on view in the museum at the **Palazzo Gagliardi** (*open daily, 9–7; adm*). Vibo, perched on hills like most old Calabrian towns, has several kilometres below it a growing little industrial port, **Vibo Marina**; just west of here stands the rather romantically ruined Castello di Bivona. If you go into the hills above Vibo Valentia, there is a castle at **Arena** served by an unusual aqueduct that dates from Norman times. South of Vibo on the N18, **Mileto** stands next to the ruins of Mileto Vecchia, destroyed in the earthquake of 1783. The ruins are extensive, including the cathedral and the Abbazia della Trinità, also built by the Normans.

Tropea, Cape Vaticano and the 'Calabrian Riviera'

Most old road maps show the road into this peninsula as a dead end, but don't believe it. In recent years a good road has been built all around this bump on Italy's toe, opening up the choicest bit of Calabria's coastline. The first village west of Vibo is the quiet fishing port of **Briático**. **Tropea** comes next, the centre of the Cape Vaticano tourist preserve and truly the only coastal village that is a holiday destination, instead of just a place for passing through (it already attracts the Germans, who always find the good spots first, but the British are starting to come too). Tropea is built on a steep-sided rock overlooking some fine long beaches; from the belvedere at the end of the main corso you can see Stromboli, the amiable volcano that spouts off every 11 minutes, as well as other Aeolian Islands; how many depends on how clear it is.

The old town is well preserved, full of contented cats, *pizza a taglio* shops and a scattering of old noble palaces on the back streets that are quite elegant by Calabrian standards. Don't miss the **Duomo**, on the southern edge of the cliffs, an exceedingly graceful Norman work built in 1163 (but heavily restored), with blind arcades and decoration in cut stone; inside is an icon of the Madonna said to have been painted by St Luke, like many others around the Mediterranean, along with other interesting medieval tombs and relics. Tropea's main square is called **Piazza Ercole**, recalling a legend that Hercules visited here; the Romans called Tropea *Portus Hercules*. Note the war memorial, financed by the Tropeans of Montevideo, Uruguay—a reminder of how south Italy's emigrants tended to cluster in little colonies; any town you pass through is likely to have a social club for its sons in some city of the Americas.

From Tropea's beaches, you can climb up to the ruined Benedictine monastery of **Santa Maria dell'Isola**, on an island joined to the coast by a short causeway. Around the cape itself, the road rises to more spectacular views over the Aeolians and Sicily's northern coast; as far as Cape Vaticano it is lined with signs for the many holiday villages and campgrounds tucked discreetly down by the sea.

Further south, the towns along the coast are easier to reach though, except Scilla, less attractive. Gioia Tauro is a grim industrial town that squeezes out most of Calabria's olive oil. Outside **Palmi** there is a recently opened museum and cultural complex, the **Casa di Cultura Leonida Repaci**, that houses among other collections the best folk museum in Calabria, and a modern art gallery with works by de Chirico and other 20th-century Italian painters *(south of the town centre on the main SS18; open Mon–Wed, 8–2 and 3–6; Tues, Thurs, Fri, 8–2 only)*.

Scilla, at the entrance to the Straits of Messina, is a peaceful and lovely fishing town that owes its fortunes to the straits' greatest culinary treasure, the *pesce spada*. Swordfish may be tasty, but they are nobody's fools. To nab them, the Calabrians have invented one of the most peculiar styles of fishing boats you'll ever see. These delicate, insect-like craft have metal towers that can be up to 30m in length, secured by wires and swaying precariously. One stands straight up like a mast; this is for the lookout watching for schools of fish. The other projects beyond the bow, and holds a spearman who, guided by the lookout, can make the kill before the swordfish even feel the presence of the boat.

Scilla marks the spot where the mythological Scylla, a daughter of Hecate changed into a dog-like sea monster, seized some of Odysseus' crewmen near the end of the *Odyssey*. In classical times, Scylla meant the dangerous rocks of the Calabrian side of the straits, a counterpart to the whirlpool Charybdis towards the Sicilian shore. So many earthquakes have rearranged the topography since then that nothing remains of either. Still, the narrow straits are one of the most dramatic sights in Italy, with Messina and the Monti Peloritani visible over in Sicily, neatly balancing Reggio and the jumbled peaks of Aspromonte in Calabria. Not far inside the straits is the port of **Villa San Giovanni**, a suburb of Reggio and today the major ferry crossing point for Sicily.

Where to Stay and Eating Out

Vibo Valentia (℗ 0963)

Accommodation here ranges from the honest and simple ★★**Miramonti**, Via F. Proietti, ℗ 41053 (*moderate*), to the basic **Pensione Il Terrazzino**, ℗ 571091 (*inexpensive*), at Bivona on the coast near the castle. The best restaurant in the area is in Vibo Marina, a locally celebrated seafood establishment called **L'Approdo**, Via Roma 22, ℗ 572640. Elaborate *frutti di mare* antipasti, grilled fish, swordfish *involtini* invite a worthwhile splurge at about L50,000.

Pizzo (℗ 0963)

This village has a rare old establishment at its centre that, although somewhat modernized, still offers a pleasant stay, the ★★★**Murat**, Piazza della Repubblica, ℗ 534201 (*moderate*).

Tropea/Cape Vaticano (℗ 0963)

The best places are around Tropea and nearby Parghelia, 3km to the north. Here, on one of the prettiest parts of the coast, is the ★★★★★**Baia Paraelios**, ℗ 600300, ▨ 600074 (*expensive*), a group of well-furnished cottages set on a terraced hill overlooking a beautiful beach. This is one of the few places along this coast where it's usually necessary to reserve some time ahead. Beyond that, there are scores of new resort hotels in all price ranges around Tropea itself, as well as at Parghelia and Zambrone to the east, where the beaches are.

For seafood, one of the best restaurants is a bit out of the way, by the station in Nicótera: **Vittoria**, ℗ 81358, with outdoor dining (L30,000). In Tropea, **Al Centro Storico**, in the centre on Via Pietro Vanea, has a wide choice of fresh seafood, and outside tables on a little square (L35,000). On Via Roma near the Duomo, **Terra di Dentro** is a shop that offers the best in Calabrian specialities to take home, from fine wines to hot peppers and *'nduja*, the spicy hard salami that is an essential component of Calabrian soul food.

Scilla (℗ 0965)

In Scilla itself the only hotel is the ★★**Sirene**, Via Nazionale 55, ℗ 754019, with simple, inexpensive rooms, though up in the hills above the village you'll find the considerably fancier ★★★**Del Pino**, Loc. Melia, ℗ 755126, ▨ 755144 (*moderate*), with a pool and tennis courts. There is also a very popular **Youth Hostel**,

© 754033 (*inexpensive*), atmospherically housed in the castle. *Open April–Sept only.* **Alla Pescatora**, on the beach at Marina di Scilla, © 754147 (*moderate*), offers a wonderful octopus antipasto among its other seafood specialities. *Open April–Sept only; closed Wed.*

Reggio di Calabria

The last big earthquake came in 1908, when over 100,000 people died here and in Messina across the straits. Both these cities have a remarkable will to survive, considering all the havoc earthquakes have played on them in the last 2000 years. Perhaps the setting is irresistible. Fortune has favoured them unequally in the rebuilding; though both are about the same size, Messina has made of itself a slick, almost beautiful town, while Reggio has chosen to remain swaddled in Calabrian humility. Its plain grid of dusty streets and low buildings was laid out only after the earthquake of 1783, when the destruction was even greater than in 1908 and the city had to be rebuilt from scratch.

The Allies also did a pretty thorough job of bombing Reggio in the Second World War; after all that, it's not surprising that there is little left to see of the city that began its life as Greek *Rhegium* in the 8th century BC. Some bits of Greek wall and Roman baths, and some once-grand 19th-century buildings along the waterfront promenade are almost the only things in the city older than 1908. Part of Reggio's shabbiness is without question due to the corrosive social effect of the local Calabrese mafia, known in dialect as the *'ndrangheta*, which continues to have a hold here stronger even than those that its wealthier partners in crime, the Sicilian Mafia and the Neapolitan Camorra, exert over their own respective backyards. The city does still have one special attraction for the visitor—its **Museo Nazionale della Magna Graecia** (*open daily except Mon, 9–1, 3.30–7 in winter, 9–6 in summer; adm*), the finest collection of Greek art between Naples and Sicily.

The Warriors of Riace

The museum, directly north of the city centre on Corso Garibaldi, is a classic of Mussolini architecture built in chunky travertine. Containing a hoard as precious as anything in Greece itself, the museum would make a trip to Reggio worthwhile just for the **Warriors of Riace**, two bronze masterpieces that rank among the greatest productions of antiquity to have come down to us. If you haven't heard of them, it is because they were only found in 1972, by divers exploring an ancient shipwreck off Riace on Calabria's Ionic coast. They are normally kept down in the basement, in a room of their own next to a big exhibition detailing the tremendously complex original restoration job done in the seventies. These fellows, both about six-foot-seven and quite indecently virile, may perhaps have come from a temple at Delphi; no one really knows why they were being shipped to Magna Graecia. One of them has been attributed to the great sculptor Phidias.

The Warriors share the basement with a few other rare works of Greek sculpture, notably the unidentified, 5th-century BC subject called 'the Philosopher', as well as anchors and ship fittings, and amphorae that once held wine or oil—all recovered from the shipwreck, from mud well over a metre deep. The divers are convinced that the dangerous waters around Calabria may hold dozens of such treasures, so some more artefacts may have found their way to the Reggio museum by the time you arrive. And don't neglect the rest of the museum collections. Some of the most beautiful things in it are the terracotta **ex-voto plaques**, recovered from the temples of Magna Graecia. Most of these offerings show goddesses in the magical archaic Greek style—usually Persephone, who had influence over death, being abducted by Hades, receiving propitiatory gifts, or accepting souls into the underworld. Chickens are a recurring motif, not too surprisingly, since to the ancient Greeks a soul rises out of its burial urn the same way a chicken hatches from an egg. Other works help complete the picture of life and art in Magna Graecia: Greek painted ceramics from Locris and from Attica, fragments of architectural decoration from various temples—some still with bits of their original paint, records of city finances on bronze tablets, coins, some treasure recovered from tombs, and a rare early Hellenistic mosaic of a dragon, actually made in Calabria. The museum also has a collection of paintings, including two works by Antonello da Messina.

Visions of the Straits

> The opposite point seems more a tongue of land
> you'd touch with a good bowshot, at the narrows.
> A great wild fig, a shaggy mass of leaves,
> grows on it, and Kharybdis lurks below
> to swallow down the dark sea tide. Three times
> From dawn to dusk she spews it up
> and sucks it down again three times, a whirling
> maelstrom; if you come upon her then
> the god who makes the earth tremble could not save you.

Odyssey, Book XII (tr. Robert Fitzgerald)

So did Circe introduce the Straits of Messina to Odysseus. Unlike some guidebooks, we don't give out stars for memorable views, but in this case we are tempted to make an exception. The straits may lack the postcard-photogenic qualities of the Grand Canyon or Istanbul at twilight, but there is truly no place on earth quite like it. The Italian highway engineers have thoughtfully placed parking areas in all the choicest spots along the motorway north of Reggio, and so many people stop to enjoy the view they cause traffic jams in summer. Messina and much of the Sicilian coast are visible, along with Strómboli and other of the Aeolian islands on a clear day; perhaps even Mount Etna will peek out from behind its eternal entourage of clouds. Spidery swordfish boats ply the waters below, keeping company with the busy Sicily ferries, Greek or Russian tramp steamers and every other sort of ship, passing under the the two gigantic power pylons that seem to moor Sicily to the mainland, constructions as preposterous in their way as the swordfish boats.

For all that, the real wonders of the straits will never develop on your film. Nothing is left of the rock and the whirlpool, of course, but memories continue to linger. It is as if the great sea were twisted into a knot in the middle; everything that is eternally Mediterranean seems to live here, or at least pass through occasionally, like Odysseus. If you are especially lucky, you may be treated to an appearance of the famous *Fata Morgana*, the mirages of islands or many-towered cities that often appear over the straits. The name comes from the enchantress Morgan le Fay. Arthurian romance came to southern Italy with the Normans, and rooted itself deeply in these parts; old Sicilian legends have a lot to say about King Arthur. In one of the tales, Arthur sleeps and awaits his return not in Avalon, up in chilly England, but deep in the smoky bowels of Etna. Roger de Hauteville himself, a close relation of William the Conqueror, is said to have seen the *Fata Morgana*, and his learned men interpreted the vision as a divine invitation to invade Sicily. Roger demurred, thinking it would be better to wait and take Sicily on his own than do it with the aid of sorcery.

Aspromonte

All around the toe of Italy, from Palmi as far as Locri, the interior of the peninsula seems utterly impenetrable, a wall of rough peaks looming over the narrow coastal plain. In fact all of the toe is really one great round massif, called **Aspromonte**. The tortuous mountain roads allow few easy opportunities for climbing inland, but from the north end of Reggio a 30km route, the SS184, will take you up to **Gambarie**, with pine forests and views over the straits and Sicily (from Reggio, take the Gallico exit on the motorway and follow the signs). In winter Gambarie is Calabria's unlikely ski resort, with just enough snow to get by in an average year; in summer it's a good starting-off point for walkers. There is little to Gambarie but a collection of faintly alpine-looking hotels and a communications tower, but the forests around it are lovely. This area was the haunt of the chivalrous 19th-century bandit Musolino, a sort of Calabrian Robin Hood still remembered in these parts. His well-tended grave is in the cemetery in his birthplace, **Santo Stefano**, on the way to Gambarie.

Aspromonte is a world in itself, with its 22 summits and its Greek-speaking villages. It has four levels of altitude, called the *piani* or *terrazze di Aspromonte*. The lowest grow the jasmine and bergamots; further up come groves of some of the biggest olive trees you'll ever see. On top, there are still wide expanses of virgin forest: mostly beech and pine, along with some white birches. Ceps and other mushrooms abound; the locals put up roadside stands in the autumn and sell them by the basket. Hiking trails are marked, mostly starting from Gambarie. One popular summer excursion follows a passable road to **Montalto**, just under the tallest summit of Aspromonte, with incredible views that take in two seas and three volcanoes (Strómboli and the nearby island of Vulcano, along with Etna). Seven km from Montalto is the **Santuario di Polsi**, a popular pilgrimage site for the 'Madonna della Montagna'.

Like the Albanians, the Greeks—called *Grecaneci*—of Aspromonte are a Calabrian cultural minority; scholars who have studied their language speculate that they may be descendants of the original Greek population of Magna Graecia, holding on to their cultural identity thanks only to the barely accessible locations of their mountain villages. Finding these will require some effort. Most are on the southern part of Aspromonte: **Bova**, **Roccaforte del Greco** and **Chorio** are the largest. From Roccaforte you can find another called Galliciano, which can only be reached by mule. Serious hikers, or people equipped with mules, can also seek out the Grecaneci in Roghudi, east of Roccaforte, built on a nearly vertical cliff, and nearly a ghost town.

Where to Stay and Eating Out

Reggio di Calabria (℗ 0965)

Most of the hotels are in the north part of town, clustered around the archaeological museum. The poshest is the modern ★★★★**Excelsior**, Via Vittorio Veneto 66, ℗ 812211, ✉ 893084 (*expensive*), with fully air-conditioned rooms, but you can get by just as well at the more modest ★★★★**Lido**, Via III Settembre 6, ℗25001, ✉ 899393 (*moderate*), just around the corner. In the *inexpensive* range, you can try the pleasant ★★**Eremo**, on Via Eremo Botte, ℗ 22433, one of the few hotels in the vicinity that has access for wheelchairs, or else the funky but friendly ★★**Diana**, VIa Vitrioli just off the Corso, ℗ 891522, in a mouldering, fascinating pre-earthquake palazzo.

The **Ristorante Rodrigo** at Via XXIV Maggio 25, ℗ 20170 (*moderate*), is one of the best places in Reggio's centre for seafood, including its speciality *ravioli Rodrigo*, stuffed with fish. *Closed Sun.* For something a bit more elegant, there's the **Collina della Scioattolo** on the Via Provinciale, ℗ 682255 (*moderate*), just outside town with a view of the straits, which has first-class swordfish and *aragoste*. *Closed Wed.* Or maybe something less elegant—**L'Ancora** at Via Tripepi 126, ℗ 813274 (*inexpensive*), not far from the tourist office, offers typical local home cooking. *Closed Sun.* A select few readers may also experience the **Trattoria-Vini Pratico**, facing the FS station on the left. This is a time capsule, one of the last survivors of the '50s-style *vino e cucina*, with its hospital-room ambience perfectly preserved. You can get a tolerable dinner here for less than L20,000.

Aspromonte (℗ 0965)

Gambarie has almost all of the hotels on Aspromonte, and there isn't a lot of difference between them; fortunately all the rooms have heating. The ★★★**Centrale**, Piaza Mangeruca, ℗ 743133, will do fine, as would the only inexpensive choice, ★★**Il Ritrovo**, Via Garibaldi 15, ℗ 743021.

In the summer, look out for informal outdoor restaurants around Gambarie; just a few tables under the trees, and good simple cooking for next to nothing. In

Sant'Alessio di Aspromonte, on the road up to Gambarie, the **Ristorante Nunziatina**, ✆ 741006 (*inexpensive*), is a local favourite and a stronghold of mountain cooking, with home-made Calabrian pastries for dessert. In summer, try the **Villa Rosa** (*moderate*), on the road to Gambarie just beyond Santo Stefano—a wonderful place, with outdoor dining on a panoramic terrace, pasta with ceps and barbecue. The only problem is you have to ring Rosa in advance; ✆ 740500.

The Ionian Sea

Tourist Information

Locri, Via Matteotti 90, ✆ (0964) 29600

Crotone, Via Torino 148, ✆ (0962) 23185

Catanzaro, in the Galleria Mancuso, ✆ (0961) 743901

In addition some of the coastal resorts open local information desks during the summer season, as at:

Metaponto Lido, Viale delle Sirene, ✆ (0835) 741933

Italy's Longest Beach

From Reggio as far as Táranto, the coasts of Calabria and later the Basilicata are one long beach—about 500km of it, broken in only a few places by mountains or patches of industry. All along this route, the pattern will be the same: sleepy new concrete settlements on the shore, within sight of their mother towns, just a few kilometres up in the mountains. If you come in summer, you will see great rivers, like the Amendola, filled not with water but with pebbles; the terrible deforestation of Calabria in the 19th century (committed mostly by northern Europeans with the assistance of corrupt Italian governments) denuded much of the interior, and made its rivers raging torrents in the spring. Recent governments have worked sincerely to reforest vast tracts, especially on Aspromonte, but wherever you see bare rock on the mountains, there is land that can never be redeemed.

On the coastal plain around Reggio, snow is hardly ever seen. This is one of Italy's gardens, a panorama of lemon and orange groves. Two more exotic crops have also given some fame to the region: jasmine, which grows so well nowhere else in Italy, and bergamot, which refuses to grow nearly anywhere else. The bergamot is a small, hard, green orange, discovered and first cultivated only some 200 years ago. Now it is an indispensable ingredient in the making of the finest perfumes, and a surprisingly important source of income in this area (it's also the stuff used to flavour Earl Grey tea).

Many of the new villages and towns on the bottom of the toe have become little resorts—two *pensioni* and a pizzeria, on average; none is worth special mention, but you'll never have trouble finding clean water and a kilometre or so of empty (and usually trash-strewn) beach. Coming from Reggio, the first town (and southernmost town of mainland Italy) is **Mélito di Porto Salvo**, where Garibaldi landed in 1860. The main road into the southern

Aspromonte starts from here, leading to the land of the Grecaneci, but on any of the other roads that straggle up the massif, the main attractions are likely to be the ruins of deserted villages.

How Do Places Get Their Names?

What is the story behind Little Snoring, or Hell, Michigan and Truth or Consequences, New Mexico? Amerigo Vespucci didn't discover America, but he got the glory because one early mapmaker thought he did. Nations, cities, whole continents around the globe have been stuck with names that prove history has a well-developed sense of whimsy. As far as the scholars can tell, 'Spain' probably comes from a Phoenician word meaning 'land of rabbits'. The first settlers in Chicago would probably have named their town after one of the founding fathers had they known that in the language of the local Indians Chicago signified something like 'smelly onions'.

We call 'Greece' the nation properly known as Hellas, because the Romans did. But on the other hand the Greeks gave 'Italy' its name; the story is a reminder of just how accidental history can be. Italy was originally *Vitellia*, which came from a word that among the Bruttians down here in Calabria apparently meant 'cow pasture' (the root also survives in the modern Italian *vitello*, or calf). We can imagine one of the early Greek explorers landing on Calabria's Ionian shore. He would walk inland and find a party of Bruttian cowherds sitting by their cows. With signs, or through a bad interpreter, we can imagine the Greek asking them 'Pray tell me, what place is this?'

Locri and Gerace

About 3km south of **Locri** there are fragmentary ruins of the Greek city of the same name, a few bits of wall and bases of temples. Most of the art excavated from Locri has been taken to the Reggio museum, and further afield (including perhaps, the famous Ludovisi throne in Rome, which has recently been called a fake). Enough was left behind in Locri to make the **Antiquarium** near the sea worth a visit (*open Tues–Sat, 9–1, 4–6; Sun, 9–1*).

When pirates and malaria forced the Locrians to abandon their city in the 8th century, they fled to the nearby mountains and founded **Gerace**. Though the population of its melancholy medieval centre today is only about 300, Gerace was an important centre in the Middle Ages; it still has Calabria's biggest **cathedral**, an 11th-century Norman Romanesque work supported by columns dragged up from the ruins of Locri. The church has an interesting exhibit on the restoration, and a *Tesoro* where the star is a 12th-century cross made in Constantinople. Gerace has other churches worth a look: **San Francesco**, a big Franciscan barn of 1252, or the small **Oratorio dell'Addolorata**, with an ornate Rococo interior. The older churches, such as **Santa Cuore,** show a strong Byzantine-Norman influence in their architecture. Further inland from Gerace, **Cittanova** began as one of Italy's strange 'radial cities', a Renaissance fancy of town planning based on Campanella's mystical *City of the Sun*. Laid out as a new town after the earthquake of 1616, it never really prospered.

Back on the coast, **Marina di Gioiosa Iónica** has ruins of a small Greek theatre, while **Gioiosa** itself, 5km inland, can show excavations of a Roman villa, including bits of mosaic.

Greek Churches

Roccella Iónica is an up-and-coming little town. Its hilltop setting and half-ruined castle provide one of the few breaks in the monotony of beach along the coast road. Up in the hills above Monasterace Marina, the Greek village of **Stilo** is famous for its 10th-century Byzantine church, **La Cattolica**, with five small domes and remains of medieval frescoes. This church appears on almost every Calabrian tourist brochure, but there is another one nearby that is just as good: **San Giovanni Theresti** stands just outside the village of Bivongi, a delightful little building with blind arcading and a cupola over a drum and fake columns, all made of brick. The caretaker here is a Greek monk; the village of Bivongi invited Mount Athos to send one over to keep old memories alive. Also near Bivongi is a beautiful and surprisingly big waterfall on the Torrente Stilo, called the **Cascate del Marmárico** (don't expect to see much water falling in summer, though).

Inland from Stilo, almost in the centre of the peninsula, is **Serra San Bruno**, an unexpectedly pretty and refined village surrounded by forests. It grew up around the 11th-century Charterhouse, the second one founded (after Grenoble's). The founder of the Carthusians himself, Bruno of Cologne, lived and died here. The **monastery**, 2km outside the village, has the remains of a lavish Baroque complex destroyed in the earthquake of 1783, including a **museum** (*open daily, 9–1, 3–8, in winter daily exc Mon, 9–1, 3–6; adm*), and one church façade now freestanding like a stage prop. In the village itself, the Rococo **San Biagio**, or *Chiesa Matrice*, has reliefs with scenes from Bruno's life, and one very unusual altarpiece of the Virgin.

Where to Stay and Eating Out

Marina di Gioiosa Iónica (*©* 0964)

None of the various tiny 'lidos' on Calabria's Ionian shore is particularly inviting for more than a short stopover. This is one of the more pleasant spots, just north of Locri, where the **★★★San Giorgio**, Via I Maggio, *©* 415064 (*moderate*), has a nice garden, beach and pool.

Gerace (*©* 0964)

A Squella, *©* 356086 (*inexpensive*), just at the entrance of the town on the Locri road, offers good pizza as well as a full menu with traditional favourites like bean and chicory casserole and pasta with chick peas and hot peppers. *Open for lunch only out of season.*

Stilo (*©* 0964)

There is just one hotel in Stilo, but one with an unusual degree of character: the **★★San Giorgio**, at Via Citarelli 8, *©* 731153 (*moderate*). It occupies a former cardinal's palace and is furnished partly in period style, as well as having a pool and a terrace with panoramic views. Just outside of Bivongi, near the Cascate del Marmárico, you can try mountain trout and pasta with a sauce made from stewed kid at **La Vecchia Miniera**, ✆ 731869 (*moderate*); the management also organizes tours of the falls and other sites in the area.

Catanzaro

Further north, there is little out of the ordinary to detain you along the shore of the Gulf of Squillace as far as Catanzaro; scanty Greek and Roman ruins can be seen at **Caulonia** on the coast near Stilo; the church of San Zaccaria has a 13th-century fresco of Christ Pantocrator in the apse. More ruins await at **Roccelletta di Borgia**, the ancient town of Scolacium, just south of Catanzaro Marina. Between the two at **Soverato**, a small museum contains a *pietá* and other works of the noted Renaissance sculptor Antonello Gagini, collected from local churches (ring the Pro Loco at ✆ (0967) 22243 to see it).

After you have been here for a while you will begin to understand why **Catanzaro** is the Calabrian capital. Make a wrong turn on a mountain road anywhere, and Catanzaro is where you will end up. Really an overgrown mountaintop village that has straggled gradually down to the sea since the war, it is a piquant little city, the kind of place where the young men call you *capo* or *cavaliere* and ask for a light while they give you the once-over. The city park, called the Villa Trieste, has nice views and there is a recently opened **museum of carriages** (*loc. Siano north of town, open weekdays, 8.30–12 and 4–6; adm*), but there is little else in Catanzaro to see.

Crotone—The City of Pythagoras

Heading into the gulf of Táranto, the ghost cities of Magna Graecia make the only distractions along a lonely coast; after Catanzaro there is nothing to see for another 40km, until **La Castella**, where the 16th-century castle on a tiny island, accessible by a short causeway, makes a picturesque sight. **Crotone**, the Greek Croton, is no ghostly ruin, but a dismal middle-sized industrial city. All those dams up in the Sila were built to provide electricity for Crotone's new chemical plants, in a big scheme started by Mussolini in 1925. Along with Vibo Valentia, Crotone is a new provincial capital, governing a bit of the coast and an obscure inland *paese* called the Marchesato around Cutro. The new government likes to spell the name with a K, the way the Greeks did, which adds another touch of strangeness to what is already a vortex of weirdness. Crotone suffered badly from flooding in 1996, and immediately there was an oucry for an investigation. Few new cities have been so poorly planned and built, and a disaster was bound to happen.

The old Croton was often the most powerful of the Greek cities in Calabria, though it was more famous in the ancient world as the home of the philosopher Pythagoras. With his scientific discoveries, mathematical mysticism and belief in the transmigration of souls, Pythagoras cast a spell over the Greek world, and particularly over Magna Graecia. He was hardly a disinterested scholar in an ivory tower; around the middle of the 6th century BC, he seems to have led, or merely inspired, a mystic-aristocratic government in Croton based on his teachings. When a democratic revolution threw him out, he took refuge in

Metapontum. Croton had a reputation, too, for other things: its medical school, the success of its athletes at the Olympic games, and especially its aggressive and unyielding attitude towards its neighbours. From all this, nothing is left but the **Museo Archeologico** (*open July–Sept only, Tues–Sat, 9–1 and 3.30–7; Sun, 9–1*), with a large collection of terracotta ex-votos like those at Reggio. On a promontory south of Crotone, a single standing column from a temple of Hera makes a romantic ruin on **Cape Colonna**. Travellers in the 1600s reported about 50 columns on the site; they must have been carted off since for building stone.

Rossano

North of Crotone, the dry climate around **Melissa** and **Cirò** makes this Calabria's biggest and best wine-growing region. Further up, you can dip easily into the mountains at **Rossano**, a hill town only 7km from the coast. Rossano claims to have invented licorice candy; they have been making it since 1731. The town's particular treasure, originally in the **cathedral**, is a beautiful 6th-century manuscript called the *Purple Codex*, believed to be the oldest illuminated gospel anywhere, made in Syria and almost certainly brought here by eastern monks fleeing their Muslim invaders. It can now be seen in the **Museo Diocesano** (*open Mon–Sat, 10–12 and 5–7; adm*), next to the cathedral. Rossano is worth a look around; even though many of the houses are empty, the old town is brightly colourful and one of the best preserved in Calabria. It's steep and complicated enough; with luck (don't ask us for directions, just keep climbing!) you will find a small Byzantine church similar to Stilo's: five-domed **San Marco**, at the highest point of the town.

The Coast of Ruined Cities

Past Rossano, the mountains recede into the plain of **Sybaris**, named after the Greek city so renowned for luxurious decadence that even today it is echoed in the word *sybarite*. Sybaris' only misfortune was to have jealous Croton for a neighbour. Croton besieged Sybaris and took it in 510 BC. After razing the city to the ground, the Crotonites diverted the River Crati over the ruins so that it could never be rebuilt. They did such a good job, in fact, that until a few years ago modern archaeologists could not even find the site; some scholars became convinced the whole story of Sybaris was just a myth. Now that they've found it, excavations are feverishly under way, and it is hoped that the richest city of Magna Graecia may yield the archaeologists something worth the trouble it has caused them. So far, they have learned that the Crotonites did not do as thorough a job of destruction as had been thought. Above Sybaris proper, levels of excavation reveal ruins of *Thurii*, an Athenian colony and base in the Peloponnesian Wars, and a Roman town above that called *Copia*.

The first finds are now on display at the **excavation site** (*open Mon–Sat, 9–2 and 4–7*), but so far they consist only of items from the Roman town that was later built over the parts of old Sybaris that had not been covered by water. Sybaris stands at the mouth of the Crati, which is now a wildlife preserve for a small colony of that increasingly rare species, the Mediterranean seal.

Policicoro and Metapontum

Nearing the northern boundaries of Calabria, there are castles frowning down over the sea at **Roseto** and **Rocca Imperiale**, the latter built by Frederick II. The Basilicata's share of the Ionian coast opens into the broad Piano di Metaponto, one of the largest of the new coastal agricultural regions that DDT opened up after the war in southern Italy. The new town of **Policoro** stands near the ancient city of Heraclea, and its **Museo Nazionale della Siritide** (*open daily, 9–7; Oct–Mar, 9–6; adm*) has a good collection of Greek vases and terracottas, as well as surprises like a little pendant of the smiling god Bes—the Phoenicians visited here too. There are a number of molds for the making of terracotta ex-votos; in all the Greek cities, the faithful would leave these in great numbers in the sanctuaries of the goddesses Demeter and Persephone. *Siritide* refers to this section of the coast. Taras (Taranto) and Thurii fought over it for a long time, and finally agreed to share it and co-found the city of Heraclea in 434 BC. Its scanty ruins, built on a long, narrow ridge, can be seen beyond the gardens of the museum. Two areas have been excavated, showing a long, tidy grid of streets with foundations of houses but, so far, no important temples.

From the museum you can detour 11km inland, through some newly prosperous farm-lands to the ancient religious site of **Santa Maria d'Anglona**. Set on an isolated hilltop with a wide view, Anglona was inhabited from the Bronze Age until about 1546, the year the bishop moved to the nearby village of Tursi. It stands above a hamlet called *Troyli*, recalling a local legend that Trojans once settled this place. At the top of the hill nothing is left save the impressive 11th-century church, in a style reminiscent of Pisan Romanesque and decorated with strange carved reliefs on the façade and apse, and some original frescoes inside (to get in ask at the Policoro museum).

North of Policoro, **Metapontum** was another rich city. It based its prosperity on growing and shipping wheat; today its famous silver coins, always decorated with an ear of wheat, are especially prized by collectors. Even by the standards of Magna Graecia, though, Metapontum suffered bad luck. Among numerous sackings was one by Spartacus and his rebel army. In the Punic Wars the city had sided with Hannibal, who upon his retreat courteously evacuated the entire population, saving them from a bloody Roman vengeance.

Metapontum today is, like Policoro, a brand-new settlement, with the disconcertingly over-planned air of an army base. Though it has more ruins to show than any of the other Calabrian sites, do not expect anything like Paestum or Pompeii. At the centre of the archaeological zone there is an **Archaeological Museum** (*open Tues–Sun, 9–1 and 3.30–6.30; adm*). Like so many others built by the government in southern Italy, it is brand new and already under serious restoration. The museum contains Greek ceramics and local Lucanian imitations, along with relics of the Oenotrians, a Lucanian tribe that inhabited the area before the Greeks arrived. The city's scanty remains, including the outlines of a horseshoe-shaped classical theatre, lie all around, including a 6th-century Sanctuary of Apollo Lykaios ('wolf-like Apollo') and a theatre, as well as some foundations of buildings from the Roman *castrum* that succeeded the Greek city. On the banks of the

Bradano, facing the coastal SS106, stands the **Temple of Hera** that used to be called the *Tavole Palatine* by locals—the Round Table of King Arthur. Fifteen of its columns remain.

Catanzaro (℗ 0961)

If you are passing through, there are a few simple hotels in Catanzaro: the modern and attractive ★★★**Grand Hotel**, Piazza Matteotti, ℗ 701256, ✆ 741621 (*moderate*), in the centre of town, or the cheaper but still comfortable ★★**Belvedere** at Via Italia 33, ℗ 720591 (*inexpensive*).

Down in Catanzaro Lido, by all means stop for dinner at the **Due Romani**, on Via Murano at the coastal SS106, ℗ 32097 (*moderate/inexpensive*), which specializes in seafood, including the best and most copious *griglia mista* we've ever had in Italy, at bargain prices. In the city itself, there is little choice and little seafood; at **La Corteccia**, Via Indipendenza 30, ℗ 746130 (*inexpensive/moderate*), you can eat traditional cuisine for very reasonable prices. The wine shop (with no name; *inexpensive*) on Vicolo San Rocchello is another, more rough-and-ready place to sample some powerful local specialities.

Tiriolo (℗ 0961)

This pretty village on the southern end of the Sila, once famed for the costumes of its women (you still may see one), offers a nice alternative to staying in nearby Catanzaro, and it also makes a good base for exploring the interior. It has three good hotels, of which the most inexpensive is the welcoming, family-run ★**Coniglio d'Oro**, Loc Vaccariti (on the main street north of the centre), ℗ 991056; the 'golden rabbit' also has a good and cheap pizzeria-restaurant. So does the ★★**Autostello Chiarella,** Viale Mazzini (the main street coming from the south), ℗ 991005, which is just as good but slightly more expensive.

Crotone (℗ 0962)

Along the Ionian coast, dining is simple—perhaps a little seafood shack that is only open in the summer, or a small but lively pizzeria with a little terrace and dinners in the L20,000 range. There are some exceptions, such as **Da Annibale** in a pretty spot called Le Castelle on Cape Rizzuto, not far south of Crotone, at Via Duomo 35, ℗ 795004 (*moderate*), where the swordfish *involtini* is a rare treat. In Crotone, where you would least expect it, there is one very good restaurant: **Il Girrarosto**, Via Vittorio Veneto 30, ℗ 22043 (*moderate*), which specializes in roast lamb and kid, but also knows what to do with swordfish and other seafood. There is a nice terrace, too.

Policoro and Metaponto (℗ 0835)

Along the Basilicata's short stretch of Ionian coast, Policoro makes the most convenient place to stop over. You'll find a number of respectable middle-range hotels, including the ★★★**Calla**, Corso Pandosia 9, ℗ 972129, and the ★★★**Motel Due**

Palme, on the coastal road just north of Policoro at Scanzano Iónico, ✆ 953024, 🖂 954025 (*both moderate*). There are also hotels by the beach at Metaponto Lido, including the **★★★Kennedy**, Viale Jonio 1, ✆ 741960, 🖂 741960 (*low moderate*), a good bargain. In Policoro, there is a good family trattoria called the **Ragno Verde**, Via Colombo 13, ✆ 971736.

The Basilicata Inland

The interior of the Basilicata has never been one of the more welcoming regions of Italy. Divided about equally between mountains and rolling hills, the isolation of this land has usually kept it far from the major events of Italian history. The territory may be familiar if you have read Carlo Levi's *Christ Stopped at Eboli*, a novel written when the Basilicata was a national scandal, the poorest and most backward corner of all Italy. None of the famous 18th- and 19th-century travellers ever penetrated deeply into the region, and even today it is a part of the country few foreigners ever visit.

Even though the Basilicata counts more ruined and vanished cities than live ones, things are looking up a bit. The countryside and most of the villages may seem lonely and empty, but on the coast, in Potenza and Matera you will see some modest signs of prosperity.

Tourist Information

Matera: Via Viti de Marco 9, ✆ (0835) 333 541. You can also find out about this surprisingly switched-on city from MATERANET (www.hsh.it).

Potenza: Via Cavour 15, ✆ (0971) 34594.

Matera, City of the *Sassi*

Of all the Basilicata's towns, the only one that offers a real reason for stopping is **Matera**, a lively provincial capital of some 55,000 people that has become famous for a kind of freak show attraction. Matera was an inhabited town since before recorded history in these parts began, and for centuries, probably millennia, its people built cave-homes and cave-churches in the easily worked tufa stone. Until recently, the city had a certain notoriety as the most desperately poor provincial capital in Italy—and the scene of Carlo Levi's chilling book. Times are better now, but Matera has chosen to preserve rather than obliterate its terrible past by turning its poorest sections, the **Sassi**, into a sort of open-air museum— one that has made UNESCO's list of World Heritage Sites. *Sassi* are the cave neighbourhoods that line the two ravines between which Matera is built. Visitors as recently as 40 years ago reported people living in their cave homes in almost inconceivable poverty, sharing space with pigs and chickens, their children imploring outsiders not for money, but for quinine.

Most of the buildings (and all of the caves) in the Sassi are abandoned today—Matera and its province have benefited from the good works of the *Cassa per il Mezzogiorno* as much as any part of the south. You may think it somewhat macabre, visiting the scenes of past

Matera

misery, but the Sassi are indeed fascinating in their own way. Don't be surprised to see a group tour of bewildered foreigners being dragged through the cave neighbourhoods' steps and winding lanes. You can get a good view over the Sassi from the overlooks at the top of the town; note that people are actually starting to rehabilitate some of the houses—including a few quite trendified ones with roof terraces.

There are two Sassi, the *Sasso Barisano*, north of the town centre, and the *Sasso Caveoso*, to the east. If you visit, before long a child or old man of the neighbourhood will come up and approach you with the offer of guide service—worth the trouble and slight expense if you have the time and find the Sassi interesting. They know where the old churches with the Byzantine frescoes are (some as old as the 9th century), and, if you can pick out enough of their southern dialect, they have plenty of stories to tell. Local guides are also probably a better option than the maps and itineraries you can pick up from the tourist office—it's very easy to get lost in the Sassi, or to miss some of the most interesting sights, even with a map.

Don't get the idea that the Sassi are just plain caves. They started that way, but over the centuries they evolved into real neighbourhoods, with quite normal-looking façades, like the cave houses of southern Spain. The predominant stone of the area is tufa, a volcanic rock that is easier to cut and shape than wood; in Matera it was always easier to dig out a house or church than build one. Opposite the Sassi, along the other side of the Gravina ravine, you will see the real caves, many of them with traces of habitation from prehistoric times.

Matera of the Churches

What makes Matera such a compelling destination is the contrast between the lost weird world of the Sassi and the more favoured parts of town. Matera never had much money, but it did have a sense of style, and whatever pennies its rulers could squeeze out of the *paisani* went into an ironically grandiose ensemble of churches and piazzas. Matera still has style, though it is subtle and you'll have to stay around awhile to see it. On a Sunday evening, when nearly all the Materesi descend to participate in one of south Italy's most enthusiastic *passeggiatas*, Matera can look wonderfully urbane.

The centre, and the most gracious square in town, is **Piazza Vittorio Veneto**, decorated with the smallest and most peculiar of the churches: **San Domenico**, with a shallow Byzantine-style dome, AVE MARIA spelled out in plain light bulbs across the front and a medieval rose window carved into a kind of wheel of fortune. Near this is the entrance to the recently rediscovered **hypogeum** that underlies most of the city centre. Like the 'underground cities' of Cappadocia, this is believed to have been used for storage and as a refuge in times of trouble. It is usually open, as the city and a local cultural organization use the singular setting for exhibits of modern art and local crafts.

Other churches nearby include **San Giovanni Battista** (1223), just up Via S. Biagio, and two others that can be found by following Via delle Beccherie/Via Ridola eastwards, a route provided with views over the Sassi. These two mark the extremes of southern religiosity: **San Francesco d'Assisi**, with a sunny, delightful late Rococo façade, and an eccentric 18th-century church called the **Purgatorio**, sporting a leering skull over the main portal. Further down Via Ridola, the ornate **Palazzo Lanfranchi** from the same period has a small collection of paintings and sculpture—a chance to see the sort of art that was made to accompany this architecture (*open daily exc Mon 9–1, Sun 9–12; adm*).

Matera has a first-class local archaeological museum, the **Museo Ridola** (*open daily 9–7; adm*), housed in the Baroque former convent of Santa Chiara just around the corner on Via Lucana. From outside the museum, you can see the gloomy **Castello Tramontano** on a hill dominating the city. Begun by an exceptionally piggish boss of Matera called Count Tramontano ('Count Twilight'), the works were abandoned in 1515 and never taken up again after the count was murdered in a revolt.

Two more of Matera's Baroque façades can be seen in the Sassi themselves, set in proper piazzas among the cave homes: **Santa Maria di Idris**, in the Sasso Caveoso, and **San Pietro Barisano**, in the Sasso Barisano. The façades of these churches go back to the 1200s; these and some of the others have remains of their original frescoes.

The Duomo

Right at the top of the town, at the top of a narrow hill between the two Sassi, is the 13th-century **cathedral**, a fine Apulian Romanesque building with a square campanile that can be seen all over Matera. The Duomo has quite an interior, with brilliantly carved medieval capitals, and lots of gilding and some richly decorated chapels from later centuries; one wonders what the poor children from the caves thought of it in the old days. There is also a *trompe l'oeil* ceiling; noticeable if you stand at the centre of the nave. Near the entrance is a spectacular *pietra dura* altar; opposite, another chapel has been removed to reveal an excellent bit of original fresco in a decidedly Byzantine style. The entire west end of the church must have been painted as a Last Judgement; only a bit of Purgatory remains, along with a scene of the sea giving up its drowned souls.

The main altar is a carved and polychromed Renaissance work, an introduction to the wealth of art from the same period in the two chapels to the left of it. One of these, with frescoes of sibyls and prophets from the 1530s on its ceiling, contains a strange, folkloric carved *presepe*. From here (if the door is open) you can find your way to a tiny, older church hidden inside this one: Santa Maria di Costantinopoli, with a 13th-century relief over the door showing a procession with an image of the Madonna—the *Madonna della Bruna*, to be specific, who then as now gets a ride around town on a float every 2 July—in her current artistic incarnation, she looks a lot like Merle Oberon. A new float is made every year, covered in papier-mâché Baroque frippery, and at the end of each procession the townspeople destroy it.

A narrow opening in Piazza del Duomo leads to a street called Via del Riscato, 'Redemption Street'—it was here that the Materese got even with Count Twilight in 1515.

Cave Churches

The dry, austere countryside around Matera is full of tufa quarries, caves and churches. Across the Gravina ravine from the Sasso Caveoso (the one south of the cathedral), the cliffs called the **Murgia Timone** hold a number of interesting cave churches, some with elaborate fronts, even domes, cut out of the tufa, and medieval frescoes. You'll need a map and some help from the provincial tourist office, or else a guide, to find them. Among the most interesting are those of **Santa Maria della Palomba, La Vaglia, the Madonna delle Tre Porte** and **Santa Barbara**. Near Santa Maria della Palomba you can see a functioning tufa quarry; the easily cut stone is still used for houses, though it is well hidden under the stucco. There are more of these half-forgotten churches in parts of neighbouring Apulia, but none anywhere else in Italy; indeed, they can only be compared to the similar Byzantine rock churches of Cappadocia in Turkey.

Determined explorers can spend weeks here, seeking out the rest of the churches in the forbidding countryside around Matera. One set lies in a 20km stretch of the Gravina south of the city, the **Parco delle Chiese Rupestre del Materano**, which begins at the Murgia Timone. Another section of this park, just as long, follows the Torrente Gravina di Picciano, east of Matera around the village of **La Martella**.

Matera ☎ (0835) **Where to Stay and Eating Out**

Two very pleasant hotels have recently opened in fine old residences in the city centre: the ★★★**Piccolo Albergo**, Via di Sariis 11, ☎ 330201, and the ★★★**Italia**, Via Ridola 5, ☎ 333561 (*both high-moderate*); some rooms in the Italia have views over the Sassi. Also on Via Roma, there is a clean and spartan budget choice (the only choice), the ★**Roma**, Via Roma 62, ☎ 333912 (*inexpensive*).

Matera also has some good restaurants—at **Al Casino del Diavolo**, Via La Martella 48, © 261986 (*moderate-inexpensive*), they lay on lots of *peperoncinis* if you let them, in fearfully hot dishes, one called 'souvenir of Lucania', that explain the restaurant's devilish name. **Il Castello**, Via Castello 1, © 333752 (*moderate*), has interesting *orechiette* with mushrooms and sausage, as well as good fish and meat. *Closed Wed.* **Basilico**, in the centre at Via San Francesco 33, © 336540 (*moderate*), looks a bit out of place in Matera with its hypermodern pastel decor and *cuisine soignée*, but in fact most people come here for really good pizza at reasonable prices. For a wide choice of simple but piquant Basilicatan dishes, and a terrace overlooking the Sassi, there is **Il Terrazzino** (*moderate*).

Southern Basilicata

South of Matera, route 175 descends to the coast and Metaponto, a scenic route of pines and wild flowers that passes the attractive whitewashed village of **Montescaglioso**; at the top of this town is an impressive medieval monastery, the Abbazia de Sant'Angelo. To the southwest route 7 passes an artificial lake, Lago di San Giuliano, and **Miglionico**, where there is a grim mouldering castle and also perhaps the best painting in the Basilicata: a glorious 18-section altarpiece by the Venetian Renaissance artist Cima del Conigliano.

The valley of the Basento is one of the Basilicata's comparatively modern and prosperous regions, due largely to government industrial schemes—and the discovery of some modest gas reserves. The region's main road is route 407, which locals call the *Basentana*, following the river up to Potenza. Along the way, **Ferrandina** is one of the prettier villages; its neat rows of sun-bleached, gabled terrace houses, similar to many places in Apulia, offer an example of the Basilicata's traditional style of building. West of Ferrandina on the back roads you will see a picturesquely ruined castle on a round hill, the Castello di Uggiano. Pisticci, down the river, is the largest town south of Matera, though by no means the most pleasant; the weirdly eroded gullies around the town make a fitting introduction to the sad landscapes you will see in much of this region.

Craco, overlooking a steep cliff west of Pisticci, is one of the more recent of the south's many ghost towns, today almost completely abandoned after landslides made the site unsafe—a recurring problem in the region thanks to deforestation. **Tursi** and **Stigliano**, two otherwise unremarkable villages, both have remarkable churches. Tursi's is the sanctuary of Santa Maria d'Anglona (*see* above, Policoro). In Stigliano, it is the 17th-century church of San Antonio, with an odd waffle-iron Rococo façade even better than the one on the Gesù Nuovo in Naples. South of Stigliano, the wild countryside around **Aliano** offers some of the more outlandish scenery in southern Italy. Deforestation and consequent erosion have turned parts of it into a lunar landscape, exposing weirdly twisted rock formations called *calanchi*. Aliano itself is the village where Carlo Levi actually stayed during the time he describes in *Christ Stopped at Eboli*. The house in which he lived is at the bottom of the village, and now houses a **museum** (*open Mon–Sat, 10.30–12.30 and 5–7; Sun, 9.30–12.30*), dedicated to the writer and to local folklore, customs and traditional life.

Monte Vúlture and the Castles of Emperor Frederick

Eastern Basilicata is a province to itself, with a capital at **Potenza**, a plain modern hilltop city regularly rattled to pieces by earthquakes. Although present on this site since it was Roman Potentia, Potenza consequently has little to show: a few medieval churches and a small Archaeological Museum, on Via Cicotto. There are mountains on all sides, with some humble skiing areas to the south.

To the east, you'll find some startling landscapes in the mountains dubbed (by some tourist official, most likely) the **'Basilicatan Dolomites'**, a patch of jagged and sinister limestone peaks around the equally sombre villages of Pietrapertosa and Castelmezzano; the former has a ruined castle built by the Arabs, who were a power in this region back in the heyday of the Emirate of Bari. **Campomaggiore**, nearby, is entirely new; the original, higher up in the mountains on a dirt track, became a ghost town like Craco after a landslide in 1885. Its ruins are still visible.

Route 7, passing through Potenza, follows the course of the Appian Way. There's little point in taking it westwards, towards Benevento and Avellino in Campania; this area also suffered badly in the 1980 earthquake. In the other direction, the road passes through **Tricárico**, a pleasant village under the round donjon of a Norman castle. Further north, near the Apulian border, **Acerenza** was the Basilicata's capital when Potenza was still an insignificant mountain village. Acerenza's quite impressive 10th–13th-century **cathedral** contains, along with some good Romanesque sculptural work, the drollest fraud in the Basilicata, a venerable bust believed for centuries to represent the town's patron, San Canio; instead, the little icon has been identified as none other than that devout pagan, Emperor Julian the Apostate.

The northern end of the province, astride the important routes between Naples and Apulia, was a very busy place in the Middle Ages, full of castles and fought over by Normans, Angevins and Holy Roman Emperors. Frederick II, in particular, haunted these bleak hills; he spent his last year at the well-preserved castle of **Lagopésole**, halfway between Potenza and Melfi. Although this castle had a military role, a strong redoubt against the frequent rebellions of the Basilicata's barons, it was largely intended as a residence. Its austere rectangularity looks strangely abstract and sophisticated, along the lines of the beautiful castle Frederick built in Prato, near Florence. Some good capitals and other sculptural details survive inside, including an image believed to be the Emperor's grandfather, Frederick I Barbarossa—wearing ass's ears.

Earlier in his reign, the great Hohenstaufen had spent some time at the castle at **Melfi**, a fortress that two centuries before had been the first headquarters of the de Hautevilles in Italy, where Robert Guiscard was crowned Duke of Apulia and Calabria. The castle, recently restored, is well up to cinematic standards—none of Frederick's geomantical mysticism here; unlike Castel del Monte this one was built strictly for defence. Little remains of the original furnishings, but there is a small Archaeological Museum (*open daily except Mon 9–2; Sun 9–1; adm*). Melfi itself is a sleepy town, with little but the castle and its 11th-century cathedral to remind it of times when it often occupied the centre stage of European politics. Several minor Church councils were held here, and here

Frederick promulgated his famous Costitutiones Melfitanes, perhaps the first proper written constitution in history. In the environs of Melfi you can seek out two Roman bridges, and also the villages of Barile and Ginestra, largely populated by Albanians. Between Melfi and Rapolla are a number of small cave churches cut in the tufa, some with frescoes.

Looking out from Melfi's castle, the horizon to the south is dominated by the ragged, faintly menacing outline of **Monte Vúlture**, a long-extinct volcano with a forest where once it had a smoking crater. Around the back side of the mountain, the Basilicata keeps one of its few beauty spots, the little **Lakes of Monticchio**, with lovely woods and a funicular to the top of the mountain. Much of the mineral water you've been having with dinner across the south comes from the springs here—*Gaudianello* and other labels.

Out east from Melfi, there is another old castle at **Venosa**, an important town in Roman times and the birthplace of the poet Horace (also, 1100 years later, of King Manfred, son of Frederick II). Venosa was *Venusia* back in the days when it was republican Rome's most important base in the south, and the goddess Venus must have had a sanctuary here— you can still find churches in the region dedicated to Santa Venere. Venosa's Roman past shows itself in the relief fragments built into the walls of the cathedral, last rebuilt in the 1600s, and even more in the scanty ruins of baths, an amphitheatre, and a 5th-century basilica, just outside the town, on the road to Apulia.

Next to the ruins, you can visit what has survived of one of the most ambitious church building projects ever undertaken in the south. The Benedictine **Abbazia della Trinità**, begun in the 1050s, was never completed, but it became the resting place of four of the five famous Norman brothers: William, Drogo, Robert (Guiscard), and Humphrey de Hauteville. Their tombs are in the older, completed church, along with some very fine surviving frescoes and carved capitals; among the heaps of stones tumbled about you may notice some Hebrew inscriptions; ancient and medieval Venosa both had important Jewish communities, and some Jewish catacombs have been discovered along with Christian ones on the hill east of the abbey.

Where to Stay and Eating Out

This is an isolated region, and Matera and Potenza are the only places really equipped for visitors; expect only simple accommodation everywhere else.

Along the SS407/Basentana (© 0835)

In Ferrandina, 25km south of Matera, there is only one tiny *locanda*, but the ★★★★**Degli Ulivi**, ©/⊜ 757020 (*moderate*), outside the town itself on the SS407, makes a comfortable stopover if you are passing through on the way to Táranto. In Stigliano, where no one ever goes, you can sample the modest charms of the ★**Margariello**, at Corso Umberto 55, © 561225 (*inexpensive*), for a rock-bottom price, though you have to accept that there are only two bathrooms to share between the eight bedrooms.

Potenza (© 0971)

This is the kind of place where you will share a quiet hotel with a small group of government inspectors and travelling salami salesmen. They're all on expense accounts, so there are no bargains. If you do find yourself there, try the straightforward **★★Miramonti**, Via Caserma Lucana 30, © 22987/411623 (*inexpensive*), which has rooms with or without baths.

Console yourself perhaps with dinner at Potenza's one exceptionally good restaurant, the **Oraziana**, Via Flacco 2, © 21851 (*expensive*), where fine fresh pasta and local produce are used to recreate traditional old local recipes. *Closed Sun, Aug.* Alternatively, try the singular, employee-owned **Fuori le Mura** at Via 4 Novembre 34, © 25409 (*moderate*), renowned locally for its enormous choice of antipasto treats and good roast pork and lamb. *Closed Mon.*

Melfi (© 0972)

The people who run the hotel **★★★Due Pini**, © 21031 (*moderate*), outside town at the railway station, work hard to give you a pleasant stay, and some rooms have TV. For dining, the family-run **Vaddone**, Corso da Sant'Abruzzese, © 24323 (*moderate*), offers good regional cuisine washed down with local Aglianico and Vúlture wines. *Closed Sun evenings, Mon.*

Viggianello (© 0973)

Accommodation is hard to find in the villages of the Pollino National Park, and most of it is in this village, including the **★★★Parco Hotel Polino**, Via Marcaldo, © 664018 (*inexpensive*), which has a pool and organizes trips into the mountains for its guests. There are other hotels here, in S. Severino Lucano to the south, and at Terranova del Pollino, a village in the remotest corner of the park.

Apulia

In many ways, this region will be the biggest surprise of Italy's south. From the forests and shining limestone cliffs of the beautiful Gargano peninsula in the north, through the long plain of the *Tavoliere* to the southernmost tip of Italy's heel, Apulia (Puglia) offers the most variety of any of the southern regions, not only in nature, but in its towns and in its art: in Apulia you can see Byzantine art around Táranto, a score or so of Europe's finest Romanesque cathedrals, Santa Claus' tomb, the end of the Appian Way, the loveliest Baroque city in the Mediterranean, and a town of buildings with roofs shaped like oilcans.

Ancient Apulia was home to a number of quiet, modestly cultured and prosperous nations, notably the Daunii around Fóggia and the Messapians in the south. Under Roman rule it was a quiet and pre-dominantly agricultural province, Rome's gateway to the east, and one of the parts of Italy most heavily influenced by the proximity of Greek culture. In the Middle Ages, Apulia was the home of a unique culture influenced by Normans, Arabs and Greeks. In a brief but intense period of prosperity, helped along greatly by the Crusades, Apulia's cities were fully equal in wealth and artistic talent to those of the north.

Don't come expecting the familiar Italy of hill towns and tiny farms. Italy's second-biggest expanse of flatness (after the Po valley) is made for more serious agriculture—tons of wheat, oceans of excellent olive oil and wine (which gets better every year), all grown on the big estates called *masserie* that have provided the pattern of rural life since Roman times. Around the fringes of the long plain, with its die-straight Roman roads, there are plenty of hill towns too, some that would not look out of place in Tuscany, and others covered in gleaming whitewash that would be more at home in Greece or North Africa.

Fóggia and the Capitanata

Getting Around

Fóggia's **railway station** is on Piazza Veneto, at the end of the central Viale XXIV Maggio (information ℗ (0881) 621015). It is an important junction for north–south trains—you may often have to change there—and there will usually not be a long wait for trains to Bari, Naples, Bologna or Rome. Some trains also run from Fóggia to Manfredonia, though it is only a branch off the main east-coast line.

Two separate companies operate **buses** to different points around the province, all of which leave from the side of the Piazza Veneto opposite the station, where there is also a bus ticket office. There are several buses a day to Manfredonia, Monte Sant'Angelo and Vieste, and also to Troia and Lucera.

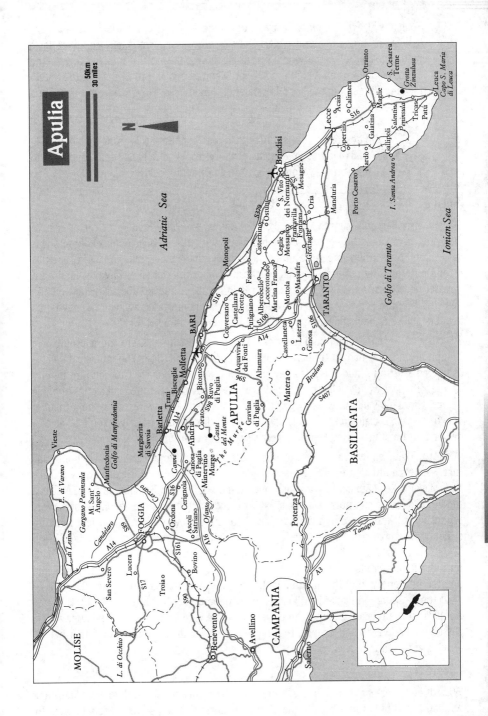

Fóggia is also well connected by **road**, as the A14 Adriatic coast *autostrada* runs just to the north. Around Fóggia there is a ring road, unusually complete for a medium-sized city, that connects up all the roads that run into the town—the SS16, parallel to the A14, the SS89 for Manfredonia and the Gargano, the SS655 for the south and the SS17 to Lucera and Campobasso. For Troia, take the SS546.

Tourist Information

The Fóggia tourist office is at Via Sen. Emilio Perrone 17, © (0881) 723141. It is quite some distance from the railway station and hard to find, on the second floor of an apartment block.

Fóggia

Fóggia, after Bari and Táranto the third city of Apulia, was once Frederick's capital, where between campaigns he enjoyed quiet moments with his English wife, his harem, his falcons and his Muslim sorcerers. It must have been quite a place, but old Fóggia has since been obliterated by two of the usual southern plagues: earthquakes have levelled it on several occasions, and the French sacked it in 1528. Allied bombers finished off the remains, and the Fóggia you see today is a newborn—homely and awkward as newborns are, but still somehow endearing if you come in the right frame of mind.

Its citizens haven't forgotten Frederick, but these days they seem more proud of a composer of operas named Umberto Giordano, born here in 1867. The municipal theatre is named after him, and there is a big statue of him in the Piazza Giordano in the city centre, among a wonderfully eccentric set of more statues representing characters from his works. Giordano's big hit was *Andrea Chenier*; another of his works, with the intriguing title of *Fedora*, is claimed as the only opera that calls for bicycles on stage. You'll be able to see one or the other during Fóggia's opera season, in the autumn.

Modern Fóggia shows you broad, planned boulevards and low, earthquake-proof build-ings. There's a little left of old Fóggia to see; a charming **cathedral** divided neatly in half, like a layer cake, 12th-century Romanesque on the bottom and Baroque on top. The early medieval door on the north side was rediscovered only during the Second World War, when bombs knocked down the adjacent building that was hiding it. A few twisting streets to the north, on Piazza Nigri, is Fóggia's **Museo Civico** (*open Mon, Wed–Sun, 9–1; Tues, 9–1 and 5–7*), with a collection devoted to archaeological finds and exhibits on folk life and crafts from around Apulia. The single portal with an inscription incor-porated into one side of the building is the last surviving remnant of Frederick's palace. Near the museum, on Piazza Sant'Egidio, the **Chiesa della Croce** (1693–1742) is one of Apulia's more unusual churches: an elegant Baroque gate leads to a long avenue, which passes under five domed chapels that represent stages in the passion of Christ before arriving at the church itself.

Lucera

Why does Lucera have a cathedral from the 14th century, while almost all the other Apulian towns built theirs back in the 12th or earlier? Well, sir, there's a story for you. In the 1230s, Emperor Frederick II was hard pressed. Excommunicated by his devious rival, Pope Gregory IX, and at war with all the Guelph towns of Italy, Frederick needed some allies he could trust. At the same time, he had a problem with brigandage in some of the predominantly Muslim mountain areas of Sicily. His solution: induce 20,000 Sicilian Arabs to move to Apulia, with land grants and promises of imperial employment and favours. The almost abandoned town of *Luceria*, once an important Roman colony, was the spot chosen, and before anybody knew it Frederick had conjured up an entirely Muslim metropolis 290km from Rome. The Emperor felt right at home in Lucera, and the new city became one of his favourite residences; later it would be the last stronghold of his son Manfred, in the dark days that followed Frederick's death. Charles of Anjou took the city in 1267; attempts at forced Christianization, and the introduction of settlers from Provence, caused a series of revolts among the population, which the Angevins finally settled in 1300 by butchering the lot.

Little remains of Muslim Lucera, or even of the Lucera of the French; most of the Provençals could not take the summer heat, though some of their descendants still live in the hills to the south. Still, it's a well-kept and attractive town, with an elegant centre around the simple, Gothic **cathedral** of 1300, built by Charles II directly after the massacre of the Saracens—the site probably once held the town's Great Mosque. The cathedral does its best not to look out of place (it's the only genuine Gothic church in Apulia); inside are some good Renaissance details, including a carved ambo (pulpit) and a baldachin over the baptismal font, along with big showy frescoes by Corenzio (the one who fell off his scaffolding in Naples) that no one has bothered to restore. Other monuments include the church of **San Francesco**, a typical barn-like Franciscan church built from recycled Roman ruins, as well as parts of a gate and an amphitheatre from Roman *Luceria* on the edge of town. Smaller fragments reside at the **Museo Civico** (*open Tues, Thurs, 9–2; Wed, Fri, 9–2 and 3–6; Sat, Sun, 9–1; adm*), just behind the cathedral.

Frederick's **castle** (*follow the signs; 2km north of the centre; open Tues–Sun, 7.30–2.30*), one of the largest ever built in Italy, was begun in 1233, the same year as the importation of the Saracens. It is still an impressive sight, with its score of towers and walls nearly a kilometre in circumference, set on a hill looking out over Lucera and the Fóggia plain. Only ruins are left of Frederick's palace inside.

Troia and its Cathedral

Fóggia's province is commonly known by its old Byzantine name, the *Capitanata*. The flatter parts of it, the *Tavoliere*, were until recently too dry to be of much use to agriculture. One of Mussolini's big projects, as important as the draining of the Pontine marshes, has made it one of the Mezzogiorno's most productive corners. The **Apulian aqueduct**, carrying water from the Apennines in northern Campania, is the longest and most capacious in the world.

South and west of Fóggia, in the foothills of the Apennines bordering the Molise and the Basilicata, you might consider a side trip to **Troia**, a cosy village atop a steep hill commanding the *Tavoliere*. Its famous **cathedral** is one of the oldest and most spectacular in Apulia, and a good introduction to the glories of the Apulian Romanesque. Troia, once the Roman town of *Aecae*, was refounded in 1017, and prospered from the start. Popes held two small church councils here in the 11th and 12th centuries; the cathedral was begun in 1093, though not finished until the time of Frederick.

Much of the inspiration for the Apulian style came from Pisa, and the Pisan trademark—blind arcades decorated with circle and diamond shapes—is in evidence here, and also the most beautiful **rose window** in Italy, a unique, Arab-inspired fantasy from Frederick's time; the circle is divided into 11 sections, each with carved stone lattice-work in a different geometric design. This eclectic building has some other surprises, beginning with a set of **bronze doors**, done in the 1120s by an artist named Odisarius of Benevento and embellished with bronze dragon door handles and incised figures of saints. Along the top of the north wall, note another Islamic contribution, intricately carved geometric arabesques that would not look out of place in the Alhambra. This cathedral has quite a bestiary carved into it; if you look closely, besides the usual lions you'll find all sorts of other creatures, including a mermaid and a bunny.

Inside, the cathedral is dark, austere and tremendous, with a narrow nave that accentuates its great height; some of its windows are the original alabaster models, which don't let in much light. Like so many other Apulian cathedrals, it is also strangely and intentionally asymmetrical, with everything on the right side just slightly out of alignment.

If you should be doing any more travelling through the pretty hills south of Fóggia, two more places of interest are **Bovino**, a resolutely medieval-looking village with a 13th-century cathedral and some Roman remains, and **Ascoli Satriano**, where a very well-preserved triple-arched Roman bridge still spans the River Carapelle. You can also see substantial remains of the abandoned Roman town of *Herdonio*, near **Ordona**.

Where to Stay and Eating Out

Fóggia ✆ (0881–)

Expect nothing special here; the best is the ★★★★**Cicolella** at Viale XXIV Maggio 60, ✆ 688890 (*expensive*), near the station. This old establishment is Victorian on the outside, but remodelled within; the restaurant is also one of the best in town. Two reasonably inexpensive places near the station are the ★**Venezia**, Via Piave 40, ✆ 770903, and the slightly more expensive ★**Centrale**, Corso Cairoli 5, ✆ 771862.

The same family that runs the **Cicolella Hotel** (*see* above) also operates three fine restaurants; the one in the hotel itself (*expensive*) is a rare find, and a good place to introduce yourself to Apulian specialities like *orecchiette*, little 'ears' of pasta that lately are becoming fashionable all around Italy. The fish here is very good, and also the roast lamb. *Restaurant closed Sun.* A wide range of local and seasonal specialities can also be sampled at **Il Grottino**, Vico Teatro, ✆ 671331 (*moderate*), an old favourite near the Teatro Giordano that also makes good pizza. *Closed Sun.* For far fewer lire, you won't do better than the anachronistically good, cheap and friendly **Trattoria Santa Lucia**, at Via Trieste 57, which has a fixed price menu at L25,000.

Lucera ✆ (0881–)

The place to stay in Lucera is the characterful and friendly **★★Al Passetto**, Piazza del Popolo 26–30, ✆ 520821 (*inexpensive*), next to the bus station. If they're full, the **★★La Balconata,** just across the piazza, Viale Ferrovia 15, ✆ 546725, will do fine. There's also a nice hotel further north in San Severo, the **★★★Milano**, Via Appulo 15, ✆ (0882) 375643 (*moderate/inexpensive*), with showers and TV in all rooms, and a lock-up garage.

The **Albergo Al Passetto** (*see* above) has a fine and inexpensive restaurant, with average prices of L30,000. *Closed Mon.* Even San Severo has a restaurant that can make it worth stopping over. **Le Arcate**, Piazza Cavalotti 28, ✆ (0882) 322146 (*moderate*), uses lighter variations on rustic cuisine, and offers lamb done in all kinds of interesting ways. *Closed Mon.*

The Gargano Peninsula

It looks a little out of place, being the only stretch of scenic coastline between Venice and the tip of Calabria. The 'spur' of the Italian boot is, in fact, a lost chip of the Balkans, left behind when two geological plates separated to form the Adriatic, several million years ago. For a long time, before silt washed down by the rivers gradually joined it to the mainland, the Gargano was an island. It might as well have remained so, for the Gargano is as different from the adjacent lands in attitude as it is in its landscapes.

Getting Around

The Gargano has a little private **railway**, called the *Ferrovia del Gargano*, that clatters amiably from San Severo, 30km north of Fóggia, up the western edge of the peninsula to Rodi Garganico and Peschici (about six trains a day; information ✆ (0884) 707495). Connecting **buses** will take you from Peschici to Vieste along the coast road (SP52). Buses are less frequent between Vieste and Manfredonia and Fóggia. There are several buses a day from Fóggia and Manfredonia to Monte Sant'Angelo, and to San Giovanni Rotondo, but seeing the Foresta Umbra and the interior of the Gargano will be hard without a car; there is only one bus early in the morning, from Monte Sant'Angelo.

There is also a regular **ferryboat service** around the peninsula from Manfredonia that calls at Vieste, Peschici, Rodi Garganico and the Tremiti islands, with one sailing daily between June and September, and more infrequently in spring and early autumn. It does not operate between October and March.

Manfredonia is the main port for the **Tremiti islands**; the steamer departs several times a week (5 hours). In summer departures are daily, and there are additional services from Vieste (3 hours), Pugnochiuso (4 hours) and Péschici (2 hours). Summer hydrofoils run from Ortona (2 hours), Vasto (1 hour), and Termoli (45 minutes).

Manfredonia

If you are coming from the north, you will enter the Gargano by way of Lesina and the Gargano's two lakes: the **Lago di Lesina** and the **Lago di Varano**, two large lagoons cut off from the sea by broad sand spits. From Fóggia, the logical base for attacking the Gargano would be **Manfredonia**, a port town with a beach and a pretty centre at the southern end of the peninsula. It is the base for ferries to the Tremiti islands and the towns of the Gargano, as well as being a small resort in its own right. As its name implies, this town was founded by Frederick's son Manfred, and it prospered well enough until Dragut's Turkish pirates sacked and razed it in 1620. (One of the hometown girls ended up as the favoured wife of the sultan.) Of old Manfredonia, all that is left is Manfred's **castle**, rebuilt and extended by Charles of Anjou. It now contains a small archaeological museum where the star exhibits are the steles of the ancient Daunii, stones carved into warlike figures with weapons and strange warlike designs; similar steles are found in Corsica, northern Tuscany and parts of southern France (*open daily, 8.30–1.30, 3.30–7.30; closed the first and last Mon of each month; adm*). The town also has a brash **cathedral**, which dates from the 17th century, although it manages to look much newer, thanks to a recent cleaning.

Along the Fóggia road, about 2km south of the centre of Manfredonia, you can see the ruins of **Sipontum**, a Roman town that was finally abandoned to the malaria mosquitoes when Manfred moved the population to his healthier new city. The much more recent town of **Siponto**, next to it, is now a popular beach resort. As evidence of how important Sipontum was in the early Middle Ages, there is the impressive 11th-century church of **Santa Maria di Siponto**, in the same style of decoration as the cathedral at Troia, only built on a square, Byzantine-Greek plan. It is built over a much earlier underground Christian building, from around the 5th century. Another 11th-century church, very similar to Santa Maria, survives another 9km up the road to Fóggia—**San Leonardo**, an even better work, with finely sculpted portals and a small dome.

Monte Sant'Angelo

The tourists who come to the Gargano for the beaches probably never notice, but this peninsula is holy ground, and has been perhaps since the time of the ancient Daunians. Sanctuaries, ancient and modern, are scattered all over it; there are many stories of apparitions of saints and angels, and even 25 years ago, a holy man who received the stigmata lived at San Giovanni Rotondo.

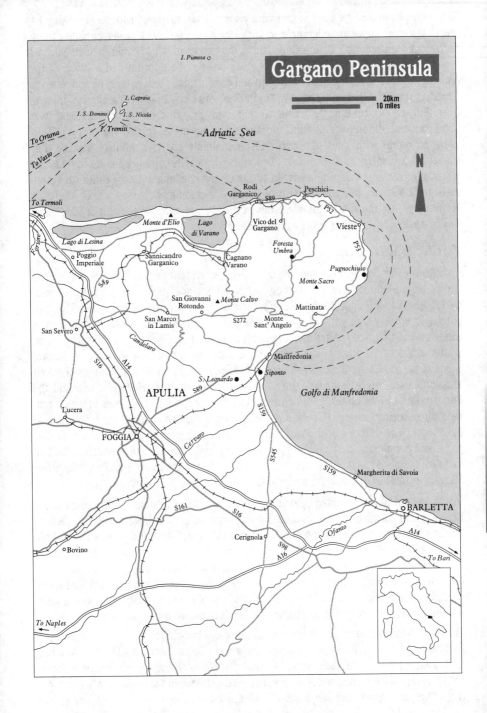

Gargano Peninsula

20km
10 miles

I. Pianosa

I. Capraia
I. S. Domino
I. S. Nicola
I. Tremiti

To Ortona
To Vasto

Adriatic Sea

To Termoli

N

Rodi
Garganico
S89
Peschici
P52

Monte d'Elio
Lago di Lesina
Lago
di Varano
Vico del
Gargano
Vieste

Fortore
Poggio
Imperiale
Sannicandro
Garganico
Cagnano
Varano
Foresta
Umbra
P53

San Giovanni
Rotondo
Monte Calvo
Pugnochiuso
Monte Sacro

San Marco
in Lamis
S272
Monte
Sant' Angelo
Mattinata

San Severo
Candelaro

Manfredonia

APULIA
S89
S. Leonardo
Siponto

Golfo di Manfredonia

S16
A14

S159

Lucera
Cervaro

FOGGIA
S545

S159
Margherita di Savoia

S161
S16

BARLETTA

Bovino
Cerignola
S98
A16
Ofanto
A14
To Bari

To Naples

225

The centre of all this, for the last thousand years at least, has been **Monte Sant'Angelo**, one of the most important pilgrimage towns in Italy (and thus well served by public transport, from Manfredonia). Before Christianity, the cavern now dedicated to Saint Michael was the site of a dream oracle; a 5th-century bishop of Sipontum had a vision of the archangel, who left his red cloak as a token and commanded the sanctuary be converted to Christian worship. Early on, the new Monte Sant'Angelo was attracting pilgrims from all over Europe—continuing a tradition that had begun long before the site was Christianized. Among the pilgrims were the first Normans, in the 9th century. They returned home with tales of a rich and fascinatingly civilized Apulia—a place they suspected just might be a pushover for mounted, heavily armoured knights. The first Norman adventurers were not slow in taking up the challenge. All the other sites dedicated to St Michael around the coasts of Europe—including of course Mont St Michel in Normandy—are the spiritual descendants of this one, founded as the cult of St Michael spread across Christendom in the early Middle Ages.

Terrible is This Place...

That Monte Sant'Angelo is a special place becomes evident even before you arrive. The trip up from Manfredonia passes through an uncanny landscape: chalky cliffs dotted with caves, ancient agricultural terraces, and a strange clarity in the light and air. The road climbs so quickly that you seem to be looking straight down into Manfredonia, even though it is 14km away. After much twisting and grinding of gears, you arrive at a quiet, whitewashed city, a maze of steps and tunnels. The medieval centre of town, the **Junno**, is one of the most beautiful old quarters in southern Italy, a nonchalant harmony of colour and form that only a few coast towns in Apulia can achieve. Here you will find the **Sanctuary of St Michael**, behind an eight-sided tower built by Charles of Anjou that reproduces the proportions (on one level) and much of the decoration of Frederick's Castel del Monte. The exterior of the sanctuary seems to be a normal church, with a Gothic porch and portals (mostly built in the 19th century; see if you can guess which of the two identical portals is the original 12th-century work). Above the doors is a Latin inscription: 'Terrible is this place; this is the house of God and the Gate of Heaven'.

Inside, instead of the expected church, there is a long series of steps leading down to the cavern, passing a beautiful pair of bronze doors made in Constantinople in 1076, perhaps by the same artists who did the ones at Amalfi Cathedral. In the darkness most of the scenes are difficult to make out, but Jacob's ladder and the expulsion from Eden stand out clearly. Down in the cave, it is chilly and dark; in the old days pilgrims would come down on their knees, shuffling through the puddles to kiss the image of the archangel. The grotto is laid out like a small chapel. There are plenty of bits of medieval sculptural work around, but the best is a wonderful crazy-medieval bishop's chair, from the 12th century.

The town records give us an almost endless list of celebrity pilgrims: a dozen popes, King Ferdinand of Spain, four Holy Roman Emperors, Saints Bernard, Thomas Aquinas, Catherine of Siena, and so on; even St Francis, and they can show you the mark he made on the cavern wall. Behind the altar, you can see the little well that made this a holy site in the first place. Long before there was a St Michael, indigenous religions of Europe had a great interest in springs and underground streams; many scholars believe the idea of dragons began with a primeval fascination with buried streams and accompanying lines of telluric forces beneath the earth's surface; the sleepless 'eye' of the dragon is the fountain, where these forces come to the surface. In the icons of Monte Sant'Angelo, as well as in the endless souvenir figurines hawked outside the sanctuary, Michael is shown dispatching Lucifer in the form of a dragon.

Tomba di Rotari

There's more to see in Monte Sant'Angelo, and more oddities. Downhill from the sanctuary, next to the half-ruined church of San Pietro, stands the 12th-century work called the **tomb of Rotari**. The idea that this was the tomb of 'Rotarus', a Lombard chief, stems from a misreading of one of the inscriptions. It is now believed this was intended to be a baptistry—a very large and unusual baptistry, if so; it is hard to make out the original intention, since much of it has been swallowed up into the surrounding buildings. Some of the sculpted detail is extremely odd; note the figures of a woman suckling a serpent—or dragon (*see* **Topics**, p.53).

More intimate scenes of ladies and dragons await next door, in an incredible relief over the entrance to **Santa Maria Maggiore**, completed in 1198. Inside this lovely church are two odd domes, very like the *trulli* of Alberobello (*see* below), a dignified fresco of St Michael in full Byzantine court dress, and tantalizing bits of other Byzantine paintings from the 13th–14th centuries. Also in the Junno district, the town has opened a small museum of the folk arts and culture of the Gargano, the **Museo Tancredi** (*open May–Sept, Mon–Sat, 9.30–12.30 and 3.30–7.30; Oct–April, Mon–Sat, 9.30–12.30; adm*). On the top of the town, there is a romantically ruined Norman castle, rebuilt by the Aragonese kings, but left quite alone ever since.

San Giovanni Rotondo and Padre Pio

From the back of Monte Sant'Angelo, a narrow road leads into the heart of the Gargano, eventually branching off to the 'Forest of Shadows' (*see* below) or **San Giovanni Rotondo**, a little town on the slopes of Monte Calvo. Here, besides the strange round temple that gives the town its name (believed, like the tomb of Rotari, to have been intended as a baptistry), there is a 16th-century monastery that for over 50 years was the home of Padre Pio de Pietralcina, a simple priest who not only received the stigmata, the bleeding wounds of Christ, on his hands, feet and side, but also had the ability to appear before cardinals in Rome while his body was sleeping back in the Gargano. The Church always has its suspicions about phenomena like these, and it did its best, while acknowledging the honesty of Padre Pio's miracles, to keep him a little under wraps lest popular devotion get out of hand. Nevertheless, the town has become a pilgrimage destination in its own right, and before he died in 1968, Padre Pio was able to attract enough donations to build a large modern hospital, the first in the Gargano. If you've been around the south much you'll know what he looked like by now—only the Virgin Mary herself gets her picture up in more bars, petrol stations and hotels. You can visit the **Sanctuary of Santa Maria della Grazia** and Padre Pio's cell; pilgrims are asked to avoid spontaneous singing during Masses.

West of San Giovanni and, like it, an old stop on the pilgrimage route to Monte Sant'Angelo is the town of **San Marco in Lamis**, which has similarly always been a monastic centre. The present, huge Franciscan house dates from the 16th century.

Vieste

Enough of the holy Gargano. Once past Monte Sacro, on the coast north of Monte Sant'Angelo, you are in the holiday Gargano, on an exceptionally lovely coastline of limestone cliffs, clean blue sea, and good beaches decorated with old watchtowers, or stumps and columns of rock and other curious formations. **Vieste**, at the tip of the peninsula, is in the middle of it, a lively and beautiful white town on white cliffs, surrounded by beaches. Within the last ten years, Vieste has become the major resort of the southern Adriatic, and boutiques and restaurants are crowding the town centre.

On Via Duomo, near the centre of the old town, is the **Chianca Amara** or 'bitter stone', where, it is believed, 5000 of the town's people were beheaded by the Turks when they sacked Vieste in 1554. Nearby are the 11th-century **cathedral**, with 18th-century additions, and, beyond that, another **castle** built by Frederick II, with fine views over the town, and the **Grotta Sfondata** ('bottomless lagoon'), one of a few marine grottos and lagoons accessible by boat tours from Vieste. There is also a peculiar early Christian hypogeum (cave for burials) on the coast at the site of a long-disappeared town called *Merinum.*

The best parts of the coast lie to the south of Vieste: beautiful coves like **Cala San Felice**, with a little beach and a natural arch in the cliffs, and **Cala Sanguinaria**. A bit further south, at **Acqua della Rosa**, when conditions are just right, the reflection from the limestone cliffs give the water near the shore a rosy tint. Most of the tourist sprawl, with miles of beaches and campsites, extends to the north of Vieste. Near the road inland for Monte Sant'Angelo, **Mattinata** is one of the more eccentric examples of Apulian vernacular architecture, a gleaming white village of rectangular houses stacked in tidy rows like sugar cubes.

On the Gargano's northern coast, **Peschici** and **Rodi Garganico** are two other pretty fishing villages that are now fast-developing resorts, and particularly crowded in August. Boats call at both of them for the Tremiti islands, and from either village, or from Vieste itself, it is a relatively easy excursion by bus or car up the mountains to the **Foresta Umbra**, the 'forest of shadows', a thick, primeval forest of beeches, oaks, and pines, similar to those that covered most of Apulia in the Middle Ages. A visitors' centre run by the *Corpo Forestale* along the SS528, past the turning for Vico del Gargano, will help you learn more about it.

The Tremiti Islands

In winter, this minuscule archipelago 40km from the coast has a population of about 50. August, however, finds it crawling with most of the 100,000 holiday-makers who annually spill over from the resorts of the Gargano. The striking beauty of this tiny archipelago is its main attraction—the bluest waters in the Adriatic and pale calcareous cliffs much like the Gargano mainland (there's only one beach). If you can avoid coming in July or

August, when the hordes of day-trippers sail in, the Tremitis can be a perfect spot to let your watch run down.

The islands enter the history books first as a place of exile—Augustus' daughter and Charlemagne's troublesome Italian father-in-law were both confined here—or as a monkish retreat. Later the Tremitis were ruled by abbots; beginning in 1010, Benedictines from Montecassino founded an abbey on the smaller island, San Nicola. They became wealthy with treasures deposited by mainlanders fearful of the Normans, and in 1236 the Inquisition dissolved the abbey and grabbed up the booty. The Cistercians who followed lasted until the 1350s, when pirates tricked them into believing their captain was dead and desired a Christian burial. The Cistercians complied, and during the night the captain rose from the grave and let his men in at the gate to massacre the monks. In 1412 yet another order, the Lateranesi, was sent by Pope Gregory XII to restore the monastery. The Bourbons of Naples claimed the islands in 1737, ending monastic rule and creating yet another island penal colony.

San Nicola and San Domino

San Nicola is dominated by its fortress-monastery. Boats call just under its main gate where an inscription reads *Conteret et Confringet* ('crush and kill')—referring to the rights granted to the abbot by Pope Paul III to torture and kill heretics. Principal sights within the walls include the ancient church of **Santa Maria a Mare** (1045) with mosaic fragments and a large, celebrated icon of Christ, as well as its old cloister, a fine cistern, and the grand **Dormitorio Nuovo**, built by the Lateranesi.

Nearby San Domino, largest and most luxuriant of the Tremitis, was indefensible and thus uninhabited for most of its history. Its marvellous coastline of cliffs and jutting rocks, penetrated by grottoes, is easy to explore in a day either by boat or on foot. Tourist facilities are concentrated around the beach, **Cala delle Arene**. From here you can walk to the **Capella del Romito**, at the highest point of the island—all of 85m.

Along the coast are the violet-coloured **Grotta delle Ciole**, the **Grotta delle Murene**, where sea eels breed, and the Punta del Diavolo. The most spectacular feature of the island, the 75m crag known as the **Ripa dei Falconi** where falcons were bred in the days of chivalry, and the **Grotta del Bue Marino** beneath it, may seem vaguely familiar if you've seen *The Guns of Navarone*. Over 45m long, the cave is the largest on San Domino; if you go by boat, take a torch to see the rock formations.

The other two Tremiti islands are uninhabited: **Pianosa**, low and flat, used by Italian fishermen and Balkan smugglers on overnight trips, and **Caprara**, island of rabbits, with an enormous natural arch and a lovely cave called the **Grottone**, almost 30m high at its mouth.

Where to Stay and Eating Out

The Gargano has a large number of *aziende agrituristiche*—some of which are simple bed-and-breakfast places in the country, though some offer home-cooked meals at very reasonable prices. Whichever, if you have a car they make a good and inexpensive alternative to staying in hotels; complete lists can be obtained from any tourist office.

Manfredonia ℗ (0884–)

Almost all the hotels here are outside town, near the beaches, such as the comfortable, modern ★★★**Gabbiano**, Via Eunostides 20 at Siponto, ℗ 542554, ✆ 542380. In town, the choice is between the small and simple ★★★**Azzurro**, Via di Vittorio 51, ℗ 581498, and the cheaper and even more basic ★**Sipontum**, down the road at Via di Vittorio 229, ℗ 542916; both are inexpensive, agreeable places to stay over while waiting for a boat or a bus.

Manfredonia's restaurants are mostly around the port, and most specialize in seafood; **Al Porto**, Piazza Libertà 3, ℗ 581800 (*moderate*), is justifiably proud of its seafood risotto, and the linguine with clam sauce is also a treat. *Closed Mon.* There are more treats to be had in the cool modern surroundings of **Il Baracchio**, Corso Roma 38, ℗ 23874 (*moderate*), where the octopus salad has to be tasted to be believed. *Closed Mon.*

Monte Sant'Angelo ℗ (0884–)

The only hotel up here is the bizarrely named but comfortable ★★★**Rotary**, 1km from town on Via Pulsano, ℗ 562146 (*moderate*); there are also three camp sites nearby at Frazione Macchia. At **Al Grottino**, Corso Vittorio Emanuele 179, ℗ 561132 (*inexpensive*), you can get a dinner worth L50,000 for about half the price—roast lamb and kid, truly elegant antipasti, sweets and cheeses, and one memorable dish called *orecchiette in carozza*. *Closed Mon.* Another good choice for lunch is the **Garden Paradise** at Via Basilica 51 (*inexpensive*), with well-prepared seafood and good *involtini*. *Open Oct–Mar, closed Mon.*

Vieste ℗ (0884–)

The best beach hotels are slightly garish places, a little bit of Rimini on the Gargano. The ★★★★**Pizzomunno Vieste Palace**, Lungomare Enrico Mattei, ℗ 708741, ✆ 707325 (*expensive*; cheaper rooms sometimes available in the *Pizzomunno Residence*), about 1km south of the town centre, is a luxurious place that keeps holiday-makers busy with sailing, sports, a pool, a beautiful beach and a noisy disco, as well as filling them up in an exceptional, highly rated restaurant. Second choice would be the ★★★**Falcone**, Lungomare Enrico Mattei 5, ℗ 708251, ✆ 708252 (*moderate*), with a private beach, and most of the resort amenities at a much better rate. In the centre of Vieste, a good budget choice is the ★**Pensione San Giorgio,** Piazza della Libera, ℗ 708618 (*inexpensive*), which also has a good restaurant.

Some good hotels can be found along the coasts around Vieste—usually in lovely spots, but convenient only if you have a car. The ★★★**Gabbiano Beach**, ℗ 706376, ✆ 706689 (*moderate*), 7km north on the road to Peschici, is one of the better ones, with its own beach, pool and sailing facilities. A large and ever-increasing selection of hotels similar to those of Vieste will be found in nearby Peschici and Rodi Garganico. The **Peschici**, Via San Maritino 31, © 964195 (*inexpensive*), has good views and more facilities and services than most two-star hotels. *Closed Nov–Mar*. In the historic centre of Rodi Garganico is the ★★★**Albano**, Via Scalo Marittimo 33, © 965138 (*moderate, inexpensive out of season*), another well-appointed and reasonably priced option, with air-conditioning, TV in most rooms, and a good if unexciting restaurant. If you want something cheaper, try the tiny **Villa a Mare**, at Via Trieste 89, © 966149 (*inexpensive*). All rooms have showers, but there's no air-conditioning here.

Vieste is home to a restaurant considered by many to be the finest in Apulia: **Il Trabucco** in the Hotel Pizzomunno (*see* above), © 708741 (*expensive*); overwhelming seafood antipasti, and the best of Apulian wines and fresh local ingredients from the Gargano's own olive oil to grilled fish brought in by Vieste's fishermen the same morning. Not all the good restaurants are in hotels: the **Vecchia Vieste**, Via Mafrolla 30, © 707083 (*moderate*), offers seafood and specialities like *involtini alla Viestiana*. *Closed Mon, Jan, Feb*. For a similar price you can eat seafood or grilled meats at **Box 19**, Via Santa Maria di Merino 19, © 705229 (*moderate*). *Open Oct–Mar, closed Mon*. One of Peschici's best restaurants, especially for fish and seafood, although it has excellent meat dishes too, is **Fra' Stefano**, Via Forno 8, © 964141 (*inexpensive*), in the centre of the old town.

Tremiti Islands © (0882–)

Over a dozen hotels have appeared in recent years, all of them on San Domino. If you want to stay over it's worth booking in advance at the eight-room ★**Al Faro**, © 663424 (*inexpensive*), near the central square on San Domino. *Closed Oct–Easter*. Among the fancier places a good bargain is the ★★★**Gabbiano**, Piazza Belvedere, © 663410 (*moderate*), where it's equally essential to book. You tend to pay over the odds for food here, but one place where you can find value for money is the **Al Faro** hotel (*see* above), where the restaurant offers home cooking influenced by the food traditions of the San Nicola monastery, washed down with good-quality wines. You even get to choose your own fish out of the fridge. On San Domino's piazza, **La Barcaccia**, © 663453 (*moderate*), is another good place for seafood.

Down the Coast to Bari

If you take the main route, a little bit inland, you will be passing through more of the *Tavoliere*, the long, dull plain that stretches the length of Apulia. *Tavoliere* means a chessboard; 2000 years ago, when the Romans first sent in surveyors to apportion the land among their Punic War veterans, this flat plain—the only one south of the Po—gave the methodical rectangularity of the Roman mind a chance to express itself. They turned the plain into a grid of neatly squared roads and farms; many of their arrow-straight roads survive, and the succeeding centuries have managed to throw only a few kinks into the rest. If not for the olive groves and vineyards, you might think you were in Iowa.

Two different **railways** serve this area, and unusually for Apulia you're more likely to find a train than a bus to many destinations. All the coastal towns from Barletta to Monópoli are on the main FS east-coast route. From Barletta, there is an FS branch line to the south with infrequent services to Spinazzola and Altamura. In addition, one of the three private regional lines that operate from Bari, the *Ferrovia Bari-Nord* (✆ 213577), runs a very frequent service through the inland towns such as Andria, Ruvo and Bitonto. There are also reasonably regular **buses** along the coast road, and to inland destinations from Barletta or Bari. The hardest place to reach without a car is Castel del Monte: the 7am Bari-Nord train from Bari to Andria will connect you with the only bus to there, but the only return bus the same day leaves a few hours later at 11.15am.

Communications by **car** are very easy, as driving along the straight Roman roads across the flat plain is much faster than on the mountain roads of the neighbouring regions. The main trunk route is the A14, which near Canosa di Apulia is joined by the A16 *autostrada* from Naples and the west coast. Two other roads, the SS16 along the coast and the SS98 through Andria and the inland towns, run roughly in parallel with the A14 into Bari. If you are driving to Castel del Monte from Bari, turn off the SS98 on to the SS170 just west of Ruvo di Apulia. For Altamura and the Murge, take the SS96 south from Bari.

There are tourist offices along this stretch of coast in **Margherita di Savoia**, Via Cirillo 2, ✆ (0883) 654012, **Barletta**, Via Gabbiani 4, ✆ (0883) 578314, and in **Trani**, at Via Cavour 140, ✆ (0883) 588825.

Barletta's Colossus

The coastal road, though just as flat, has more to see than the inland route, passing through a string of attractive medieval port towns, each with its contribution to the Apulian Romanesque in the shape of a grand old cathedral. Each, that is, except **Margherita di Savoia**, the first town south of the Gargano, a funky urban smudge surrounded by salt pans. No one seems to remember what the old name was, but they changed it a century ago to honour the formidable wife of King Umberto I. Today it is the best place to inspect the modern Apulian fancy in architecture—houses entirely covered in colourful, patterned bathroom tiles.

Barletta, the next town southwards, is also one of the largest. Though quite a prosperous place these days, Barletta has sadly neglected its historical centre. If you pass it by, however, you will miss a unique and astounding sight. On Corso Vittorio Emanuele, beside the church of San Sepolcro, stands the largest surviving ancient bronze statue, locally known as the **Colosso**.

To come upon this 6m figure in the middle of a busy city street, wearing an imperial scowl and a pose of conquest, with a cross and a sphere in his hands, is like lapsing into a dream. Scholars have debated for centuries who it might be. It's obviously a late Roman emperor, and the guesses have included Valentinian, Heraclius and Marcian; the last is most probable, and especially intriguing, since the triumphal column of Marcian (a rather useless emperor with no real successes to commemorate) still stands in Istanbul, and the statue of the emperor that once stood on top of it was probably carried away by the Venetians after the sack of Constantinople in 1204. A ship full of booty from that sack foundered off Barletta's coast, and the Colosso washed up on a nearby beach; the superstitious citizens let it stay there for decades before they got up enough nerve to bring it into the city. The figure is surpassingly strange, a monument to the onset of the Dark Ages; the costume the emperor wears is only a pale memory of the dress of Marcus Aurelius or Hadrian, with a pair of barbaric-looking leather boots instead of imperial buskins.

San Sepolcro, finished in the 13th century, is interesting in its own right. Above the plain French Gothic vaulting, there is an octagonal dome, recalling the Holy Sepulchre in Jerusalem. Corso Garibaldi leads from here into the heart of old Barletta, passing the **Museo Civico de Nittis** (*open Tues–Sun, 9–1*), which has in its collection the only surviving statue of Frederick II—a little the worse for wear, poor fellow—as well as a large collection of works by the local, Impressionist-influenced painter Giuseppe de Nittis (1846–84). Barletta's 12th-century **cathedral** is near the end of Corso Garibaldi. Look on the left-hand wall, between the façade and the campanile, and you will see a cornice supported by thirteen strange figures. If you are clever and have a good eye, you may make out the letters on them that make an acrostic of *Richardus Rex I*—Richard the Lionheart, who contributed to the embellishment of the cathedral on his way to the Crusades.

Nearby is the 13th-century church of **Sant' Andrea**, with another fine façade, the main portal of which, from 1240, was the work of the Dalmatian sculptor Simon di Ragusa. The Third Crusade was launched from Barletta's often-rebuilt **castle**, in a great council of Frederick and his knights. The polygonal bastions you see were added in the 1530s.

Trani

The next town along the coast, Trani is a sun- and sea-washed old port that still has a large and prosperous fishing fleet. It was an important merchant town in the early Middle Ages—it once fought a war with Venice, and its merchant captains created perhaps the first code of laws of the sea since ancient times. Trani's famous **cathedral** stands in an open piazza on the edge of the sea, another excellent work of the Apulian Romanesque, and a monument to the age of the Crusades. At the centre of the façade is another pair of 12th-century bronze doors, very much like the ones in so many other cities of the south. These ones are special, though, since the artist who did them and several others in the town is a native, Barisano of Trani.

Inside, the most remarkable things are underground. This cathedral is really three buildings stacked on the same site; the lower church, called **Santa Maria della Scala**, is really the earlier, Byzantine cathedral, and below that is the **Crypt of San Leucio**, an unusual early Christian church or catacomb with solid marble columns and bits of medieval frescoes. Some of Trani's other notable buildings are the **Ognissanti**, a typical church of the 12th-century Knights Templar; the **Palazzo Cacetta**, a rare (for southern Italy) example of late Gothic architecture from the 1450s; and two small churches that were once synagogues, **Santa Maria Scuolanove** and **Sant'Anna**, converted after the Spaniards expelled Trani's long-established Jewish community in the 16th century.

From Trani, **Bisceglie** is the next town, with another good Romanesque cathedral. Then comes **Molfetta**, a city with a reputation for drugs and gangsters. Molfetta has a cathedral like Trani's on the harbour's edge, the **Duomo Vecchio**. This may be the most peculiar of them all: its plan, subtly asymmetrical like that of Troia, has a wide nave covered by three domes, the central one being elliptical. The west front is almost blank, while the back side has elaborate carved decoration, and a door that leads into the apse. Molfetta also has another cathedral, the Baroque **Duomo Nuovo**, from 1785.

Castel del Monte

In Enna, the 'navel of Sicily', Emperor Frederick built a mysterious, octagonal tower at the highest point of the town. In Apulia, this most esoteric of emperors erected an equally puzzling palace. It, too, is a perfect octagon, and if you have been travelling through the region with us, you will have noticed that nearly every town has at least one eight-sided tower, bastion or campanile, and that often enough Frederick was originally behind them. **Castel di Santa Maria del Monte** (*open Mon–Sat, 9–1 and 3–7; Sun, 9–1; adm*), to give it its original title, was begun by Frederick in the 1240s on a high hill overlooking the Apulian *Tavoliere*, south of the town of Andria.

At each of the eight corners of Castel del Monte is a slender tower, also octagonal. The building, though 24m tall, has only two storeys; each has eight rooms, almost all interconnected, and each facing the octagonal courtyard. The historians sometimes try to explain the castle as one of Frederick's hunting lodges. This won't do; the rooms each have only one relatively small window, and in spite of the wealth of sculpted stone the castle once had, it would have seemed more like a prison than a forest retreat—in fact the emperor's grandsons, the heirs of his son Manfred, were later imprisoned here for 30 years. Neither is it a fortification; there are no ramparts, no slits for archers, and not even a defensible gate. Some writers have suggested that Frederick had an artistic monument in mind. The entrance to the castle, the so-called 'triumphal arch', is a work unique for the 13th century, an elegant classical portal that prefigures the Renaissance. Inside, every room was decorated with columns, friezes and reliefs in Greek marble, porphyry and other precious stones. Almost all of these have disappeared, vandalized by the Angevins and the noblemen who owned the castle over the last five centuries. The delicately carved Gothic double windows survive, one to each room, along with a few other bits of the original decoration: grotesques at the points of the vaulting in some rooms, elegant conical fireplaces, capitals (some Corinthian, some in the Egyptian order) and in two of the corner towers, corbels under the arches carved into peculiar faces and figures.

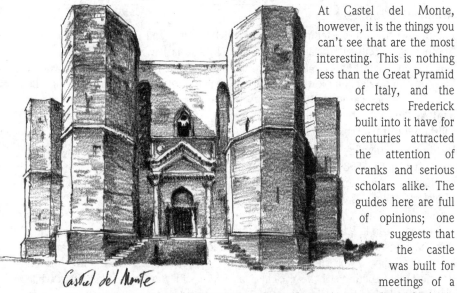

Castel del Monte

At Castel del Monte, however, it is the things you can't see that are the most interesting. This is nothing less than the Great Pyramid of Italy, and the secrets Frederick built into it have for centuries attracted the attention of cranks and serious scholars alike. The guides here are full of opinions; one suggests that the castle was built for meetings of a secret society, and considering the atmosphere of eclectic mysticism that surrounded the emperor and his court, this seems entirely possible. Whole books have been written about the measurements and proportions of the castle, finding endless repetitions of the Golden Section, its square and cubic roots, relations to the movements of the planets and the stars, the angles and proportions of the Pythagorean five-pointed star, and so on. The idiosyncrasies of the design are just as interesting. For all its octagonal rigour, the castle is full of teasing quirks. Looking from the courtyard (where there are some surviving fragments of reliefs), along the eight walls there are two large windows, two doors and two balconies, studiously arranged to avoid any pattern or symmetry; some of the windows, facing the courtyard or between the chambers, seem centrally placed from one side, but several feet off centre from the other: intentional, but impossible to explain.

The relation of the castle to the ancient surveying of the Apulian plain is a fascinating possibility. Frederick's tower in Sicily has been found to be the centre of an enormous rectilinear network of alignments, uniting scores of ancient temples, towers, and cities in straight lines that run the length and breadth of the island. The tower is believed to be built on the site of some forgotten holy place; the alignments and the vast geometrical temple they form probably predate even the Greeks. No one has yet suggested that Castel del Monte replaced any ancient site, but the particular care of Apulia's ancient surveyors, and the arrangement of the region's holy places, sanctuaries and Frederick's castles suggest that something similarly strange may be hidden here. The wildest theory so far claims that the castle marks the intersection of the two greatest alignments of them all; lying exactly halfway betwen the Great Pyramid and Stonehenge, and halfway between Jerusalem and Mont Saint Michel.

Around the *Tavoliere*

The nearest town to Castel del Monte is **Andria**, a large and thriving market centre. Another of the cities associated with Frederick, Andria has an inscription from the emperor on its St Andrea's Gate, honouring it for its loyalty. Two of Frederick's wives, Yolande of Jerusalem and Isabella of England, daughter of King John, are buried in the crypt of Andria's **cathedral**. Other churches worth a look include the 13th-century **Sant'Agostino**, built by, of all people, the Teutonic Order; and the 16th-century **Santa Maria dei Miracoli**, restored in the Baroque.

Heading back towards Fóggia, on the banks of the River Ofanto between Barletta and Canosa di Apulia (SS93 road), you can visit the site of the Battle of **Cannae**; here, in 216 BC, Hannibal trapped and annihilated four Roman legions in one of the most famous battles of history. Military strategists still study the Carthaginians' brilliant ambush, the last serious defeat Rome was to suffer for centuries. At the time, Hannibal and his elephants had already been in Italy for two years. Cannae was the opportunity he was waiting for, and historians are puzzled why he didn't immediately follow it up with a march on Rome—probably it was due to a lack of siege equipment. The chance was missed; Hannibal spent another eight years campaigning successfully but fruitlessly in Italy, while the Romans locked themselves up in their towns and sent their armies off to conquer Spain and North Africa. Cannae taught the Romans to be careful, and it could be said that Hannibal's great victory meant the defeat not of Rome, but of Carthage. A small **museum** on the site gives a blow-by-blow account, along with archaeological finds, but at the time of writing is unfortunately closed for an indefinite period.

In Roman times, **Canosa di Apulia** was one of the most important towns in the region; the reminders of its former status include three large tombs on the outskirts of town, excavated in 1843, and a collection of archaeological relics in the **Museo Civico** (*open Tues–Sun, 8–2*). Canosa isn't much today, but its otherwise undistinguished five-domed cathedral has in its courtyard the **tomb of Bohemund**, a striking marble chapel with a small cupola (octagonal, of course) that holds the remains of the doughty Crusader (if the cathedral is closed, you can at least see the tomb from the adjacent town park). Bohemund, who died in 1111, was the son of Robert Guiscard; renowned for valour and chivalry, he seized the main chance when the First Crusade was being preached and ended up Prince of Antioch. The most remarkable feature of his tomb is the pair of **bronze doors**, signed by an artist named Roger of Melfi. The one on the left, inscribed with geometrical arabesques, is a single slab of bronze. Inside the cathedral, you may notice the early medieval bishop's chair, resting on two weary-looking stone elephants. On the outskirts of Canosa, there are remains of a 6th-century church, the **Basilica San Leucio**, and a small museum.

Four Towns, Four More Cathedrals

In this corner of Bari province, there are altogether eight noteworthy cathedrals on a narrow strip of land only some 64km long. They are the only real monuments—nothing has been built ambitiously and well around here since the 14th century—and they stand as the best evidence of Apulia's greatest period of culture and prosperity. One of the best cathedrals in Apulia is at **Ruvo di Apulia**, an ancient settlement that was famous in classical times for pottery—reproducing Greek urns at a lower price, above all between the 5th and the 3rd centuries BC, when the trade was at its most flourishing. A large collection of locally made urns, and some Greek imports too, can be seen at the **Museo Jatta** (*open Mon–Sat, 9.30–12; adm*). The **cathedral** is a tall, almost Gothic work, with a richly decorated façade incorporating a fine rose window. The little arches along the sides of the building are decorated with figures of pagan gods, copied from surviving pieces of ancient Ruvo's pottery.

Bitonto is the market for the vast olive groves of the *Tavoliere*. It calls itself the 'City of Olives', and there do seem to be barrels of them about everywhere. To find the cathedral, you'll have to wind your way through the nicely labyrinthine centre where cars cannot fit. Fortunately the town has put up maps at the entrances, to help you find your way around.

Bitonto's **cathedral** is considered by many to be the classic of Apulian Romanesque; here the best features of the exterior are the side galleries and the carvings of fantastical animals and scriptural scenes over the three front portals (note the Three Kings on the lintel of the main portal, amidst mermaids, cockatrices and elephants) and on the apse, with cartoon-like lions and griffins. Inside, there is a famous pulpit of 1226 displaying a fierce-looking eagle; on one side a curious, primitive relief shows Emperor Frederick, Isabella of England, and their family. Another church worth seeking out in Bitonto is the 1670 **Purgatorio**, a bit of pious Baroque perversity of the sort common in southern (and Spanish) towns; here the façade shows a skeleton with a sundial halo, plenty of tortured souls, and crowned and mitred skulls.

Apulia's southern borders make up a distinct region, a slightly elevated jumble of plain and rolling hills called **Le Murge**. It isn't the most attractive part of Apulia—in some parts the deforested hills have severe erosion problems, making for landscapes as empty and eerie as anything in the Basilicata. Here the most important town, **Altamura**, can seem like an oasis in midsummer. Altamura was founded by Frederick on the site of an abandoned ancient city. For centuries it was a town of some distinction, even having its own university. Its advanced outlook led Altamura to support the French and the short-lived Parthenopean Republic during the Napoleonic Wars. As a result, a mob led by a cardinal and egged on by monks, called the Army of the Holy Faith, sacked and burned the city in 1799.

The university never recovered, but Altamura still has a beautiful **cathedral**, begun by Frederick in 1232; heavy damage from an earthquake in 1316 accounts for the departures from the Apulian norm. The building retains its exceptional rose window and portal, but the twin towers above were added during the Renaissance. For some reason, in the course of doing so, they turned the cathedral backwards—the old portal and rose window were carefully taken apart, and placed where the apse used to be. On the façade, note the wonderful portal of the Last Supper, along with the other excellent, well-preserved details: the relief of the Three Kings on the right, a delicate rose window and a later addition, the arms of Charles V above. Nearby, the little church of **San Nicola** has an unusual portal of 1576 with abstract, almost primitive scenes of Noah, the life of Christ, and Adam and Eve. Across from the church stands a giant, fading outdoor fresco of St Christopher (they always painted him extra large: first because in popular legends

St Christopher *was* a giant, and second so that you wouldn't miss him—it was good luck to see this saint before going on a trip).

Gravina in Apulia, on the road towards Potenza, has the fourth cathedral, but it is only a dull 15th-century replacement for the Norman original. Gravina does have other charms. The town is set above a steep ravine, lined with caves where the inhabitants took refuge from pirates and barbarians during the Dark Ages. One of the town's churches, **San Michele dei Grotti**, is a cave too, with a heap of human bones believed to be those of victims of Arab pirates during the 8th century. Other churches show somewhat eccentric versions of Renaissance styles, notably the **Madonna delle Grazie**, near the railway station. On Piazza Santomasi there is a **museum** (*open Mon–Sat, 9–2; adm*), which contains a full-size reconstruction of another ancient cave church, with fragments of Byzantine frescoes, as well as a more conventional collection of archaeological discoveries.

Where to Stay and Eating Out

Barletta and Trani ✆ (0883–)

Barletta can be a discouraging place to spend a night, but if you insist, the ★★★**Vittoria** will do, Via Brigata di Barletta near the station, ✆ 534247, (*moderate*). The province does better for restaurants than hotels, and every town has at least one place worth staying for. In Barletta, it is **L'Antica Cucina**, on Via Milano near the station, ✆ 521718 (*expensive/moderate*), for a refined plate of *orecchiette* and turnip tops or courgette flowers, seafood antipasti and a wide choice of exceptional marine concoctions and roast meats for *secondo*. Trani is a better bet for hotels— try the ★★★**Trani**, at Corso Imbriani 137, ✆ 588010 (*low moderate*), near the sea. All rooms have bath or shower, and most also TV, and there is a good restaurant too. In Trani, the place for fish and shellfish is **La Darsena**, Via Statuti Marittimi, ✆ 47333 (*inexpensive*). *Closed Mon*. The **Torrente Antico**, Via Fusco 3, ✆ 47911 (*expensive*), uses local produce, both fish and meat, in interesting ways, and has a list with the best Apulian wines. *Closed Sun evenings, Mon, Nov*. The **Ritrovo degli Amici**, on the Lungomare Cristoforo Colombo, ✆ 45439 (*expensive*), serves fish more or less straight from the sea. *Closed Mon*.

Molfetta ✆ (080–)

Like Barletta, Molfetta can seem one of the less delightful Apulian destinations. The ★★★**Molfetta Garden**, south of town on the Strade Provinciale di Terlizzi, ✆ 941722 (*inexpensive*), is a good-value hotel that has its own tennis courts. There are two restaurants worth a stop: **Bufi**, at Via Picca 24, ✆ 911597 (*expensive*), is near the fish market, and presents old and in many cases near-forgotten recipes in innovative ways. *Closed Mon, Sept*. Another adventurous but cheaper restaurant is the **Bistrot**, Via Dante 33, ✆ 915812 (*moderate*), where the specialities include the chef's own *gamberi* and *spaghetti Forza 4*. *Closed Wed*.

Around Castel del Monte © (0883–)

The closest hotel to the castle itself is the **★★★Parco Vecchia Masseria**, on the SS170, © 569806, a restored *masseria* with a pool and garden (*moderate/inexpensive*). Andria has a wider choice, and for dinner there is the excellent **Fenice**, Via Firenze 35, © 550260 (*expensive*), where the Mediterranean and local specialities on offer include sea urchins. *Closed Sun evenings, Mon, Aug*. Another of the region's best restaurants is about 3km outside Gravina in Apulia in the Murge, the homely **Villa Coluni** at Via Guardialilo (*inexpensive*), where the best local, seasonal produce is made use of in deliciously simple recipes.

Altamura © (080–)

No town in Apulia seems more in the middle of nowhere, and it's a pleasant surprise to find a distinguished and quiet old establishment like the **★★★★★San Nicola**, in the centre at Via de Samuele Cagnazzi, © 8705199 (*expensive/moderate*). If you're just stopping for lunch, the inexpensive **Trattoria Padova** on Via Luciani off the Corso offers simple seafood dishes and a chance to meet the locals.

Bari

Somehow Bari should be a more interesting place. The second city of the peninsular Mezzogiorno is a bustling town full of sailors and fishermen, and also boasts a university and a long heritage of cultural distinction. Bari nonetheless will be a disappointment if you come here expecting Mediterranean charm and medieval romance. If, on the other hand, you'd like to see a southern city that has come close to catching up with the rest of Italy economically, Bari will be just the place. It has oil refineries, a busy port, and a new suburban business centre of glass skyscrapers called the *Baricentro*. The newer districts, with their smart shops and numb boulevards jammed with noisy traffic, exhibit a thoroughly northern glitter, and the good burghers who stroll down the Corso Cavour for their evening *passeggiata* are among the most overdressed in Italy. Bari has also become one of the Italian cities most regularly visited by international rock music tours. Be warned, though—and you probably will be—that the city has one of the highest street-crime rates in the country, so take care and try to avoid carrying with you anything of particular value, including cameras, above all in the old city and at night.

Getting Around

 Bari itself is a compact city, and once there it doesn't take long to see the sights on foot. This isn't Naples, but the traffic and parking are predictably horrible.

by air

Bari's **airport**, about 8km west of the city at Palese, has regular connections to Rome, Milan, Turin, Pisa and some other destinations. There is a special bus to the airport which leaves from the Alitalia office at Via Califati 37.

For anyone in Italy discovering a sudden desire to bolt, there are regular ferries from Bari to Corfu, mainland Greece (Igoumenitsa and Patras), Albania and Egypt. All ferries leave from the **Stazione Marittima** (information ✆ (080) 5211726), on the Mole San Vito, at the opposite end of the city from the main FS rail station. Car ferry services to Greece are operated by the Ventouris line, with sailings daily from June to September and three times a week during the rest of the year. Services to ports in the former Yugoslavia will presumably be resumed when political circumstances allow.

Bari is an important junction on the main FS east-coast line, with many long-distance services, and there is also a busy branch line from Bari to Táranto (Bari FS information ✆ (080) 5216801). There are also three private **regional railways** that run from the city. The *Ferrovia Sud-Est* (FSE), ✆ (080) 5832222, runs a line from Bari's central FS station to Lecce, Táranto (in competition with the FS) and towns in the *trulli* country. Just across from the FS station on Piazza Aldo Moro, on the southern side of the town, there is another station that serves two more lines: the FCL, ✆ (080) 5725111, which has 12 trains a day to Altamura and to Matera in the Basilicata, and on the adjacent track the *Ferrovia Bari-Nord*, ✆ (080) 5213577, which runs a kind of commuter service north to Andria and the towns en route.

There are scheduled long-distance bus services from Bari to Rome, Naples and other major Italian cities, most of which also leave from the Piazza Aldo Moro. This square is also the main terminus and junction for most local city bus routes. Some bus services to destinations in the province, though, operate from Piazza Eroi del Mare, on the east side of the port.

The A14 *autostrada* reaches the outskirts of Bari, near the town's own ring road, before turning south for Táranto. Given the size of Bari, it's usually quicker and easier to walk or take buses rather than use a car within the city. Moreover, given the city's reputation for street crime, this is one of the places where it's most advisable for drivers to find a hotel with a lock-up garage and leave their car there, and above all not to leave any valuables on view in a car.

Tourist Information

The main provincial EPT office is at Piazza Aldo Moro 32/A, ✆ (080) 5242244, across from the station. There is also the local AAST, at Corso Vittorio Emanuele 68, ✆ (080) 5235186. The magazine *Eccobari*, available from the tourist offices, has a good map of the city.

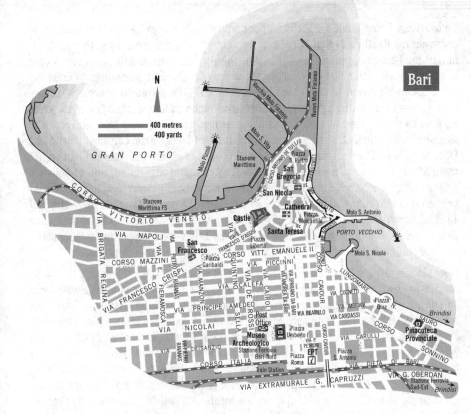

The Town That Stole Santa Claus

Bari can trace its history back to before the Romans, but it began to make a name for itself only in the 10th century. As an important trading city, and seat of a nominally independent Byzantine governor, Bari was sometimes a rival of Venice, though more often its ally. Robert Guiscard and his Normans, who took the city in 1071, favoured Bari and helped it become the leading town of Apulia.

Sixteen years later, in 1087, a fleet of Barese merchantmen in Antioch got word that some of their Venetian counterparts were planning a little raid on Myra, on what is now the southern coast of Turkey. Their intention was to pinch the mortal remains of St Nicholas, Myra's 4th-century bishop, canonized for his generosity and good deeds. Relic-stealing was a cultural imperative for medieval Italians, and the Barese sneaked in by night and beat the Venetians to their prey, something that did not happen often in those days.

The Greek Christians of Myra were disgusted by the whole affair, but the Baresi had them outmatched, and so St Nicholas went west (his sarcophagus was too heavy to move, and so you can still see it today in the museum at Antalya, Turkey). Every year, on 8 May, the Baresi celebrate their cleverness with a procession of boats in the harbour, and an ancient icon of the saint is held up to receive the homage of the crowds on shore, recreating the scene of Nicholas' arrival 900 years ago.

To provide a fitting home for such an important saint, Bari began almost immediately to construct the **Basilica di San Nicola**, at the centre of the old town. Even though this is one of the first and greatest monuments of the Apulian Romanesque, it is also a case where the original ambition overreached the ability of succeeding generations to finish the job. The two big towers remain unfinished, and much of the decorative scheme was abandoned, giving the church a dowdy, barn-like appearance. Still, this is the first of the great Apulian churches, the place where the style was first translated from Norman French to southern Italian. Inside, the only surprise is the tomb of Bona Sforza, Queen of Poland and Duchess of Bari. The daughter of a 16th-century Duke of Milan, she inherited Bari on her mother's side and as a teenager was packed off to marry Sigismund, one of Poland's greatest kings. She survived him, and had a brief but eventful career as a dowager queen before retiring to sunny Apulia in her last years. Near the main altar, note the wonderful 11th-century **bishop's throne**, one of the greatest works of medieval sculpture in Apulia; its legs, carved into the figures of **men groaning** as if they were supporting some unbearable burden, must have been a good joke on any fat bishop over the centuries.

Down in the crypt, you can pay your respects to St Nicholas. There will nearly always be somebody down there, praying or conducting a service; Nicholas' tomb has always been one of the south's most popular places of pilgrimage, as much for Orthodox Christians from abroad as for Italian Catholics. Most of the visitors today are local, but an Orthodox chapel has been added to accommodate pilgrims from Greece, and before 1917 the tomb was much visited by Russian Orthodox believers, and now may well be again. The church is also home to a centre for ecumenical studies, as the Baresi try to make amends after nine centuries. One of Nicholas' tricks is to exude gallons of a brownish liquid the faithful call *manna*, to which all sorts of miracles are attributed; half the families in this part of Apulia have a phial of it for good luck. The saint's reputation for helpfulness is certainly still current. Until a recent remodelling, the walls of the crypt were literally covered with supplications, written in ballpoint pen, along the lines of 'Dear San Nicola, please let me be married to Alfredo...'

Around Old Bari

South of San Nicola, you will find the **cathedral**, which is difficult to distinguish from San Nicola, although it was begun almost a century later. The plan is the same, as is the general feeling of austerity broken by small areas of richly detailed carving around some of the doors and windows. Unlike San Nicola, the cathedral still has its original beam ceiling, interrupted only by an octagonal cupola, and much more suited to its Romanesque plainness. Two unusual features are the stone baldachin over the main altar, and the *trullo*, the large round building adjacent to the north wall that once served as the baptistry. Old Bari, as we have said, is a bit drab for a medieval historic centre. There is a reason for this, in that Bari has had more than its share of trouble. The Normans levelled it once after a revolt; more recently, a plague in the 1650s wiped out nearly the entire population, and the port area was heavily bombed in the Second World War. As a result, old Bari in some parts has the air of a new town. The buildings in the old centre may be all rebuilt or restored, but at least the labyrinthine old street plan survives—it's famous, in fact, for being one of the easiest places in all Italy to get lost. There will be no trouble, however, finding the **castle** (*open Tues–Sat, 9–1 and 3–7; Sun, 9–1; adm*), just across the Piazza Odegitria from the cathedral. The Normans began it, Frederick II completed it, and later centuries added the polygonal bastions to deflect cannonballs. Inside, some sculpted reliefs and windows survive from Frederick's time, along with bits of sculpture and architectural fragments from all over Apulia. Excavations are currently under way on the castle grounds; apparently the centre of Roman Bari lies directly underneath.

Modern Bari

On your way up towards the railway station, you will be crossing the Corso Vittorio Emanuele—site of both the city hall and Bari's famous fish market, and also the boundary between the old city and the new. When Bari's fortunes began to revive, at the beginning of the 19th century, Joachim Murat's Napoleonic government laid out this broad recti-linear extension to the city. It has the plan of an old Greek or Roman town, only with wider streets, and it fits Bari well; many of the streets have a view open to the sea.

Via Sparano di Bari and Corso Cavour are the choicest shopping streets. Bari's two museums are in the new town. The **Pinacoteca Provinciale** (*open Tues–Sat, 9–1 and 4–8; Sun, 9–1*) is in the Palazzo della Provincia on Lungomare Nazario Saura, and has a good selection of south Italian art—few Neapolitans are represented, though there is a genuine Neapolitan *presepio* (crib). The **Museo Archeologico** (*open Tues–Sun, 9–1*) occupies a corner of Bari University's sprawling, crowded palace on the Piazza Umberto I, near the railway station. As is usual in southern museums, the star exhibits are classical ceramics: painted vases from Attica, including one very beautiful figure of the *Birth of Helen* from Leda's egg, and also several Apulian copies, some of which are as good as the best of the Greeks. Much of the rest of the collection is devoted to the pre-Greek Neolithic cultures of Apulia.

Bari Ⓒ (080–)   ***Where to Stay***

Bari makes the most convenient base for seeing the whole region, but be careful; the city is a major business centre, and full of dull hotels at outrageous prices for expense-account travellers. Two unremarkable places that can provide a pleasant night's accommodation are the ★★★**Grand Hotel Moderno** at Via Crisanzio 60, Ⓒ 5213313, Ⓔ 5214718 (*moderate*), and the ★★★**Costa**, at Via Crisanzio 12, Ⓒ 5219015, Ⓔ 5210006 (*moderate*). Both are within a few streets of the railway stations.

There are plenty of cheap hotels around the station area and the Via Calefati, towards the centre, though some of them are pretty awful. If you want to spend as little as possible, there are two good choices in the centre: the ★★**Serena** in a stately old building at Via Imbriani 69, Ⓒ 5540980, and the ★★**Romeo**, Via Crisanzio 12 near the archaeological museum, Ⓒ 5237253, both well kept and very inexpensive.

Bari is a city famous for fish, which, like all the smaller towns around it, still sends its own fishing fleet out each morning. **La Pignata**, Corso Vittorio Emanuele 173, ✆ 5232481 (*expensive*), has long been considered the city's best restaurant, with remarkable seafood risotto, as well as another kind of risotto made with chicken livers called a *sartù*; the chef also likes to innovate, and you shouldn't be surprised to find your fish done up in saffron or mint sauce. *Closed Wed.* **Ai Due Ghiottoni**—the 'two gluttons'—at Via Putignani 11, ✆ 5232240 (*expensive*), is a little more formal than the name might imply, but the food is good and the wine list extensive. *Closed Sun, Aug.* Another of Bari's best is the **Executive**, Via Amendola 197, ✆ 5486025 (*expensive/moderate*). At lunchtimes it's usually crowded with business people taking a quick meal, but the food is always good, and in the evening the ambience is more relaxed. *Closed Fri, Sun evenings.* For excellent fish in informal surroundings try **Al Pescatore**, Via Frederico II di Sveia 8 (no phone; *moderate*).

For less expensive places worth the trouble, you'll need to go out along the shore a bit. The **Taverna Verde**, Largo Adua 19, ✆ 5540870, near the Molo San Nicola, is a popular place where fish and beer go down together very well, and **Da Tommaso**, outside town on the Lungomare Massari at Palese Marina, is another good place for seafood (*both inexpensive*). On Via Principe Amadeo, just off the main Corso Cavour, the **Porta d'Oro** (*inexpensive*) offers bargain seafood dinners, and good pizza in the evenings.

The *Trulli* Country

Southwest of Bari is a small but especially attractive region of little towns set amid an extraordinary, unique man-made landscape, given its character by one of the oldest forms of building in Italy still in regular use—the strange, whitewashed dome-roofed houses known as *trulli*.

The Love of *Trulli*

It takes you by surprise. Turning a corner of the road or passing the crest of one of the low hills of the Murge, all at once you meet a kind of land-scape you have never seen before. Low stone walls neatly partition the countryside, around acres of vines propped up on arbours, covering the ground like low flat roofs. The houses are the strange part, smooth white-washed structures in a bewildering variety of shapes and forms, each crowned with one or more tall conical stone roofs. These are the *trulli*, and when there are enough of them in one place, they make a picture that might be at home in Africa, or in a fairy tale, but certainly nowhere else in Italy.

The *trulli* are still built these days; the dome is easier to raise than it looks, and the form is adaptable to everything from tool sheds to petrol stations. It is anybody's guess as to their origins; some scholars have mentioned the Saracens, others, less probably, the Mycenaean Greeks. None of the *trulli* you see today are more than a century or two old. They are exotically beautiful, but if the form has any other advantage, it would be that the domes give warmer air a chance to rise, making the houses cooler in the broiling Apulian summers. Beyond that one modest tangible contribution, there is no real reason for building *trulli*—only that they are an inseparable part of the lives of the people who live in this part of Apulia. There is no special name for the area around Alberobello where most of the *trulli* are concentrated; people simply call it the '*trulli* district'.

Trulli are built of limestone, with thick, whitewashed walls and only a few tiny windows. The domes are limestone too, a single row of narrow slates wound in a gradually decreasing spiral up to the top. Most have some sort of decoration at the point, and a few of the older ones are embellished with some traditional but obscure symbols, painted like Indian tepees. *Trulli* seem only to come in one size; when a *trullo*-dweller needs more room, he simply has another unit added on. In this way, some of the fancier *trullo* palaces come to resemble small castles—Loire châteaux built for hobbits. Grandest of all is the one on Piazza Sacramento in Alberobello, the only specimen with a second floor; they call it the *Sovrano*, the Supreme Trullo.

Getting Around

One of the best ways to see the area is on the *Ferrovia Sud-Est* **rail** line between Bari and Táranto or Lecce, which stops at most of the *trulli* country towns such as Putignano, Alberobello, Locorotondo and Martina Franca. At Martina Franca the Lecce and Táranto lines divide. The FSE also operates **bus** services to the area from Táranto and Bari. The most attractive **road** route through the district is the SS172—to get on to it from Bari, take the main Táranto road (SS100) south to Casamassima (about 20km), and turn left on to the SS172.

Tourist Information

The tourist offices in the area are in the larger towns of **Ostuni**, at Piazza della Libertà 63, © (0831) 301268, and **Martina Franca**, at Piazza Roma 37, © (080) 705702. Martina Franca is also the first village in southern Italy with its own web site (in Italian), and a very professional and informative one it is: *http:www.tno.it/Rete-Civiche/MARTINA/*

Fasano, between Alberobello and the coast, has a helpful office at Piazza Ciaia, © (080) 713086, and also runs information booths in summer at Selva di Fasano, Viale Toledo, and at Torre Canne lido, on Via del Faro.

Alberobello

The **Valle d'Itria**, between the towns of Putignano and Martina Franca, is the best place for *trullo*-hunting. **Alberobello**, the *trullo* capital, has over a thousand of them (and nearly as many souvenir stands and craft shops). For all that, Alberobello is the best base for visiting the *trulli* country, a gracious and lovely white village, one where people never seem to lose their surprise that people would come all the way from Rome (let alone other countries) to visit them.

Modern (not-too-modern) Alberobello stands atop a hill. Here you can find the aforementioned **Sovrano**, which was once the headquarters of a group of *carbonari* (secret progressive political societies of the early 19th century) and is now home to a church group. The **Zona dei Trulli**, well-signposted, lies on the slope opposite, and consists of two adjacent neighbourhoods called the Rione Monti and the Ala Piccola, where most of the hobbit-houses now house shops or restaurants. Here also the modern church of **Sant'Antonio** has been built *trullo*-fashion; there is a small museum next door.

Locorotondo and Ostuni

Trulli look pretty out in the countryside too, and particularly so around **Locorotondo**, a town on a hill with views all around the Itria valley. Locorotondo itself is stunning, a gleaming white town topped not with *trulli*, but tidy rows of distinctive gables. The street plan, from which the town takes its name, is neatly circular, built around an ancient well dedicated to St George. Nearby, at the top of the town, the pretty church of **Santa Maria Graecia** has a carved altarpiece and bits of frescoes, and views around the valley.

Not just Locorotondo, but many others of the towns and villages in this district must be counted among the most beautiful in southern Italy. In each of them, white arches and steps climb the hillsides, sometimes punctuated by *trulli* and topped with surprisingly grand Baroque churches. You can spend as much time exploring these little towns as you care to. **Ostuni** is one of the loveliest, with an ornate 16th-century cathedral and a handful of other Renaissance and Baroque confections standing out among its white streets—including even a Neapolitan-style *guglia* (spire). Ostuni also has the advantage of being near the sea, at the centre of the long strip of very modest but peaceful beach resorts that line the coast between Monópoli and Brindisi.

Martina Franca, the highest town in Apulia, is a lovely Baroque town with a garland of Baroque monuments, including the old Palazzo Ducale, a number of other palaces and a cathedral at the top, which towers over the city like a castle. In July and August Martina Franca becomes an important point on the cultural map when it hosts the Valle d'Itria Festival, an international music festival that attracts major opera, classical and jazz performers from around the world. The tourist office has information on how to obtain tickets.

Castellana Grotte and Fasano

Nor are the attractions of this area limited to *trulli* and white towns. The people around **Castellana Grotte** never tire of bragging that their famous grotto is the most beautiful in Italy. They may be right; the deepest section of the grotto tour, called the *Caverna Bianca*, is a glistening wonderland hung with thousands of bright glassy stalactites (*open April–Sept, daily, 8.30–12.15 and 2.30–6; Oct–Mar, daily, 9–12 and 2–5; tours every hour; adm very exp*). Like much of Apulia, this region is what the geologists would call karst topography: built mostly of easily dissolving limestone, the territory is laced with every sort of cave, accompanied by such phenomena as streams and rivers that disappear into the ground, only to pop back up to the surface a few miles away.

In the Middle Ages, the more inviting of the caves filled up with Greek Basilian monks. Here, following their burrowing instinct just as they did in Asia Minor and elsewhere, the Greek hermits turned literally dozens of caves into hidden sanctuaries and chapels. The best are around Táranto, but there are a couple—**Grotto di San Biagio** and **Grotto di San Giovanni**—outside the town of **San Vito dei Normanni**, and some more along the ravines near the town of **Fasano**, where they are called *laure*; four of these can be sought out near Fasano's rail station.

Fasano is an up-and-coming little town that fancies itself a tourist centre for the region. Its big attractions are the **Selva di Fasano**, a wide and beautiful forest on the hills south of town, and the nearby **Zoosafari-Fantasilandia**, an amusement park and zoo (*hours change monthly, but it's generally open every day 9.30–5 or later; adm L15,000 for each attraction, or L20,000 for both*). Some of the old *masserie* (the big estate houses that dominate the countryside in many parts of Apulia) welcome visitors, such as the **Masseria S. Angelo de' Graecis**, at Contrada S. Angelo (*open Fri, Sat and holidays, 5.30–8; adm*) where you can learn eveything you ever wanted to know about olive oil.

Also near Fasano, just off the Ostuni road at the village of Montealbano, you can visit what may be the most impressive **dolmen** in the south. Apulia's earliest cultures were not often great builders, but they could be counted among the most sophisticated of all the Mediterranean Neolithic peoples. Much of their geometric pottery, which you can see scattered among Apulia's museums, is distinctively beautiful. This dolmen, a chamber formed by one huge slab of rock propped horizontally over two others, has acquired an odd local nickname: the **Tavole Palatine**, or Table of the Knights—the Round Table of King Arthur.

Along the coast near Fasano is the small resort of Torre Canne, and north of that, in an isolated setting by the sea, straddling the coastal road, the ruins of the Messapian-Roman town of **Egnazia**. The most impressive parts of the scanty ruins, excavated in 1912, are the massive late-Roman walls facing the sea; foundations behind it include those of two early Christian basilicas, a forum and amphitheatre, and some Messapian tombs cut into the rock; there is also a small museum, currently closed for restoration. The largest town on this part of the coast, **Monópoli**, is a modern and nondescript place, with some medieval sculpture surviving in its Baroqued cathedral and in the church of Santa Maria Amalfitana.

Where to Stay and Eating Out

Alberobello ℰ (080–)

Because the *trullo* towns are easily accessible by rail from Bari or Táranto, not many people stay over. But Alberobello's unaffected hospitality makes it one of the most pleasant bases imaginable, and there is a wide choice of both hotels and restaurants. At the top of the list is the ★★★★★**Hotel dei Trulli**, Via Cadore 32 in the *zona dei trulli*, ℰ 9323555, ✆ 9323560 (*expensive*), a group of *trulli* cottages set in a garden and beautifully furnished, each with its own terrace. There is also a pool, and a fair restaurant. In the village centre, you have an even choice between the ★★★**Lanzilotta**, Piazza Ferdinando IV, ℰ 721511, ✆ 721179, the ★★★**Miniello**, Via Balenzano 14, ℰ 721188, and the ★★★**Didi**, Via Piave 30, ℰ 9323432. All are excellent and inexpensive. Whichever you choose, have dinner at the Lanzilotta, where you can meet everybody in town and enjoy good home cooking at rock-bottom prices. For a snack, stop in at the **Casa della Focaccia** in a *trullo* on Via Monte Nero and try lovingly-made *focacce* in several varieties each day, and a glass of white wine from Locorotondo.

Alberobello also has one of Apulia's finest restaurants in **Il Poeta Contadino** ('The Peasant Poet'), at Via Indipendenza 21, ℰ 721917 (*very expensive*). It's not cheap, but the atmosphere is soothing and sophisticated, and both food and wine are among the best you'll find. *Closed Sun evenings, Mon, Jan.*

Locorotondo ℰ (080–)

This village is the centre of Apulia's most famous wine region, and you can sample some of its best at the **Cantine Callela**, via Martiri della Libertá on the way to Alberobello. For dinner, a bottle of Locorotondo wine is mandatory: a pale, dry white, much more delicate than most of the strong wines of Apulia. They'll be glad to slip you a bottle with the stuffed peppers or *coniglio al forno* at **Casa Mia**, on Via Cisternino, ℰ 9311218 (*inexpensive*). At the small, intimate **Centro Storico**, Via Eroi di Dogali 6, ℰ 9315473 (*moderate*), the owner's love of food is obvious in the care taken with the cooking and presentation. *Closed Wed.*

Ostuni ✆ (0831–)

Ostuni and its stretch of coast are well equipped with hotels; the pleasant ★★**Tre Torri**, Corso Vittorio Emanuele 298, ✆ 331114 (*inexpensive*), is fine for a short stay. Along the shoreline, the sharp modern design of the ★★★★**Rosa Marina**, ✆ 350411, ✉ 350411 (*expensive*), and its surrounding holiday village stand out at Rosa Marina, on the SS379 north of Ostuni. It's a comfortable place too, with a pool, private beach and all the amenities.

Martina Franca ✆ (080–)

The ★★★**Dell'Erba**, Via dei Cedri 1, ✆ 901055 (*expensive/moderate*), has a garden, childminding facilities and TV in each room, as well as an excellent restaurant. In addition, all across this area there are dozens of privately owned *trulli* whose owners rent them out to visitors as part of the local *Agriturismo* programme. You can get more information and a list from tourist information offices or from the Associazione Nazionale per l'Agriturismo, Palazzo Ducale, Martina Franca, ✆ 701096.

Castellana Grotte ✆ (080–)

At the friendly **Taverna degli Artisti**, at Via Matarrese 23, ✆ 8968234 (*inexpensive*), you might try the *canneloni* or the lamb *torcini. Closed Thurs.* And if you don't mind spending a bit more, the **Fontanina**, on the Alberobello road outside the town, ✆ 8968010, is another welcoming restaurant that serves generous portions of traditional food. *Closed Mon.* There is a choice of modern hotels around the village, including the ★★★**Le Soleil** on the road to Conversano, ✆ 4965133, ✉ 4961409 (*moderate/inexpensive*).

Táranto

According to legend, Táranto was founded by Taras, a son of Poseidon who came riding into the harbour on the back of a dolphin. According to the historians, however, it was only a band of Spartans, shipped here in 708 BC to found a colony. They chose a good spot: probably the best harbour in Italy, and the only good one at all on the Ionian sea. Not surprisingly, their new town of Taras did well. Until the Romans cut it down to size, Taras was the metropolis of Magna Graecia, a town feared in war but more renowned in philosophy. Taras, now Táranto, is still an interesting place, with an exotic old quarter, a good museum, and maybe the best seafood in southern Italy. It wears a decidedly north Italian air—this is the one city in the Mezzogiorno where things work, and where not quite all the public's money goes down the drain. Nevertheless, the best part of the story is all in the past.

History: Rotten Shellfish, Sheep with Overcoats

With its harbour, and with the help of a little Spartan know-how on the battlefield, Taras had little trouble acquiring both wealth and political power. By the 4th century BC, the population had reached 300,000. In its palmiest days, Taras' prosperity depended on an unusual variety of luxury goods. Its oysters were a highly prized delicacy, as far away as Rome. Another shellfish, the murex, provided the purple dye—really a deep scarlet—used for the robes of Roman emperors and every other style-conscious ruler across the Mediterranean. This imperial purple, the most expensive stuff of the ancient world, was obtained by allowing masses of the murex to rot in the sun; an enormous heap of the shells, with perhaps the mollusc who coloured Caesar's cloak somewhere near the bottom, was mentioned by travellers only a century ago. For a similarly high price, the Tarantines would have been happy to provide you with the cloth, too. Their sheep were known for the softest and best wool available, and the Tarantine shepherds actually put coats on their flocks to keep it nice.

If contemporary historians are to be believed, Taras managed to avoid most of the terrible inter-city conflicts of Magna Graecia simply by being much larger and more powerful than its neighbours. And it was spared civil troubles by a sound constitution, with a mix of aristocratic and democratic elements. Pythagoras spent part of his life in Taras, an exile from his native Croton, and he helped to set a philosophic tone for the city's affairs. The height of Taras' glory was perhaps the long period of rule under a Pythagorean mathematician and philosopher named Archytas (*c.* 400 BC), a paragon of wisdom and virtue in the ancient world. Plato himself came to visit Archytas, though he never mentions Taras in his writings.

When Taras and Rome went to war in 282 BC, they did so as equals. Taras called in Pyrrhus of Epirus as an ally, but after 10 years of inconclusive Pyrrhic victories, the Romans gained the upper hand and put an end to Taras' independence. Rome graciously refrained from razing the city to the ground after Taras helped Hannibal in the second Punic War; just the same, the Tarantines felt the iron grip of the victors, and their city quickly dwindled both in wealth and importance. Of all the Greek cities of the south, Taras, along with Reggio, proved to be the best survivor. Throughout the Dark Ages the city never quite disappeared, and by the time of the Crusades it was an important port once more.

The modern city, Italianized to Táranto, substantially industrialized and a major base for the Italian navy, has known little of philosophers or well-dressed sheep, but still manages to send its fame around the world in other ways. The city gave its name to the country quick-dance called the *tarantella*, and also to the *tarantula*. Before you change your travel plans, there really are no large hairy poisonous spiders in Apulia, just a few innocent little brown ones. Their bite isn't much, but a little notoriety still clings to them, thanks to the religious pathology of the south Italians. Throughout antiquity and the Middle Ages, various cults of dancing were current around the Mediterranean. Everything from the worship of Dionysus to the medieval Dance of Death touched this region, and when the Catholic church began to frown on such carrying on, the urge took strange forms. People bitten by spiders became convinced they would die, and that their only salvation was to dance the venom out of their system—dance until they dropped, in fact. Sometimes they would dance for four days or more, while musicians played for them, and their friends sought to discover the magic colour—the 'colour' of that particular spider—that would calm the stricken dancer. *Tarantism*, as 19th-century psychologists came to call it, is rarely seen anywhere in the south these days, and for that matter neither is the *tarantella*, a popular style of music that took its name from this bit of folklore, and was first in vogue around the beginning of the 1800s.

Getting Around

There are two **railway** lines, but both use the central station in Táranto, at the far western end of town—between the old town and the steel mills—on Piazzale Duca d'Aosta. Regular FS trains leave for Lecce, Brindisi, Bari and further north, as well as for the horrible endless trip around the Ionian sea to Reggio di Calabria (Táranto FS information ✆ (099) 4711801). On one or another of the FS lines you can get to Massafra, Castellaneta, Grottaglie or Manduria. FSE (*Ferrovie Sud-Est*) local trains, which operate from one side of the station, will take you to Locorotondo, Martina Franca, and Alberobello on the way to Bari (✆ (099) 4704463).

The FSE also operates a large proportion of the province's **bus** services. Several a day for Massafra, Alberobello, Bari or Lecce leave from Piazza Castello. Their buses for Ostuni and Manduria leave from Via di Palma. SITA buses to Matera also leave from Piazza Castello, and there are daily buses to Naples run by the Miccolis company from the Corso Umberto. Buses to Metaponto and Potenza leave outside the train station.

The A14 *autostrada* comes to an end just north of Táranto and all major roads from the north meet up with an outer ring road through the western part of the city, part of the Via Appia (SS7) for Brindisi. The only trunk route that involves crossing over to the older, southern part of Táranto is the SS7 *ter*, for Lecce.

Tourist Information

The Táranto EPT is at Corso Umberto 113, ✆ (099) 4532392. On the internet, **Táranto Online** offers lots of cultural and practical information, current events and old photographs, at *http://italia.freeworld.it/taranto/*

The Città Vecchia

Perhaps unique among cities, Táranto has two 'seas' all to itself. Its harbour consists of two large lagoons, the **Mare Grande,** separated from the Mediterranean by sand bars and a tiny archipelago called the **Isole Chéradi** (one of which is big enough to hold a farm), and the **Mare Piccolo.** The city is on a narrow strip of land between them, broken into three pieces by a pair of narrow channels. Today, the westernmost section, around the railway station, is almost entirely filled up with Italy's biggest steel plant, begun as the showpiece project of the *Cassa per il Mezzogiorno* in the early fifties. This gargantuan complex provides an unexpected and memorable sight if you enter the city by night. Directly below the station along the Via Duca d'Aosta, a bridge takes you over to the old town, a nearly rectangular island that is only four blocks wide, but still does its best to make you lose your way. The ancient Tarantines, lacking any sort of hill, made the island their acropolis—

though in those days it was still attached to the mainland. Most of the temples were here, along with a famous gold-plated bronze statue of Zeus that was the second-largest piece of sculpture in the world, surpassed only by the Colossus of Rhodes. Today all that remains of ancient Taras are some columns from a **Temple of Poseidon**, which have been re-erected in the main square next to Táranto's **Castello**, built in the 1480s by King Ferdinand of Spain, and now the navy headquarters. From the square, a **swinging bridge**, something rare in Italy, connects the old town with the new. The Mare Piccolo, besides being an enormous oyster and mussel farm for the fishermen of Táranto, is also the home of one of Italy's two main naval bases. If you come by very early in the morning when the bridge is open, you may see big warships waiting their turn with little fishing boats to squeeze their way through the narrow channel.

Follow the fishermen home, and you'll end up in the **fish market** on Via Cariati, near the docks at the opposite end of the Città Vecchia. In sometimes slick and up-to-date Italy this is one of the places where you can most truly believe you are in the Mediterranean: a wet and mildly grubby quay awash with the sounds and smells of the sea, where tired fishermen appear each morning at dawn to have coffee, sort out the catch, and bang the life out of octopuses on the stones. Of course there are plenty of cats around; true 'aristocats' they are, the descendants of the first cats of Europe. Ancient historians record how the ancient Tarantines imported them from Egypt.

From the fish market, pick your way a short distance across the Città Vecchia to the **cathedral**, built and rebuilt in a hodgepodge of different styles, beginning in the 11th century. Most of the last, florid Baroque remodelling has been cleared away, saving only a curious coffered ceiling, with two golden statues suspended from it. Roman columns and capitals support the arches, and there is a good medieval baptismal font under a baldachin. Some bits of mosaic survive on the floor, which must originally have been similar to the one in Otranto; one of the figures still visible is a centaur blowing a horn. Táranto's cathedral is dedicated to St Cataldus, a Munster Irishman who did good works here on his way to the Crusades; you can see his tomb down in the crypt, as well as the chapel dedicated to him upstairs, the ornate 18th-century **Capellone**, with fantastical (and fantastically expensive) decoration in *pietra dura*—vases of flowers cut out of stone. From outside the cathedral, you can get an idea of its original appearance on the north side, with Norman blind arches, and a small cupola on a drum of columns, similar to some of the Byzantine churches in Calabria.

The rest of the Città Vecchia is residential and ancient, a series of parallel alleys and stairways connecting the Mare Grande and Mare Piccolo sides. The area was down at heel and half-forgotten for a long time, but with Táranto's new-found prosperity the city is putting a good deal of money into housing rehabilitation and restoring old palaces and other monuments, a process that is finally beginning to make a difference.

The Museum of Magna Graecia

As in Bari, crossing over from the sleepy old town into the hyperactive new centre is a startling contrast. Táranto has no need to envy Bari these days; its new town is surprisingly bright, busy and sprawling, with as many grey-suited businessmen as blue-clad sailors. As in Bari, the showcase of the new town is the **Lungomare**, built over an embankment over the Mare Grande; also like Bari, this leads to a Mussolini-era civic centre, including a striking **Palazzo del Governo** from the twenties. Taranto has some good modern buildings too, including the witty, postmodernist (1992) **Monte dei Paschi** bank offices on Via d'Aquino, built to look as if it is falling down. There aren't many other sights here, but the best of Magna Graecia is on display at the **Museo Nazionale** (*open daily, 9–2; adm*), on Piazza Archita, just two streets west of the swinging bridge.

The people of old Taras may have been Spartans, but they had an eye for pretty things. With building activity going full blast around Táranto, new discoveries are being made all the time; already the collection rivals those of Reggio and Naples, and there is always the possibility that some new discovery, like that of the Warriors of Riace, will turn up to broaden our appreciation of the ancient world. There are some fine pieces of sculpture from temples and funeral sites, including the well-preserved 6th-century BC tomb of an athlete, a head of Aphrodite and several other works attributed to the school of Praxiteles, and also a wonderful bronze of the god Poseidon, in the angular, half-oriental Archaic style, not to mention curiosities like a monkey-headed statue of the Egyptian god Thoth.

The museum also has what is believed to be the largest collection of Greek **terracotta figures** in the world. They are fascinating in their thousands, the middle-class *objets d'art* of antiquity. The older ones are more consciously religious images of Dionysus, Demeter or Persephone that served the same purpose as the crucifix on the wall of a modern Italian family. Later examples give every evidence of creeping secularism; the subjects range from ladies at their toilette to grotesque theatre masks, comic dancers, and figures from mythological stories. A few are copies of famous monuments; one figurine reproduces a statue of Nike, or Victory, erected in Taras after one of Pyrrhus' defeats of the Romans—and later moved to the Roman forum after the war went the other way.

Among the fragments from Taras' buildings, there is an entire wall of leering Medusas, protection against the evil eye—as much a preoccupation among the ancient Greeks as it is with southern Italians today. Besides large collections of delicate, exquisite jewellery, glass trinkets, cosmetic cases and mirrors, and coins (many minted with the city's own symbol of Taras riding his dolphin), there is also an important selection of **Greek ceramics**. The vases include fine examples of the earlier, less-common black figure-work, and are admirably laid out according to motifs, such as funerals, war, and athletics, near a case full of such odd finds as javelin points, and a genuine ancient discus (on the vases and accompanying explanations you can learn anything you ever wanted to know about the ancient Greek games). They are particularly fascinating to see, with their figures of humans and gods fighting, taking part in sports or revelling. In one room, a rare evocation of Magna Graecia at play is provided by scenes on vases of Athene and contending athletes.

Táranto © (099–) **Where to Stay and Eating Out**

Most of the better hotels are inconveniently located on the far eastern edge of town. One well-run spot in the centre is the **★★★Plaza**, facing Piazza Archita at Via d'Aquino 46, © 4590775 (*moderate*). All of the rooms are air-conditioned, and most have a balcony over the square. For an inexpensive hotel, you can't do better than the immaculate and welcoming **Pisani**, in the new centre at Via Cavour 43, ✆ 4530487, 🖷 4707593. If they are full, the **Imperiale**, Via Pitagora 94, ✆ 433019, is a bit more expensive, basic but clean and quite friendly. The other bargain places are in the old town, in the picturesque environs of the fish market, like the **Ariston**, Piazza Fontana 15, ✆ 407563 (*cheap*)—a bit grotty, but with great views over the Mare Piccolo.

Táranto is still a wonderful place to eat seafood, but many of the old favourites in the city centre seem to be closing down, and not much is appearing to replace them. One that remains is **Al Gambero**, just across the channel from the fish-market at Vico del Ponte 4, ✆ 4711190 (*moderate*), a place that has earned a high reputation with its creative dishes involving nearly all the fantastic array of marine delicacies the Ionian sea has to offer. *Closed Mon, Nov.* One of the best and newest places to eat in Táranto is the sophisticated **Le Vecchie Cantine**, Corso da Carelli, ✆ 7772589 (*expensive*), where the speciality is swordfish with spaghetti. *Open Oct–April, closed Wed.* Right by the swinging bridge on the new town side, **Da Giovanni**, Corso Due Mari, ✆ 4590706 (*moderate*), is a dependable seafood place that does an especially good *spaghetti vongole*. All of these places feature prominently the local speciality: a variety of mussels called *mitili* that are farmed in Táranto's two 'seas'.

There are many good inexpensive places in the new city: the **Ristorante-Pizzeria Mario** at Via Acclavio 68, ✆ 26008, besides good pizza, has seafood dinners for under L30,000; even better is the **Ristorante Basile**, Via Pitagora 76, ✆ 26240, across from the main city park, which cooks fine dinners at rock-bottom prices. Pass up the *menu turistico* and go for a good fish dinner for L20,000 or so.

As an alternative to staying in the city, follow the Lungomare out eastwards, and then the signs for the *Litoranea* (coastal road); for almost 20km, this is lined with lidos and small resorts where you can find a wide choice of hotels, camp grounds and pizzerias around the beaches.

Towns Around Táranto

Grottaglie, just 15 minutes by train to the east of the city, is the ceramics capital of south-east Italy. The town's potters continue to produce plates, vases and pots in enormous quantities today, and attract throngs of visitors on summer weekends, eager to buy their traditional, and sometimes more modern, styles.

The Potters of Apulia

Ceramics and terracotta have been two of the main products of Apulia since the days of the ancient Greeks. The museums of southern Italy all have thousands of examples of mass-produced terracotta ex-votos, plaques with an image of a god or symbols that were left as religious offerings at a temple (usually temples of Demeter and Persephone). Today the region's pots may be put to different uses from those for which they were originally designed, but their forms and shapes remain much as they have always been.

Terracotta production is centred around Bari, but Grottaglie is the capital of Pugliese pottery, boasting an unbroken tradition of working in ceramics since at least the Middle Ages; the thousands of plates and vases stacked on the pavements and rooftops make an arresting sight. As well as producing copies of ancient Greek wine bottles and amphorae (all glazed with flowers and abstract patterns), the town still makes the huge plates that were traditionally used for communal eating on the threshing-room floor during harvests, while the giant vases that now make good plant pots or umbrella stands were originally intended to hold soaking laundry before wash day. Grottaglie pottery is found on sale all over Italy, but at its source it's available at almost half the price: a great bargain, especially if you're travelling by car.

Further along the road and rail line towards Brindisi is **Francavilla Fontana**, which takes its title of 'free town' from a favour granted by King Ferdinand IV. The town conserves several 14th–18th-century palaces, including a small one belonging to the 18th-century Bourbon kings, as a reminder of its days as a feudal stronghold. Nearby **Oria** has a history much the same. Oria is a lovely town, with brightly-coloured tile domes over its churches; many of its old gates survive, as do its medieval *contrade*. Like Siena, and so many other Italian cities, Oria is divided into legally chartered communities, each with its special festival, colours and symbols. These *contrade* may date back to the tribes of pre-Roman times. Frederick II built a strong **castle** for Oria in 1227–33, with three tall round towers, which now resembles a toy fortress. It's one of the few such castles you can visit, and the city has assembled a collection of antiquities and bric-à-brac inside (*open Tues–Sun, 8–12 and 4–6; adm*). In the Middle Ages, Oria had an important Jewish community; the ghetto and its buildings are still intact.

Oria is believed to have been the capital of the ancient Messapians, a quietly civilized people who suffered many indignities at the hands of the Greek colonists, and finally succumbed to the allure of classical culture. **Ceglie Messapico**, south of Ostuni, was another of their cities, and it is here you can see the *specchie*, the Messapians' note-worthy surviving monuments.

A Messapian Mystery

The *specchie* are conical stepped towers; they get their name intriguingly from the Latin *speculum*, a mirror, but no one has the faintest idea what they are or what purpose they served. Many of them are found on heights, and it is possible that they were used for sending messages over long distances by some sort of signals. One is in Ceglie itself, and the other two out in the country. Of these, the easiest to track down is the most impressive, the 9m Specchia Miano, halfway between Ceglie and Francavilla.

As you will learn, the real mystery is finding the things. Coming from Ceglie, make the first left after the petrol station 3km south of town (there's a *trullo* on the corner). Then turn right directly after you cross the railroad tracks. Take the next dirt track on the left, and follow it until you come to a paved road, where a yellow sign directs you the rest of the way.

It's worth the trip. You're back in *trullo* fairyland here, a green rolling landscape covered in wild flowers where everything is on a tiny scale: tiny farms and tiny *trullo* farmsteads on every side (most of their owners now live in the towns, and use them for summer houses; the electricity cables seem strange and incongruous). Behind one of these stands the Specchia Miano, an irregular, much-eroded terraced heap of small stones. Climb it, and you'll notice that part of the *specchia* seems to be collapsed, as if there had been a chamber inside. From the top, you can see the hilltop centres of Oria and Ceglie clearly; the *specchia* seems to be exactly on a line between them, and in the distance you can see parts of an old track that follows the line.

Manduria and Massafra

Manduria was another Messapian city, mentioned in the histories as fighting continuous wars with the Greeks of Taras. Ruins of its fortifications can still be seen—three concentric circuits of which the outermost is 5km around—along with caves, necropoli, and a famous well mentioned in Pliny's *Natural History*. To find the well, turn right in front of the church of the Capuccini, on Via Sant'Antonio. The new city has an interesting **cathedral**, with a beautifully carved Renaissance rose window and portals. Old Manduria is a somewhat gloomy place, an effect heightened by its ensemble of mouldering Baroque churches and palaces, and especially by the paving stones of black volcanic basalt, like those of towns in Sicily; Manduria is also one of the towns, like Oria, where the streets and some of the buildings of the old Jewish ghetto still survive.

West of Táranto, a very short distance back toward Le Murge and Matera, you can visit one of the most unusual cities of Apulia. **Massafra**, even more than Matera, was a city of troglodytes and monks. A steep ravine, the **Gravina di San Marco**, cuts the city in two. The ravine and surrounding valleys are lined with caves, and many of these were expanded into cave-chapels, or *laure*, by Greek monks in the early Middle Ages. Between the caves and the old church crypts, it has been estimated that there are over a hundred medieval frescoes in, around, and under Massafra—some of considerable artistic merit. One of the best is a beautiful Byzantine Virgin called *La Vergine della Scala*, in a sanctuary of the same name, reached from Via del Santuario in the old town of Massafra by a long naif-Baroque set of stairs. The Madonna is shown receiving the homage of two kneeling deer, the subject of an old legend. Adjacent to the sanctuary, some more, this time 13th-century paintings can be seen in the **Cripta della Bona Nova**.

Apart from these well-visited examples, you will have to rely on the locals' considerable goodwill towards strangers to find the rest of the caves, crypts and frescoes. None of the sites is well marked. At the bottom of the ravine is the **Farmacia del Mago Greguro**, a now rather neglected complex of caves that it is believed were used by the monks to store and prepare medicinal herbs.

Other cave churches and frescoes can be seen at **Mottola**, **Palagianello** and **Ginosa**, built like Massafra over a ravine full of caves. **Laterza**, perched on a 200m-deep gorge near the border with the Basilicata, has about 180 caves and *laure*, of which some 30 can be visited. **Castellaneta** also has a ravine, the steepest and wildest of them all, and some cave churches, but this town cares more to be known as the birthplace, in 1895, of Rudolph Valentino. There's a monument to him in the main square, with a life-size ceramic statue of the old matinée idol dressed as the Sheik of Araby.

Where to Stay and Eating Out

Ceglie Messapico Ⓒ (0831–)

Nobody ever comes here, but if you're in the neighbourhood Ceglie can make a pleasant enough stopover. There are a number of inexpensive hotels, including the simple **★★Tre Trulli**, Via Carducci, Ⓒ 377557, and restaurants from the **Trattoria Messapica**, on Piazza del Plebescito (*inexpensive*) with simple home cooking, to **La Taverna dei Dominicani**, Via Dante 15, Ⓒ 384910 (*moderate*), with sophisticated cuisine in a restored pilgrims' hostel.

Castellaneta Marina Ⓒ (099–)

Táranto is a comfortable city in which to spend a few days, and there is little reason to try and find accommodation out in the hinterlands. West of the city, at Castellaneta Marina, the **★★★★Golf Hotel**, Riva dei Tesseli, Ⓒ 6439251, @ 6439255 (*expensive*), is a resort complex of cottages in a grove near the links—not much of a course, really, but a full 18 holes, and a genuine novelty in these parts.

Francavilla Fontana Ⓒ (0831–)

On the way to Brindisi, Francavilla Fontana has a good restaurant, **Al Piccolo Mondo**, Via San Francesco d'Assisi 98, Ⓒ 943618 (*expensive*), where fresh pasta, grilled meats and excellent fish are imaginatively prepared. *Closed Mon, July.*

The Salentine Peninsula

It has lovely Lecce and dowdy Brindisi, some flat but unusual countryside, the sun-bleached and sea-washed old towns of Gallípoli and Otranto, lots of caves and Neolithic remains. Its coastline, while not as ruggedly beautiful as that of the Gargano, does have its charms, not least of which is that it is relatively uncrowded. Not many tourists, even among the Italians, make their way to this distant Land's End. If you are beachcombing or backpacking, and can resist the temptation presented by the ferries to Greece, this might be a perfect place to spend a lazy week or so.

Getting Around

by air

Brindisi's Casale **airport** is 4km north of the city and has regular flights to Rome, Milan, Verona and some other destinations. There is a frequent bus service between the airport and the main FS rail station in the city centre.

by sea

Brindisi is the most important Italian port for ferries to Greece, and has daily connections almost the year round to Corfu, Patras and Igoumenitsa, with several a day in the busy summer season. All ferries leave from the **Stazione Marittima**, in the centre of the port. Schedules, prices, and even the names of the lines change all the time—as fairly insubstantial companies sometimes set up from one year to the next just for the summer season—but the EPT office should have up-to-date information. That may not be much help in summer—frequently as the boats run, it is a good idea in July and August to book a passage before you get to Brindisi. If you do need to buy a boat ticket here, avoid absolutely the ticket touts clustered around the train station and the Stazione Marittima. There is an enormous number of agencies in Brindisi offering ferry tickets, but many of them too are notoriously unreliable. It is always advisable to look around and to buy tickets from the boat companies themselves or an approved agent. The two most established ferry companies and their main agents in Brindisi are **Adriatica**, Stazione Marittima, ✆ (0831) 523825, and **Hellenic Mediterranean**, Corso Garibaldi 8, ✆ (0831) 528531. They are not as cheap as some ferries, but are reliable.

Between June and September ferries also operate between the little port of Otranto and Corfu and Igoumenitsa. They are faster than many of the Brindisi boats, but more expensive.

by rail

Lecce, despite its location, is well served by rail; the city is a terminus for long sleeper runs across Italy to Rome and Milan. All of these trains also pass through Brindisi, and both towns have very frequent trains heading for Bari or Táranto (Lecce FS information ✆ (0832) 301016). In addition, there is always the tired but game FSE, which has services from Lecce to Otranto, Gallípoli and Nardo, as well as some to Bari and Táranto via Manduria (Lecce FSE information ✆ (0832) 41931).

by bus

In Brindisi, buses to all provincial towns and nearby cities leave from the Viale Porta Pia. In Lecce, most buses to towns in the Salentine, run by the Sud-Est Company, leave from Via Adua near the old western walls. There are also daily long-distance services from Lecce and Brindisi to Rome, Naples and many other Italian cities.

by road

The Via Appia (roughly following the modern SS7) reaches its end in Brindisi, as it has done for over 2000 years. Traffic leaving the port can be very slow in summer, and a more leisurely way to get away from the city can be along the SS16 to San Vito dei Normanni and the *trulli* country, or along the coast road.

In **Brindisi** the EPT is at Lungomare Regina Margherita, ✆ (0831) 562126. On the peninsula there are offices in **Lecce**, Via XXV Luglio in the Castello Carlo V, ✆ (0832) 248092; **Otranto**, at Via Rondachi 8, ✆ (0836) 801436; and **Santa Cesarea Terme**, at Via Roma 209, ✆ (0836) 944043.

Brindisi

The word *brindisi* in Italian means to toast. It's just a coincidence; the name comes from the original Greek colony of *Brentesion*, and it isn't likely that anyone has lately proposed any toasts to this grey and dusty port. Brindisi today is what it was in Roman times: the gangplank to the boat for Greece. On the Viale Regina Margherita, to the right of the port, a small piazza at the top of a formal stairway holds a magnificent **Roman column**, once topped by the statue of an emperor, that marked the end of the Appian Way (it is currently under treatment to protect it from the elements). For six centuries, all of Rome's trade with the East, all its legions heading toward new conquests, and all its trains of triumphant or beaten emperors and generals passed through *Brundisium*. From the 11th century on, the city reassumed its old role when it became one of the most important Crusader ports. A memory of this survives too; if you enter the city from the north or west, you will pass the **Tancredi Fountain**, an Arab-inspired work built by the Norman chief Tancred. Here the Christian knights watered their horses a last time before setting out for the Holy Land.

As a city where people have always been more concerned with coming and going than settling down, Brindisi has not saved up a great store of monuments and art. Travel agents and shipping offices are more in evidence than anything else, helping expedite the hordes of tourists flowing to and from Patras, Corfu and Igoumenitsa. If you're staying, there are a few things to look at. Alongside the 12th-century **cathedral**, rebuilt in warmed-over Baroque, there is a small exotic-looking portico with striped pointed arches; this is all that remains of the **Temple**, headquarters church of the Knights Templar, and closely related to the Temple in London. Nearby, a small collection of ancient Apulian relics has been assembled at the **Museo Archeologico** (*open daily, 9–1.30; adm*). Down Via San Giovanni, a few blocks south, another curious souvenir of the Templars has survived, the round church of **San Giovanni al Sepolcro**, built in the late 11th century, with fanciful carvings of dancers and lions on the portal. Back on the waterfront, on Viale Regina Margherita, there is a small local ferry that runs across the harbour to the 45m **Monument to Italian Sailors**, erected by Mussolini in 1933. A lift goes up to the top, from where there are good views of the comings and goings of the port.

Santa Maria del Casale

The greatest of Brindisi's attractions, however, lies just north of the city, near the sports complex on the way to the airport. **Santa Maria del Casale** is a church unlike any other in Italy; built in the 1320s, in an austere, almost modern economy of vertical lines and arches, the façade is done in two shades of sandstone, not striped as in so many other

Italian churches, but shaped into a variety of simple, exquisite patterns. The church makes use of many of the features of Apulian Romanesque, but defies classification into any period or style; neither is any foreign influence, from the Saracens or Greeks, readily apparent. Santa Maria is a work of pure imagination.

The interior, a simple, barn-like space, is painted with equally noteworthy frescoes in the Byzantine manner. The wall over the entrance is covered with a remarkable visionary **Last Judgement** by an artist named Rinaldo of Táranto, full of brightly coloured angels and apostles, saints and sinners; a river of fire washes the damned into the inferno while above, the fish of the sea disgorge their human prey to be judged. Many of the other frescoes, in the nave and transepts, have become badly faded, though they are still of interest.

Brindisi Ⓒ *(0831–)* **Where to Stay**

Brindisi's hotel-keepers, accustomed to folks staying just overnight while waiting for the boat to Greece, have not been inspired to exert themselves, and there are no really outstanding places in the city. The best is the ★★★★**Internazionale**, at Lungomare Regina Margherita 26, Ⓒ 523473, ✉ 523476 (*high moderate*), which is very convenient for the ferry docks. This is an older hotel, though very well kept; you're likely to encounter grandmotherly furnishings, and maybe you'll get one of the rooms with a marble fireplace. The ★★★**Barsotti**, Via Cavour 1, Ⓒ 560877, ✉ 563851 (*moderate*), is a plain but acceptable place, near the train station.

The ★★**Europa**, Piazza Cairoli 5, Ⓒ 528546, is of reasonable quality yet inexpensive and centrally located, on one of the two main squares between the train station and the ferry terminal. Brindisi also has a **Youth Hostel**, at Via Brandi 2, Ⓒ 413123, which is 2km to the west of the city centre (*both inexpensive*).

Brindisi Ⓒ *(0831–)* **Eating Out**

Behind the Appian Way column in Brindisi is the city's most elegant restaurant, which manages to mix traditional and newly invented ways of cooking and presenting meat, seafood and pasta—La **Lanterna**, at Via G. Tarantina 14, Ⓒ 524950 (*moderate*). *Closed Sun.* For something simpler, but still good, try **La Camelia**, at Via G. Bruno 11, Ⓒ (0831) 563071 (*inexpensive*), for tasty *orecchiette* or seafood risotto. *Closed Sat.* Otherwise, if you're waiting for a train or ferry, there are any number of pizzerias and trattorias along the Corso Umberto and Corso Garibaldi where you can find something cheap, filling and quick.

Lecce

Unfortunately for the traveller, you will have to come a long way, to the furthest corner of Apulia and the last city in this book, to find the most beautiful town in southern Italy. Unfortunately for Lecce, its pretty streets and Baroque monuments are currently being drowned in traffic that is worse than Naples'. A distinguished but sleepy university town

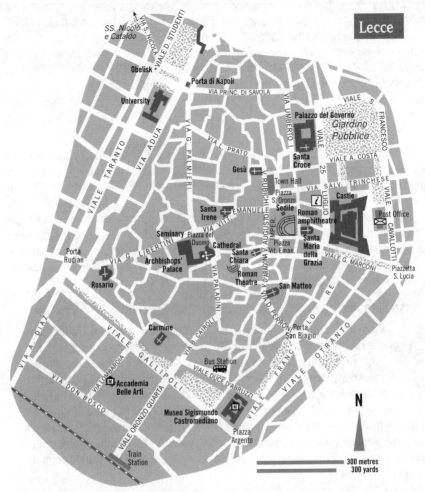

only a decade ago, it has been transformed almost out of recognition by modern times and a modicum of prosperity. Nevertheless, Lecce is worth a visit. Its history, and its tastes, have given it a fate and a look different from any other Italian town. First and foremost, Lecce is the capital of southern Baroque—not the chilly, pompous Baroque of Rome, but a sunny, almost frivolous style Lecce created on its own.

History

Lecce started as a Messapian town, and flourished as the Roman *Lupiae*, but really only came into its own during the Middle Ages, as the centre of a semi-independent county comprising most of the Salentine peninsula. The last Norman king, Tancred, was Count of Lecce, and he favoured the city, founding SS Nicolò e Cataldo. This is one of the few buildings left from the Middle Ages, but only because Lecce, uniquely among Apulian cities, was prosperous enough to replace them in later centuries when styles changed. Lecce enjoyed royal favour under the Spaniards in the 16th century; with its location near the front lines of the continual wars between Habsburg and Turk, Lecce often found itself the centre of attention even though it was not a port. Somehow, during the Spanish centuries, while every other southern city except the royal seat of Naples was in serious decline, Lecce was enjoying a golden age. In these centuries, the city attained distinction in literature and the arts, giving rise to such unfortunate nicknames as 'The Athens of Apulia'. Lecce also found the wealth virtually to rebuild itself, and took the form we see today with the construction of dozens of palaces, churches and public buildings in the city's own distinctive style.

Even though Lecce was doing well under the Spaniards and Bourbons, it hardly enjoyed the privilege of being ruled by them. On the contrary, perhaps more than any other city in Italy, Lecce's resistance to the new order manifested itself in four serious revolts. First, in 1648, came a popular revolution coinciding with Masaniello's revolt in Naples and, like it, bloodily repressed by Spanish troops. A second rebellion, in 1734, almost succeeded; the rebels were tricked into submitting by the Bourbons, who offered them reforms that were later withdrawn. In the wake of the French revolution, another revolt occurred, and the last came in 1848; the Leccesi worked hard for the unification of Italy, and contributed to the fight both men and ideas.

Leccese Baroque

One critic has called Baroque the 'most expensive style of architecture ever invented'. Considering all the hours of skilled labour it took to carve all those curlicues and rosettes, it's hard to argue. Lecce, like southern Sicily, some parts of Spain, and Malta—all places where southern Baroque styles were well developed—was fortunate to have an inexhaustible supply of a perfect stone. *Pietra di Lecce* is a kind of sandstone of a warm golden hue, possessing the additional virtues of being extremely easy to carve, and becoming hard as granite after a few years in the weather. Almost all of Lecce is built of it, giving the city the appearance of one great, delicately crafted architectural ensemble.

The artists and architects who made Lecce's buildings were almost all local talent, most notably Antonio and Giuseppe Zimbalo, who between them designed many of Lecce's finest buildings in the mid-17th century, and carried the style to its wildest extremes. Leccese Baroque does not involve any new forms or structural innovations; the ground plans of the Zimbalos' buildings are more typical of late-Renaissance Italy. The difference is in the decoration, with an emphasis on vertical lines and planes of rusticated stonework, broken by patches of the most intricate and fanciful stone-carving Baroque ever knew. These churches and palaces, along with the hundreds of complementary little details that adorn almost every street—fountains, gates, balconies and monuments—combine to form an elegant and refined cityscape that paradoxically seems all gravity and restraint. Leccese Baroque owes more than a little to Spanish influences, and the city itself still has an air of Spanish reserve about it. As a king of Spain once described a similar Baroque city—Valetta, in Malta—Lecce is a 'town built for gentlemen'.

Piazza Sant'Oronzio

A Baroque city was conceived as a sort of theatre set, its squares as stages on which these decorous gentlemen could promenade. An odd chance has given Lecce's main piazza something even better—a genuine arena right in the middle. In 1901, much to the surprise of the Leccese, workmen digging the basement for a new bank building discovered a **Roman amphitheatre**, with seats for some 15,000, directly under the city centre. In the thirties, the half that lay under the piazza was excavated; occasionally the city uses it for concerts and shows. Only the lower half of the grandstands have survived; the stones of the top levels were probably carted away for other buildings long ago, allowing the rest to become gradually buried and forgotten.

In Brindisi, by the column that marked the end of the Appian Way, you may notice the pedestal of a vanished second column. Lightning toppled that one in 1528, and the Brindisians let it lie until 1661, when the city of Lecce bought it and moved it here, attaching a copper statue of their patron, Sant'Oronzio, or Orontius, the first bishop of Lecce, and supposedly a martyr during the persecutions of Nero. What appears to be a small pavilion in the middle of the square, overlooking the amphitheatre, is the **Sedile**, an elegant early masterpiece of the Leccese style (1596) that once served as the town hall. The lovely portico, now glassed in, houses meetings and official functions. Around the square, the church of **Santa Maria della Grazia** is one of its few Baroque buildings that has survived; much of the rest dates from the Fascist era.

Whenever you see a digital clock, you can thank (or curse) Lecce; a hometown boy invented them in the twenties, and one of his original models used to stand in this piazza near the Sedile. It must have finally bust, for the city has done away with it.

Santa Croce and San Matteo

North of Piazza Sant'Oronzio, the most outrageous Baroque of all awaits along Via Umberto I. **Santa Croce** was begun in 1549, but not completed until 1680, giving Lecce's Baroque berserkers a chance at the façade. The lower half of it is original, done mainly in a sober Renaissance style. The portal, however, and every thing above it, is a fond fancy of Zimbalo and his colleague Cesare Penna. Among the florid cake-icing decoration the rose window stands out, made of concentric choirs of tiny angels. Look carefully at the figures on the corbels supporting the second level: among the various cartoon monsters can be made out Romulus' and Remus' she-wolf, a few dragons, a Turk, an African, and an equally exotic German. Santa Croce's interior is one of Lecce's best, with beautiful altars in the transept chapels by Penna and Antonio Zimbalo. Giuseppe Zimbalo also designed the **Palazzo del Governo** next door, originally a monastery.

Behind Santa Croce, the pretty **Giardino Pubblico** and the nearby **castle** built by Emperor Charles V mark old Lecce's eastern edge. The castle is now used for conferences and exhibitions, although it becomes the busiest place in town for the colorful **market** that takes place here on Friday mornings. For another interesting walk through the old town, start from the Piazza Sant'Oronzio down Via Augusto Imperatore (Augustus was in Lecce when he got the news of Julius Caesar's assassination). This street passes another

Baroque church, **Santa Chiara**, currently under restoration, and a Salesian convent with a skull and crossbones over the portal—the ultimate Spanish touch. Even better, in a small garden opposite the church there is the **most preposterous statue of Vittorio Emanuele in all Italy**, surpassing even the bronze colossus on the Altar of the Nation in Rome. This Vittorio is smaller, but the contrast between his ponderous moustaches and jaunty stance leaves him looking half a pirate, half the leader of the firemen's band.

The next Baroque church is the recently cleaned **San Matteo** (1700), one of the last, and architecturally the most adventurous of the lot, with an elliptical nave and a complex façade that is convex on the lower level and concave above. Continue straight down Via Perroni, and you will come to one of Lecce's fine Baroque town gates, the **Porta San Biagio**. To prove that this city's curiosities are not all Baroque, we can offer the neo-classical **war memorial**, across Piazza Roma near the gate, and off to its right a block of mansions, built around the turn of the century, in a style that imitates the Alhambra in Spain, complete with pointed arches, minarets and Koranic inscriptions.

Piazza del Duomo

Leaving Piazza Sant'Oronzio by Via Vittorio Emanuele, you pass the church of **Santa Irene**, a relatively modest Baroque church of the 1720s, with a splendid statue of the saint above the main portal. If you're not careful you may entirely miss the little alley off to the left that leads to the **Piazza del Duomo**, one of the finest Baroque architectural groups anywhere, and, as with many of Lecce's historic buildings, recently restored. It was the plan of the designers to keep this square cut off from the life of the city, making it a sort of tranquil stone park; the alley off Via Vittorio Emanuele is the only entrance. The kids of the neighbourhood appreciate the plan more than anyone; the piazza has become the most popular football venue in town, one where you can't break any windows or lose the ball.

The **cathedral** is one of the finest works of Giuseppe Zimbalo (1659–70). To make the building stand out in the L-shaped medieval piazza, the architect gave it two façades: one on the west front and a second, more gloriously ornate one facing the open end of the piazza. The angular, unusually tall campanile (73m), with its simple lines and baby obelisks, echoes the Herreran style of imperial Spain. If you can find someone to let you in, the long climb is worth the trouble, with an exceptional view over the city and most of the Salentine peninsula; on a clear day you can see Albania. Adjoining the cathedral are the complementary façades of the **Archbishops' Palace** and the **Seminary**, the latter the work of Giuseppe Cino, a pupil of Zimbalo.

Behind the cathedral, in the back streets off Via Paladini, there is a small but well-preserved **Roman theatre**. In the opposite direction, Via Libertini passes several good churches, including the unique **Rosario** (1691–1728), also known as **San Giovanni Battista**, the last and most unusual work of Giuseppe Zimbalo. Just beyond it, the street leaves the city through the **Porta Rudiae**, the most elaborate of the city's gates, bearing yet another statue of Sant'Oronzio. Leading away to the right from here, Via Adua follows the northwestern face of this diamond-shaped city, passing the **University** (the *Università Salentina*) and some remains of the walls Charles V rebuilt to keep out Turkish corsairs; further up, at the next gate, the **Porta di Napoli**, you don't need to read Latin to recognize another relic of Charles' in the **triumphal arch**, erected in 1548. Most destructive and least modest of monarchs, Charles erected monuments like this around the Mediterranean, usually after unsuccessful revolts, to remind the people who was boss. This one, featuring crowned screaming eagles and a huge Spanish coat of arms, is a grim reminder of the militaristic, almost totalitarian government with which the Habsburgs tried to conquer Europe.

From here broad Via Palmieri leads back toward the cathedral, passing the delightful **Piazzetta Ignazio Falconieri**, facing a palace decorated with whimsical caryatids and corbels in a style that approaches Art Nouveau.

SS Nicolò e Cataldo

In a little park in front of the Porta di Napoli, there is an attractive monument to the less grisly, though thoroughly useless King Ferdinand I, called the **Obelisk**. From here, a road off to the right leads to the city **cemetery**, home to a tribe of contented cats who pass in and out through a quite elegant 19th-century neoclassical gate; next to it stands the church of **SS. Nicolò e Cataldo**, founded in 1180 by Count Tancred. The façade is typical Baroque, but if you look carefully you will notice that the portal and rose window are much older. Behind the 18th-century front hides one of the best Apulian Romanesque churches, and one of the only medieval monuments to survive in Lecce. The nave and the dome are unusually lofty, with a strong Arab-Norman look about them; the carvings on the side portal and elsewhere are especially good, with a discipline and tidiness that is unusual for medieval sculpture (to see these, you'll have to enter the cemetery, around the left side of the church).

The Museo Sigismundo Castromediano

The founder of this collection, now Lecce's city museum, was a duke, and also a famous local patriot who fought against the Bourbons and earned long spells in the Neapolitan dungeons. His prison memoirs shocked Europe in the 1850s, and moved William Gladstone to a few rousing anti-Bourbon speeches. Duke Sigismundo would be happy if he could see his little collection, now become one of the best-arranged and most modern museums in Italy—a corkscrew-shaped ramp through its middle makes it accessible to wheelchair users, and virtually all the exhibits are clearly labelled. The most prized works are several excellent Apulian and Greek vases, found all over the Salentine Peninsula, though there is also a good collection of medieval art and architectural fragments, and a small picture gallery. The museum is on Viale Gallipoli, at the southern end of the old town and not far from the railway station (*open Mon–Fri, 9–1.30 and 2.30–7.30; Sun, 9–1.30; closed Sat*).

Lecce ℭ (0832–) ***Where to Stay and Eating Out***

Lecce's hotels are like the town itself, tasteful and restrained—if you can find one; inexpensive accommodation is sadly lacking here. There are two fine old establishments. The ★★★**Risorgimento** is in the centre at Via Augusto Imperatore 19, ℭ 242125, ✉ 245571 (*moderate*). Near the station, the ★★★**Grand Hotel**, Viale Quarta 28, ℂ 309405, ▣ 309891 (*moderate*), offers a tiny bit of old-fashioned elegance at very reasonable rates. For anything cheaper the only choice is the ★★**Cappello**, Via Montegrappa 4, ℂ 308881, south of the town centre and the tiny, spartan ★**Oasi**, Via Mangianello 3, ℂ 351359 (*both inexpensive*).

Although Lecce is an inland city, the sea is not far away, and many of its restaurants have always specialized in fish. One popular place, in the northern part of the old town, is **I Tarocchi**, Via Idomeneo 14, ℂ 239212 (*moderate*), known for its seafood antipasti and crêpes. *Closed Tues.* Near the town hall on Via L. Prato, **Donna Papera,** ℂ 241336 (*inexpensive*), is a delightful restaurant run by two women, simple refreshing cuisine in a wonderful atmosphere—but you'll have to ring ahead. Another winner, though a little bit distant from the centre, is **Gino e Gianni**, Via Adriatica, km 2, ℂ 399210 (*moderate*), with a long list of seafood dishes prepared following the local traditions. *Closed Wed.*

Inexpensive places in the centre of town are not lacking. You can enjoy a good pizza or an inexpensive full dinner in a pretty enclosed garden at the **Pizzeria Dominga**, Corso Vittorio Emanuele 48. On Via Palmieri north of the cathedral, **La Locanda** tries hard to give you a solid dinner for L25,000, and the house special *orrecchiete* is a treat. You can find another good and unpretentious trattoria near the Castello on Via XXV Luglio: **Guido e Figli** (*inexpensive*).

The Tip of the Salentine

Italy's furthest southeastern corner is one of the quieter parts of the country. It offers a low, rocky coastline, rather like that of the Gargano only without the mountains, a number of towns embellished in the Leccese Baroque style, and a lonely beach or two. One of the most noticeable features of the countryside—and this is true for all of the Salentine peninsula—is the eccentricity of the rural architecture. There aren't many modern *trulli* here, but a few of their ancient predecessors, low-domed houses of unknown age, in addition to little houses with flat roofs curled up at the corners, some recent artistic do-it-yourself experiments in cinder-block, and many tiny pink Baroque palaces, sitting like jewel-boxes in a prairie landscape of olive trees, tobacco and wild flowers, even in December.

Flying Saints and Greeks

The towns here show an almost African austerity, excepting perhaps **Nardò**, decorated with a lovely square called the **Piazza Salandra**, in which there is a *guglia* (spire) as frilly as those in Naples; on the same square **San Domenico** sports a wild, Leccese-style façade. Nardò's much-rebuilt 11th-century **cathedral** retains some medieval frescoes. Near the town walls, on Via Giuseppe Galliano, is a strange, unexplained circular temple called the **Osanna**, built in 1603. Among the other interesting towns and villages around Lecce are **Acaia,** with a romantically ruined Renaissance castle, and **Calimera**, one of the centres of Apulia's tiny Greek community—oddly enough the town's name means 'good morning' in

Greek. Very few people anywhere in Apulia actually still speak Greek, though their thick dialect has led many writers into thinking so; any Greeks left are more likely to be descendants of 16th-century refugees from Albania than survivors of Magna Graecia.

Nearby **Copertino**, in the early 17th century, was the home of the original flying monk. St Joseph of Copertino, a carpenter's son born in a stable, was a simple fellow, if his many biographers are to be believed, but he got himself canonized for his nearly effortless talent for levitating. Thousands saw him do it, including the pope's emissaries, a king of Poland, and a Protestant German duke, who immediately converted. Joseph's heart is buried under the altar of the little church named after him. Copertino also has a large Angevin **castle**.

Florentine Frescoes in Apulia

Galatina, smack in the middle of the Salentine, is a rambling old town that makes a sort of a living from wine. Its fanciest church is **SS Pietro e Paolo** on the main square, with a grand Leccese-style façade outside and clouds of gloom inside, but the real reason for stopping here is one of the Mezzogiorno's most unusual artistic treasures, in the Franciscan church of **Santa Caterina**. In 1389, Pope Boniface IX charged the Franciscans with the task of 'Latinizing' the Salentine; even at this late date most of the peninsula was still strongly Greek in language and religion. They built this church for their convent, and made terrible nuisances of themselves proselytizing the population, but it was left to their French patroness, Marie d'Enghien de Brienne, to pay for the frescoes that would provide the artistic side of the Church's propaganda. Marie was the wife of Raimondello Orsini del Balzo, the most powerful lord in the Salentine (whose tomb can be seen here), though after his death she married Ladislas of Durazzo and became Queen of Naples.

No one knows the names of Marie's artists, but most likely they were southerners who had been up north to see the revolutionary new style of painting that was taking shape in Tuscany; the result is a strange marriage of influences—a little Giotto, a little Byzantium. Whoever they were, they had talent, and they covered the walls of Santa Caterina with an acre or two of scenes that, but for their intense southern expressiveness (emphasized by the night-time backgrounds of many of the frescoes), would look entirely at home in Florence or Assisi. The first bay, by the entrance, has scenes from the *Apocalypse*; the second, *Genesis*; the third, the *life of Christ*; and the fourth, by the main altar, the *life of St Catherine*. Some of the best work, though, is in the shadows of the right aisle, a brilliant and eccentric *life of Mary*; bring a flashlight. The grand decorative scheme was never finished; perhaps Marie lost interest when she went to Naples. Consequently, some of the frescoes here are still in the cartoon state (*sinopie* in Italian), and you can see only the artist's sketch of a planned fresco on the bare walls of the church.

The Ionian Coast: Gallípoli

On the Ionian coast, **Porto Cesario** is a peculiar little resort, facing two islets inhabited entirely by rabbits. Further south, **Gallípoli**, like its namesake on the Hellespont, was once thought of highly by somebody; the name comes from the Greek *kalli polis*, or 'beautiful city'. The name still fits. Well whitewashed and resolutely cheerful, the old quarter still has a Greek air about it, with houses scoured by the sea air and fishermen folding their nets in the port. Children bounce around the narrow steets, while their mothers boil *orecchiete* with the doors and windows wide open, stopping now and then to stand in the doorway and talk to the neighbours across the way.

The oldest part, once an island, is now bound to the mainland by a short causeway. At the landward end stands the **nymphaion**, a trough-like fountain decorated with classical fragments: caryatids and badly faded mythological reliefs. Across the causeway, the huge **castle** with squat rounded bastions dates back in part to the Byzantines. Lately the town has put it to use as an open-air cinema. Just up the corso, there is a Baroque **cathedral** that would look right at home in Lecce; behind the well-frosted façade, though, is a light and airy interior—quite shipshape, as churches in old port towns often seem to be.

Gallípoli has the best sort of **museum** (*open April–Sept, daily, 9–1 and 5–7; Oct–Mar, daily, 9–1 and 4–6*), on Via De Pace—nothing pretentious, nothing even labelled, but good fun, in a big atrium lined with dusty bookshelves and full of cutlasses, whalebones, old cannonballs, coins, amphorae, an arrow from Tierra del Fuego, and even a crocodile skeleton. Elsewhere around old Gallípoli you will find a couple of huge old olive presses, still ready for use, and by the beach on the back side of town, the delightful little church of **Santa Maria della Purità**, with a floor of painted ceramic tiles and almost-naive paintings of Judith and Holofernes, and Moses parting the waters.

Down the coast, the Salentine's southern tip, not surprisingly, is called Land's End— *Finibus Terrae*. The spot is marked by the church of **Santa Maria di Leuca**, built over the ruins of a temple of Minerva that must have been a familiar landmark to all ancient mariners. The church's altar stone fulfilled the same purpose in the original temple. As in the Land's Ends of Celtic Europe, this corner of the Salentine has quite a few standing stones and dolmens, left from the days of the Messapians or perhaps even earlier. The most important Neolithic monument is called the *Centropietre*—'hundred stones'—near the village of **Patù**; it is a small temple of two aisles divided by columns, with flat stone slabs for a roof.

Coming back up the Adriatic side towards Otranto, the coastal road passes through some of Apulia's prettiest scenery: limestone cliffs like those of the Gargano, and *maquis* that seems to be in bloom all the time. There are also plenty of caves, many showing evidence of Stone-Age habitation or later religious uses. The **Grotta Zinzulusa**, hung with stalactites, may be the one worth visiting. Just to the north is a thermal spa, **Santa Cesarea Terme**, built around an old neo-Moorish bath-house.

Otranto

Readers of Gothic novels might choose to leave **Otranto** out of their itineraries, but there's no reason to be afraid. Horace Walpole, when he was writing his *Castle of Otranto*, knew nothing about the place; he merely picked the name off a map. There really is a **castle**, built by the Aragonese in the 1490s, but it is partly in ruins. Otranto today, (stress on the first syllable, as for most Apulian towns), is an austere and arch-

Mediterranean town draped over bare hills, one probably most familiar to outsiders as a better option than Brindisi for ferries to Greece.

Although originally a Messapian settlement, the city first appears in history as Greek *Hydruntion*, conquered and probably resettled by Taras, and its proud citizens still refer to themselves as *Idruntini*. It rivalled Brindisi as Rome's window on the east, and reappeared in the 11th century as one of the leading Crusader ports. Otranto's finest hour came in 1480, during Naples' wars with the Turks and their Venetian allies; according to a delicately embroidered legend, Turkish pirates sacked the city, killing some 12,000 or so, and massacred the 800 survivors when they refused, to a man, to forsake Christianity; the last victim, according to the legend, was the executioner, who declared himself a Christian after witnessing the steadfast faith of the Idruntini. The place hasn't been the same since; only recently, thanks to the tourist ferry business, is Otranto beginning to regain some of the importance it had in the Middle Ages.

The Mosaic on the Cathedral Floor

If you're not bound for Greece, the best reason for visiting will be the **cathedral**, begun in the 11th century by the Normans, and the only one in the south to have conserved an entire medieval **mosaic pavement**. H. V. Morton wrote that coming here felt like 'walking on the Bayeux tapestry' (they won't let you walk on it any more, but you can get close enough to see almost all the figures well). The vigorous, primitive figures are the work of a priest named Pantaleone, from about 1165. Pantaleone is a Greek name—or Apulian Greek—and we might expect the work of a 12th-century Pantaleone to show at least some Byzantine influence. Instead what we get is 100 per cent Germanic fancy and anarchy, as if the Norman conquerors had taken pains to make the Italians draw badly, the way they liked it. The pavement really is closer to the Bayeux tapestry than anything in southern Italy. Nevertheless, whatever the sources of Pantaleone's inspiration, his art is a subtle one, making good use of a limited palette of reds and browns to make a unified composition against the cream-coloured tesserae of the background.

Three great trees stand at the centre of his composition, supporting small encircled images that encompass all creation: scriptural scenes, fantastic animals, heroes, symbols of the months and seasons. These are 'trees of life', a common motif in early Christian and Islamic art, as well as in Middle Eastern and Germanic mythology—and therefore a perfect symbol for the syncretic, tolerant world of southern Italy under the Normans. All of the myriad figures in the mosaic above are connected to its branches, as if to demonstrate the interconnectedness of nature, and the common source of all life. The trees have a common root, balanced on the backs of two strong elephants; below the one on the right you can see where the artist Pantaleone signed his name in mosaic.

If you look carefully, you can find Alexander the Great (at the lower right, below Noah's Ark), and even King Arthur, *Re Artù*, above the twelve circles with scenes of the *Labours of the Months*, each pictured with its astrological sign. These will teach you a farmers' year, still the same in Apulia, that is very different to anything known in Britain or America:

January, Capricorn: a man warming himself by the fire
February, Aquarius: pouring his water into the pot of a woman who is making *porchetta* (roast pork), just as country women do today
March, Pisces: a man cleaning his feet (apparently there isn't much to do in March)
April, Aries: a shepherd taking the flocks to summer pasture
May, Taurus: a woman in costume for the summer festival
June, the Twins: the grain harvest
July, Cancer: threshing the grain
August, Leo: the wine harvest
September, Virgo: stamping the grapes
October, Libra: ploughing for next year's crop
November, Scorpio (as a lizard): woodcutting
December, Sagittarius: with his arrows, helping the men out with a boar hunt

The strangest parts are in the choir, which common folk would probably not often see: above the trees of life lies an utterly incomprehensible composition of sixteen rings, some with Latin or Arabic inscriptions, enclosing Adam and Eve, fantastical beasts (a unicorn, a centaur, a camel, a griffin). At the top are King Solomon and the mystic Mermaid, the same one pictured at Monte Sant'Angelo and so many other places in Apulia, surrounded by another inscription in Arabic. Beyond this ensemble, in the apse, the composition dissolves into total anarchy; among the scenes here are Samson and the lion, a King of Nineveh, a very large serpent crushing a reindeer, prophets and men fishing.

With so much on the floor to wonder at, it's easy to miss the other attractions: a beautiful wooden coffered ceiling, and some fine Renaissance carved detail on the pillars and side portal, all done around 1480. The cathedral **crypt** seems a church in itself, and a museum of columns and capitals: classical Corinthian, Byzantine and medieval among others. Some frescoes can be seen, including a 12th-century Madonna, along with an exquisite early Renaissance relief of two angels at the rear. Across the street from the cathedral, note the plaque on the town hall commemorating two local boys who died at Adowa in 1898, in the unsuccessful campaign to subjugate Ethiopia; only Italians could come up with the ironic inscription describing the soldiers as *vittimi delle dovere*, 'victims of duty'.

Not far away in the old town, **San Pietro** is the city's oldest church (the key is at 1 Piazza del Popolo); like its Byzantine predecessor it is oriented towards Jerusalem. Another ancient church, now in ruins, can be seen just behind San Pietro, built into the city wall. Back by the port the **town park** on the seafront is the centre of what action there is in Otranto. In summer a shuttle bus from here takes visitors around the beaches, and to the small wooded lakes up in the hills. For Neolithic fans, a map in the park points you to the dolmens and other monuments—the area around Otranto, especially around the neighbouring villages of Giurdignano and Bagnolo, probably has a denser population of these than any place in Italy.

Galatina ✆ (0836–)

In town there isn't much: a few trattorias and the ★★**Palas**, Via Piave 39, ✆ 565422, a good inexpensive hotel. But out north of town on the SS476 towards Lecce, the ★★★★**Hermitage**, ✆ 565422, ✆ 528114 (*moderate*), is a luxurious hotel in an unlikely setting, with a pool, tennis and the best restaurant in the area, offering innovative dishes that marry the delights of sea and the land; good desserts too (*expensive/ moderate*).

Gallípoli ✆ (0833–)

You won't regret spending a few days here. The town itself has plenty of accommodation, including the ★★**Mini Hotel**, with modern rooms with TV on a quiet street in the new town, and ★★**Al Pescatore**, Riviera Columbo 39, ✆ 264331 (*both inexpensive*). There are some modern resort hotels at Baia Verde, on the Via Litoranea: the ★★★★**Costa Brada**, ✆ 202551 (*expensive*), and ★★★**Le Sireneuse**, ✆ 202536 (*moderate*), are both typical white Mediterranean palaces, and both have good restaurants. For restaurants, Gallipoli has an embarassment of riches. **La Pazziarella**, Via Petrelli off Corso Roma in the new town, ✆ 264300 (*moderate*), offers some new seafood ideas, including an *orecchiete* with five or six different sorts of shellfish, and *sarago*, one of the best fishes in these parts, baked in salt (like they do in Istanbul). *Closed Fri.* Down on the harbour, the **Marechiaro,** ✆ 266143, in an attractive building with a view and an outdoor terrace, has been in business over a century, and has a wide range of seafood at moderate prices. And there's yet another worthy seafood palace: **Il Capriccio**, at Viale Bovio 14, ✆ 261545 (*expensive*). *Closed Mon, Oct*.

Santa Cesarea Terme ✆ (0836–)

This spa town has most of the accommodation, should you be stopping on this nicely languid stretch of coast. On Via Roma near the waterfront, you have a choice between two charming ancient spa hotels, the ★★★★**Grand Hotel Mediterraneo**, ✆ 944008, ✆ 944032 (*moderate*), and the inexpensive ★★★**Palazzo** next door, ✆ 944316, ✆ 944319.

Otranto ✆ (0836–)

Otranto has several newly opened hotels, including the ★★★**Albania**, Via S. Francesco di Paola 10, ✆ 801183 (*inexpensive*), with bathrooms in all of its 10 rooms, or, nearer the beaches, the ★★**Miramare**, Viale Lungomare 55, ✆ 801024 (*inexpensive*). In and around the centre you will find a dozen or so other similar places in the same price range. Otranto's best restaurant is **Da Sergio**, at Corso Garibaldi 7, ✆ 801408 (*moderate*), even though the Sergio of the title prides himself on having a local clientele, and is inclined to be patronizing to foreigners. His father is a fisherman, and the restaurant has particularly good fish. *Closed Wed, Nov, Feb*.

Architectural, Artistic and Historical Terms

Acroterion: decorative protrusion on the rooftop of an Etruscan, Greek or Roman temple. At the corners of the roof they are called *antefixes*.

Ambones: twin pulpits in some southern churches (singular: *ambo*), often elaborately decorated.

Atrium: entrance court of a Roman house or early church.

Badia: *abbazia*, an abbey or abbey church.

Baldacchino: baldachin, a columned stone canopy above the altar of a church.

Basilica: a rectangular building, usually divided into three aisles by rows of columns. In Rome this was the common form for law courts and other public buildings, and Roman Christians adapted it for their early churches.

Borgo: from the Saxon *burh* of San Spirito in Rome: a suburb.

Bucchero ware: black, delicately thin Etruscan ceramics, usually incised or painted.

Calvary chapels: a series of outdoor chapels, usually on a hillside, that commemorate the stages of the Passion of Christ.

Campanile: a bell-tower.

Campanilismo: local patriotism; the Italians' own word for their historic tendency to be more faithful to their home towns than to the abstract idea of 'Italy'.

Camposanto: a cemetery.

Cardo: transverse street of a Roman *castrum*-shaped city.

Carroccio: a wagon carrying the banners of a medieval city and an altar; it served as the rallying point in battles.

Cartoon: the preliminary sketch for a fresco or tapestry.

Caryatid: supporting pillar or column carved into a standing female form; male versions are called *telamones*.

Castrum: a Roman military camp, always neatly rectangular, with straight streets and gates at the cardinal points. Later the Romans founded or refounded cities in this form, hundreds of which survive today.

Cavea: the semicircle of seats in a classical theatre.

Cenacolo: fresco of the Last Supper, often on the wall of a monastery refectory.

Ciborium: a tabernacle; the word is often used for large freestanding tabernacles, or in the sense of a *baldacchino* (q.v.).

Comune: commune, or commonwealth, referring to the governments of the free cities of the Middle Ages. Today it denotes any local government, from the Comune di Roma down to the smallest village.

Condottiere: the leader of a band of mercenaries in late medieval and Renaissance times.

Confraternity: a religious lay brotherhood, often serving as a neighbourhood mutual-aid and burial society, or following some specific charitable work. (Michelangelo, for example, belonged to one that cared for condemned prisoners in Rome).

Cosmati work: or *Cosmatesque*: referring to a distinctive style of inlaid marble or enamel chips used in architectural decoration (pavements, pulpits, paschal candlesticks, etc.) in medieval southern Italy. The Cosmati family of Rome were its greatest practitioners.

Cupola: a dome.

Cyclopean walls: fortifications built of enormous, irregularly polygonal blocks, as in the pre-Roman cities of Latium.

Decumanus: street of a Roman *castrum*-shaped city parallel to the longer axis, the central, main avenue called the Decumanus Major.

Duomo: cathedral.

Forum: the central square of a Roman town, with its most important temples and public buildings. The word means 'outside', as the original Roman Forum was outside the first city walls.

Fresco: wall painting, the most important Italian medium of art since Etruscan times. It isn't easy; first the artist draws the *sinopia* (q.v.) on the wall. This is covered with plaster, but only a little at a time, as the paint must be on the plaster before it dries. Leonardo da Vinci's endless attempts to find clever short-cuts ensured that little of his work would survive.

Ghibellines: one of the two great medieval parties, the supporters of the Holy Roman Emperors.

Gonfalon: the banner of a medieval free city; the *gonfaloniere*, or flag bearer, was often the most important public official.

Grotesques: carved or painted faces used in Etruscan and later Roman decoration.

Guelphs: (*see* **Ghibellines**). The other great political faction of medieval Italy, supporters of the Pope.

Hypogeum: underground burial caverns, usually of pre-Christian religions.

Intarsia: work in inlaid wood or marble.

Narthex: the enclosed porch of a church.

Naumachia: mock naval battles, like those staged in the Colosseum.

Opus Reticulatum: Roman masonry consisting of diamond-shaped blocks.

Palazzo: not just a palace, but any large, important building (though the word comes from the imperial *palatium* on Rome's Palatine Hill).

Palio: a banner, and the horse race in which city neighbourhoods contend for it in their annual festivals. The most famous is at Siena.

Pantocrator: Christ 'ruler of all', a common subject for apse paintings and mosaics in areas influenced by Byzantine art.

Pietra Dura: rich inlay work using semi-precious stones, perfected in post-Renaissance Florence.

Pieve: a parish church, especially in the north.

Predella: smaller paintings on panels below the main subject of a painted altarpiece.

Presepe: a Christmas crib.

Pulvin: stone, often trapezoidal, that supports or replaces the capital of a column; decoratively carved examples can be seen in many medieval southern cloisters.

Putti: flocks of plaster cherubs with rosy cheeks and bums that infested much of Italy in the Baroque era.

Quadriga: chariot pulled by four horses.

Quattrocento: the 1400s—the Italian way of referring to centuries (*duecento, trecento, quattrocento, cinquecento*, etc).

Sinopia: the layout of a fresco (q.v.), etched by the artist on the wall before the plaster is applied. Often these are works of art in their own right.

Stigmata: a miraculous simulation of the bleeding wounds of Christ, appearing in holy men like St Francis in the 12th century, and Padre Pio of Apulia in our own time.

Telamon: *see* **Caryatid.**

Thermae: Roman baths.

Tondo: round relief, painting or terracotta.

Transenna: marble screen separating the altar area from the rest of an early Christian church.

Travertine: hard, light-coloured stone, sometimes flecked or pitted with black, sometimes perfect. The most widely used material in ancient and modern Rome.

Triclinium: the main hall of a Roman house, used for dining and entertaining.

Triptych: a painting, especially an altarpiece, in three sections.

Trompe l'oeil: art that uses perspective effects to deceive the eye—for example, to create the illusion of depth on a flat surface, or to make columns and arches painted on a wall seem real.

Tympanum: the semicircular space, often bearing a painting or relief, above the portal of a church.

Italian words are pronounced phonetically. Every vowel and consonant is sounded. Consonants are the same as in English, except the *c* which, when followed by an 'e' or 'i', is pronounced like the English 'ch' (*cinque* thus becomes cheenquay). Italian *g* is also soft before 'i' or 'e' as in *gira*, or jee-ra. *H* is never sounded; *z* is pronounced like 'ts'. The consonants *sc* before the vowels 'i' or 'e' becomes like the English 'sh' as in *sci*, pronounced shee; *ch* is pronouced like a 'k' as in *Chianti*, kee-an-tee; *gn* as 'ny' in English (*bagno*, pronounced ban-yo; while *gli* is pronounced like the middle of the word million (*Castiglione*, pronounced Ca-stee-lyon-ay).

Vowel pronunciation is: *a* as in English father; *e* when unstressed is pronounced like 'a' in fate as in *mele*, when stressed can be the same or like the 'e' in pet (*bello*); *i* is like the 'i' in machine; *o*, like 'e', has two sounds, 'o' as in hope when unstressed (*tacchino*), and usually 'o' as in rock when stressed (*morte*); *u* is pronounced like the 'u' in June.

Useful Words and Phrases

yes/no/maybe	*si/no/forse*
I don't know	*Non lo so*
I don't understand	*Non capisco*
Does someone here speak English?	*C'è qualcuno qui che parla inglese?*
Speak slowly	*Parla lentamente*
Please	*Per favore*
Thank you (very much)	*(Molte) grazie*
You're welcome	*Prego*
It doesn't matter	*Non importa*
All right	*Va bene*
Excuse me	*Scusi*
How are you?	*Come sta?*
What is your name?	*Come si chiama?*
Hello	*Salve* or *ciao* (both informal)
Good morning	*Buongiorno* (formal hello)
Good afternoon/ evening	*Buona sera* (also formal hello)
Goodnight	*Buona notte*
Goodbye	*Arrivederla* (formal), *arrivederci, ciao* (informal)

Italian Menu Vocabulary

Antipasti

antipasto misto	mixed antipasto
carciofi (sott'olio)	artichokes (in oil)
frutti di mare	seafood
funghi (trifolati)	mushrooms (with anchovies, garlic, and lemon)
gamberi al fagiolino	shrimp with white beans
mozzarella (in carrozza)	buffalo cheese (fried with bread in batter)
prosciutto (con melone)	raw ham (with melon)
salsiccia	dry sausage

Minestre e Pasta

agnolotti	ravioli with meat
cannelloni	meat and cheese rolled in pasta tubes
cappelletti	small ravioli, often in broth
crespelle	crêpes
frittata	omelette
gnocchi	potato dumplings
orecchiette	ear-shaped pasta, usually served with turnip greens
panzerotti	ravioli filled with mozzarella, anchovies and egg
pappardelle alla lepre	flat pasta ribbons with hare sauce
pasta e fagioli	soup with beans, bacon, and tomatoes
pastina in brodo	tiny pasta in broth
penne all'arrabbiata	quill shaped pasta in hot spicy tomato sauce
polenta	cake or pudding of corn semolina, prepared with meat or tomato sauce
stracciatella	broth with eggs and cheese
tortellini al pomodoro/panna/ in brodo	pasta caps filled with meat and cheese, served with tomato sauce/cream, or in broth
vermicelli	very thin spaghetti

Second Courses—Carne (Meat)

agnello	lamb
arista	pork loin
arrosto misto	mixed roat meats

bocconcini	veal mixed with ham and cheese and fried
bollito misto	stew of boiled meats
brasato di manzo	braised meat with vegetables
bresaola	dried raw meat similar to ham served with lemon, olive oil and parsley
carne di castrato/ suino	mutton/pork
carpaccio	thin slices of raw beef in piquant sauce
cassoeula	winter stew with pork and cabbage
cotoletta (alla milanese/alla bolognese)	veal cutlet (fried in breadcrumbs/with ham and cheese)
fegato alla veneziana	liver and onions
involtini	rolled slices of veal with filling
maiale (al latte)	pork (cooked in milk)
manzo	beef
ossobuco	braised veal knuckle with herbs
petto di pollo	boned chicken breast
pizzaiola	beef steak with tomato and oregano sauce
pollo (alla cacciatora/alla diavola/alla Marengo)	chicken (with tomatoes and mushrooms cooked in wine/grilled/ fried with tomatoes, garlic and wine)
rognoni	kidneys
saltimbocca	veal scallop with prosciutto and sage, cooked in wine and butter
scaloppine	thin slices of veal sautéed in butter
spiedino	meat on a skewer or stick
tacchino	turkey
vitello	veal

Pesce (Fish)

aragosta	lobster
aringa	herring
branzino	sea bass
calamari	squid
cozze	mussels
fritto misto	mixed fish fry, with squid and shrimp
gamberetto	shrimp
granchio	crab
insalata di mare	seafood salad
merluzzo	cod
ostriche	oysters
pescespada	swordfish
polipo	octopus
pesce San Pietro	John Dory
rombo	turbot
sgombro	mackerel
sogliola	sole
tonno	tuna
triglia	red mullet (rouget)
trota	trout
trota salmonata	salmon trout
vongole	small clams
zuppa di pesce	mixed fish in sauce or stew

Contorni (Side Dishes, Vegetables)

asparagi (alla fiorentina)	asparagus (with fried eggs)
broccoli (calabrese, romana)	broccoli (green, spiral)
carciofi (alla giudia)	artichokes (deep fried)
carote	carrots
cavolfiore	cauliflower
cavolo	cabbage
fagioli	white beans
fagiolini	French (green) beans
funghi (porcini)	mushrooms (boletus)
insalata (mista, verde)	salad (mixed, green)
melanzana (al forno)	aubergine/eggplant (filled and baked)
patate (fritte)	potatoes (fried)
peperoni	sweet peppers
piselli (al prosciutto)	peas (with ham)
pomodoro	tomato
spinaci	spinach
zucchini	zucchini (courgettes)

Dolci (Desserts)

coppa gelato	assorted ice cream
crema caramella	caramel-topped custard
crostata	fruit flan
gelato (produzione propria)	ice cream (homemade)
granita	flavoured ice, usually lemon or coffee
panettone	sponge cake with candied fruit and raisins
semifreddo	refrigerated cake
tiramisù	mascarpone, coffee, chocolate and sponge fingers
torta	tart
zabaglione	whipped eggs, sugar and Marsala wine, served hot
zuppa inglese	trifle

Index

*Chapter titles and main page references are in **bold**; page references to maps are in italics.*